The New Science of Swimming

James E.
Brian E.

Gil Eva

PRENTICE HALL, *Englewood Cliffs, New Jersey 07632*

Library of Congress Cataloging-in-Publication Data
Counsilman, James E.
   The new science of swimming / James E. Counsilman & Brian E.
Counsilman.
      p.   cm.
   Includes index.
   ISBN 0-13-099888-5
   1. Swimming.   I. Counsilman, Brian E.
GV837.C796   1994
796.2′1—dc20
                                              93-29229
                                                 CIP

Acquisitions editor: Ted Bolen
Editorial/production supervision: Alison D. Gnerre
Cover design: Design Solutions
Cover photo: Paul Barton/The Stock Market
Production Coordinator: Peter Havens

Learning Resources
Centre

Printed in the United States of America

10 9 8 7 6 5 4 3 2 1

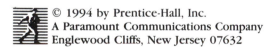

ISBN 0-13-099888-5

Prentice-Hall International (UK) Limited, *London*
Prentice-Hall of Australia Pty. Limited, *Sydney*
Prentice-Hall Canada Inc., *Toronto*
Prentice-Hall Hispanoamericana, S.A., *Mexico*
Prentice-Hall of India Private Limited, *New Delhi*
Prentice-Hall of Japan, Inc., *Tokyo*
Simon & Schuster Asia Pte. Ltd., *Singapore*
Editora Prentice-Hall do Brasil, Ltda., *Rio de Janeiro*

Contents

Preface   IX

1

The Mechanical Principles Involved in Swimming   1

Resistance and Propulsion, 5
Action-Reaction, 8
The Effect of Lift, 10
Hand Speed and Acceleration, 22
The Evenness of Application of Propulsion, 29
Transfer of Momentum, 30
The Theoretical Square Law, 30
Buoyancy, 31
Footnotes, 32

2

The Crawl Stroke   33

Body and Head Position, 34
The Flutter Kick, 38
The Arm Stroke, 47
The Mechanics of Breathing, 60
Footnotes, 64

3

The Back Crawl Stroke   65

Body Position, 67
The Kick, 67
The Arm Pull, 70
Arm Recovery, 79
Breathing, 85
Footnotes, 85

4

The Butterfly Stroke   86

Body Position, 87
The Dolphin Kick, 88
The Arm Pull, 91
The Arm Recovery, 95
Hand Pitch in the Butterfly, 98
Breathing Action and Timing, 99
Acceleration in the Butterfly, 103
Footnotes, 103

5

The Breaststroke   104

Body Position, 110
The Kick, 111
The Arm Stroke, 118
Breathing and Head Action, 122
Coordination of the Kick and Pull, 123
The Long Pull after the Dive and Turn, 126

Common Mistakes in the Breaststroke, 130
Footnotes, 131

6

Starts, Turns, Relay Exchanges and Pace   132

Starts, 133
Turns, 143
Relay Exchanges, 146
Pace, 146
Footnotes, 157

7

The Physiological Basis for Training Swimmers   158

The Three Energy Systems, 159
The Neuro-Motor System, 164
Physiological Adaptations to Specific Means and Methods of Training, 165
The Chronobiology of Stress and Adaptation, 169
Muscle Fiber Typing, 182
Footnotes, 185

8

International Sports Training Theory   187

Fundamentals of Sports Training Theory, 188
Fundamentals in the Development of Endurance Abilities, 197
The Classification of Endurance Abilities, 198
The Difference Levels of Endurance Preparation, 199
Means and Methods of Endurance Preparation, 200
Repetition Methods, 202
Special Endurance Methods: Their Load Factors and the Theoretical Approach
   to Their Effect, 203
Fundamentals in the Development of Speed Abilities, 215
Psychological Preparation, 220
Footnotes, 227

9

Advanced Theories in the Planning of Training   229

Training Theories Involved in the Planning Process, 230
Footnotes, 255

10

Fundamentals in the Development of Strength Abilities and Flexibility in Swimmers   256

The Nature of Strength, 256

Identifying the Different Strength Abilities, 257

Special Strength Training for Sport, 258

The Means of Strength Training, 259

The Methods of Strength Training, 260

Regimes of Work in the Utilization of Specific Resistance, 267

Strength Exercises, 269

General and Special Strength Exercises for Swimmers, Using a Barbell, 278

Shock Exercises/Pliometrics, 290

The Vertical Jump as a Measure of Explosive Power and Speed, 290

Flexibility, 295

Footnotes, 296

11

A Practical Guide to Organizing a Season's Program   302

The Use of Intermittent Work and Its Application, 303

Types of Sets, 304

Measurable Indices as Guidelines for the Use of Methods, 309

The Type of Activity Executed in the Use of Endurance Methods, 313

A Mixed Program of Training, 319

Planning a Year's Training Program, 320

Planning Each Week, 321

Training the Distance Swimmer, 328

Training the Sprinter, 329

Training the Individual Medleyist, 330

Adjusting Workouts to Fit the Various Age-Group Levels, 330

Masters Swimming, 332

Warm-Up, 335

The Taper, 337

Sample Workouts, 339

Suggested Reading, 354

12

Train with the Experts   355

Eddie Reese, Men's Swimming Coach, University of Texas, 357

Sample Workouts from Eddie Reese, 364

Richard Shoulberg, Swimming Coach, Germantown Academy and
 Foxcatcher's Farm, 370

Sample Workouts from Richard Shoulberg, 376

Chen Yeung Chi, National Head Coach, People's Republic of China, 379

Skip Kenney, Men's Swimming Coach, Stanford University, 382

Jack Simon, Coach, U.S. Swimming Club, 384

Sample Workouts from Jack Simon, 386

Richard Quick, Women's Swimming Coach, Stanford University, 387

Appendix 1

Roster of Elite Swimmers Pictured in Text   393

Appendix 2

Theoretical Considerations in Special Strength Training   396

Footnotes, 403

Glossary, 405
Index, 411

Preface

Because there were no models from which to begin developing concepts, swimming in humans advanced primarily through trial and error. We are 65 percent water, so they say, but when humans enter the water it is a foreign element in which we are poorly designed for efficient locomotion. While fish and other aquatic animals are equipped with flippers and fins that are relatively small by comparison to their body size, humans have two sets of long, thin limbs which present little surface area to apply against water. We can only attain top speeds of about six miles per hour, whereas dolphins and some fish reach speeds five times that fast. It has taken tens of thousands of years for techniques to evolve to the point at which we find them now, and we still don't understand fully whether or not we are on the right track.

The first edition of this book was published in 1969. When the editors at Prentice Hall suggested a revision, I, as the original author, invited my son, Brian, to coauthor it with me. Brian had been my assistant for the final eight years of my career, and I believed that together we could make a contribution to the sport of competitive swimming by pooling our interests. Brian had developed considerable expertise in the theory and methodology of training, while I had lately concentrated more on the biomechanics of swimming. It has taken us over two years to update the book, and we are here to say that it is harder to revise than to write from scratch. We have replaced many of the photographs from the original, traveling to competitions and training centers to shoot them, sometimes under adverse lighting conditions. Among those who allowed us to come to their facilities to photograph their swimmers were Jon Urbanchek of the University of Michigan, Jack Nelson of the Greater Fort Lauderdale Swim Club, Skip Foster of the University of Florida, Dennis Dale of the University of Minnesota, and Gary Conelly of the University of Kentucky. John Collins of the Badger Swim Club and Skip Kenney of Stanford University also permitted us to photograph their swimmers. Their swimmers cooperated in the photographic sessions, for which we thank all coaches and swimmers. Some photographic sessions occurred at inconvenient times, such as when the swimmers were warming up for the Olympic Trials and were very nervous. We tried not to distract them. Through the cooperation of Glen Patton, coach of the University of Iowa Men's Team, and Brad Flood, who was then Mr. Patton's distance assistant, we photographed Artur Wojdat in our own pool.

Other coaches helped us in other ways. Dick Shoulberg, coach of the Germantown Academy Foxcatchers, went so far as to travel to Bloomington for his interview. For his kindness to me and his interest in the project, including follow-ups in the form of many phone conversations and a review of his part of the manuscript, we thank him most heartily. Our thanks also go to Eddie Reese of the University of Texas; Jack Simon, U.S. Swimming Club coach; Skip Kenney and Richard Quick, respectively the men's and women's coach at Stanford, all of whom are identified in the text, for their time and trouble in either submitting to personal interviews or replying to the questionnaires sent to them. Chen Yeung Chi, the Chinese National Coach, happened to make Bloomington his center of operations as he traveled around the United States, visiting a number of this country's swimming centers. In the course of several conversations, he provided some interesting insights into the recent swimming success of his country. For this we thank him also.

Peder Dahlberg, former Indiana University swimmer and present Masters world champion in the breaststroke in his age group, provided sample workouts from his log. For this Brian and I thank him.

Dave Tanner, former Indiana butterflyer and present world champion in the 200 fly as well as computer programmer for the Division of Research and Development at Indiana University, provided unremitting support and advice on the project over the past two years. The photographic skills of Mike Lindsay, former member of the Indiana University Swim Team, were much appreciated. He did several of the still shots that appear in the book; Brian Counsilman did the rest.

Joel Stager, Ph.D., exercise physiologist and director of the Exercise Physiology Laboratory at Indiana University, kindly agreed to read and correct the chapter devoted to the physiology of training for swimming. Dr. Stager was a sprinter at the University of Miami in his undergraduate career.

Thanks go to Jesus Dapena, Ph.D., biomechanist at Indiana University, for his considerable help in resolving questions on the biomechanics of swimming.

Gil Evans was responsible for the artwork in the original version of this book. His clear and concise illustrations have been borrowed, with or without permission, by more authors of swimming publications than even we know about. This number includes their use in an authorized instructional brochure issued by U.S. Swimming under the Prentice Hall copyright. We are grateful that Gil agreed to be the artist for this revision.

Gil was a world-class diver in his college days, making the All-American Team each of the four years he competed. After graduating from the University of Michigan School of Design, Gil became a free-lance illustrator. He later worked for major publishers as art director or creative director, before starting his own design group in 1982.

My wife and Brian's mother, Marge, was involved in all phases of this revision. She traded her typewriter for a word processor this time; she says it made all the difference. Father and son were free to make as many changes as we wanted without fear of an outbreak of rebellion.

James E. Counsilman
Bloomington, Indiana

CHAPTER 1

The Mechanical Principles Involved in Swimming

What factors separate gifted swimmers from the less gifted? This question has been the proper concern of swimming coaches and their athletes for more than a century. Are there particular requirements for working effectively in water; or, given enough determination and hard work, can anyone become a swimming champion? The authors and other swimming coaches think we have made some progress in answering these questions, but the complex of variables is so great that it may be more accurate to say we have arrived at some principles to guide our thinking in the search for answers.

For instance, it has been known for a relatively short time that certain traits are genetically acquired. Among them are physical abilities which enable their possessors to excel in certain specific physical skills. Talent for swimming may be one of those which requires certain specialized abilities, variations in which follow a normal curve distribution. In the course of our careers, the authors have observed and trained literally hundreds of swimmers whose talents cover the full range. Researchers have helped our understanding of why the technique of one swimmer is better than that of another. Swimming teachers have used this information to help poor swimmers become adequate, average swimmers to become good, and good swimmers to become highly skilled; but we have been unable to make champion swimmers out of poor swimmers.

The desire to swim fast is as old as swimming itself. It is just one of a myriad of activities that gives rise to aggressive zeal in humans. Yet swimming does not fall among those activities that appear to be programmed into human behavior, such as walking or running. Human infants walk at about a year and run before they are two; but they do not swim without external guidance. Swimming skill must be acquired through instruction or imitation. This may account for the wide variation in technique seen among swimmers; walking and running, on the other hand, display only minor variations in technique from one individual to the next.

There is evidence that humans took to the water thousands of years ago. In the British Museum in London is an Assyrian bas-relief, dating to 880 B.C., which shows three warriors swimming across a stream. Two are supported on inflated skins or bladders; the third is using a technique that looks similar to today's crawl. British explorer James Cook, writing about his 1778 voyage to the Sandwich Islands, described people who "swam and dove like fishes."

There was a period in the 1800s, when Europeans were reluctant to enter the water. Their attitude toward swimming was summed up in Bartholomew Parr's *London Medical Dictionary*. "Swimming is a laborious exercise and should not be continued to exhaust the strength. It is not natural to man as to quadrupeds; for the motions of the latter in swimming are the same as in walking."[1]

This and the next four chapters contain photographs and drawings which depict both good and poor technique. It is a fact that poor technique, detrimental to performance, is often seen among world-class swimmers. This is evidence of several points: once a stroke pattern becomes ingrained, it is hard to change; talented swimmers often perform well despite certain mechanical flaws, mechanics being merely one facet of technique; and there is still a lot to be learned about the fluid mechanics of swimming.

Of the first point, many coaches shy away from tampering with the stroke of a successful swimmer because they know there is a strong likelihood that a period of time will follow when the swimmer will swim slower than before and will question the change. It is easy to understand why elite swimmers especially resist such change, and why some coaches like to say about stroke flaws in such cases, "If it ain't broke, don't fix it."

On the other hand, swimmers often develop good technique without any guidance. Others—even the very talented—slip easily into certain minor stroke flaws. Their coaches state that they must be monitored constantly for such backsliding. Still others are coached into techniques that are almost completely artificial. Their coaches appear to have assigned the same value to stroke idiosyncrasies as to important principles.

All these possibilities are due to the complex nature of swimming movements and the problems associated with operating in the medium of water itself. It is for this reason that it is necessary to understand the fluid mechanics of swimming.

Regarding future improvements in swimming performance, the authors wish to predict that most will result from a better understanding of swimming mechanics. Thus, in addition to recognizing the role of guided trial-and-error learning, students of swimming need at least an elementary knowledge of fluid mechanics. Graduate students, who are interested in the biomechanics of swimming, need to know not only what techniques good swimmers adopt through trial and error, but why. Fluid mechanics is the study of how bodies behave as they move through air or water. These future researchers are sure to be disappointed at first. They will find themselves studying propeller design or the behavior of fluids as they are pumped through tubes. Such studies will seem to have little relevance to swimming. Eventually connections will be made and students will see that all objects, including the bodies of swimmers, behave in predictable ways in air and water. It will then be up to them to apply these principles to the particular problems they will confront as researchers and coaches.

There are two major forces involved in swimming, both of which exploit the resistance (or drag) of the water. The first is the resistance of the water to forward progress (passive drag). Water must be pushed aside or pulled along in order to achieve that progress. The second is the resistance against which the swimmer exerts force (active drag) in order to move forward. If the swimmer is to go faster, he must upset the balance between the forces either by increasing propulsion or decreasing resistance.

Propulsion is achieved by moving the arms and legs so that the resistance of the water and the inertia of the body are overcome. Inertia is the tendency of a body to remain in one state, either in motion or at rest. If humans were shaped more like seals, we could take advantage of inertial force once set in motion. As it is, given the small surface area of our source of propulsion (hands and arms, feet and legs) we are condemned to relative inefficiency and to speed fluctuations which vary widely with every stroke.

When we apply force, we must overcome the inertia of our bodies and the decelerating effect that the resistance of the water exerts as the propulsion of the previous stroke phases out. Just as stop-and-start driving uses more gasoline, the repeated speed fluctuations of swimming use more energy than if the force were applied evenly. Streamlining the body as much as possible, while disturbing alignment only enough to create propulsive force, is the most energy-efficient way to swim.

By understanding the physical laws that govern propulsion and resistance in water, errors in stroke mechanic recommendations can be avoided.

A simple example is that of the swimmer who raises his head out of water in order to reduce frontal resistance, but fails to take into account that he will affect the alignment of his body so seriously that total resistance will be increased rather than reduced.

Coaches can ignore these forces and counterforces when dealing with extremely talented athletes—mistaken advice about stroke mechanics has little effect on them—but the effect can be disastrous for marginal swimmers. Gifted swimmers make necessary adjustments despite misinformation; the less talented do not. Even so, there have been cases of good swimmers whose careers were permanently derailed by well-meant, but mistaken, advice about stroke.

On the other hand, there are coaches who believe there is nothing to good-versus-bad stroke mechanics. This attitude reinforces our opinion that uninformed coaching is worse than no coaching at all. Unquestionably, swimmers develop better stroke mechanics if left alone, than if taught incorrectly. It behooves coaches of swimming to learn enough about the laws of physics which govern

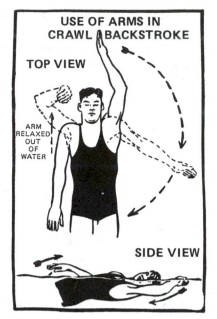

FIGURE 1–1 BACKSTROKE: THEN AND NOW

A. For the first half of this century, coaches recommended the elbow be bent on the recovery and held straight on the arm pull.

B. The current recommendation is just the opposite: The elbow should be straight on the recovery in order to preserve streamlining and to prepare for the arm pull, and the bent-arm pull allows the most effective application of force.

movement in the water to avoid fundamental mistakes. Informed guidance, early in the swimmer's career, is very important. This is the major reason for our conviction that the technical education of grass-roots coaches is more critical than that of the collegiate coaches in terms of the ultimate effect on performance results over a swimmer's career.

Figure 1–1–A is a drawing from a book published in 1924.[2] It depicts a backstroker bending his elbow on the recovery and keeping a straight elbow on the pull. This is precisely the reverse of what we recommend today. We now think the straight-arm pull causes a misapplication of force, and that the bent-arm recovery places the arm in a poor position to begin to apply force backward. This is not to say unequivocally that all swimmers should have the same degree of elbow bend. Swimming movements are complex. They are influenced by anatomical, morphological, and strength variations unique to each individual. Yet, within a fairly narrow range of variations, the bent-arm pull, as illustrated in Figure 1–1–B, permits a more efficient application of force and is an example of a better understanding of fluid mechanics than the straight-arm pull. With variations, the bent-arm pull is used by all current champion backstrokers and, in fact, in all four competitive strokes by all good swimmers.

Those who are interested in only the "how" of the various strokes and not the "why" miss a lot of the fun of coaching. It is the engagement of the intellect, as much as of the body, that makes swimming so challenging. It is for this reason that as much of this chapter is devoted to describing "why" as to describing "how." James Hay said it well when he stated, "... improvement comes so often from careful attention to detail that no coach of sports in which techniques play a major role can afford to leave those details to chance or guesswork. For him, a knowledge of biomechanics might be regarded as essential."[3]

Each of the following sections describes a particular mechanical principle which applies to one or all of the competitive strokes. They are intended as guides toward a better understanding of the succeeding four chapters.

RESISTANCE AND PROPULSION

A swimmer's forward speed is the result of two forces: *resistance* (or drag), which tends to hold him back and is caused by the water he has to push out of his way or pull along with him; and *propulsion*, which drives him forward and is created by the muscular contractions of the arms and legs as they exert pressure against the resistance of the water (Figure 1–2).

In order to swim faster, a swimmer must either decrease resistance or increase propulsion, or do a combination of the two. In essence, swimming biomechanists try to improve streamlining or increase propulsion through strength and power gains or better application of force. The greatest improvements in stroke mechanics in recent years have been in the area of increasing forward propulsion. Increased general and specific strength and power have enabled swimmers to create greater propulsive force. Nearly all competitive swimmers now use some form of supplemental exercise designed to improve endurance-strength and speed-strength. This is a dramatic reversal from the days when it was thought that increased strength would have a detrimental effect on flexibility (see Figure 1–3[4]).

Conditioning plays a substantial role both in decreasing resistance and increasing propulsion. It enables the swimmer to maintain the highest possible level of propulsion and the least possible amount of resistance throughout the race. As a swimmer fatigues, his body gradually loses its streamlining. The better the ability to keep propulsion high and resistance low, the better the performance will be. This is a training effect rather than a biomechanical one, but it should not be forgotten by coaches and researchers as they pursue the study of the "why and how" of the strokes.

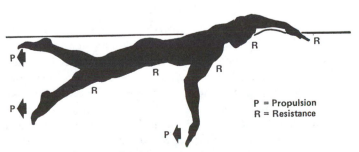

P = Propulsion
R = Resistance

FIGURE 1–2   PROPULSION AND RESISTANCE: THE TWO FORCES WHICH ACT ON THE SWIMMER'S BODY AS HE MOVES THROUGH THE WATER.

FIGURE 1–3 LONG, SOFT, PLIABLE MUSCLES VERSUS SHORT, SNAPPY MUSCLES? THIS OPINION IS DIRECTLY OPPOSED TO THE CURRENT ONE.

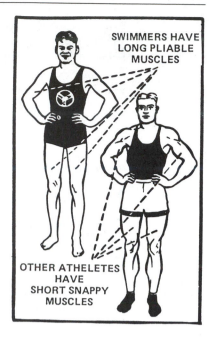

What difference is there between the muscles developed by a swimmer and those of other athletes?

Other athletes develop a short, snappy set of muscles. Quick starting and stopping requires tense contraction and expansion of muscles like the coiling and releasing of a spring. Swimmers work in a different element and require an easy pull for the liquid solid. They require yielding muscles and develop the long, soft and pliable variety. Their muscles are differently distributed. The thigh muscles in the leg and the biceps in the upper arm are most noticeably different, being long and snaky instead of humped.

Resistance (or Drag)

Three types of water resistance (or drag) have been identified: frontal or head-on resistance, surface drag or skin friction, and eddy resistance or tail suction (Figure 1–4).

1. *Frontal resistance* is the resistance to forward progress that is created by the water immediately in front of the swimmer or any part of his body. A consideration of this type of resistance is crucial in any discussion of stroke mechanics.

2. *Surface drag* is the resistance caused by the water immediately next to the body. While this type of resistance is important in airplanes, boats, and high-speed objects, it is of less consequence in swimming. Swimmers shave their legs and arms—some even remove the hair on their heads—in an effort to reduce surface drag. Swimsuit companies rise and fall on the basis of their ability to produce swimwear that is perceived as diminishing surface drag.

   The ritual of "shaving down" coincides with tapering, which is the process of resting and otherwise preparing for peak performance. The introduction of an additional factor makes it hard to attribute improvements in performance results to shaving alone. Nevertheless, it has become a universal practice among swimmers. They reserve this ritual for the special competitions when they want to achieve peak performance because they believe the effect will be lost if they shave down too often. By itself, this belief is the best evidence that *shaving down* is ritualistic. The drops in times are real, but there are several factors which could be responsible: decreased

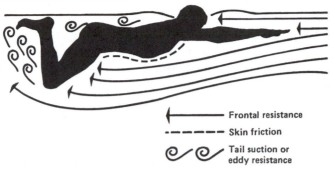

Frontal resistance
------- Skin friction
Tail suction or
eddy resistance

FIGURE 1–4 THREE TYPES OF RESISTANCE

resistance, resulting in increased propulsion; a better feel for the water, resulting in improved stroke mechanics; or the tapering process. Research on the subject is inconclusive, and there are inconsistencies in the lines of reasoning that have been put forward. Since shaving down appears to work, the authors recommend it.

3. *Eddy resistance* is caused by the water that is not able to fill in instantaneously behind poorly streamlined parts of the body. The result is that the body is forced to pull along large numbers of water and air molecules.

Eddy resistance is an important consideration in the design of boats, cars, and airplanes. Designers have spent as much time streamlining the backs of these vehicles as they have their fronts. Insofar as swimming is concerned, too little attention has been given to the effect of this type of resistance. In an effort to decrease frontal resistance there is the theoretical possibility that eddy resistance may be increased.

Engineers can change the shape of a vehicle, but nothing can be done to change the shape of humans, except through diet and body building. Body position can be improved by streamlining the body more effectively, thus creating less resistance. Frontal resistance and eddy resistance are particularly susceptible to being decreased by streamlining.

A swimmer's body can also create greater resistance through poor streamlining in the lateral plane. If the hips and legs sway laterally, for example, both frontal and eddy resistance will increase. When underwater films of champion swimmers are compared with those of average swimmers, it is quite obvious that good swimmers maintain a much more streamlined position in the water than mediocre swimmers, and that they create far less frontal drag and fewer eddies.

Propulsion

Created by the swimmer's arms and legs, propulsion is the force that drives the swimmer forward. Paradoxically, propulsion is created by the resistance offered by the water against which the hands, arms, legs, and feet push backward in order to move forward.

ACTION-REACTION

The second principle to be considered in all the competitive swimming strokes is Newton's *Third Law of Motion*. It states that every action has an equal and opposite reaction. When a runner moves forward, he pushes the ground backward and downward with his back leg, and the reaction pushes him forward and upward with the same amount of force.

It is the same in swimming. When a swimmer pushes backward with his hands, the resultant force drives him forward. Action-reaction is also involved when a swimmer tries deliberately to *climb* on top of the water in the crawl in an effort to reduce frontal resistance. This is ill-advised for two reasons:

1. The swimmer must change mechanics in order to apply force more vertically. This results in superfluous movement, an action-reaction response, which typically manifests itself in a bobbing action.
2. The elevated position of the head created by the downward application of force cannot be maintained indefinitely because the swimmer cannot apply downward force effectively in the second half of the pull. The moment of force created by the head in the raised position causes the head to drop. The end result is a disturbance in body position.

The ability to sustain a more elevated body position is probably a function of relatively greater buoyancy and, perhaps, of faster speed. Otherwise it is energy costly due to a greater proportion of the force generated having to be used to overcome the increased resistance of the superfluous movement and to correct the poor streamlining of the lower extremities. One attribute of talent appears to be the ability to make adjustments which compensate for the cost of such superfluous movements. Less talented athletes pay excessively in both effectiveness and energy for disturbances in streamlining because they do not make the automatic adjustments seen among talented swimmers. If this important fact did not have to be kept constantly in the minds of coaches, it would not be necessary to mention stroke anomalies in a book such as this.

The ability to maintain streamlining of the lower extremities is seen as a probable means of achieving an advantage from the elevation of the upper body. This could be the crucial factor in achieving performance benefits in the more undulating styles of breaststroke (the pop-up and wave-action). Without the necessary flexibility in the spine and appropriate use of the erector spinae muscles, this effect may not be achieved and the style may prove less advantageous for such swimmers than the traditional flat style of breaststroke.

As a swimmer increases his speed, the water resistance beneath his body increases without a corresponding increase in the water resistance above it. The body of a good swimmer acts as an airfoil, and he rises slightly higher in the water. This effect is similar to what happens to water-skiers when a boat pulls them at increasingly faster speeds and they rise in the water until they are literally skimming over it. Given the low speeds at which humans swim, it is better for them to try to optimize a factor they can influence, than to work on one that will disturb

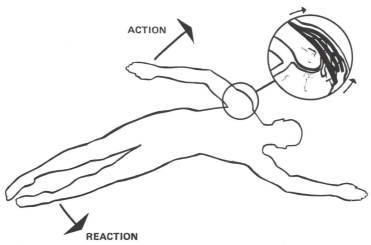

FIGURE 1–5   ACTION-REACTION: AN EXAMPLE OF NEWTON'S THIRD LAW OF MO-
TION

their streamlining. Observing a swimmer from underwater will convince the
viewer of the futility of trying to swim on top of the water or skimming over it.

On the other hand, swimmers can definitely ride too low in the water. Crawl
swimmers, who push the water upward with their hands at the finish of the pull,
experience a reaction that pushes their bodies downward. They may also carry
their heads too low in the water, causing increased resistance.

When the force applied by the hand is directly downward, it tends to push
the swimmer upward, in which case the force is acting against gravity. This force
would be better applied in a more backward direction, resulting in forward
progress. These effects are examples of action-reaction.

What happens out of water is also important. The mechanics of the recovery
of the arms, which in three of the four competitive strokes is out of water, affect
the efficiency and speed of the swimmer. An improper recovery can break the
rhythm of the swimmer's stroke, causing him to pull too fast or too slow, to
shorten his pull too much, or to introduce too long a glide into his arm stroke.

A poor recovery can also increase a swimmer's frontal and eddy resistance.
In another instance of the distorting effect of action-reaction, a wide recovery in
a counterclockwise direction in the crawl, as in Figure 1–5, causes a movement
of the feet in the opposite or clockwise direction. The muscles that recover the
arm attach at the shoulder. When they contract, they exert an equal force at each
end. The lateral movement caused by a wide recovery can be demonstrated to
the swimmer by having him lie in the water, supporting his feet with a tube or
kick board, and perform a wide recovery action. In both the crawl or backstroke
the result will be a readily observable movement of the feet in the opposite
direction.

In the backstroke the arms should be recovered directly overhead. This will
nearly eliminate the lateral reaction of the body.

Lateral reaction in the crawl stoke can be minimized by decreasing the
radius of rotation of the recovering arm, that is, by lifting the elbow up and

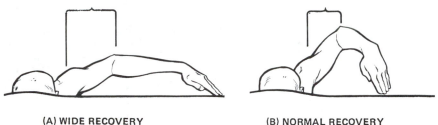

(A) WIDE RECOVERY   (B) NORMAL RECOVERY

FIGURE 1–6   SHORTENING THE RADIUS OF ROTATION
  A. Wide Recovery
  B. Normal Recovery

bringing the hand in, (the change being shown from 1-6-A to 1-6-B). In the butterfly stroke the distorting effect of one recovering arm is canceled by the same effect of the other arm. Lateral body movement is obviously not a concern in this stroke.

THE EFFECT OF LIFT

An understanding of the fluid mechanics of swimming was radically altered when the role of lift in swimming was identified in 1969,[5] 1970,[6] and 1971[7] (see Figure 1–7). Before then it had been generally assumed that the propulsive force created by the swimmer's hand was purely one of drag.

The terms *lift* and *Bernoulli effect* are synonymous. The word *lift* implies work against gravity; it follows that it may be construed as applying only to upward movements. Lift is a force which can be exerted in any direction—upward, downward, forward, backward, and sideways—as it is in swimming.

Oars to row a boat, paddles to propel a canoe, and the old-time paddle wheel to move a river boat are examples of the use of drag (Figure 1–8). The forward thrust in these three cases results from the difference in pressure between the posterior side of the paddle or oar, where the pressure is high, and the anterior side of the paddle or oar, where the wake is formed and the pressure is low (Figure 1–8–A). In this type of propulsion the presence of a wake is crucial. If the flow were completely streamlined, the pressure on the paddle would add up to zero, and movement would not take place.

Examples of lift propulsion are found in the sculling paddles of the gondolas of Venice and in propeller-driven boats and airplanes (Figure 1–8–C). Dolphins, whales, and most large fish depend on lift for propulsion. These creatures propel themselves with large winglike flukes or caudal fins with which they scull their way through the water.

During the period when it was theorized that good crawl swimmers pulled their arms through the water in a line straight down the midline of their bodies, they were thought to be using their arms as paddles, with their hands forming a wake. Drag (resistance) was then assumed to be their only source of propulsion. Accordingly, in an example of Newton's Third Law (action-reaction), if they wanted to move straight forward, swimmers had to push the water straight back. Underwater motion pictures of great swimmers provided the first clues that this

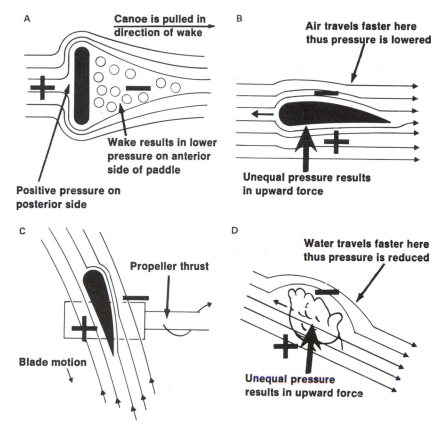

FIGURE 1–7 FOUR APPLICATIONS OF LIFT PROPULSION

A. Wake formation from a paddle. The canoe is pulled in the direction of the wake.

B. A wing provides aerodynamic lift through the camber (curvature) of its surfaces. Because the upper surface is more highly cambered than the lower surface, the air moving over the top surface is forced to move more quickly. This results in a lower pressure on the upper surface as compared with the lower surface and results in aerodynamic lift (Bernoulli's Principle).

C. The propeller of a boat uses Bernoulli's Principle in the same manner, except that the blade moves in a vertical plane and the lift effect is used to push the boat in a horizontal plane.

D. The hand of a swimmer can use lift to propel the swimmer forward by using Bernoulli's Principle instead of relying on wake formation, as the paddle does in (A). The pressure differential between the palm and the back of the hand is determined more by the pitch of the hand in relation to its path through the water than by its camber.

was not happening, but for a long time this evidence was construed as a stroke anomaly and it was disregarded or attempts were made to eliminate it.

In all four strokes such movies reveal an elliptical or curvilinear pull pattern similar to an inverted question mark or S shape. Figure 1–9 shows the arm pull pattern of four champions swimming the four competitive strokes. The dotted line represents the path of the middle finger. A study of these pull patterns reveals that champion swimmers are not pushing directly backward in a straight line, but

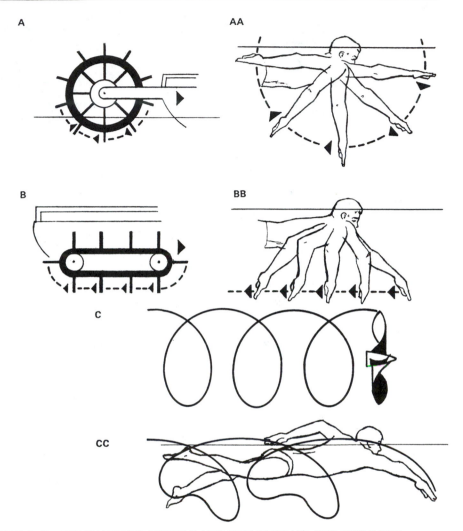

FIGURE 1–8   COMPARISONS OF DRAG AND LIFT IN BOATS AND SWIMMERS

Both an old-fashioned paddle wheel (A) which pushes backward in two dimensions and a swimmer who pulls straight down the midline of his body with no elbow bend (AA) are examples of an inefficient application of force because both are pushing water backward that is already moving backward.

Even less efficient is the moving tread of a caterpillar tank (B), which, if it were used in water, could be compared with a swimmer who bends his elbow in order to push straight back (BB). The continuous tread works when it is applied against a solid, such as the ground, but not against a fluid, such as water, etc.

As the blades of a propeller move forward (C), they constantly encounter still air or water; as the swimmer's body moves forward (CC), it too encounters still water against which to apply more effective force than if the water were already moving backward. This is the reason swimmers use some form of elliptical pull, either in two or three dimensions, but never in a single dimension.

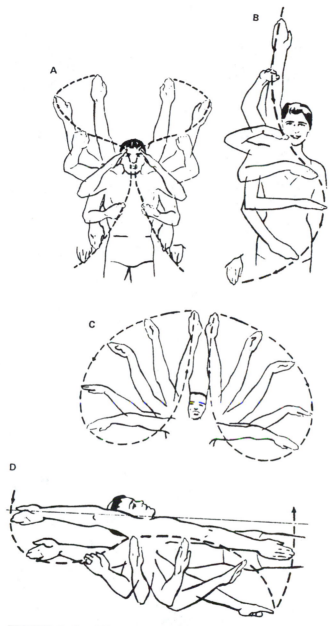

FIGURE 1–9 ARM PULL PATTERNS OF THE FOUR COMPETITIVE STROKES WITH RELATION TO THE BODY

A. Butterfly
B. Crawl
C. Breaststroke
D. Backstroke

The arm strokes of all these swimmers have a number of components in common. They are not straight-line pulls. The arms start the pull with the elbows straight, then, during the pull, the bend of the elbow is increased until the arms are halfway through the pull, at which point the elbows are bent about 90 degrees. From this halfway point onward (except in the breaststroke) the elbows extend until the pull is completed and they are again almost completely straight.

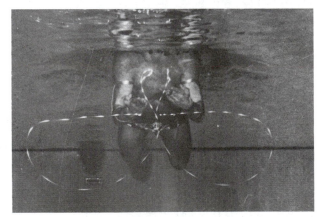

FIGURE 1–10   TWO-DIMENSIONAL VIEW OF THE PATH OF THE MIDDLE FINGER OF
THE FOUR COMPETITIVE STROKES WITH RELATION TO STILL WATER

    A. Butterfly
    B. Crawl
    C. Breaststroke
    D. Backstroke

FIGURE 1–10   *(continued)*

are using some form of zigzag or elliptical pattern. It must be remembered that such illustrations are two dimensional, while the movements they depict are three dimensional. They also show the path of the hand through the water in relation to the swimmer's body, not in relation to still water.

The writers cannot stress too much the flattening effect of photographs and drawings on three-dimensional movements. This is the reason light tracings from the side are better at revealing the true nature of the pull and its relation to water. Regardless of how the pull pattern is depicted, it is elliptical, or, to be more precise, helical (spiral) in shape.

This relationship can be shown by taking a time exposure with a still camera, in a darkened pool, of a swimmer with a flashing light attached to the middle finger of each hand. Another method is to photograph the swimmer with a movie camera held in a static position as the swimmer moves past the camera. These methods are illustrated in Figures 1–10 and 1–11, respectively.

If, indeed, good swimmers use their hands as propellers rather than paddles during at least part of the pull—this concept has been substantiated by other studies and has gained major acceptance[8,9]—the contribution of lift is a significant factor, especially in some swimmers and in some strokes. Among crawl swimmers with relatively little elliptical movement in their pull, lift may be minimal and drag may dominate. Among breaststrokers who display an effective sculling action of the hands and feet, lift probably dominates and drag is minimal.

A sequence of pictures in Chapter 2 (Figure 2–14) presents a freestyler who exhibits very little sculling movement in his pull. This is an elite swimmer, who apparently uses drag as his primary source of propulsion; even so, the combined frontal and side views of his stroke reveal the three-dimensional nature of his pull which enables him to contact still water against which to exert force. Thus he fulfills one of the criteria for efficient production of force. There are elite crawl swimmers who use more of a sculling action, introducing considerable lateral movement in the first half of the pull (see Figure 2–18, which is a series of drawings of the actual stroke of an elite swimmer). Such crawl swimmers probably exploit more lift than drag in their force production.

These authors believe it takes greater power and endurance to employ drag propulsion effectively in the crawl than to exploit lift. Anatomical variations may also influence the type of pull that is most effective for a given swimmer. All these considerations leave coaches in a quandary: Should swimmers be forced into a pattern for the first half of the pull or should they be allowed to evolve a pull, unguided by their coach? The answer may be different for an age-group coach than for a seniors coach, but the common-sense answer is to allow the stroke to evolve, guided by a coach who understands that lateral movement in the freestyle pull is not a stroke flaw.

To understand the principle of lift, it is important to know that fluid pressure diminishes as the speed of flow increases. For example, an airplane wing is so designed and its pitch so inclined in relation to the direction it is traveling as to produce a greater speed of airflow over its upper surface than over its lower surface. This difference in the speed of flow causes a greater pressure on the lower surface and a lesser pressure on the upper surface (Figure 1–7–B) and results in a lift or upward push on the wing.

The propeller of a boat acts in the same manner, exploiting lift to supply the forward thrust (Figure 1–8–C). Similarly, the hand of the swimmer, if it is pitched or inclined in the proper manner in relation to its path through the water, can serve the same function as a propeller (Figure 1–8–C). This effect is consistent with Newtonian physics, being an example of action-reaction.

Another concept is also operating which is appropriate to the discussion of swimming, and that is that *greater efficiency in water is achieved by moving a large amount of water a short distance than by moving a small amount of water a great distance.* Sculling movements therefore permit swimmers to achieve greater efficiency than do straight-line movements.

The propeller of a boat or airplane never pushes the water or air directly backward. It is designed in such a way as to contact stationary water or air with every revolution. This also happens in swimming movements, especially during the early part of the arm pull.

If the swimmer pulls his hand in a straight-line pattern, he is pushing a little water a long distance with great acceleration. Once the water around the hand has been started backward by the movement of the arm, the swimmer can get little traction from this backward moving water. He must therefore move his hand in an elliptical or at least a curvilinear pattern in order to continue encountering still water. In this manner he observes the principle stated above.

Since the swimmer cannot gain much propulsion from water already moving backward, he must solve the following problems: (1) how to evolve a stroke pattern that, once he has started the water moving backward, will allow him to get away from that water and work against still water, and (2) how to pitch his hands in such a way that they will serve as propellers, not paddles. In observing the pull patterns of good swimmers, it can be seen that some do this effectively, while others, especially in the crawl, do not.

Because there is a significant change in the pitch of the hands during the pull in the butterfly and because the zigzag pattern of the arm stroke is pronounced, the butterfly is well suited to illustrate the lift phenomenon. The dotted line follows the pattern of the hands in relation to the body in Figure 1—9—A, which also reveals the relative position of the arms and the degree of bend of the elbows. The pull is often referred to as the hourglass or keyhole pull and it is used with slight variations by all world-class butterflyers.

The pull in relation to still water is shown in Figure 1—11. A tracing of the pull pattern of a world-ranked swimmer was superimposed over a single photo from a sequence of twenty-five frames, in which a 35mm camera was held in a static position on the bottom of the pool, while the subject swam directly over the camera. The motion of his hands with respect to still water was drawn into each frame. The sequence of pictures was taken at twenty-four frames per second. From the time the hands entered the water at Frame 1 (not shown) until they left at Frame 25 (not shown), the elapsed time was slightly over one second. Only one frame of this sequence of twenty-five frames is necessary to illustrate the various hand and arm positions.

The motion of the hands in Frames 1 through 17 suggests the possibility that the force exerted by the water on the hand is one of lift rather than drag. During the outward push of the butterfly arm pull, through Frame 11, the swimmer has the impression he is pulling back on the water. The pictures tell a different story. His hands are actually moving forward. It is likely that a forward thrust, due to lift, is present during this phase of the stroke. This is the case with a propeller blade and a dolphin's flukes, both of which exert a forward thrust while moving forward through the water. Figure 1—12 shows the hand pitch of a good butterflyer.

FIGURE 1—11   THE PATH OF THE HANDS DURING THE PROPULSIVE PHASE OF THE BUTTERFLY ARM PULL IN RELATION TO THE WATER

Note that the hands exit at nearly the same point at which they entered. (Each dot along the pattern represents the position of the hands in each of the twenty-five frames.)

FIGURE 1–12 A DIAGONAL
VIEW OF THE BUTTERFLY
STROKE, SHOWING CHANGES
IN HAND PITCH

A. During the first part of the
pull the palms face diagonally
down and outward

B. The orientation of the hands
changes to face almost directly
backward

C. During the insweep the
palms face diagonally inward

D. As the hands begin to push
back and outward, the pitch
changes once again so the palms
are facing diagonally outward.

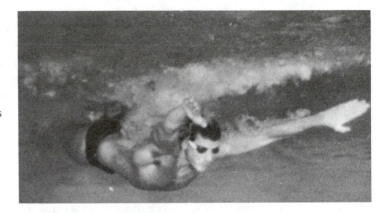

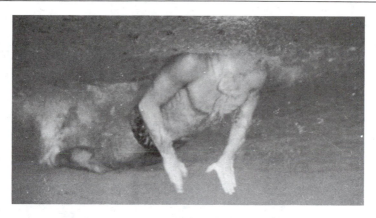

FIGURE 1–12
(continued)

Pull and Hand Position.   In order to achieve the maximum amount of forward propulsion from the arm pull, a high elbow during the first half of the pull is desirable. This action is accomplished through inward (medial) rotation of the upper arm. When the pull is half finished, the elbow should be bent about 90 degrees. This elbow-up position permits the pressure differential between the greater force (+) on the palm of the hand and the lesser pressure (−) on the knuckle side of the hand to push the swimmer horizontally and in a forward direction. It is also possible to achieve some pressure differential by flexing the wrists, and this technique is an option for swimmers who are not strong enough to achieve inward rotation of the upper arm and elbow flexion. But the application of force is less favorable than that achieved by medial rotation of the upper arm because the proper combination of hand pitch and backward thrust are not easy to achieve.

The high elbow position seen in Figure 1–13–A (butterfly), B (crawl), and C (breaststroke) is desirable and is typical of the stroke mechanics of good swimmers. In the backstroke (D) the swimmer bends his elbow and rotates his upper arm in the same manner as that of the other three strokes; but since he is in a supine rather than a prone position, his arm position should be described as elbow-down (Figure 1–13–D).

Hand position during the pull should be flat as opposed to cupped. Studies of the cupped hand versus the flat hand have concluded that the flat hand presents a larger surface area and is able to push more water than the cupped hand. In many photographs in this book the swimmer's thumb is held away from the fingers. This position seems to be neither detrimental nor beneficial.

Concerning minor deviations in finger position, it is wise to heed two maxims: *(1) never subordinate fundamental principles to minor details, and (2) know the difference.* For instance, in positioning the hand for the pull, it is fundamental that it be flat, not cupped; but holding the thumb out at the side, away from the fingers, is a minor detail. On the basis of present knowledge, it appears to provide no advantage or disadvantage.

It is a fact that even the best swimmers have stroke defects. They do well either in spite of these defects—because they have enough ability, strength, or conditioning to overcome them—or because the defects are not important

FIGURE 1–13 HIGH ELBOW
POSITION IN THE FOUR
COMPETITIVE STROKES

   A. Butterfly
   B. Crawl
   C. Breaststroke
   D. Backstroke

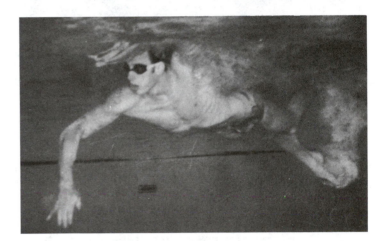

FIGURE 1–13
(continued)

enough to have much effect on performance. Even so, they are deficits not worth imitating consciously.

An aspect of hand position that is critical, if the swimmer is to maximize the role of lift in his forward propulsion, is *hand pitch*. Although the direction of pitch varies at different stages of the pull, the critical angle remains approximately 30 to 40 degrees in relation to the path of the hand through the water in the crawl and butterfly and 90 degrees in the back. Another important element in this context is the swimmer's ability to maintain the critical inclination or angle of pitch. The longer he can do so in the face of the increasing demands of a race

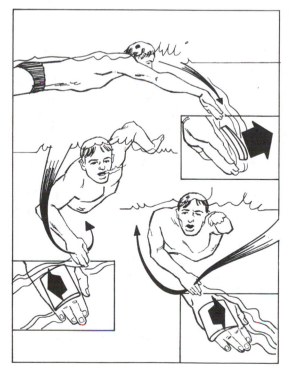

FIGURE 1–14 ANGLE OF ATTACK IN RELATION TO THE WATER'S SURFACE

(fatigue) the better. This is a function of his strength and endurance. Underwater films reveal this essential factor: As a swimmer tires, his ability to maintain correct pitch diminishes. Successful swimmers are able to hold the correct pitch longer (see Figure 1–14).

As the path of the hand changes during the course of the pull, the orientation of the hand must also change in order to maintain the desired pitch. An analysis of underwater films of great swimmers reveals that most of them make these precise changes. A plausible explanation of how they develop desirable patterns is that they are sensitive to changes in water pressure against their hands. In its search for an effective means of applying pressure, the neuromuscular system probably determines the pull pattern and hand pitch through trial-and-error learning, with minimal cerebral involvement.

HAND SPEED AND ACCELERATION

One of the biomechanical influences which affects sports performance is the ability to accelerate. It has been a common assumption that the swimmer who can pull his hand against the water the fastest, without slipping or spinning, would create the greatest forward velocity. Still, no one had tried to equate hand speed with mean velocity or tried to find out if the ability to produce hand speed could be taught to swimmers who lack it. Neither could the authors find any studies that measured hand speed from the beginning of the propulsive phase to the end and that tried to quantify the speed of each segment of the total movement.

Sometime around 1976, in discussing these speculations with Robert Schleihauf, the man who did so much to legitimize the lift theory by measuring the contributions of lift and drag in swimming, the senior author of this book mentioned his ideas about the possible role of acceleration in the exploitation of lift in swimming. Schleihauf had already presented some pull patterns of Olympian Mark Spitz in his article, "A Biomechanical Analysis of Freestyle Aquatic Skill,"[8] and had charted their velocities in three separate planes. These charts are reproduced in Figure 1–15. Schleihauf had also showed the pull patterns in relation to the body of the swimmer, but from underneath, and with relation to the water. Schleihauf's reason for presenting all these aspects was to demonstrate the complexity of the interaction between the pitch of the hands, the velocity being developed, and the mode of propulsion (lift or drag), depending on the phase of the stroke.

Although Schleihauf's primary interest was in identifying lift and drag forces, this study led to the observation that good swimmers apparently *do* accelerate their movements and that this is an important, performance-enhancing effect.

It was decided to examine the hand-speed patterns of several world-class swimmers in the four competitive strokes, looking for elements they might hold in common and for ways the patterns might vary from those of less able swimmers. The force created by the hand varies directly with the speed of the hands. The decision was made not to try to measure this force, but to measure hand speed only.

It was clear from the studies that swimmers apply force in alternating periods of acceleration and deceleration.

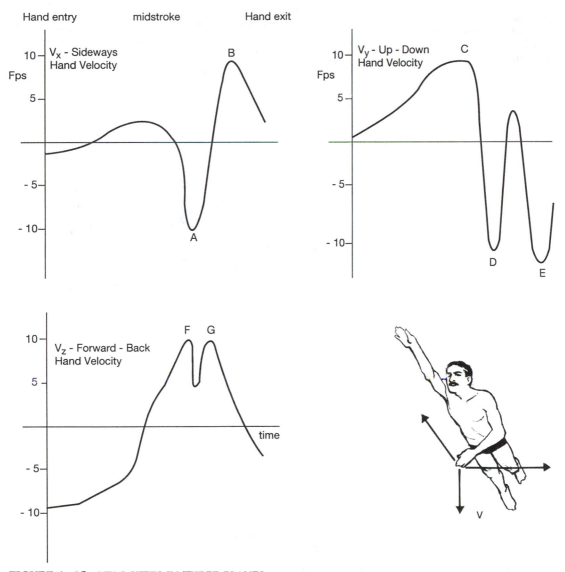

FIGURE 1–15 VELOCITIES IN THREE PLANES

Showing that the velocity curves in each of the planes of the same stroke are very different

Figure 1–16 shows how the hand actually moves in relation to the water as seen from a side view, the hand entering the water at point A and exiting at point B. The figure is shown here, not because it is helpful in promoting the learning process, but because it shows pictorially that lift *does* occur. Otherwise the hand would not exit ahead of the point at which it entered.

Figure 1–17 illustrates the arm pull pattern of Mark Spitz from the side, plotted in segments of one-tenth of a second each. The curve is described by the third finger of the pulling hand and is in relation to the body.

FIGURE 1–16 MARK SPITZ'S
HAND PATTERN IN THE CRAWL
STROKE IN RELATION TO THE
WATER

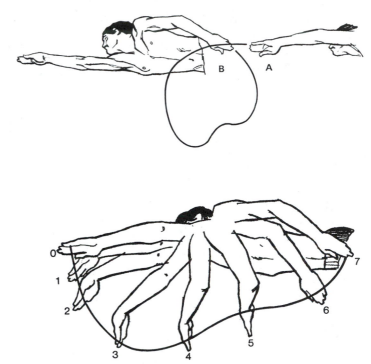

FIGURE 1–17 MARK SPITZ'S HAND-ACCELERATION PATTERN IN RELATION TO HIS
BODY

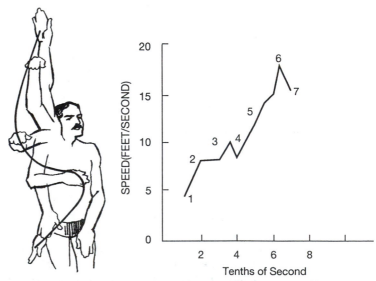

FIGURE 1–18 A. MARK SPITZ'S HAND-SPEED PATTERN FROM UNDERNEATH AND IN
RELATION TO HIS BODY
B. GRAPHIC EXPRESSION OF THE HAND-SPEED PATTERN SHOWN IN (A).

Figure 1–18–A is the pull pattern of Mark Spitz, shot from under the body, and Figure 1–18–B is the hand-speed curve of Mark Spitz developed from measurements in such acceleration patterns as shown in Figure 1–17 and 1–18–A, that is, as the hand moves in relationship to the body. This curve is typical of world-class swimmers. It was thought these illustrations would be helpful in teaching proper pitch of the hands and in understanding how acceleration might be attained.

Such hand-speed curves and acceleration patterns are easier for the average swimmer to interpret than those which relate the pull pattern to the water against which it is applied, as in Figure 1–16.

Hand Speed in Good Swimmers in the Four Strokes

Figure 1–19 is Rowdy Gaines's hand speed curve, when swimming the crawl stroke at maximum effort. Each arm position, starting with point A, represents the distance the arm traveled in one-tenth of a second, the propulsive phase of each arm stroke lasting a little over five-tenths of a second. The figure reveals that the hand follows a pattern in which the three-dimensional speed continuously increases, except between points D and E where there is a dip in the curve. This finding confirms that of Schleihauf.[10] The same deceleration pattern is apparent in the speed patterns we have examined of other world-class swimmers, such as Jim Montgomery, who owned the 100 meter record just prior to Rowdy Gaines, and Matt Biondi, who broke Gaines's record.

Alex Baumann's backstroke (see Figure 1–20) at slow speed is the only representation in this section of the hand speed of a swimmer *not* swimming at maximum effort. It is presented here to show that world-class swimmers tend to have similar hand-speed patterns even at moderate speeds, the difference being the time it takes to complete the pull.

Figure 1–21 depicts Nobutaka Taguchi's hand-speed pattern in the breaststroke. Taguchi is swimming at maximum effort. The entire propulsive phase of the arm pull takes slightly less than four-tenths of a second. The bimodal pattern is similar to that of the other strokes in many respects. The dip in the speed curve indicates deceleration of hand speed between points C and D, when the hands change the direction of the pull from outward to inward. Maximum speed is

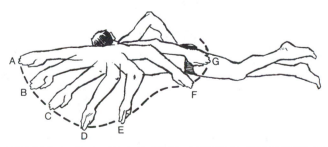

FIGURE 1–19 ACCELERATION PATTERN OF ROWDY GAINES'S CRAWL STROKE IN RELATION TO HIS BODY

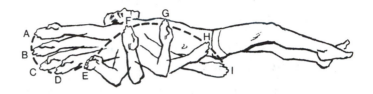

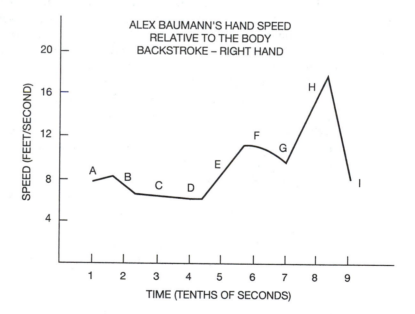

ALEX BAUMANN'S HAND SPEED
RELATIVE TO THE BODY
BACKSTROKE – RIGHT HAND

FIGURE 1–20 A. ACCELERATION PATTERN OF ALEX BAUMANN'S BACKSTROKE IN RELATION TO HIS BODY
B. GRAPHIC EXPRESSION OF (A)

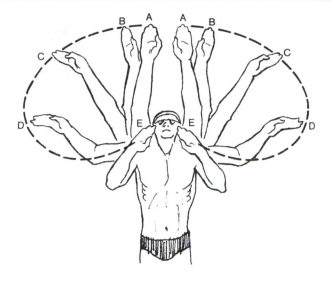

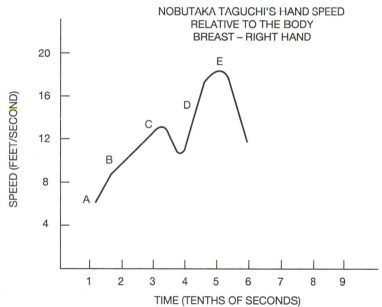

NOBUTAKA TAGUCHI'S HAND SPEED
RELATIVE TO THE BODY
BREAST – RIGHT HAND

TIME (TENTHS OF SECONDS)

FIGURE 1–21 A. ACCELERATION PATTERN OF NOBUTAKA TAGUCHI'S BREAST-STROKE IN RELATION TO HIS BODY
B. GRAPHIC EXPRESSION OF (A)

achieved with the inward sculling action of the hands from points D to E. In coaching breaststroke technique, it is a good policy to have swimmers emphasize hand acceleration during this phase of the stroke.

Figure 1–22 depicts Jim Halliburton's hand-speed pattern when swimming butterfly at fast speed. The time involved in applying propulsive force is approximately five-tenths of a second. The decrease in hand speed, causing the dip in the

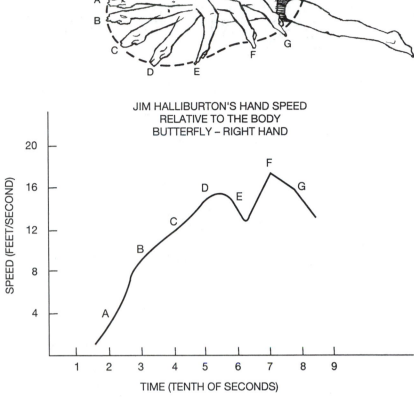

FIGURE 1–22 A. ACCELERATION PATTERN OF JIM HALLIBURTON'S BUTTERFLY IN RELATION TO HIS BODY
B. GRAPHIC EXPRESSION OF (A)

speed curve near point E, occurs when the hands scull inward. Peak hand velocity of 18 feet per second is reached at point F, when the arms are finishing the pull.

Hand Speed in Poor Swimmers

Poor swimmers, regardless of their deficiencies, tend to exhibit inappropriate patterns of hand speed and acceleration. Although the hand-speed patterns of exceptionally poor swimmers reveal that they achieve some acceleration, they seldom attain even 60 percent of the magnitude of hand speed of good swimmers. In this study, the hand-speed patterns of several high school swimmers of marginal ability were studied. Their graphs are not presented here, but each was unlike those of world-class swimmers in one or more of the following respects: (1) too much hand speed early in the pull, (2) too little hand speed at the end of the pull, (3) erratic hand-speed patterns with two or more dips in the curve, and (4) good hand-speed pattern with one hand and poor hand-speed pattern with the other.

For more information on the role of acceleration in swimming, the reader may want to consult the footnotes 11, 12, and 13 at the end of the chapter.

THE EVENNESS OF APPLICATION OF PROPULSION

Ideally, an even application of force is preferable to a fluctuating one in all so-called cyclic activities, which feature repetitive movements. In reality, the evenness of application cannot be termed a principle because it is unattainable. Nevertheless, speaking relatively, coming as close as possible should be the goal.

In specialized strength training for swimming, deviations in force production are plotted against a so-called ideal force curve which conceptualizes or advocates an even application of force (see Figure 8 in Appendix II).

The primary reason the crawl stroke is faster than the butterfly or breast-stroke is its evenness of application of force relative to the other two strokes. Although there is more total propulsive force when both arms are pulling during the butterfly than at any time during the crawl stroke, there is also a phase in each cycle of the butterfly when there is no propulsion from the arms. That, of course, is the recovery phase. The crawl stroke does not contain a phase of profound deceleration.

The mechanics of a stroke should be designed to permit the body to travel at as even a forward speed as possible. If a swimmer moves repeatedly from acceleration to deceleration, much of the force he could be using to overcome water resistance is lost in overcoming inertia. This would happen if he were using the "catch-up" style of crawl stroke, for example.

The idea of evenness of application should not be confused with the concept of increasing acceleration throughout the stroke. Once again, these are matters of relativity. Fluctuations in propulsive force in swimming are inevitable. The catch-up crawl stroke, in which one arm completes its pull and recovery before the other begins, causes fluctuations in propulsive force which are overly profound and which are very costly in their "stop-and-go" effect.

Fluctuations, being inevitable, should be minimized as much as possible. If there appears to be a paradox in that swimmers are being advised to accelerate the arm pull, beginning with a slow entry and accelerating throughout the pull, the seeming paradox may be resolved by emphasizing that, while swimmers should try to accelerate as described, they should avoid excessive deceleration.

In the crawl and backstroke, avoidance of excessive deceleration can be accomplished by beginning to pull one arm before or immediately as the other arm finishes the pull, providing a smooth, constant application of forward propulsion of the arms. In the butterfly stroke, the arm pull should begin almost as soon as the arms enter the water. Any prolonged glide of the arms up front will cause the body to decelerate. In the breaststroke, there should be a slight glide after the arms are extended forward, since that timing provides the best use of the momentum developed by the kick. This momentum causes the body to plane or level off and create less resistance. If the swimmer waits too long in this glide position, his forward momentum will decrease too greatly, his feet will drop, and he will have to pay an excessive price for his next acceleration. The only exception would be the case of a swimmer who has a relatively poor kick and a very strong pull. Such a swimmer should eliminate the glide and begin to pull as soon as the arms become fully extended. Two former world-record holders, Chet Jastremski and Nobutaka Taguchi, were examples of this type of swimmer.

TRANSFER OF MOMENTUM

It is quite easy to *transfer the momentum* of one part of the body to another part or to the rest of the body. This principle is used in many movements performed in and out of water. In the wind-up start—now used primarily in relay exchanges—the momentum developed by the arms during the wind-up and prior to leaving the starting block is transferred to the swimmer's entire body and helps achieve greater distance in the dive (see Chapter 6, Figure 6–3).

This principle also applies to the recovery of the arms in the crawl, butterfly, and backstroke. In the backstroke recovery the arms develop momentum in a circular motion. Immediately before the recovering arm goes into the water, it has developed momentum in a downward direction (Figure 1–23–A). If the speed of the arm is checked immediately before it enters the water (Figure 1–23–B), the momentum of the arm is transferred to the body, forcing the upper body and head downward (Illustration A). A person can hardly see a backstroke race without noting at least one swimmer whose head bobs up and down as a result of this stroke defect. To avoid it, the backstroker needs merely to let the arm continue into the water with the momentum it developed during the recovery. The water resistance will tend to dissipate most of this momentum (Illustration B).

Slowing the speed of the recovering arm or arms in the crawl or butterfly stroke immediately before the hands enter the water also has detrimental effects. This will be discussed in subsequent chapters.

THE THEORETICAL SQUARE LAW

The resistance a body creates in water (or any other fluid or gas) varies approximately with the square of its velocity. To illustrate this fact, consider an airplane going 100 miles per hour and creating 1000 pounds of resistance. When the airplane doubles its speed to 200 miles per hour, it does not simply double its

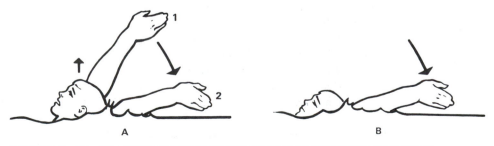

FIGURE 1–23   TRANSFER OF MOMENTUM IN THE BACKSTROKE RECOVERY

resistance. Rather, the resistance increases by four times, or to 4000 pounds. If the plane increases its speed to 300 miles per hour, it now increases its resistance by nine times. This law also applies to a swimmer's speed and resistance in water. A direct and practical application of this law to the swimming strokes is found in the speed with which the recovering arm enters the water.

If a swimmer makes his entry twice as fast as he does normally, in what is called a rushed recovery, he creates four times more resistance to forward progress than he would otherwise. A rushed recovery, therefore, not only breaks rhythm but, by increasing the resistance to forward progress, tends to have a braking effect. What should determine the speed of recovery? The swimmer cannot delay placing his hand in the water just for the purpose of creating less resistance. That would quickly become counterproductive, destroying the rhythm of the total stroke. The speed of the recovering arm should correspond to that of the pulling arm. It may be a bit faster in some cases, but not significantly so, and the difference can be adjusted by allowing the hand to sink into the water slightly before beginning to pull. It is difficult to recover quickly with one arm and, simultaneously, pull steadily with the other. A close parallel in the speed of the pull and the speed of the recovery is an important factor in stroke rhythm.

When a swimmer doubles the speed with which his arms move through the water, he creates four times as much propulsion, providing his stroke mechanics remain the same. A corollary to the theoretical square law is a physiological law which says that the energy expenditure of a muscle approximately cubes with the speed of the muscle's contraction. In other words, when the speed of the pulling arm is doubled, the energy expenditure is increased eight times. Thus, while a faster arm pull does increase propulsion, it also increases energy expenditure and oxygen consumption disproportionately. This explains why swimmers, who spin their arms while swimming, tire quickly. It is also the reason that middle-distance and distance races should be paced.

BUOYANCY

It is common knowledge that a lightly loaded boat is easier to pull or push through the water than a heavily loaded one of the same size and shape. It displaces less water, floats higher, creates less resistance, and has less inertia to overcome.

A light, buoyant swimmer also floats higher and creates less resistance than a heavier, less buoyant swimmer of the same size. Swimmers vary greatly in body type, bone size, muscular development, weight distribution, relative amounts of fat tissue, lung capacity, and so on. All these factors affect individual *buoyancy* and floating position. A large-boned, heavily muscled male floats lower in the water than a small-boned, lightly muscled female; but he has more muscular force available to move him through the water, thus somewhat canceling her advantage.

Both extremes in buoyancy have been observed among swimmers: some who are so buoyant they can float on their backs in a horizontal position, others who cannot float in any position. Yet swimmers of each extreme can be and have been world-record holders.

FOOTNOTES

1. Bartholomew Parr, M.D., *London Medical Dictionary*, Vol. II (Philadelphia: Gilbert Marshall, 1902), p. 5.

2. William Bachrach, in collaboration with Clarence A. Bush, *The Outline of Swimming: An Encyclopedia of the Sport* (Chicago: J. B. Bradwell Publishers, 1924), p. 129.

3. James Hay, The Biomechanics of Sports Technique (Englewood Cliffs, NJ: Prentice-Hall, Inc., 1973), p. 5.

4. Bachrach, *Outline of Swimming*, p.149.

5. James E. Counsilman, "The Role of Sculling Movements in the Arm Pull," *Swimming World*, Vol. X, No. 12 (Dec. 1969), pp. 6, 7, and 43.

6. James E. Counsilman, "The Application of Bernoulli's Principle to Human Propulsion in Water," Swimming I: Proceedings of the First International Symposium on the Biomechanics of Swimming, Water Polo, and Diving; L. Lewillie and J. P. Clarys, eds. (Baltimore: University Park Press, 1970), pp. 59–71.

7. R. M. Brown and James E. Counsilman, "The Role of Lift in Propelling the Swimmer," *Selected Topics on Biomechanics*, J. M. Cooper, ed. (Chicago: Athletic Institute, 1971), pp. 179–88.

8. Robert Schleihauf, "A Biomechanical Analysis of Freestyle Aquatic Skill," *Swimming Technique* (Fall 1974), pp. 89–96.

9. Bodo Ungerechts, "Optimizing Propulsion in Swimming by Rotation of the Hands," Swimming III: Proceedings of the Third International Symposium on the Biomechanics of Swimming; J. Terauds and E. H. Bedingfield, eds., R. C. Nelson and C. A. Morehouse, series eds. (Baltimore: University Park Press, 1979), pp. 55–61.

10. Schleihauf, *A Biomechanical Analysis*, (Fall 1974), 11:89–96.

11. John M. Wasilak, "Training at Various Velocities on the Biokinetic Swim Bench, Related to the Three-Dimensional Hand-Speed Patterns of the Front Crawl" (submitted in partial fulfillment.of the requirements for the PED Degree, School of Health, Physical Education, and Recreation, Indiana University, Bloomington, IN (1988).

12. James E. Counsilman, "The Importance of Hand Speed and Acceleration in Swimming the Crawl Stroke," *Swimming Technique* (1981), 18(1) 22–26.

13. James E. Counsilman and John M. Wasilak, "Hand Speed and Hand Acceleration Patterns in Swimming Strokes," *American Swimming Coaches Association, World Clinic Yearbook* (1981), pp. 41–55, Ft. Lauderdale, FL.

CHAPTER 2

The Crawl Stroke

The origin of the crawl stroke is lost in the past. It is probable that some version of an alternating, overarm stroke evolved in nearly every society since the emergence of modern humankind, especially among those who settled along oceans, seas, and other bodies of water. In some cases, the crawl seems to have appeared, disappeared, and reappeared, all in response to the vagaries of custom, chance, imitation—all the influences that affect human activity. For instance, there is evidence in art and literature that some form of the crawl developed in the countries surrounding the Mediterranean, only to be rejected later when belief in the dangers of complete immersion in the water prevailed and then revived again when explorers took note of its efficiency among the Polynesians and brought it back to Europe. The stroke has gone through many stylistic variations to reach its present form. It now consists of an alternating, overarm action combined with some form of flutter kick.

The rules for competition in the freestyle, which to all intents means the crawl, are simple and few:

1. Start—The forward start shall be used.
2. Stroke—Freestyle means that in an event so designated the swimmer may

swim any style; except that in a medley relay or individual medley event, freestyle means any style other than butterfly, breaststroke, or backstroke.

3. Turns—Upon completion of each length the swimmer must touch the wall.

4. Finish—The swimmer shall have finished the race when any part of his person touches the wall after completing the prescribed distance.[1]

BODY AND HEAD POSITION

The principles discussed in Chapter 1 regarding body position also apply in the crawl stroke.

Horizontal Body Alignment

Body position in the crawl stroke should be as streamlined as possible, while still permitting the feet to be deep enough in the water for effective action. Any disturbance of streamlining that creates additional drag decreases the swimmer's speed and increases energy cost. Coaches must constantly keep in mind how a swimmer's energy is distributed. If a choice must be made, it should always be towards driving the swimmer forward rather than lifting him up.

To measure the difference in drag (negative resistance) between the head held in Position A, in which the waterline broke at the hairline level, and Position B, in which the waterline broke at the eyebrow level, several swimmers were towed by an apparatus in which the tension created on the towing line was recorded.[2] The drag measurements in Figure 2–1 are an average of three trials at each position. They show that Position A created less resistance than Position B at all speeds measured. These speeds ranged between 1.1 feet per second and 7.03 feet per second. As the swimmer was dragged at the higher speeds, there

FIGURE 2–1   DRAG MEASUREMENTS WITH THE HEAD IN TWO POSITIONS

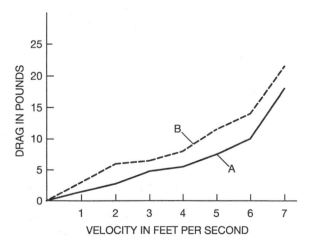

Position A. Drag created by subject with head held in normal position, with water line at hairline level.
Position B. Drag created by subject with head held in a high position, with water line at eyebrow level.

FIGURE 2–2   BREATHING INTO THE CONCAVITY BEHIND THE BOW WAVE
   A. Preserving streamlining by breathing into the concavity behind the bow wave.
   B. Disturbing streamlining by raising the head too high during breathing.

was correspondingly less difference in the amount of drag between the two positions.

   The head should be carried with a slight posterior flexion of the neck. If the head position is correct, it will create a bow wave that will leave a trough or concavity in the water at the side of the head where the swimmer will be able to breathe without having to roll too far or lift the head too high (see Figure 2–2–A and B).

   Unfortunately, this study did not measure the drag created at a position between the two extremes. Nevertheless, it did reveal a significant increase in drag at Position B, which most coaches would agree is somewhat high. The study reinforces majority opinion that the head should be carried closer to Position A than to Position B.

Another practice which disturbs horizontal body alignment without contributing to forward propulsion is to turn the palm up as the hand leaves the water and enters the beginning of the recovery phase. This occurs after the propulsive phase has ended and the hand can no longer apply appreciable backward force but it can create an upward force that disrupts streamlining. The swimmer should prepare the hand for exit from the water by turning the palm inward toward the body. Hand pitch at this point should look as though the swimmer were removing the hand from a side pants pocket, that is, angled slightly with the little finger leaving the water first.

Body position may also be affected by velocity, but the effect is negligible. Fish and dolphins reportedly attain swimming speeds of 20 miles per hour or more, while the swimming speed of humans reaches less than 5 miles per hour. When marine animals reach those speeds of 20 miles per hour they are in their most streamlined and horizontal body position and their entire bodies are completely submerged. When they "porpoise," that is, rise above the water, it is *not* for the sake of increased speed. Biologists believe they are either looking for food or engaging in a social activity.

The point is that the key to faster swimming is not in trying to lift oneself higher in the water but in streamlining and applying forward propulsive force as effectively as possible. This premise being widely accepted, it is agreed that swimmers should avoid excessive up-and-down movements.

To correct the three defects described earlier and illustrated in Figure 2–3: (1) the swimmer should carry his head so the hairline is approximately at the waterline, rotating his head on its axis when breathing, rather than lifting and

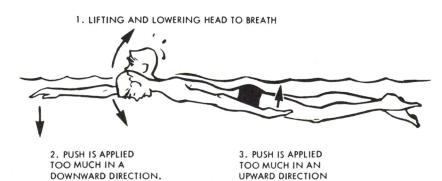

1. LIFTING AND LOWERING HEAD TO BREATH

2. PUSH IS APPLIED
TOO MUCH IN A
DOWNWARD DIRECTION.

3. PUSH IS APPLIED
TOO MUCH IN AN
UPWARD DIRECTION

FIGURE 2–3   THREE STROKE DEFECTS WHICH CAUSE EXCESSIVE UP-AND-DOWN MOVEMENTS OF THE BODY

The horizontal alignment of the body in the vertical plane is most frequently disturbed by the following defects: (A) Lifting the head out of the water to breathe, which causes the rest of the body to drop. Lowering the head causes the body to rise slightly.

(B) Directing the force of the first part of the pull straight down, which results in an elevation of the upper torso.

(C) Keeping the elbow straight at the end of the pull, and the palm pushing upward, directs the force of the armstroke upward, which causes the hips to drop.

lowering it, taking the breath as nearly as possible in the trough in back of the bow wave; (2) the swimmer should press his hands in a more backward direction when beginning to pull, rather than directly downward, and the hand should be pitched diagonally outward at entry, rather than parallel to the surface of the water; and (3) as the swimmer ends the propulsive phase and prepares for the recovery, the palm should be turned inward to face the hip and the hand should be slipped out of the water, little finger first, as though the hand was being pulled from the pocket, rather than finishing with a vigorous upward push. (See the arm-pull in the sequence of pictures at the end of this chapter.)

Lateral Body Alignment

Good lateral body alignment is as important as horizontal alignment in the crawl stroke. Since side-to-side movement of any part of the body distorts alignment and increases resistance, excessive movements in this plane should be minimized. A swimmer whose head, shoulders, hips, and feet weave back and forth sideways is easy to spot. Viewing a swimmer frequently from directly in back and at a height of 10 to 20 feet is helpful in making the diagnosis.

A good way to describe this fault to the swimmer is to tell him he is dragging along half of the water in his lane, whereas, if he corrects the cause of the lateral movement, he will be moving less than a quarter of the water in his lane. The less water a swimmer has to push out of his way or drag along with him, the better. Movies or videotapes taken from the vantage point described above will also help the swimmer realize how much he is *wiggling or swaying*.

Although a swimmer appears to move in an almost straight line, swimming movements are circular or variations of circular movement. Swimmers in the water are not exempt from the laws that apply to all bodies suspended in fluids, including air. Any circular movement of the arm or legs, either during recovery or pull, will tend to have a reaction which will distort body alignment in the opposite direction. This manifestation of Newton's Third Law of Motion (the action-reaction principle), is discussed in Chapter I.

To demonstrate action-reaction, have the swimmer place both feet in an inner tube and lie face down in the water, both hands at his sides. As he recovers one arm in a wide circular motion, he will notice his feet swinging to the opposite side. This motion of the feet can be minimized by changing the arm recovery from a wide sweeping motion to one with a high elbow and the hand close under the elbow. (See Chapter 1, Figure 1–5.)

While it might seem that the best way for a crawl swimmer's arm to pull through the water would be in a line directly under the body, good swimmers don't. Rather they pull in a curvilinear pattern near, across, and around the midline of the body. Good lateral alignment of the body can nevertheless be disturbed by pulling the arm too far across either side of a line running vertically and directly under the center of gravity of the swimmer's body. (See Chapter 1, Figure 1–9.)

The lateral or sidewards flexion of the head off the longitudinal axis of rotation—an action frequently seen among crawl swimmers when they breathe—not only throws the head out of alignment, but also affects the alignment of the rest of the body. Figure 2–4 depicts this action-reaction phenomenon.

FIGURE 2–4 LATERAL FLEXION OF THE HEAD PRO-
DUCES MOVEMENT OF THE LEGS IN THE OPPOSITE
DIRECTION

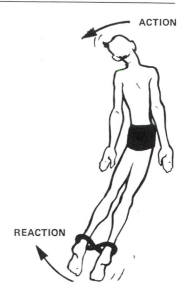

Another stroke error which causes excessive lateral movement, particularly of the shoulders, is checking or slowing the speed of the recovering arm by muscular effort before the hand and arm enter the water. When this occurs, much of the momentum of the recovering arm is transferred to the upper body, resulting in lateral movement.

Obviously many factors can operate to destroy good body alignment (streamlining), however, lateral movement is easily discernible when the swimmer is viewed as he swims directly away from or toward the observer. Coaches need to frequently observe swimmers from this vantage point.

If it is possible to combine one force that distorts the body alignment in one direction simultaneously with another force that affects it in the opposite direction, providing they are equal, they will cancel each other and the body will remain in relatively straight alignment. An example of this technique is the two-beat crossover kick (see Figure 2–5, p. 42). In this style, the reaction to the recovery of the arm in a clockwise direction throws the feet out of alignment in the opposite (counterclockwise) direction, while the kick of the foot in a sideward direction keeps the hips and feet in.

THE FLUTTER KICK

The Role of the Kick: Propulsive or Stabilizing?

The main source of propulsion in the crawl is the arm stroke. The primary function of the kick is to stabilize and keep the feet from dropping, thus preserving streamlining. The lateral thrust of the kick serves to cancel the tendency of the recovering arm to disturb body alignment. It is possible that some very fast swimmers create propulsion with their kick. They would necessarily be six-beat kickers. To maximize that possibility, it is important that the kick not be so high that the entire foot is out of water at any point in the kick. Such an action causes the foot to bring air bubbles into the water on its downward path, thus diminishing the density of the medium against which the kick is exerting force.

A comparison between the crawl stroke and an automobile with a separate front- and rear-wheel drive may serve to illustrate the point that the kick is not usually propulsive. The front wheels are turning at a rate of 30 miles per hour, while the rear wheels are turning at a speed of only 20 miles per hour. What will be the total speed of the car? Will the rear wheels contribute anything to the speed of the car?

This illustration applies because the swimmer can pull himself faster than he can kick himself through the water. In the case of the car, the rear wheels add nothing to its total speed but, instead, serve as a drag. The total speed of the car, therefore, is less than 30 miles per hour. The comparison is not precise in that the swimmer's arms and legs do not have a similar amount or kind of traction with the water that the tires have with the road; thus, they slip. It *would* be accurate if the car were on an icy road and the forward speed were only 15 miles per hour, while the speed of the front and rear wheels remained 30 and 20 miles per hour, respectively. In this case, the rear wheels would be turning faster than the road was going under them and would then contribute to the total speed of the car.

Whether the swimmer gets any propulsion from the kick depends on whether the feet can push the water backward faster than the swimmer's total speed through the water. Some swimmers can achieve this speed, but the energy cost is enormous and not worthwhile except among sprinters with a very strong kick. All others are better off using this energy to pull themselves through the water with their arms, expending only enough energy in kicking to maintain body alignment.

To test whether a swimmer receives any propulsion from the kick, an apparatus was devised to tow the subjects at various speeds, while measuring the tension on the towing line. Subjects were towed while in a glide position without kicking and again in a glide position while kicking. The tension was measured to see if it was greater, the same, or less when kicking than when just being towed in a glide position. Generally, at the lower speeds of under 5 feet per second, when the swimmer kicked at maximum effort, the tension on the line decreased. However, when the swimmer was pulled at speeds greater than 5 feet per second, the kick did not contribute anything, and, in some instances, actually created an increased drag.[3]

The weakness of this experiment is that the data can be interpreted various ways. No distance crawl swimmer is capable of kicking the full distance of an event such as the 1500-meter freestyle at full effort. The tendency is exactly opposite: The longer the race, the less the swimmer kicks. The kick decreases because the heart can supply only so much blood to active muscles. If a swimmer kicks and pulls equally hard, the pulling muscles will have to share a disproportionate amount of the available blood supply with the kicking muscles, since active muscles get their share of the fuel whether they deserve it or not on the basis of their contribution to total forward propulsion. The result will be the earlier fatigue of the arms. The authors believe a reduced kick is advisable, particularly in distance events. World records have been set in the distance events by swimmers with reduced kicks, some of whom kicked as few as two beats per arm cycle. The great Russian, twice Olympic champion, Vladimir Salnikov is an example of such a swimmer, as is Janet Evans, world-record holder in the women's 1500-meter freestyle. Many two-beat, distance kickers switch to four or six beats into and out of their turns. Salnikov and Evans are examples of this sort of swimmer.

As for swimmers who switch to a more vigorous kick at the end of a distance race, we say they employ a final "kick." If this seems to contradict what has just been said about the nonpropulsive nature of the kick, these authors don't believe it is. The final "kick" can involve either increased kicking frequency, kicking amplitude, or both. Or by eliciting a matching pickup in the frequency and power of the pull, it can become more a tactical device than a substantive contribution to the end of the race.

The situation is just the opposite for sprinters. Since a sprinter rides slightly higher in the water, if she does not increase the tempo and effort of her kick to match that of the pull, the front part of her body will rise and her legs will drop deeper into the water. It is not uncommon to see swimmers who use a two-beat kick (two beats per arm cycle) in the distance events switch to a six-beat kick when sprinting.

Adrian, Singh, and Karpovich determined the energy cost of the leg kick, arm stroke, and whole crawl stroke of twelve subjects of both sexes. They summarized on the basis of their data:

> The energy cost of the leg kick is greater than that of the arm stroke and the whole stroke. The energy cost of the arm stroke is less than that of the whole stroke at the low velocities, but becomes greater than the whole stroke as the velocity increases.
>
> Formulas for the prediction of oxygen requirement for the leg kick and arm stroke were determined for the group and for the best swimmer. A similar formula for the whole stroke from data of the best swimmer was also determined.
>
> Evidence was obtained to substantiate the belief that the leg kick should be kept at minimum velocity when competing in the 1500 meter crawl.
>
> In general, the efficiency of the leg kick is less than 1 per cent, whereas the arm stroke average efficiency is 2.24 per cent. The efficiency of the whole stroke was slightly higher than that cited in other studies, ranging from 1.71 to 3.99 per cent.[4]

The data in this study indicated that the kick became an increasingly important factor as the swimmer went faster and approached top speed, a result that should not be surprising (see page 39 and footnote 3 in this chapter).

Swimmers can kick too much, but they can also kick too little. The degree of effort should be evaluated individually, with the swimmer selecting the technique that allows him to swim the fastest. Regardless of the foregoing, leg action is important. If the legs are not conditioned, they will become fatigued and less effective in their stabilizing role. If the kick is mechanically poor, failing to move the swimmer effectively on kick board drills, it will be less effective as part of the total stroke and may even create additional drag.

The Timing of the Kick

Coordination of the kick with the arms is important because, if the hips are permitted to roll with the shoulders, the feet will be in a good position to thrust diagonally sidewards at the proper time, and the kick will be fulfilling its neutralizing role.

The sequence of drawings at the end of the chapter illustrates the proper relationship of kick to arm stroke. The lateral thrust is apparent in underwater movies and videos of good crawl swimmers. There it is easier to recognize that as the arm swings forward in an arc by action of the deltoid muscle at the beginning of the arm recovery there is a movement of the legs in the opposite direction, which neutralizes the effect of the recovery.

Another important point regarding the timing of the arms and legs concerns the end of the pull. As the arm finishes its pull, it is pushing backward and upward. This action causes the hips to be pulled further underwater if the downbeat of the kick does not correspond with the upward movement of the arm. The authors have studied underwater movies of many great crawl swimmers and, in every case, this particular timing has been evident regardless of whether they were using a two- or six-beat kick.

Kicking Patterns

Three different kicking patterns are seen with the crawl stroke: the six-beat kick, the two-beat, and the two-beat crossover.

The Six-Beat Kick in the Crawl Stroke.   The timing of the leg kick and arm stroke is illustrated in Figure 2–5. This timing is common to the crawl, regardless of kicking style. Although a slight majority of swimmers develop a six-beat kick per arm-stroke cycle, there are minor variations in the kick and the manner in which the diagonal thrust of the feet is made within the six-beat context. Some six-beat kickers use a hesitation and drag of their feet on every third kick at the point at which each foot is at the bottom of the kicking cycle. This *drag* kick serves as a rudder in keeping straight body alignment. Certainly the drag effect of the feet creates increased resistance, but it may be more than compensated for by the resultant advantageous effect on general body alignment. Although Figure 2–5 does not show it, the downward thrust of the kick occurs during the end of the arm pull. This timing is common to nearly all elite swimmers. The purpose of this timing is to allow the downward thrust of the kick to counteract and neutralize the tendency of the arm pull to pull the body downward. In the sequence of drawings presented at the end of the chapter (Figure 2–18), the swimmer is using the six-beat kick that is normal among most crawl swimmers.

The Straight Two-Beat Kick in the Crawl Stroke.   The straight two-beat flutter kick is characterized by two beats per arm cycle, or one beat per arm pull. When a two-beat kick is used by crawl swimmers who also use a high elbow recovery, a large lateral thrust of the legs, such as that illustrated in Figure 2–6, becomes unnecessary. Among swimmers with a high elbow recovery, the leg

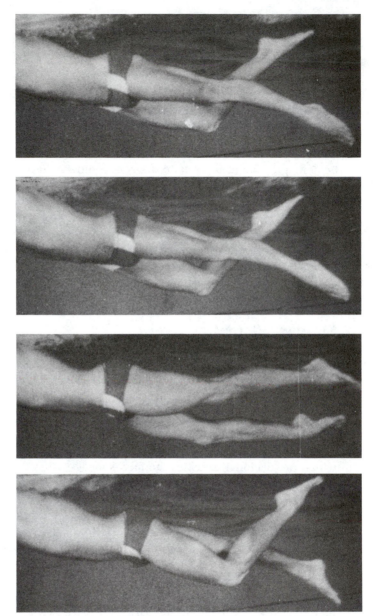

FIGURE 2–5   THE TIMING OF THE KICK AND PULL IN THE CRAWL

A. The leg closest to the viewer is completing the downbeat and right leg is finishing the upbeat. The feet are at or near maximum spread.

B. The upward beat of the left leg is made with a straight knee. The downward beat of the right leg begins with the knee bending; a definite spread of the legs at the knee is noticeable.

C. The left leg continues its upbeat with very little bend at the knee. The right knee is almost fully extended. Notice the knee separation.

D. The left knee bends significantly, causing the foot to continue upward to its highest point. The right leg extends fully and reaches its lowest point. Propulsion is derived primarily from the downward movement.

action is similar to that of the two-beat crossover kick except that the legs do not cross one above the other. Straight two-beat kickers have relatively buoyant legs and do not require a lot of kicking action to keep their legs in a high, horizontal position. This is probably why most straight two-beat kickers are women. The fact that few men use the straight two-beat kick, and few women use the two-beat crossover kick implies the responsibility of some anatomical difference or the role of some variation in buoyancy, flexibility, or strength.

The leg kick and arm pull action is timed so the downward thrust of the leg coincides with the upward thrust of the arm on the same side, as the pull is being finished. Thus, the tendency of the arm to pull that side of the body down is partly canceled by the tendency of the downward thrust of the leg kick to raise that side of the body. Some coaches believe the two-beat kick, properly executed with some vigor, can assist body roll and acceleration. They feel the two-beat does not *cancel* an undesirable feature but contributes a positive one.

Since a straight two-beat crawl swimmer kicks so few times per arm cycle, it sometimes appears that movement of the legs has stopped. Underwater movies of both two-beat crossover and straight two-beat crawl swimmers reveal that the legs continue to move constantly in some swimmers, the movement being so slight that the legs seem relaxed and merely drifting with the water currents; in others, the legs appear to stop completely at times and to be held rigidly, serving as rudders to keep the body in straight alignment (see Figure 2–6). This pause comes at a point when the legs have reached maximum spread. Swimmers using this type of stroke generally fall into the proper timing without conscious effort. The pause at this point would seem to cause an increase in drag and therefore to be detrimental. As the authors have watched the kick in underwater movies, we have gained the impression that the pause does rudder or hold the body in position, possibly to maintain alignment and prevent wiggling. Research and some good conceptual thinking about the fluid mechanics of the two types of kick are needed to validate or refute the different opinions.

FIGURE 2–6   THE STRAIGHT TWO-BEAT KICK IN THE CRAWL STROKE
A U.S. Olympian demonstrates the straight two-beat kick. The downbeat of the right foot is ready to begin at the same time as the right arm begins its back and upward pull.

The Two-Beat Crossover Kick in the Crawl Stroke.   The role of the two-beat crossover kick is to cancel the distorting effect upon hips and legs of the act of recovery. In this style one kick is given by each leg during each arm pull, or two kicks per complete arm cycle. At a certain point in the kicking phase one leg crosses on top of the other, and during the next kick, the leg position reverses. This variation of the flutter kick has been used by many great swimmers, most of whom were not aware of it until they saw their movies. Yet it is so common that we cannot recall watching a meet in which no swimmer used it. This doesn't mean that the two-beat crossover kick is suited to all crawl swimmers. A tally of recent Indiana University men's teams showed as few as 30 percent and as many as 50 percent of the swimmers were two-beat crossover kickers in given years. Figure 2–7 and the accompanying descriptions depict and describe this type of kick. If a swimmer uses it and is swimming well, we believe he should be encouraged to continue.

The two-beat crossover kick tends to be seen in swimmers with a wide, flat arm recovery. They probably resort to it unconsciously because they lack sufficient shoulder flexibility to recover with a high elbow. The authors have observed such swimmers often have large shoulder blades, which restrict arm and shoulder movement. The wide, flat arm recovery causes greater lateral movement of the hips, which can be more effectively canceled by a horizontal and lateral thrust of the leg than by the diagonal and upward thrust of the six-beat kick. These athletes would probably benefit from shoulder stretching exercises to improve shoulder flexibility in order to recover with a high elbow in which the hands are held closer to the body and lateral movement of the legs thereby diminishes. Even so, anatomical restrictions may limit improvement.

It is virtually impossible to imitate the two-beat crossover kick on the kick board in kicking drills. The swimmers who use this kind of kick should condition their legs by kicking in the same way as other crawl swimmers, that is, by kicking the conventional flutter kick on the board and by practicing some breaststroke kick each day. This latter drill will strengthen the knee and hip flexors and the extensors of the thighs and knees.

The Mechanics of the Flutter Kick

A swimmer kicks differently on a kick board than when he is swimming. The body rolls when swimming, but remains relatively flat during kicking drills. It appears to be impossible to simulate the rolling motion during kicking drills. Some coaches have eliminated the board from their kicking drills because of this problem as well as their conviction that swimmers acquire more overload without the board. It also takes the shoulder out of the impingement position.

Beginning competitive swimmers often kick too hard and too high. In fact, it is rare to watch an age-group or Masters meet without seeing a lot of water being splashed high into the air by the kick. The swimmers are usually bending their knees too much and involving their upper legs too little. While performing kicking drills, the swimmer should try to minimize the rocking motion of the shoulders. The feet should not break the surface of the water, but should merely

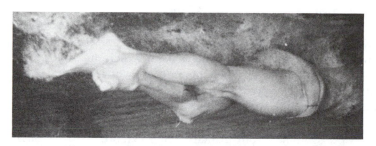

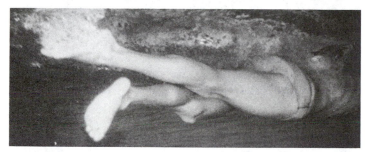

FIGURE 2–7 THE TWO-BEAT CROSSOVER KICK IN THE CRAWL STROKE

A. The right leg crosses on top of the left leg as the left arm finishes its pull.

B. The right leg kicks laterally and cancels the effect of the recovery of the left arm.

C. The legs are at their widest spread.

D. A light tracing of the two-beat crossover kick shows how complicated the pattern of the kick becomes in its stabilizing role.

churn the water up as they kick upward and approach the surface. The feet should separate on the vertical plane between 10 and 16 inches.

Many swimmers kick more efficiently with their toes pointed inward than with the feet pointed straight back. However, no conscious effort should be made to *toe in*. The natural torsion of the femur or the angle at which the bone of the upper leg is set into the hip joint determines the angle at which the upper leg and foot are held. If the swimmer merely *plantar-flexes* or points the toes backward, the amount of *toeing in* that is desirable for him will have been attained. Figure 2–8–A shows a swimmer with superior ankle flexibility. A lack of ankle flexibility may prevent a swimmer from plantar-flexing (Figure 2–8–B). Such swimmers may be able to stretch their ankles, allowing them to become flexible enough to push the water backward with the instep.

FIGURE 2–8 EXAMPLES OF GOOD AND POOR ANKLE FLEXIBILITY IN THE FLUTTER KICK
  A. Good Plantar Flexibility
  B. Poor Plantar Flexibility

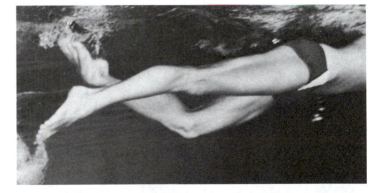

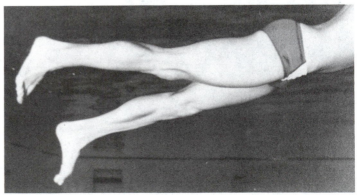

THE ARM STROKE

It is traditional to divide a discussion of the crawl arm stroke into two phases: the pull and the recovery. In this chapter, the recovery will be discussed first.

The Recovery

It is an oversimplification to believe that what swimmers do out of water is unimportant, and what they do under water is all that counts. It is only necessary to recall that a wide sweeping recovery causes excessive lateral movement of the hips and legs (see Chapter 1, Figure 1–5).

The recovery of the arm begins before the pull has finished. That is, there is a transitional phase in which the elbow of the recovering arm is out of the water, while the hand is still under water pushing backward and outward. The backward and outward push towards the side of the body rounds out the pull, transforming it into the beginning of the recovery. This rounding-out motion conserves the momentum developed during the last part of the pull.

The elbow should leave the water first and start to swing upward and forward with the hand trailing behind it. Another common style of recovering is to keep the elbow almost stationary after it lifts and to rotate the upper arm forward, allowing the hand to swing forward with the elbow as a pivot and pass in front of the elbow before the elbow passes the shoulder. The hand is usually then driven deeply into the water. It is the writers' contention that this arm recovery causes the arm to lose the momentum acquired during the last part of the pull and to increase the amount of work the recovery muscles must do.

Except in all-out efforts such as a 50-yard/meter sprint, the arm recovery should be a controlled, relaxed movement, using only enough muscular tension to prevent centrifugal force from pulling the hand outward. As the first part of the recovery finishes, the recovery muscles (primarily the deltoid and trapezius) contract to provide the momentum to recover over the water. After this initial contraction phase, the recovery muscles decrease their degree of contraction, and the momentum developed during this early phase is almost enough to carry the arm through the rest of the recovery. This action can be thought of as a *controlled ballistic movement*, while the action described above is less controlled. In other words, there is sufficient contraction to prevent the arm from flopping loosely, but not so much that it is a sustained, vigorous contraction of these muscles. The latter would be unduly costly in terms of energy expenditure. The swimmer who complains of having tight shoulders has probably been exerting too much tension during recovery.

Top swimmers use their recovery muscles less vigorously and for a shorter period than poorer swimmers do. Good swimmers also use three of the arm depressor muscles (the latissimus dorsi, teres major, and triceps brachii) longer and more vigorously than do poorer swimmers.[5]

In the case of the swimmer who must use a wide, flat recovery due to lack of shoulder flexibility, the movement may be more ballistic than is desirable, but this throwing motion permits the centrifugal force of the initial part of the recovery to carry the arm forward.

During the first part of the recovery the hand should be carried with the palm facing almost backward and slightly upward, and with the wrist in a relaxed position. As the hand swings forward past the shoulder, it should be in line with the elbow. This action keeps the radius of rotation close to the body and results in less lateral displacement of the hips and legs. At this point the hand should start to lead the elbow and, even though the wrist does not flex or extend, the palm should start to face the water, but with the thumb entering first and the hand inclined at about 40 degrees to the surface of the water (see Chapter 1, Figure 1–7–D). Gravity will accelerate the movement of the arm slightly at this point. The swimmer should be careful not to accelerate the speed of his arm movement during its recovery due to muscular effort. If the arm recovery is rushed, the rhythm of the stroke will be disturbed, and the swimmer will tend either to rush the pulling arm and drop the elbow or to delay the beginning of the pull until the recovering arm enters the water. The consequence will be the development of an excessive glide in the stroke, resulting in a dead spot in propulsion.

It is also nearly impossible to recover one arm fast and to pull the other arm more slowly. A rushed recovery creates additional resistance, which holds the swimmer back. The resistance to forward progress which the recovering arm creates as it enters the water varies approximately with the square of the speed at which it is placed in the water. Thus, when a person doubles the speed with which the recovery arm enters the water, the resistance to forward progress is increased by four times.

Another error seen commonly in the recovery is that of swinging the hand higher than the elbow, as in Figure 2–9–A. This causes body displacement, uses more energy, and may break stroke rhythm. Figure 2–9–B is a shot of the normal, high-elbow recovery.

The Pull

The hand should enter the water immediately before the elbow becomes fully extended. When observing a mixed group of good and less good swimmers, it is very noticeable that good swimmers execute this action perfectly, while less good swimmers lay in part of the forearm with the hand or actually immerse the elbow before the hand on the entry. The palm should be facing diagonally down and outward with the little finger higher than the thumb. This is the ideal angle in terms of preparing for lift production. It also minimizes the entrapment of air, thus preventing the formation of excessive bubbles in back of the hand. Air bubbles decrease the efficiency of the arm pull by presenting a less dense medium for the hand to act against.

The entry described above is called the *normal reach entry*, and it is recommended over either digging deeper or *overreaching*.

Overreaching is a technique favored by coaches and swimmers who believe in stretching or reaching out with the hand as it enters the water. They are of the opinion that stretching produces a longer and more powerful stroke. It is true that the elbow should be almost completely extended by the time the hand enters the water, but there should be no elevation of the shoulder by rotating and moving the shoulder blade and collarbone upward. This action disturbs the swim-

FIGURE 2–9 TWO STYLES OF RECOVERY IN THE CRAWL

A. In which the hand is higher than the elbow

B. Normal, high-elbow recovery

mer's lateral body alignment and weakens his pull. To prove this to a swimmer, have him do a supine straight arm pullover with a weight he can just lift. He will find that the same weight is harder or impossible to lift when the shoulder is elevated and the scapula rotated. In fact, rotation of the scapula is poor technique in any of the four competitive strokes.

Another effective method of communicating this idea is to tell the swimmer that elevation of the shoulders is forbidden except on racing dives and push-offs. *Elevation of the shoulders* is clearer terminology than *rotation of the scapula*. A swimmer is likely to fall into this mechanical defect of lifting the shoulder blades if his coach uses the term *reach*. Once the swimmer's elbow is completely extended, the only way he can reach or stretch his hand further forward in front of his body is through elevation of the shoulders. The term *reach* should be banned from the lexicon of stroke mechanics sessions.

The Application of Propulsive Force. Once the arm is in the water, it should pause just long enough for the hand to sink a few inches, then begin to pull. At this point, most elite crawl swimmers initiate a three-dimensional pull which contains the elements that allow it to develop some lift: optimum pitch of the hand in relation to the water and sufficient lateral movement to be able to get away from water that is moving backward and to contact water that is still. A few great crawl swimmers, however, use a more two-dimensional pull, which contains very little lateral movement. They may be exploiting propulsive drag more than lift. Kieren Perkins, who stunned the swimming world with his 1500-meter swim in the Barcelona Olympics, and Artur Wojdat are examples of the sort of stylist who uses a drag-dominated pull. The authors theorize that despite the fact that they do not pitch the hands on the entry and do not achieve much lateral movement in their pull, they do obey the requirement of contacting still water as the pull progresses and avoiding water that is already moving backward.

Of the four competitive strokes, the crawl *always* possesses the potential for exploiting more drag than lift. These authors nevertheless believe that Perkins and Wojdat would be better off to incorporate more lateral movement into their strokes. We have photographed many good swimmers, who, while using elliptical pull patterns in a myriad of variations, never pull in a perfectly straight, one-dimensional pattern. Figure 1–9–B in Chapter I shows the elliptical pull pattern of a champion swimmer. Some swimmers use a variation of this pattern in which the S shape is more or less pronounced than this one. The width of the pattern may also vary slightly from one swimmer to the next, due perhaps to variations in strength, flexibility, or some other factors which we do not yet understand (see Figure 2–10).

Beginning of the Pull and Flexion of the Wrist.   When the hand and arm have become completely submerged, the palm is turned from the diagonal position by rotation of the forearm, the action occurring between the radius and ulna bones. In movies of some great swimmers, the authors have observed a marked flexion of the wrist at this point. This places the palm in a more favorable position to push the water backward than if the wrist were to remain in straight alignment. This wrist flexion is shown in Figure 2–11, along with an elbow bend which,

FIGURE 2–10 ARM PULL PATTERNS OF THREE GOOD CRAWL SWIMMERS, SHOWING EXTREMES OF ELBOW BEND
  A. Too little elbow bend
  B. Too much elbow bend
  C. Beyond the outside of the body

FIGURE 2–10 *(continued)*

ideally, should fall between A and B in Figure 2–10. Swimmers should be instructed to flex the wrists as they bend the elbow.

Elbow Bend and When It Occurs. In order to engender an effective pull pattern, the arm begins with the elbow straight or almost straight. As the hand pulls under the body, the elbow begins to bend, reaching its maximum degree of bend when the arm is approximately perpendicular to the body, or halfway through the pull. The amount of bend at this point may vary slightly from one good swimmer to the next, but the average is about 90 degrees (see Figures 2–12 and 2–18).

The elbow bend is maintained for only a short time during the pull. As the hand pushes further back, the angle of the elbow increases steadily until the

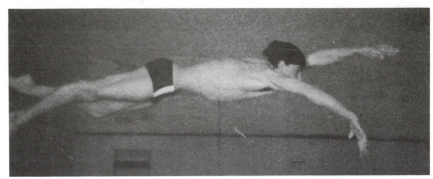

FIGURE 2–11   WRIST FLEXION DURING THE FIRST PART OF THE ARM PULL
(Note: This is the first pull following the push-off after the turn)

FIGURE 2–12   A SEQUENCE OF A CLASSIC CRAWL STROKE

A. The left arm begins to pull. Note the wrist flexion.

B. The elbow flexes and the upper arm rotates medially. The result is achievement of a high elbow, which permits the force generated by the arm to be directed backward.

C. As the left arm reaches halfway through the pull, the fingers of the right hand are just entering the water.

D. The left hand pushes the water backward diagonally in a slight sculling action; the right hand begins to pull.

E. As the left hand finishes the most propulsive phase of the pull, the swimmer is making a conscious effort to maintain high hand acceleration.

F. The pull finishes and the palm begins to turn inward in preparation for the beginning of the recovery.

G. The arm is in recovery and the hand withdraws from the water. The right hand begins its pull.

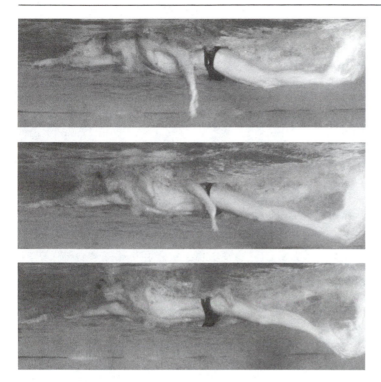

FIGURE 2–12   *(continued)*

elbow is almost fully extended. This type of pull has been referred to as the bent-arm pull, but the term would be more fully descriptive if it were called the straight-bent-straight pull.

A search of the literature since the reintroduction of the crawl into Western society reveals that for nearly a century the most highly recommended pull pattern was the straight-arm, straight-line pull directly beneath the midline of the body. This was a logical belief which had a basic flaw.

Examination of the path of the hand under the bodies of great swimmers shows that nearly all follow the same general pattern: that of the modified S shape described earlier or, more accurately, an elliptical pattern. Since there is less lateral movement in the crawl stroke than in the other three competitive strokes, this is not apparent to observers, who form their opinions about stroke technique by watching swimmers from out of the water. This is probably why coaches were misled for so long into believing that the pull in the crawl should follow a straight line down the midline of the body. Body roll introduced another variable, which complicated the issue. Lateral movement in the butterfly and breaststroke is more obviously a sculling action, since there is no possibility of confusing it with roll (see Figures 1–11 and 1–12). Doubtless that is why it took a combination of the butterfly stroke of a highly talented swimmer and the technology of underwater high-speed photography to suggest another conceptual path.

High Elbow in the Pull.   Films show that all good swimmers use some form of elbow-up pull, featuring an elbow that is bent and held higher than the hand

FIGURE 2–13 HIGH ELBOW
POSITION IN THE FIRST HALF OF
THE ARM PULL OF FOUR
WORLD-RANKED SWIMMERS

FIGURE 2–13
(continued)

throughout the first part of the pull. Figure 2–13 depicts the high elbow of four world-ranked swimmers. The high elbow is also demonstrated in Figure 2–14. (These sets of matching head-on and side views of a classic stroke have been included to show the unusual symmetry of the arm pulls of both arms.) Poor swimmers on the other hand drop their elbows, as the swimmer is doing in Figure 2–15. The elbow-up pull, plus a curvilinear pull pattern, permits maximum backward thrust during the first half of the pull, thus providing maximum forward propulsion.

As the arm is pulled down and back by the three main arm depressor muscles (the latissimus dorsi, pectoralis major, and teres major, with some help from the triceps), it is also rotated medially by the same muscles plus the subscapularis. This action increases the strength available to pull the arm backward. Because of anatomical differences, not all swimmers are capable of swimming with their elbows as high as the swimmer in Figure 2–12.

Medial Rotation of the Upper Arm.   This action requires that the upper arm be rotated inwardly toward the midline of the body. Medial rotation plus a constantly increasing flexion of the elbow continues throughout the first half of the pull. A better understanding of this rotating action can be had by reading the section on dry land exercises for swimmers, specifically the *arm rotator* drills, in Chapter 10. This action is shown clearly in the elbow-up pull in Figure 2–12. *Medial rotation* of the upper arm should be distinguished from *supination* of the forearm. Medial rotation of the upper arm causes an increase in pulling strength by adding the strength of the arm rotator muscles to the strength of the arm depressor muscles; supination of the forearm merely turns the palm over.

Medial rotation occurs naturally in many swimmers, probably because people tend to use their muscles in the most effective manner. It is not natural to all, however, and must be taught to those who do not incorporate it on their own. Medial rotation also facilitates the zigzag pull pattern. For years this was called *feathering* and was discouraged by swimming coaches and teachers. We now believe it contributes to the development of lift.

To demonstrate the importance of medial rotation to improve the strength of the pull, have the swimmer hang onto the side of the pool, submerged to the shoulders, then have her place her hands on the pool deck and climb out of the

FIGURE 2–14 AN UNUSUAL
DISPLAY OF SYMMETRY IN THE
ARM PULLS OF EACH ARM IN
THE CRAWL STROKE

A. & AA. Matching set of the
left arm

B. & BB. Right arm

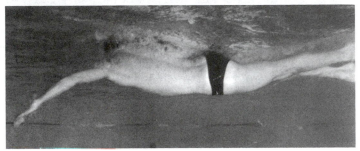

A. & AA.

pool by pushing the hands down on the deck. Most swimmers will rotate their
upper arms as they push downward. Their elbows will turn out in a movement
that largely duplicates the one advocated for the freestyle arm pull.

The effectiveness of the arm pull to achieve optimum propulsion involves
two considerations: (1) the most effective application of force insofar as the laws
of motion are concerned and (2) the most efficient application of force insofar
as anatomical function is concerned. Within those limits the swimmer must try
to satisfy both requirements. She may have to settle for a slight deviation from
the absolute observation of each in order to do this. Medial rotation of the
upper arm is an important action. The role it plays in the mechanics of all four
competitive strokes will be discussed in each of the chapters involved with a
particular stroke.

FIGURE 2–14
(continued)

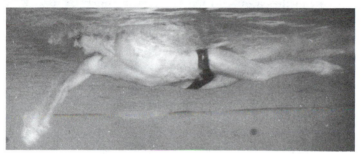

B. & BB.

FIGURE 2–15   DROPPED ELBOW IN THE CRAWL STROKE

Shoulder and Body Roll.   Shoulder and body roll vary somewhat among great swimmers, but the variations are slight, seeming to be due primarily to differences in shoulder flexibility. Generally, the greater the flexibility of the shoulders, the smaller the amount of roll. This roll, being on the longitudinal axis of the body, is not to be confused with lateral movement. Obviously, the swimmer will roll more to the side on which he breathes, the amount of roll at this point being about 45 degrees, plus or minus 5 degrees.

The amount of roll of the body to the nonbreathing side should be only 10 to 15 degrees less than that on the breathing side. The amount of total roll in degree, as approximated from underwater observation, varies as much as 30 degrees among good swimmers. The roll of the shoulders, hips, and body should be synchronized. It is a mistake to try to hold any of these flat. It is also wrong to roll just to be rolling. When correctly exploited, the roll serves several purposes: (1) It makes recovery of the arm easier and permits a shorter radius of rotation of the recovering arm; (2) it places the strongest part of the arm pull more directly under the center of mass of the body; (3) it places the hips in such a position that the feet can thrust at least partly sideward during the kick, thus canceling the distorting effect of the recovery arm; and (4) it facilitates breathing.

The coach and swimmer should work together to determine the amount of roll that is best for that swimmer. Although the swimmer will roll naturally as he strokes, it cannot be assumed he will always roll the right amount naturally. Frequently such stroke defects as a dropped elbow or delayed breathing may upset this balance and cause too much roll, or, conversely, those defects may be caused by excessive roll. If in such a case the swimmer is instructed not to roll at all, the real cause of his excessive roll will not be eliminated, and he may be worse off than before.

A forced, completely flat position of the body is neither possible nor desirable. If the swimmer tries to remain flat, he will discover that his horizontal alignment has been destroyed by the lateral movement of his hips.

It has been suggested that body roll can be used to enhance force output in the arm pull. This line of reasoning goes so far as to suggest that hip rotation is the "power source" of arm movement in the crawl stroke. This idea has been extrapolated from the use of hip rotation in swinging a baseball bat or a golf club. Aside from the unique biomechanics of these activities, the use of hip rotation as the primary means of generating movement in the baseball and golf swing is possible because the lower extremities are in contact with the ground. Such activities constitute what is known as a *closed kinematic chain*. Swimming, on the other hand, is considered to be an *open kinematic chain* because water is not a solid enough medium against which the feet can plant themselves. This makes it unlikely that hip rotation can contribute to the generation of significant force in the arm pull of the crawl stroke. It is even less likely to occur in the strokes in which no body roll occurs, such as the breaststroke and butterfly.

The Importance of Hand Acceleration in the Crawl Stroke.   Reference to the importance of hand acceleration was made in Chapter 1. The significance of this factor in swimming can hardly be overstated. Swimming is not an activity for which humans have a natural predisposition. Consequently, only a small fraction of learners automatically accelerate their arms fast enough for optimum effect. Most swimmers must be taught to incorporate it through the use of specific drills.

Evidence for this opinion can be found in the study "The Importance of Hand Speed and Acceleration in Swimming the Crawl Stroke."[6] Of sixteen competitive swimmers, only two had exploited optimal acceleration into their pull to the extent that specific instructions in its inclusion did not result in improvement. Fourteen improved by being guided to include acceleration. Very poor, noncompetitive swimmers also improved, but not so greatly. Therefore, it bears repeating that stroke drills, such as those devised for the study, should be an important part of the practice of technique.

The Lift (Bernoulli) Principle Applied to the Crawl.   The role of the lift effect in swimming propulsion has been discussed exhaustively in Chapter I.

Figure 2–16 shows the way the pull pattern in the crawl stroke exploits lift by its sculling movements. Figures 1–16, 17, and 18 confirm the role of lift in the crawl.

The reason an elliptical pull pattern is more effective is that once a swimmer starts moving water backwards she must change the path of her pull if she is to continue to contact still water against which to create force. Sculling enables her to do that, and sculling is only possible in the crawl stroke with an angle of attack produced by a high elbow.

The pitch of the hands in relation to their path through the water is also crucial to the creation of force in the crawl. It should be at or near 40 degrees to the path of the hands. It would appear to be more efficient if the hands were pitched at 45 degrees, but it has been found in some studies of propellers pitched

FIGURE 2–16   LIGHT TRACING STUDY OF THE CRAWL STROKE, FEATURING A HIGH-ELBOW PULL

A flashing light is attached to the swimmer's middle finger and he is photographed in a darkened pool as he moves in front of a stationary still camera, whose shutter is left open. A single strobe light is fired as the swimmer traverses the width of the pool. Note the high-elbow pull.

at 45 degrees or more that *curling* occurs. Curling refers to the formation of vortices in back of the propellers. These vortices may interfere with the creation of optimal lift. Some swimmers, particularly very young ones, may not have enough strength to maintain the requisite 40-degree angle during the first half of the pull. A study of champion swimmers shows that most do maintain that approximate angle.

Of the two propulsive forces in swimming, lift and drag, drag is the major contributor to total stroke propulsion in the crawl. As the force diminishes toward the end of the stroke, it is almost completely composed of drag. It is also the case that the better the swimmer the better she sustains hand speed at the end of the stroke. Good swimmers achieve greater hand acceleration than their less-talented counterparts, and that also enables them to conserve more momentum.

THE MECHANICS OF BREATHING

A swimmer with proper head placement will breathe below the normal surface of the water by pulling the mouth toward the breathing side of the face by action of the facial muscles rather than by additional rotation of the head. The swimmer should experiment with different head positions in an effort to find the bottom of the bow wave, when rolling the head to the side to breathe.

Late breathing is a flaw commonly seen among swimmers who train in a rough and choppy pool. Many swimmers develop this habit in an effort to avoid swallowing water. It is also often seen among marathon and rough-water swimmers. Late breathing *does*, in fact, protect them from the consequences of rough water. Figure 2–17 shows the late-breathing phenomenon.

The effect of late breathing is that the swimmer fails to breathe at the point of maximum body roll. This disturbs the rhythm of the stroke caused by a rushed arm recovery on the breathing side.

It is important that the swimmer turn his head to the side by rotating his neck on its longitudinal axis rather than by lifting or flexing it laterally. Either of these actions causes distortion of body alignment. The roll of the head should be timed with the roll of the body. Maximum roll of the head to the breathing side should be achieved at exactly the same time as maximum roll of the body to that

FIGURE 2–17 LATE BREATH-ING IN THE CRAWL STROKE

side. This action also applies to the opposite side. The head does not work independently of the body or the arms, but it does travel further in terms of degrees of rotation on the longitudinal axis.

Independent head action has been emphasized by some swimming experts. They advocate this technique because they believe the head should be snapped to the side, independent of body roll, the breath taken quickly, and the head snapped back to center, also independent of body roll. Coordination of the various parts of the body is interrelated. If a swimmer snaps his head back quickly, this will invariably cause an increase in the speed of the recovering arm, and the swimmer will develop a jerky rhythm in his stroke. A rushed arm recovery can often be corrected by elimination of this fast head action.

Once the breath has been taken, the head should return, not just to the midline under the body, but to a point at least 15 degrees past center. This assures balance in the stroke, and avoids one-sided swimming as seen in swimmers who do not return their heads past the center line. Stopping the head at the center line after breathing usually results in a shortened pull and a wider, more difficult recovery of the arm opposite the breathing side. A good way for the coach and swimmer to check if the head is coming back far enough is to make sure that the ear on the nonbreathing side is out of the water at some time during each arm cycle.

Inhalation occurs in the very short period of time that the mouth is out of the water. Almost immediately after the swimmer inhales and returns his mouth underwater, he should begin to exhale, allowing a steady trickle of air to leave the mouth and the nose. The swimmer should not eject the air forcefully at this point. If he does, he will have exhausted the supply of air before he turns his head again to inhale. Swimmers usually inhale and exhale a little over a pint of air with each breath; therefore, they must distribute it over the time their mouths will be underwater. Excessively deep ventilation does not increase the amount of oxygen picked up by the lungs, but it does contribute to fatigue of the respiratory muscles. Excessively shallow breathing fails to accomplish an adequate exchange of oxygen and carbon dioxide in the blood at the lungs.

A steady flow of air from the mouth and nose should be maintained until the swimmer's mouth is ready to break the water again. At this point exhalation becomes somewhat more vigorous. This action is automatic among most swimmers and serves to blow away the water which is rolling off the face and onto the mouth and nose, leaving the area around the mouth and nose clear for the split second required to inhale.

Beginning swimmers and sometimes even those at the competitive level may find it helpful to practice a drill featuring this action.

The type of breathing known as *explosive breathing* is not advocated by the authors. In this method, the breath is held most of the time the head is underwater and is expelled just before the head breaks the surface to take another breath. The rationale behind this practice is to increase the swimmer's buoyancy. The authors believe that the style of breathing described earlier in this section, which is rhythmical yet includes a sufficient increase in air expulsion at the very end of exhalation, best conforms with other aspects of the stroke to ensure natural rhythm and avoidance of idiosyncracies in the stroke.

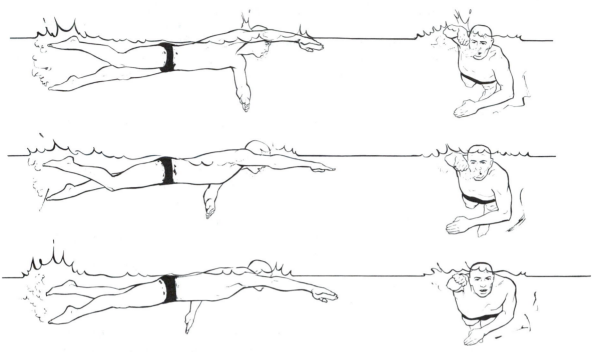

FIGURE 2–18   A SEQUENCE OF THE CRAWL STROKE: SIDE VIEW AND HEAD-ON

This sequence of drawings shows the swimmer performing a conventional six-beat flutter kick and continuous arm action.

A. As the right hand enters the water at shoulder width, the hand is pitched so the thumb enters the water first. The left arm has finished half of its pull. Air is being exhaled from the mouth and nose in a steady trickle, indicating a rhythmical breathing pattern.

B. The momentum developed by the hand during the recovery causes the right hand to sink downward for its catch. The pulling arm continues to pull with the palm still facing backward.

C. The right hand continues to move downward slowly as the pulling hand starts to return to the center line of the body.

D. The depressor muscles of the right arm begin to contract actively, depressing the right arm downward

E. The left arm has almost completed its pull and the swimmer is now applying force with both hands. The force of the right hand is not as yet directed backward sufficiently to contribute any forward propulsion to the body. It is at this point that the lowest level of forward propulsion occurs.

F. As the left arm finishes its pull, the left leg thrusts downward vigorously. This action cancels the effect that the upward action of the arms has had on depressing the swimmer's hips.

G. As the right hand presses downward, the elbow starts to bend.

H. The pulling hand has accomplished half its pull, and the head starts to rotate on its longitudinal axis. The amount of air being exhaled begins to increase.

I. The head continues to turn to the side, with the chin appearing to follow the action of the elbow as it goes backward. The pulling hand starts to round out and come back toward the center line of the body.

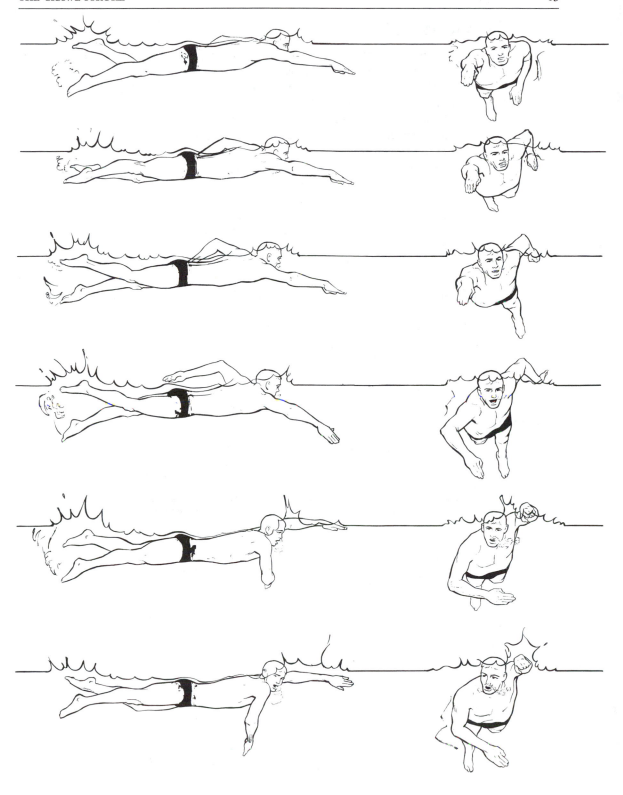

How Often to Breathe?

A breath should be taken with every complete arm cycle in the freestyle distance events. The only exception occurs among swimmers who maintain a very rapid tempo and have a short arm pull. Such swimmers get enough air by breathing every one-and-a-half or two complete arm cycles.

In sprints the breathing pattern that provides the best results on the basis of time trials and experience should be selected. Some great 50-yard sprinters have swum the entire distance without breathing. The general plan which suits most sprinters for the 50-yard distance in a 25-yard pool is to take one breath before going into the first turn and another one or two breaths on the second length. Since age-group swimmers stroke faster than their older counterparts, they may breathe every three or four strokes and still breathe enough.

It often happens that a swimmer with faulty breathing habits, such as a pause in the stroke at the time a breath is taken, chooses not to correct the mistake. The swimmer may try to compensate for the error by breathing less often. If the breath is taken properly, it need not result in a pause in the stroke. Many swimmers are able to sprint nearly as fast when breathing every complete arm cycle as they can when breathing less often. Among them are top 100-yard sprinters who have achieved their best times while breathing this way. Once again, the method selected should be the one which gives the best results.

In all freestyle races, including distance events, the swimmer should take at least two arm strokes before breathing. In the sprints the number of strokes between breaths can and should be increased.

FOOTNOTES

1. U.S. Swimming, Inc., *1992 Rules and Regulations.* Colorado Springs, CO: 1992.

2. James E. Counsilman (unpublished study, University of Iowa, 1950).

3. James E. Counsilman, "Theory of the Flutter Kick," *Beach and Pool*, XXIV, No. 6 (June 1949), 17–18.

4. Marlene Adrian, Mohan Singh, and Peter Karpovich (unpublished research project, and personal correspondence with Peter Karpovich, Springfield College, Springfield, MA, October 1965).

5. Michio Ikai, Kibashi Ishii, and Mitsumasa Miyashita, "An Electromyographic Study of Swimming," Laboratory for Physiologic Research in Physical Education, School of Education, University of Tokyo, *Research Journal of Physical Education*, 7, No. 4 (April 1964), 47–54.

6. James E. Counsilman, "The Importance of Hand Speed and Acceleration in Swimming the Crawl Stroke," Proceedings of the Biomechanics Symposium, Indiana University, October 26–28, 1980, John M. Cooper and Betty Haven, eds.

CHAPTER 3

The Back Crawl Stroke

The practice of swimming on one's back has a very obscure beginning in the history of humankind's aquatic adventures. As early as 1794, Bernardi described, albeit inadequately, what was apparently a form of the elementary backstroke.

> For a perfectly horizontal position of the body lying on its back and parallel with the surface, the head must be under water up to the ears—the legs are crossed along the tibia and over the instep, to make them figure as pointed an extremity as possible. If they were kept apart or widely stretched, when advancing head forward, they would meet the water's resistance proportionately with the angle of their opening, thus impeding or at least retarding the pace.[1]

In 1871, in London, the Marquis Bibbero reportedly swam a mile on his back in 39½ minutes. The exact style he used was not mentioned.

> Before leaving London 13 Nov '71 he was "prevailed upon" to take a benefit, when he was described as of Manchester and "Inventor of the Life-saving dress." He then swam a mile on his back in 39½ minutes (they did not trouble with fifths of a second in those days).[2]

Backstroke was popular but saw limited use as a competitive stroke until 1906, when swimming races were divided into three classes in national and international competition: breaststroke, backstroke, and freestyle. From this time until about 1912, when the back crawl was introduced, the elementary backstroke (double overarm backstroke with either the frog or scissor kick) was used in races. After the introduction of the back crawl stroke, the other forms of backstroke gradually disappeared from competitive swimming and are now taught and used only as utility strokes.

As of March 1991, current rules governing the backstroke are:

1. Start—(A) The swimmers shall line up in the water facing the starting end, with both hands placed on the gutter or on the starting grips. (B) Prior to the command "take your mark" and until the feet leave the wall at the starting signal, the swimmer's feet, including the toes, shall be placed under the surface of the water. Standing in or on the gutter or curling the toes over the lip of the gutter is not permitted at any time before the start. A backstroke starting block may not be used.

2. Stroke—Standing in or on the gutter or curling the toes over the lip of the gutter is not permitted. The swimmer shall push off on his back and continue swimming on the back throughout the race. Some part of the swimmer must break the surface of the water throughout the race, except it shall be permissible for the swimmer to be completely submerged during the turn and for a distance of not more than 15 meters (16.4 yards) after the start and each turn. By that point, the head must have broken the surface of the water.

3. Turns—Upon completion of each length, some part of the swimmer must touch the wall. During the turn the shoulders may turn past the vertical toward the breast. If the swimmer turns past vertical, such motion must be part of a continuous turning action and the swimmer must return to a position on the back before the feet leave the wall.

4. Finish—The swimmer shall have finished the race when any part of the swimmer touches the wall at the end of the course.[3]

Within the context of these rules any form of backstroke can be used, but the back crawl with alternate arm action and a flutter kick is so superior to other forms that no other style is seen among good competitive backstroke swimmers. Some swimming authorities still advocate a straight arm pull with the shoulders held level, but most recommend the S pull pattern with varying amounts of body roll. Among good swimmers the body rolls at least 45 degrees to each side.

The mechanical principles which apply to swimming the back crawl are the same as those that apply to the other strokes. This is hard to visualize because the swimmer's body is inverted, thus, the high elbow becomes a low elbow and, with regard to the pitch of the hand, the little finger becomes the leading rather than the trailing edge.

FIGURE 3–1   POOR BODY POSITION IN THE BACK CRAWL

BODY POSITION

In the backstroke the effort to streamline the body has to be moderated by another consideration. A completely horizontal body position would place the legs too high for an effective kick. When viewing underwater movies of themselves for the first time, most backstrokers are surprised at how low in the water their body position is. They—as do the swimmers of all strokes—swim *through* the water, not on top of it. Their coaches may want to convey the impression that their backstrokers are swimming high in the water, but the reality is otherwise. Coaches merely want them to think in terms of a streamlined body that minimizes resistance.

Far from swimming too high and flat, there is a tendency to do just the opposite. Backstrokers tend to sit in the water. This placement is the result of excessive piking or jackknifing at the hips, often coupled with a forward flexion of the neck. Low hip position is referred to as *sitting up* in the water (Figure 3–1).

Although some coaches have advocated this body position, these authors believe it is detrimental due to creation of excessive drag and because it results in a poor application of force.

THE KICK

The six-beat flutter kick is used by nearly all backstroke swimmers. It is remarkably similar to the flutter kick used in the freestyle. In Chapter II it was postulated that the function of the kick is primarily that of a stabilizer, which keeps the body in good horizontal position and decreases the lateral movement of the body caused by the action of the arm recovery. While it is likely that the flutter kick provides some propulsion in the backstroke, it serves primarily the same function as in the freestyle. The difference is that the lateral movement being canceled is due to movement occurring at the end of the pull, not to the arm recovery. This action is shown and discussed in the backstroke sequence pictures (Figure 3–5) on p. 75.

It is well known that a *part* of a total skill, such as the kick, when learned separately, will transfer more easily if it closely emulates the exact movement as it occurs in the whole stroke. But in doing kicking drills on the back, the swimmer uses a slightly different kick from the one used when swimming the whole stroke. Body roll and kick are not always in the vertical plane. Up to this time no way has been found to emulate this roll during kicking drills. Some coaches and swimmers have tried to solve the problem by kicking without a board, alternating the kicking drills as follows:

On the first length, flutter kick with the body turned on the left side; on the second length, flutter kick with the body on its back; on the third length, with the body turned on its right side; and on the fourth length, with the body on its back, repeating this process until the end of the drill.

Since much of the backstroke event is now swum underwater, with the arms extended overhead and the legs kicking a dolphin action, dolphin kicking on the back should be included in kicking drill sessions. To emphasize the importance of this relatively new technique, it is only necessary to mention these points: (1) Contrary to kicking in the total back crawl, dolphining on the back with no arm pull is very propulsive; and (2) prevailing rules permit only 15 yards of underwater dolphining after the start and each turn. In response to a recent rule change and to general acceptance of the new technique, most coaches have adapted by organizing short drills of 25 yards or less.

The limitation stems from the fear that there is a physical danger inherent in extending the technique too far. It is recommended that swimmers confine such practice drills to distances at or under 25 yards or meters. While kicking 25 meters without breathing may not be hazardous to a well-trained, mature swimmer, it could be dangerous for a beginning or very young competitor. Back flutter kicking drills and underwater dolphining drills remain the best way to condition the legs. They also provide a good opportunity for the coach and swimmer to work on the mechanics of the kick.

Both types of kicking drill on the back are best performed with the arms overhead, elbows extended, hands clasped, and the upper arms pressed against the ears.

The back flutter kick is done at or near the surface of the water. This helps the swimmer develop good body position. As the swimmer lies in the water and kicks, he should try to keep his feet just churning the water's surface on the upbeat without actually breaking it. At their greatest depth the feet should extend 18 to 24 inches below the surface. The head should be held back in the water with the ears submerged, but with the face out of water.

Depending on the swimmer's buoyancy and the strength of his kick, he should adjust his head position by flexing or extending the neck, thus enabling him to achieve the same approximate position in kicking drills as in actual swimming. When the swimmer does his kicking drills with his hands at his sides, his hips tend to drop. This tendency probably transfers to the complete stroke. Kicking with both arms overhead can be difficult for a person with poor shoulder flexibility or with a poor kick. It may be preferable for such a swimmer to practice the kick with one arm held overhead and the other at the side.

When the kick is integrated into the stroke, it varies in size, with two of the six beats per complete cycle being larger than the other four. This adjustment appears to be automatic. On every third kick of a stroke cycle one foot kicks diagonally across the other. This action cancels the tendency of the hip to move laterally. This lateral movement is a reaction to the last part of the pull. If the swimmer tries to keep his body from rolling, the kick will not be diagonal and the canceling effect will not occur (see Figure 3–5).

The primary propulsive force of the flutter kick in the backstroke occurs on the upbeat, which is the reverse of the case in the front crawl stroke. The knees are bent on the upbeat and are kept straight for a major part of the downbeat. Many swimmers have difficulty keeping their legs straight for long enough on the downbeat. They tend to kick from the knees, failing to bring the thighs sufficiently into action. Swimmers who kick in this fashion find their knees breaking the water's surface on the upbeat, rendering the kick less effective.

Figure 3–2 depicts the backstroke flutter kick as it should be done in kicking drills.

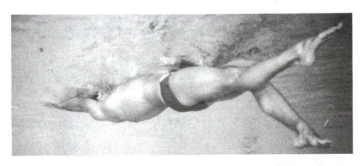

FIGURE 3–2 BACK FLUTTER KICK

A. The legs are at their widest spread, with the left leg finishing the downbeat and the right the upbeat. Note the bent knee at the end of the downbeat. The hands are clasped over the head and the body is streamlined.

B. The left leg begins the upward and backward thrust, which provides the main source of propulsion of the kick, and the right leg starts its downard thrust. Note the plantar flexion of the right foot.

FIGURE 3–2 *(continued)*

C. The left leg continues upward by extending the knee vigorously. The right leg is moving downward.

D. The legs continue the action described in C.

E. The right leg bends with a vigorous action, while the left leg continues upward. The legs are now in the same position as in (A), except they are reversed.

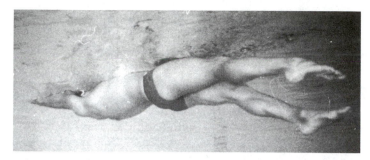

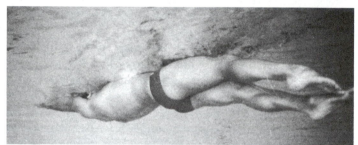

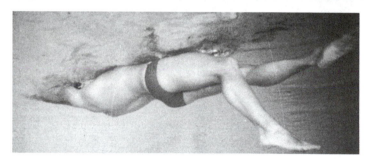

As for the back dolphin kick, Figure 3–3 is a sequence and description of a swimmer performing it with good technique.

THE ARM PULL

When first introduced into competitive swimming the backstroke featured a double overarm action and a variety of kicks, including the frog kick, the scissor kick, and the flutter kick.

By the 1920s, most backstrokers had adopted an alternate arm action pull and flutter kick. The result was termed the *back crawl stroke*. The changes occurring during the next forty-plus years were primarily those of fine-tuning, until the 1980s, when dolphining off the start and each turn began to be seen. This practice grew in popularity after David Berkoff set a world record using the dolphining technique. Dolphining provides an obvious advantage to the swimmer having an effective dolphin kick.

The essentials of the arm pull have not changed greatly since the 1960s, when it was discovered that the straight arm pull was not used by good swimmers. Rather they used a straight-bent-straight pull. This was contrary to earlier opinion that swimming propulsion was exclusively a drag force, whose recommended stroke pattern in the backstroke had been to fully extend the arms and allow the hands to prescribe a semicircular movement in which they would pull against

FIGURE 3–3 BACK CRAWL UNDERWATER DOLPHIN KICK

A. The rules permit an underwater dolphin kick after the push-off for a maximum distance of 15 meters (16.4 yards). Swimmers with a good dolphin kick benefit from this technique. In this picture the swimmer has slowed down to swimming speed, following the push-off and is about to begin dolphining.

B. The knees bend to begin the dolphin action.

C. The feet are at the lowest point and are ready to begin their upward and backward thrust. The arms remain firmly clasped overhead.

FIGURE 3–3 *(continued)*

D. The legs thrust upward vigorously until they are fully extended.

E. The knees continue to extend in a vigorous action. The upward thrust of the feet causes the hips to drop in the typically undulating dolphin style.

the water, moving the body forward by exerting pressure backward (action-reaction).

Another theory propounded during the 1940s held that the hands should be pulled in a straight line, by bending the elbows in the first half of the pull. Time trials and force measurements showed this technique to be slower and to create less forward propulsion than the fully extended arm. Good swimmers, however, didn't do either of these pulls. It took another dozen years to identify the primary source of propulsion among most good swimmers in all strokes as being lift rather than drag.

It must be kept in mind that both drag and lift obey Newton's Third Law of Motion (action-reaction). The reason for emphasizing this point is that it explains why the angle of attack is so important in teaching the backstroke and, in fact, all the strokes.

The term *bent-arm pull* is not really descriptive, since merely bending the elbow does not assure a proper pull. Rather, as the recovery ends, the arm is extended in a straight line directly over the shoulder. The hand enters the water in a vertical position, little finger first. The arm should be allowed to sink into the water to a depth of 6 to 8 inches. This is a result of the momentum achieved by the ballistic action of the recovery and should not be impeded or stopped through muscular force, since it allows the swimmer to begin the pull from an advantageous arm position. The rationale is explained more fully later in this chapter in the section on the arm recovery.

At this point, the elbow should still be straight, the transition from the end of the recovery to the beginning of the pull taking place in a smooth conversion as the momentum of the recovery dissipates and the pull begins. As the pull progresses, the elbow begins to bend and, simultaneously, the upper arm rotates medially. Medial rotation of the humerus is the action the backstroker should emphasize during the first half of his pull. It occurs as the elbow bend is increasing. The hand is then in a position directly opposite the swimmer's shoulder and within a few inches of the surface of the water. The elbow is at a point of maximum bend, or approximately 90 degrees, and the pull is just over half complete. This motion is circular and it places the hand in a good position to push downward towards the bottom of the pool.

The last half of the pull is accomplished by extension of the elbow, continued medial rotation, and adduction of the upper arm. The downward push causes the body to roll on its longitudinal axis. This lateral roll, in turn, places the arm in a more advantageous position to create force than if the shoulders remained level. The push of the hand toward the bottom of the pool continues, finishing about 1½ to 2 feet below the surface of the water. If the palm is not facing downward as the arm ends the pull, the hand will have to go deeper in order to achieve its goal of causing the swimmer to roll. The hand of some swimmers finishes a foot or more below the hip because the palm is facing inward toward the thigh as it pushes downward. This seems to be a poor application of force, but there are some world-class swimmers doing it, so it must be examined. It may be that it provides the potential for developing greater hand speed and, consequently, greater forward propulsive force and greater opportunity to develop lift through a more advantageous angle of attack.

The pull, from beginning to end, describes a flattened S pattern. Figure 3–4 shows the pull pattern of a great backstroker. Notice the depth of the hand at the end of pull and also the position of the hand at this point. The push downward is a fast movement, close to a throwing action in terms of its acceleration. Because of its close similarity to the motion used in cracking a whip, it has been referred to by some coaches and backstrokers as the "buggy whip" pull. The term is an

FIGURE 3–4 A RECENT TREND IN THE ARM PULL OF SOME ELITE SWIMMERS TO PUSH DEEPER IN THE WATER AT THE FINISH OF THE PULL

(Notice Fig. 3–5 in which the swimmer does not push as deep.)

apt one in describing the action. The authors have photographed the movement in good age-group swimmers as young as six years of age who have not been taught it purposely. We think it may be an unconscious response to the need for a strongly propulsive finish, at least in some highly talented swimmers.

In order to fully exploit this downward press of the hand towards getting the shoulder up, the swimmer must allow only one shoulder to rise as the hand pushes downward. If the swimmer tries to hold the body flat, she can cause the downward thrust to have its effect on the whole body—not just on one side— through muscular tension. Since this is undesirable and the rolling motion is desirable, such muscular tension should be avoided.

The roll of the body at this point achieves three purposes: (1) It causes the shoulder on the side of the pulling arm to elevate, with the result that it will not create unnecessary drag during the arm recovery; (2) it places the opposite arm at a better angle for strong lift production; and (3) it allows the swimmer to bend her elbow to the desired angle without having her hand break the surface of the water.

Due to some rule changes which have proven favorable to backstroke events, times in the backstroke have come very close and, in some cases, surpassed those of the butterfly, but the fact remains that the pull must be made from a very disadvantageous position by comparison with that of the butterfly and the crawl. The further the arms are placed in back of a line parallel to the side of the body and posterior to the line of the shoulders, the weaker their depressor action will be. By rolling the body, the angle between the pulling arm and the shoulder can be decreased, thus strengthening the pull.

As in the crawl, the swimmer should not roll just to be rolling. It is easy to roll too far. The amount of roll to each side is usually slightly less than 45 degrees among swimmers with normal shoulder flexibility, and is somewhat greater (45 to 65 degrees) among those whose flexibility is less than normal.

The shoulders and hips should roll simultaneously. If the swimmer allows his shoulders to roll, but tries to keep his hips flat, he will find himself experiencing a considerable amount of lateral movement in his legs (*wiggling*). When the hips roll properly, the legs are in position at the right time to kick diagonally up and across the center line of the body, canceling the distorting effect on body align-ment of the second half of the arm pull. The head should remain stationary as the rest of the body rolls around it. Among good backstrokers the head appears neither to roll nor to have any lateral movement.

After the hand pushes downward, the pull ends and the arm recovery begins with the hand at a depth of approximately 1½ feet below the surface or deeper. In fact, in the case of several elite swimmers photographed by the authors, the hand can finish as deep as 3 feet (see Figure 3–4).

The underwater recovery phase of the arm stroke should be accomplished with a minimum of resistance created by the hand as it moves upward. To achieve that end, most swimmers either flex the wrist or rotate the forearm so the palm is facing inward toward the thigh and almost touching it. To convey an impression of how the hand should be recovered out of the water, the swimmer should be told that his thumb should come out of the water first as his hand leaves the water. Lifting the arm during this period can cause the body to be pulled downward into

A. & AA.

B. & BB.

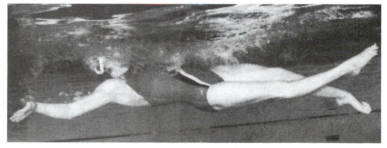

FIGURE 3–5 TOTAL STROKE OF AN ELITE BACKSTROKER

A & AA. The left arm has begun the underwater portion of its recovery, and the right arm has just entered the water, little finger first.

B & BB. The pull of the right arm begins with a pressing-out-and-down action. The hand is pitched diagonally down and back, thus achieving the best angle of attack for lift to occur. At this point in the stroke, her pull would throw her body out of alignment were it not for the diagonal thrust of the foot opposite the pulling arm.

the water, merely as a reaction to the lift. It is very important that the swimmer kick downward with the leg on the same side as the recovery arm at this point of the arm's recovery. The downward thrust of the leg will cancel the effect of the upward lift of the arm. This is but another example of equal and opposite forces canceling each other, and it usually occurs automatically. Figure 3–5 is a remarkable sequence of photographs in which the side and rear views match precisely.

C. & CC.

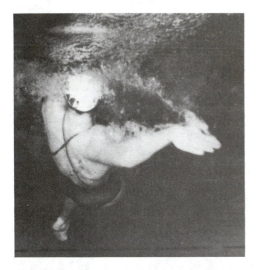

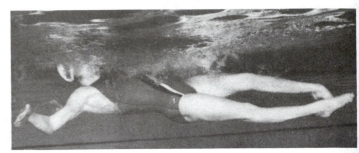

D. & DD.

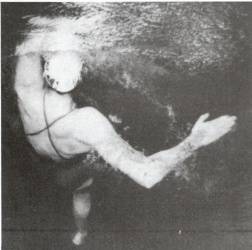

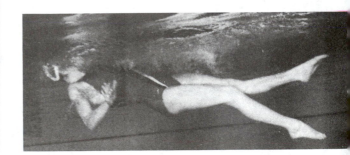

FIGURE 3–5 *(continued)*

C & CC. The body rolls further to the side as the pull continues, stabilized by the diagonally sideward thrust of the kick.

D & DD. The elbow bend continues, reaching its most extreme point in this picture. Notice the hand position in which the wrist is slightly extended as the hand sculls up and backward.

As in the other three strokes, the hand speed of good backstrokers continues to increase during the course of the pull, up to a point about three-quarters through it (see Figure 1–22 in Chapter I). This acceleration permits the pull to generate more propulsion. In the backstroke the hands should be pitched at a 40-degree angle in relation to the pull pattern, thus creating more propulsion due to the effect of lift than if they pushed straight backward and obtained propulsion due to the effect of drag.

E. & EE.

F. & FF.

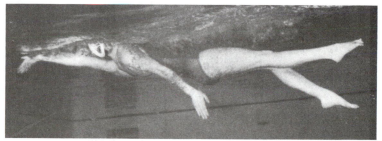

FIGURE 3–5 *(continued)*

E & EE. The left hand enters the water as the right hand pushes downward in its final sculling motion. Notice the body roll caused by the downward push of the pulling arm.

F & FF. The shoulder continues to roll to the left. The left arm is now in the same position as the right arm was in (A) and vice versa.

Figure 3–6 is composed of two light tracings of the backstroke arm pull: one photographed from the side, the other from behind. A flashing light was attached to the middle finger of each hand and the swimmer photographed as he swam across a darkened pool in front of a stationary camera, whose lens was left open. A single strobe light was flashed during the pass in order that the swimmer's image might appear. The photograph shows the swimmer sculling his way through the water in a curvilinear pattern, thus revealing that he is generating a combination of lift and drag force in which lift dominates. This is demonstrated by the

G. & GG.

FIGURE 3–5 *(continued)*

G & GG. The swimmer starts to stroke with the left arm in the second half of a complete pulling cycle.

fact that his hand entered the water only slightly in front of the point at which it exited.

Before summarizing the most common errors in the back crawl arm pull, it seems appropriate to issue a warning. Experience shows that it is hard to change such complex movements as those that comprise this pull. When a coach finally decides it must be done, he should make certain he knows how to communicate effectively with his swimmer.

The most common mistakes are: (1) pulling with a straight elbow; (2) pulling with a straight-line pull, as opposed to an S-shaped pattern; (3) dropping the elbow rather than using an inverted high-elbow action; and (4) failing to finish the pull with a downward push.

As touched upon earlier in this chapter, we have recently seen not just one but several world-class swims in the back crawl by swimmers who use a variation

FIGURE 3–6 LIGHT TRACING STUDY OF THE BACKSTROKE ARM PULL IN RELATION TO THE WATER

A. Showing the path of the hand from a side view
B. Showing the path of the hand from behind

of the bent-arm pull in which the pull finishes much deeper than usual and the elbow bend is less pronounced. At this time it is difficult to evaluate why times have dropped so dramatically in the backstroke. The introduction of a faster turn and the effect of dolphining off the start and turns have confused the issue. Nevertheless, the authors have to consider the possibility that this stroke anomaly has played a role in producing the fast times. Further study is needed to explain how this pull can be so effective, since it appears to be a misapplication of force. Figure 3–7 depicts this technique.

ARM RECOVERY

The arm recovery should be up and forward in a perfectly straight and vertical line. Any deviation from this line will result in a lateral reaction in the body. If the arm is swung wide in a low, flat, circular movement, there will be a reaction

FIGURE 3–7   AN EXAMPLE OF THE DEEPER ARM PULL AND LESS-PRONOUNCED EL-BOW BEND IN THE BACK CRAWL OF A WORLD RECORD HOLDER

A. Upon surfacing after the underwater dolphining action, the swimmer immediately begins to flutter kick. The right arm has completed its pull and is about to recover. The left arm has entered the water and is ready to begin to pull.

B. As the right arm recovers, the elbow of the left arm starts to bend and the body to roll to the left.

C. The left arm sweeps wide to the side as the body continues to roll in a counterclockwise direction.

of the legs in the opposite direction. To prove this, a person need only float in the water on his back with his feet supported by a tube and his arms held at his sides. As he recovers one arm sidewards, he will note the sideward movement of the feet in the opposite direction. If he repeats the same recovery motion, but with the arm recovery made on the vertical plane, he will find there is no lateral movement of the legs.

FIGURE 3–7 *(continued)*

D. At this point the elbow has reached maximum flexion of approximately 115 degrees. This is a departure from the flexion of the traditional backstroker, who attains about a 90-degree flexion. The torquing effect of the pull is offset to some extent by the lateral and upward force of the kick of the left leg.

E. The left arm begins to extend, pushing downard and inward.

F. The palm of the left hand has turned toward the body. The hand has reached its lowest point, well below the hips.

This reflects a stroke philosophy that is quite different from the one which has prevailed for the past twenty years. In that concept the palm faced downward at the end of the propulsive phase, the intent of which was to allow the downward push to cause the body to roll toward the opposite side, thus placing the shoulder in a good position to recover, and the opposite arm in a good position to create force at the beginning of the pull. If the stroke pictured here is indeed a more effective one, the authors are unable to determine why. Perhaps it is better suited for some swimmers than for others, or perhaps it exploits lift better than the traditional style.

FIGURE 3–8 A SEQUENCE OF DRAWINGS OF THE BACK CRAWL

A. The downward momentum developed by the left arm during the last half of the recovery phase causes the arm with the elbow still extended to sink into the water. The right hand moves upward at the same time as the left foot. This timing is seen in most good backstrokers.

B. The left elbow begins to flex as the arm is pulled downward and sideward. The right leg which is at the bottom of its downbeat is at a slight diagonal angle and is ready to begin the upbeat.

C. As the left hand passes by the shoulder, the elbow reaches maximum flexion of 90 degrees. The recovering arm starts to rotate, turning the palm outward away from the body. This action facilitates arm recovery.

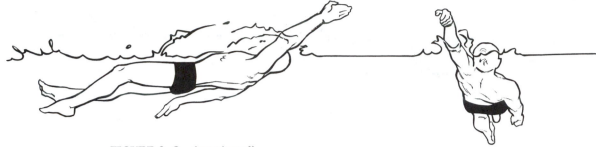

FIGURE 3–8 *(continued)*

D. The left hand position changes, bringing the palm closer to the body. This hand is ready to begin its push almost directly downward. The recovering arm continues in its vertical path.

E. As the right hand enters the water with the palm facing outward, the left arm starts its upward recovery. The swimmer pictured here is lifting his arm upward with the palm facing downward. Many swimmers rotate this arm so the palm faces inward toward the midline of the body. Both techniques are acceptable. At this point in the stroke neither hand is applying any propulsive force.

F. The catch of the right hand is made with a straight elbow. As the left hand starts its out-of-water recovery, the left leg is kicked diagonally downward. Once again, the upbeat of the leg on the opposite side coincides with the final lift of the arm from the water.

G. The right hand directly opposite the shoulder is applying its force directly backward. The left shoulder is lifted up and over the water, due primarily to the roll of the body.

H. As the right arm starts its downward push, the left leg continues to thrust diagonally upward.

I. The right arm finishes its pull, while the left hand has almost finished its recovery. The stroke cycle is now complete.

During the recovery, the elbow should be straight but not held rigid through muscular tension. The recovery should be a controlled ballistic movement, involving very little muscular tension.

As the hand exits the water, the palm should either be facing downward with a flexed wrist or be facing the thigh with the thumb up. Between this point and when the hand passes by the head (or halfway through the arm recovery), the hand should have been turned so the palm is facing almost directly outward. It should remain in this position until the recovery has ended with the little finger entering the water first, and the thumb pointing directly upward. See the sequence of drawings in Figure 3–8 at the end of this chapter.

The speed of the recovering arm should correspond almost exactly to the speed of the pulling arm, in order that there may be nearly complete arm opposition during the whole stroke. This arm opposition is more complete in the backstroke than in the front crawl. In the crawl stroke it has been shown that it is possible for one arm to start its pulling action before the other has finished. This action is not possible in the backstroke. Some backstrokers have tried to accomplish it by rushing the recovery and have only succeeded in achieving a disconnected stroke which lacks rhythm. One of the most beautiful sights in swimming is to see this flowing rhythm between the two arms, such as is seen among today's champions, whose strokes appear effortless and rhythmical, even when they swim at maximum effort.

The speed of the recovering arm should not be changed before it enters the water. If the momentum of the recovering arm is dissipated by water resistance, it will have no appreciable effect on the swimmer's body position. If, however, the momentum is slowed down through muscular effort, it will be transferred to the body, and the head and shoulders will be pulled downward.

BREATHING

Because his head is out of water at all times the backstroker has a different breathing problem than do the specialists of the other three strokes. He can breathe when he wants to, and this in itself presents a problem. He may breathe too shallowly and may enter into a *panting* or very fast breathing pattern in which he exchanges as little as a half pint of air with each breath. This happens more frequently when he gets tired. To prevent this from occurring, the swimmer should concentrate on inhaling through the mouth on the recovery and exhaling through the mouth *and* nose on the pull. He should also check on his breathing pattern occasionally to see that he is not breathing more often than one inhalation and exhalation per arm cycle. This will ensure that he does not breathe too shallowly.

Backstrokers who swim a lot of crawl do not have as great a problem with shallow breathing as those who do not. In any case it is a flaw that is easy to correct. Most breathing mechanics are reflex in nature; they need very little adjustment from the coach.

FOOTNOTES

1. Oronzio de Bernardi, *L'arte regionata del nuotare*, Parts I and II, Vol. II, 99, in Ralph Thomas, *Swimming* (London: Sampson, Low, Marston & Co., Ltd., 1904), 217.

2. Thomas, *Swimming* p. 365.

3. U.S. Swimming, Inc., *1993 Rules and Regulations*, Colorado Springs, CO: 1992.

CHAPTER 4

The Butterfly Stroke

The butterfly stroke was first swum in 1933, making it the youngest of the four competitive strokes. It was on December 16, 1933, that Henry Myers, competing for the Brooklyn Central YMCA, shocked those present by using an overarm recovery with a frog kick in a breaststroke event. The officials brought out a rule book and quickly huddled to decide whether or not the stroke conformed with the rules governing the breaststroke. Since the swimmer's arms moved forward simultaneously and since there was no mention in the rules of a requirement to keep the arms underwater, Henry Myers's stroke was deemed legal. In 1952, FINA (*Fédération International de Natation Amateur*, the governing body of international swimming) separated the breaststroke and butterfly into two events and legalized the use of the dolphin kick in the butterfly, retaining the frog kick in the breaststroke.

The butterfly resembles the crawl stroke in that the arm and leg movements are similar. The difference with the butterfly is that the arms stroke simultaneously rather than alternately, and so do the legs. The speed of the stroke has progressed to the point that there are those who believe it will some day supplant the crawl as the fastest swimming stroke. The authors see little chance of that occurring, since the butterfly possesses an inherent flaw: Its propulsive force fluctuates greatly, permitting a tremendous surge of power when the arms are pulling and suffering a correspondingly large deceleration when the arms are recovering. As described in Chapter I, there is a disproportionate amount of energy lost in this type of stop-and-go propulsion, although it can be mitigated by an effective kick.

The current rules governing the butterfly state the following:

1. Start—The forward start shall be used.

2. Stroke—After the start and after each turn, the swimmer's shoulders must be at or past the vertical toward the breast. The swimmer is permitted one or more leg kicks, but only one arm pull underwater, which must bring him to the surface. From the beginning of the first arm pull, the swimmer's shoulders shall be in line with the water surface. Both arms must be brought forward over the water and pulled back simultaneously.

3. Kick—All up-and-down movements of the legs and feet must be simultaneous. The position of the legs or the feet need not be on the same level, but they shall not alternate in relation to each other. A scissors or breaststroke kicking movement is not permitted.

4. Turns—At each turn the body shall be on the breast and the shoulders in line with the water surface. The touch shall be made with both hands simultaneously at, above, or below the water surface. Once a touch has been made, the swimmer may turn in any manner desired. The swimmer's shoulders must be at or past the vertical toward the breast when the feet leave the wall.

5. Finish—At the finish the touch shall be made with both hands simultaneously at, above, or below the water surface. The body shall be on the breast and the shoulders in line with the water surface.[1]

The butterfly is so similar to the crawl stroke in terms of the muscle groups involved and the mechanics employed that many freestylers swim excellent butterfly without much time having been spent training for it. The reverse is also true. Most top butterflyers can switch to the crawl and perform well without much problem. The butterfly is swum with both arms recovered over the water, while the legs kick up and down in a dolphin (or fishtail) kick. Among butterflyers, two kicks per arm cycle is the norm.

Chapter I contains background information which will help in understanding the basis for the stroke mechanics recommended here.

BODY POSITION

The butterfly stroke features far more vertical movement than the other three strokes. This movement is not a forced undulation but results from three main factors: (1) the downward kicking action which forces the hips up, (2) the inertia of the recovering arms which tends to pull the head and shoulders down, and (3) the first part of the pull which raises the head and shoulders upward. While some of this action in the vertical plane is desirable in that it facilitates breathing, the body must remain as streamlined as possible if the swimmer is to hold the amount of drag to a reasonable level.

Butterflyers who swim the stroke properly report that they feel a flowing motion in their bodies and a gentle but definite rhythmical rise and fall in body position. Moving or sequential pictures of good butterflyers reveal that they time the kick, pull, and head lift for breathing in such a way that body position remains relatively horizontal. The hips of a good butterflyer stay close to the surface of the water and the body angle remains relatively level. The effect which the arm pull, kick, and breathing have on body position, as well as how they should be timed in the total stroke, will be discussed in other sections of this chapter.

THE DOLPHIN KICK

The dolphin (or fishtail) kick is made by keeping the legs together and kicking them up and down in the vertical plane (see Figure 4–1). Among most flyers there are two kicks per arm stroke. The dolphin kick is faster than the other three kicking styles when performed in drills on the kick board. The kick is difficult for some swimmers because it requires superior ankle flexibility (plantar-flexion) to be effective. Ankle stretching exercise, kicking with fins, and kicking drills help to increase ankle flexibility.

The first kick downward—the one that occurs immediately after the arms enter the water—is usually the smaller and less vigorous of the two. It comes at a time when the swimmer is at his slowest speed in the stroke cycle, due to the fact that the acceleration he gained during the previous arm pull has begun to dissipate. This factor, plus the drag effect that the entry of his arms into the water has had on his forward speed, causes the swimmer to be at this lowest velocity point of the stroke. The first kick, coming as it does at this point, drives the swimmer forward, serving to elevate his hips and to place his body in an almost perfectly streamlined, horizontal position when the arm pull is made. The second kick occurs during the last part of the arm pull. It is larger and more vigorous than the first. Its function is to cancel the hip-dropping effect of the latter part of the pull on body position.

Some swimmers use only one kick thus losing the advantage of the mitigating effect of this kick against the tendency of the last part of the pull to force the hips downward. Even some good swimmers eliminate the second kick when they tire, or they make it so small and feeble as to be scarcely perceptible. Since this happens when the swimmer is tired and cannot finish his arm pull properly, the effect is to shorten the time required to finish the arm pull to the point that the swimmer doesn't have time to kick twice in each stroke. When the pull is shortened or narrowed there is less need for the second kick, whose main function is to keep the hips up. The second kick can often be kept in the stroke by having the swimmer concentrate on lengthening the stroke by pulling his arms back further. A longer pull increases the time available for a downward thrust of the feet. In addition, there is a neuromotor adaptation which further enhances propulsion: A longer, stronger finish of the pull automatically causes the swimmer to kick harder. This is the reason the second kick becomes the stronger of the two when sprinting. The combination of a strong finish of the pull and a strong second kick produces the highest peak of body velocity per stroke cycle.

When a swimmer with an exceptionally strong arm pull sprints and finishes his pull strongly, his two kicks per cycle will be almost identical in size. The first kick may even be bigger than the second. Obviously the strength or forcefulness

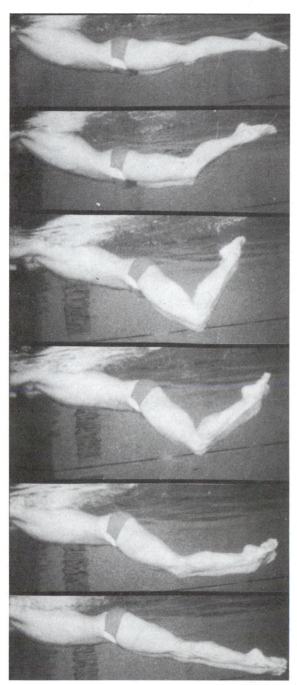

FIGURE 4–1 THE DOLPHIN KICK

A. The knees are extended as the upbeat of the kick nears completion.

B. The knees bend by an action in which the knees move downward and the feet continue upward.

C. The knees reach maximum flexion as the feet begin their downward thrust.

D. The vigorous thrust of the feet continues by extension of the knees. Notice the plantar-flexion of the ankles.

E. The propulsive phase of the kick continues as the speed of the feet accelerates.

F. The downbeat finishes.

FIGURE 4–2 A LIGHT TRAC-
ING OF THE PATH OF THE DOL-
PHIN (FISHTAIL) KICK

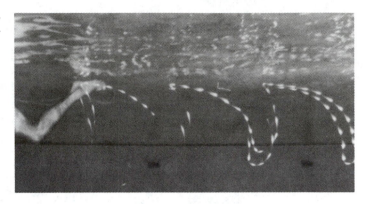

of the finish of the pull has a great deal to do with the size of the second kick. It is our belief that the coach should encourage the extra effort required to work two kicks into the stroke, but some swimmers, especially young age-groupers, may not have enough strength to pull long and work in the second kick.

Just as a runner automatically swings his arms more when he sprints, so probably does a butterflyer adjust the dolphin kick (primarily the second kick) to his stroke, particularly at the end of the pull.

Figure 4–2 shows a light tracing of the path of the dolphin kick. The feet hardly ever move backward, so the thrust of the kick must be explained in terms of the Bernoulli (or lift) effect rather than the effect of drag.

The mechanics of the dolphin kick are best learned on a kick board, but the mere fact that the swimmer can master the kick on the board does not mean he will be able to kick effectively when he combines it with the rest of the stroke. Some butterflyers prefer to do their kicking drills without the use of a board, but most like to use one. Among world-class butterflyers who do their kicking drills on their side or on their back with no board, Pablo Morales is an outstanding example. In fact, Morales's teammates at Stanford also follow this procedure. When the board is not used, the swimmer tends to undulate his body too much by alternately piking at the hips and arching the back excessively. Since the swimmer tends to do in the whole stroke what he has practiced in kicking and pulling drills, care must be taken that this stroke defect is not transferred to the whole stroke with a resulting excessive up-and-down body movement.

When the swimmer grasps the kick board, he should not press the board down with his hands, but should keep his shoulders low in the water. The board should be kept flat, not tilted upward. As he kicks on the board, the swimmer's elbows should be straight or almost straight, and he should look down the board to the opposite end of the pool. The board should remain relatively stable, not be forced up and down. As he looks at the end of the pool, the swimmer should be aware of whether or not his head and shoulders are bobbing to any great extent, and he should try to control the bobbing. He will feel his hips rise as he kicks downward and drop somewhat as he recovers his legs upward. He should not try to control this body motion rigidly but, as mentioned before, should try to prevent excessive piking action at the hips and arching of the back. Uncontrolled, these conditions introduce excessive undulating movement.

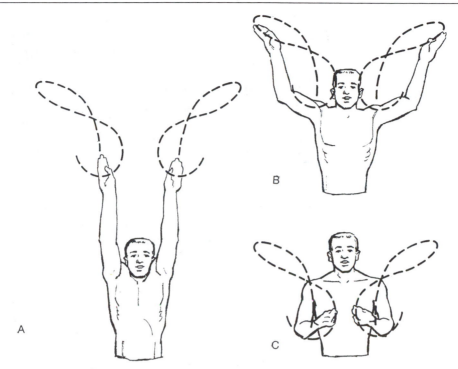

FIGURE 4–3   THE ARM PULL OF THE BUTTERFLY IN RELATION TO STILL WATER
  A. In the first part of the pull most of the propulsion derives from lift.
  B. Lift continues to be the dominant propulsive force.
  C. The primary propulsive force changes from lift to drag. As the swimmer finishes his pull, he is pushing almost directly backwards and, consequently, is exploiting drag rather than lift.

THE ARM PULL

The arm pull begins after the hands have entered the water and have sunk several inches beneath the surface. Figure 4–3 depicts the butterfly stroke as seen from directly underneath and in relation to still water. It presents the observer with a very unusual view of the near-perfect stroke mechanics of a world-class swimmer.

As can be seen in Figure 4–3, once the pull begins the arms are pressed down and outward. How wide should they press before they start inward? Figure 4–4 shows the maximum width of the arm pull of four elite butterflyers, including three world-record holders. All four attain approximately the same width of pull.

During the first half of the pull the arms are carried in a position referred to as "elbows-up" or "reaching over the barrel." This high position is accomplished by bending the elbows and then rotating the upper arms medially. Figure 4–5 shows the high elbow position of a great butterflyer, as seen from head-on and from the side. The sequence at the end of the chapter (Figure 4–10) also shows this arm position.

The narrowest point of the arm pull of three great butterflyers is shown in Figure 4–6. As can be seen, the hands of one of the swimmers nearly touch during the midpoint of the pull. In this case, if the swimmer is sculling at this point, the

FIGURE 4–4 MAXIMUM WIDTH OF THE BUTTERFLY PULL IN FOUR ELITE BUTTER-FLYERS

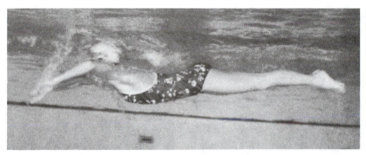

FIGURE 4–5   HEAD-ON AND SIDE VIEWS OF THE HIGH ELBOW POSITION OF A WORLD-RECORD HOLDER AND TWO-TIME OLYMPIAN IN THE BUTTERFLY.

movement may be propulsive. If the hands were pushing directly backward, this would be a drag force and the hand that is slightly in back of the other would create little or no propulsive force. Studies by the authors showed that instructing swimmers to pitch their hands and scull inward, allowing the hands to cross one above the other, resulted in improved times on the part of some of the subjects.

Since the mechanics of the fly and the crawl are nearly identical, there is little need for a detailed discussion here. It should suffice to say that the arms are pulled obliquely downward and outward, the upper arms rotated medially as the elbows are bent. Some young swimmers "rise to the catch" at this point. That is, their hands go out and up before they begin to pull due to a lack of strength. This stroke flow causes them to drop their elbows, which in turn reduces the ability of the pull to produce lift and apply force optimally. The elevation of the elbows, described earlier, imparts to the swimmer the sensation of reaching *over a barrel*, also described earlier. It permits the arms to push the water backward at an advantageous angle (approximately 40°). A *dropped elbow* during this phase of

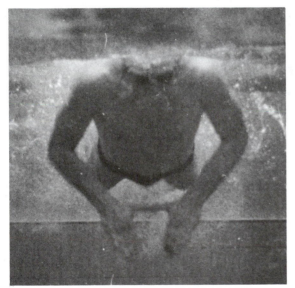

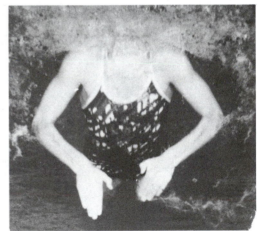

FIGURE 4–6 NARROWEST WIDTH OF THE ARM PULL OF THREE ELITE BUTTERFLY-ERS.

the pull, on the other hand, results in the force being directed more downward more than backward (see Figure 2–15 in Chapter 2).

After the hands and arms press outward, they begin to scull inward until they almost touch. This action is accomplished by bending the elbows plus increasing the medial rotation of the upper arms. Once again, this action is similar to that of the crawl arm stroke at the same point and is accomplished for the same reasons as those given for the crawl: (1) to make the arm pull stronger by adding the strength of the arm rotators to that of the arm depressors, and (2) to assure a more efficient application in terms of lift-producing effect. Figure 4-3 (A and B) shows two key positions in the arm pull to illustrate this phase.

The arms are pulled through the water in what has been called a *keyhole* or *hourglass* pattern. This is shown in Figure 1–11 in Chapter 1. The actual path of the hands through the water is best shown by taking a time-exposure picture in a dark pool with a flashing light attached to the middle finger of each hand. A strobe light is flashed at one point during the stroke in order that a picture of the swimmer may appear on the film. A sequence of six pictures of the butterfly stroke of a world-class swimmer is shown in Figure 4–7.

THE ARM RECOVERY

The butterfly arm recovery actually begins underwater, as in Figure 4–7–F, preparation for it having begun before the arms finish their pull. The overlap of the two phases occurs as the upper arms and elbows start to recover while the hands continue their backward and outward push. At this point the hands do not push directly backward so much as they sweep outward in a rounding-out motion. The effect of this rounding out is to conserve much of the momentum which the arms and hands developed during the pull. It also aids in the recovery of the arms. When the stroke is executed correctly by a powerful swimmer, it is at this point that the beauty of the stroke is most manifest.

The recovery of an outstanding swimmer is shown in Figure 4–8. These photographs, taken from just above the surface of the water, illustrate the correct mechanics of the arm recovery.

From the description in the caption of Figure 4–8, as well as from observation of the stroke from the side, it can be understood why many coaches refer to the arm recovery as primarily a ballistic movement. The force to establish such a movement need be applied for only a short period at the beginning of the movement. The momentum developed by the arms during this period carries them through the rest of the movement. In the butterfly arm recovery, the recovery muscles (primarily the deltoid and trapezius) contract vigorously during the first part of the arm swing, then relax and allow momentum rather than their sustained contraction to carry them forward. One way of conveying this idea to the swimmer is to tell him to concentrate on relaxing his arms once recovery has begun.

The palms are facing almost directly upward as they leave the water, but they should not retain that position for long. If they did, the recovery would be difficult because this position decreases the mobility of the upper arm in the shoulder joint. This is particularly true of swimmers with limited shoulder and upper arm flexibility. Almost as soon as the hands leave the water the swimmer should make a conscious effort to rotate the upper arm laterally in order that the palms may be facing downward as the hands swing forward past the shoulder. The hands should enter the water at the shoulder line or slightly outside it, with the palms facing down and slightly outward and the thumbs lower than the rest of the hand. This will establish the pitch of the hands that is necessary to facilitate propulsion from lift. Figure 4–8 shows the movement described in this paragraph.

A mistake common to many butterflyers occurs immediately before the arms

FIGURE 4–7 A SEQUENCE OF PICTURES OF THE TOTAL STROKE OF AN ELITE BUTTERFLYER.

A. The arms have finished their recovery and the hands have entered the water, pausing at shoulder width at the transition point between recovery and pull.

B. The pull begins with the hands pressing out and downward.

C. At this point the hands have reached their maximum width as the pull continues.

D. The elbow brings the hands back and inward towards the midline of the body.

E. The pull is about half completed as the hands continue to pull inward.

F. The hands push backward, completing the pull and preparing to recover.

FIGURE 4–8 THE RECOVERY OF AN OLYMPIC CHAMPION BUTTERFLYER PHOTOGRAPHED FROM THE SIDE. (A through F) The arms are swung forward in a low, flat parabola, becoming completely extended due largely to the centrifugal force generated by their circular motion. They are close to the water, yet do not drag through it. The elbows are almost straight, and there appears to be no excessive tension of the arms, that is, they are not totally relaxed and tension is controlled. The chin is carried low and the swimmer is not climbing high out of the water (a common defect). As his arms continue to swing forward from this position, they are recovered laterally over the water with the palms facing downward. The elbows are fully extended except for a slight bend of the right elbow. The inhalation is being made as the arms swing forward. As soon as they achieve a line even with the shoulders, the inhalation will end and the head will tilt downward, submerging the face.

FIGURE 4–9   HIGH AND LOW CATCH IN THE BUTTERFLY.
A. A high catch disturbs streamlining.
B. A normal catch preserves it.

enter the water. If the swimmer exercises too much control at this point and slows down, the downward momentum of the arms will be transferred to his body and he will sink further under the surface of the water than he should.

The downward momentum of the arms and hands should be absorbed by the water and not canceled by muscle action. Not only will the body drop lower into the water than it should, but the hands will stop near the surface. If the swimmer begins to pull at this point, the force of the first part of the pull will be directed downward and the swimmer will climb upward in reaction (see Figure 4–9–A). Much of the excessive up-and-down motion of some butterfly swimmers can be attributed to this defect.

On the other hand, if the swimmer allows the arm momentum developed during the recovery to cause the arms to sink slightly without pulling the head and shoulders down, he will be in a better position to apply the force of his pull in a more backward and less downward direction (see Figure 4–9–B).

HAND PITCH IN THE BUTTERFLY

The importance of hand pitch in all four strokes has been discussed in Chapter 1. To be effective in producing lift, the angle of attack must conform to the same principle of fluid mechanics that applies to propellers in airplanes and boats. The propeller must be pitched at an angle between 30 and 40 degrees in relation to its path through the air or water, and the hand must apply its force in the same manner. The closer it remains to about 40 degrees, the more effective it is in producing lift. In the butterfly, this is demonstrated in the photo sequence of Figure 4–7 and in the sequence at the end of the chapter (Figure 4–10).

BREATHING ACTION AND TIMING

Swimmers not accustomed to swimming butterfly often complain of sore muscles in the back of the neck when they begin to train the stroke. The posterior neck muscles (splenius capitis, splenius cervicis, and erector spinae) are used to lift the head by hyperextension of the neck, thus permitting the shoulders to remain lower in the water while the swimmer is breathing than he otherwise could. The butterfly is the only one of the four strokes in which these muscles are used in this way and they are not as well conditioned in swimmers of the other strokes.

If the swimmer does not hyperextend his neck, he will have to breathe with his face looking downward and his body position will be elevated during the breathing phase. We tell such swimmers to lift their heads to breathe by concentrating on hyperextension of the neck. The head-lift action should raise the head just high enough to get the mouth clear of the water, but not so high as to raise the chin very far above the surface. Some swimmers lift their heads so high that their chin is 5 to 6 inches above the water level. Kevin Berry, 1964 Olympic champion of the butterfly event, used to say that, when he was swimming well in a calm pool, he plowed a furrow in the water with his chin.

After the breath has been taken, the posterior neck muscles should be relaxed and the head should drop until it is almost in straight alignment with the body. This head action is apparent in the sequence of the butterfly stroke in Figure 4–10 at the end of this chapter.

The timing of the head lift should be such that inhalation occurs at the highest point of elevation. A common error is for the swimmer to develop a late breathing pattern in which he lifts his head to breathe after his shoulders have reached the peak of their climb and his body is on its way down. This late-breathing pattern causes him to arch his back and rush his arm recovery. In order to break such a pattern, the swimmer should begin to lift his head immediately after the catch is made (that is, at the beginning of the pull).

During the first half of the pull, the shoulders should rise as the neck continues to extend and, when the arms are past a line perpendicular to the body, the face should be almost completely out of the water and the inhalation should begin. The inhalation continues until the arms have completed their pull and begun the recovery. As the recovery is made, the head should be lowered into the water by flexion of the neck.

As the arms pass by the head on their forward swing, the face should be completely submerged, at least to eye level (see Figure 4–10). If the arms pass by the shoulders on their recovery and the swimmer is still breathing, he is breathing too late.

If the lift of the head is timed properly, it can serve to keep the body position relatively flat. Since the arm pull causes the body to rise in the water and the head lift causes the body to drop lower into the water, these two forces combine to nearly cancel each other, but the arm pull has a greater lifting force than the head lift has a lowering force, so the body does rise at this point in the stroke. In fact, the head is lifting and the neck is extending during most of the arm pull. The head drop is a fast movement, which takes approximately half the time it takes to lift the head. There are two important reasons why the head should be lowered:

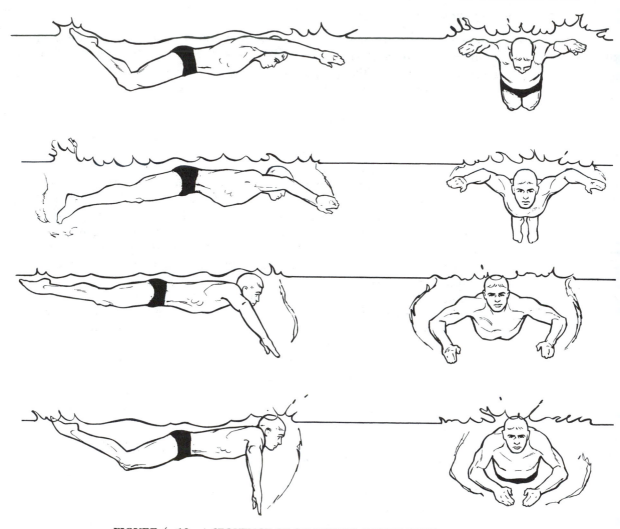

FIGURE 4–10 A SEQUENCE OF DRAWINGS OF THE BUTTERFLY.

A. As the momentum of the arms, developed during the recovery, causes the hands to sink downward, muscular effort is applied to direct the pull diagonally outward. The downward thrust of the feet has begun.

B. The feet dorsiflex at the ankles as the legs begin their upbeat. During the first part of the pull, even when the swimmer does not take a breath, he lifts his head as though he were looking forward. This action occurs naturally. Not the pitch of the hands with the thumb having entered the water first.

C. The arms start to come closer together. The line of air bubbles indicates the general path of the pull.

D. The hands approach each other as they pass directly under the shoulders. The elbow bend, still held away from the body, is approximately 90 degrees.

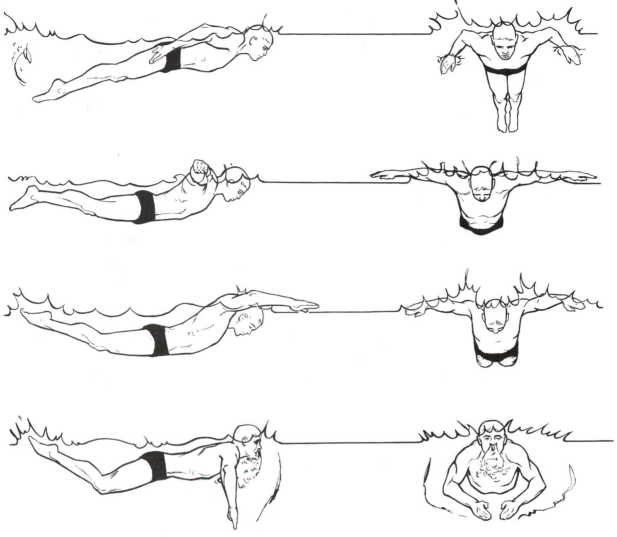

FIGURE 4–10 *(continued)*

   E. The legs complete their downbeat just before the hands leave the water. The main purpose of the second kick is to keep the hips near the surface, thus preserving streamlining. Swimmers with an exceptionally good kick may get some propulsion from the second kick.

   F. As the hands swing past the shoulders, the palms are facing downward, and the elbows are completely extended. The feet start to plantar-flex as they near the top of the upbeat.

   G. The upper arms start to hit the water as the hands enter.

   H. The exhalation is in process as the pull changes direction sharply, and the hands approach each other.

FIGURE 4–10 *(continued)*

I. The head is lifted, primarily by the flexion of the neck, and the inhalation begins before the arms complete their pull. The downbeat of the kick again coincides with the finish of the pull.

J. As the arms start to recover, the inhalation is completed, and the downbeat of the second kick also finishes.

K. After the inhalation the face is dropped back underwater, and the arms complete their recovery as the legs start upward.

(1) in order that the water may support the weight of the head, and (2) to facilitate arm recovery.

If the swimmer does not lower her head, her body position will be affected detrimentally. Her hips will drop, thereby increasing frontal and eddy resistance. On the other hand, if she lowers her head too far, she will introduce an additional up-and-down motion, which will also increase drag. Excessive lowering of the head occurs most frequently among swimmers with a poor kick—one not effective enough to keep the hips up. The action of the head is used to compensate for the weak kick, since it does cause a slight elevation of the hips.

Breathing to the Side

While there have been a few successful world-class swimmers who breathed to the side in the butterfly, there are valid reasons why this technique is not as satisfactory as forward breathing: (1) there is no lift of the head to partially cancel the upward rise caused by the arm pull; and (2) when the neck is rotated laterally, the vertebrae are placed in such a position that the neck can scarcely extend, much less hyperextend. The swimmer, in order to get his mouth clear of the water, even though he is breathing to the side in the trough formed behind the bow wave, will have to climb upward with his shoulders more than he would if he were breathing straight forward.

The deceptive feature of this type of breathing is that, because the head remains in a static position in relation to the body, it appears that the swimmer is not actually climbing as much as he does when he uses forward breathing.

How Often Should a Swimmer Breathe?

It is usual procedure for swimmers to breathe less often in the sprints, that is, to breathe once every two or three strokes in the 50- or 100-yard/meter events, as compared with once every two strokes in the 200-yard/meter events. A few have been successful breathing every stroke, even during the sprints. The breathing pattern a swimmer finally adopts must be determined by experimentation.

ACCELERATION IN THE BUTTERFLY

The butterfly inevitably produces large fluctuations in propulsive force, since both arms are pulling at the same time and then recovering at the same time. Although the arms are the main source of propulsion, the kick, if efficient and properly timed, can contribute to the propulsive force. After the hands enter the water following the recovery, there is a slight delay before the pull begins. Once the hands begin to pull, they are capable of accelerating from zero to over 19 feet per second in less than half a second (see Figure 1–24 in Chapter 1). This acceleration reaches its maximum towards the end of the stroke. In the opinion of these authors, the capacity to develop acceleration is one of the most critical factors separating great from average swimmers.

FOOTNOTE:

1. U.S. Swimming, Inc., 1993 *Rules and Regulations, Part 1.* Colorado Springs, CO: 1991.

CHAPTER 5

The Breaststroke

The breaststroke is thought to be the oldest of the competitive strokes as well as one of the oldest of the swimming styles. There is evidence of isolated cultures such as the Polynesian in which more advanced strokes developed, but it is likely that the human and animal strokes were in popular use throughout western civilization. The latter two, however, are very tiring and inefficient, and fail to provide a stable position in the water. The need must have been felt for a more effective stroke which would provide for stability even in rough water and would maintain the head out of water. As late as 1690 a Frenchman, Thevenot, wrote the following:

> To swim with the head towards heaven—to look upwards, and if we knew how to use it there would not be as many drowned as there daily are, for that happens because . . . they look downwards and embrace the water as it were with their arms.[1]

At the beginning of the sixteenth century first mention was made of a method which seemed to embody the requirements of the people of that time. In this style the simultaneous action of the arms made its appearance and, although the legs were still kicked alternately (with the propulsive force of the kick made from the instep of the foot), this method may be regarded as an initial step in the evolution of the breaststroke.

During the eighteenth century, the breaststroke became known as the frog stroke. The name indicates that there was a spread in the legs during the kick. Even though a frog kicks directly backward, primarily exploiting drag, it does spread its knees.

> Guts Muth, 1798, states that swimming on the breast was the style then used all over Europe. He says the upper surface of the feet are used not the soles of the feet and he says it is quite wrong to compare breaststroke with that of the frog.[2]

The next development must have occurred soon after Muth wrote his description. This was a change in which forward thrust derived from the sole of the foot rather than the instep. In 1842 R. H. Horne[3] concluded that the power derived from the squeezing action of the wedge kick was greater than the power derived from either the instep or the soles of the feet and, thereby, started a controversy which is still unsettled. In fact, none of the swimming strokes is the subject of as much disagreement about mechanics as the breaststroke. It is for this reason that the authors have included in this book more underwater pictures of world-record holders, Olympic champions, and other world-class swimmers of the breaststroke than of any other stroke.

Interest in competitive swimming began to develop towards the last half of the nineteenth century. It was especially keen in England. The breaststroke was the first stroke used in races, but probably not the only stroke being swum. Other strokes were tried and new ones evolved which were later to replace the breaststroke in popularity. Notable among these were the sidestroke, the overarm sidestroke, and the trudgen crawl.

On August 24 and 25, 1875, Captain Matthew Webb swam the English Channel from Dover to Calais in twenty-one hours and forty-five minutes, thereby giving impetus to swimming in general. Despite the fact that Webb swam the breaststroke in that effort, there was a trend away from it and towards the faster strokes. The turn of the century found nearly all competitive swimmers using the overarm sidestroke with a scissor kick. The advent of the Australian crawl around 1900 to 1905 caused a further loss of interest in the breaststroke because the crawl was so much faster. This is doubtless attributable to the fact that races during the period were not divided into stroke classifications. A given distance was established, and the first swimmer to reach the finish was declared the winner regardless of style. The breaststroke race was often featured in the program of swimming meets as a novelty race, and it was not until 1906 that races were divided into three classes in national and international competition. These were the breaststroke, backstroke, and freestyle. During that year A. Goersling won the 200-yard breaststroke race in 2 minutes and 52.6 seconds. Since the emphasis in competitive swimming was on the freestyle events, most good swimmers did not enter the breaststroke race. As a result, we do not know whether that time reflected the best performance possible at that juncture in the history of the stroke.

The most extreme innovation in the breaststroke occurred much later. It was the introduction of the out-of-water recovery of the arms described in Chapter 4. Coupled with the addition of the dolphin kick, the new recovery led eventually to a separation of the strokes into the breaststroke and the butterfly. Although Henry Myers[4] lost the race in which he was the first to recover his arms over the water, the news about the new stroke spread rapidly, and swimmers were intrigued by its possibilities. The 1936 Olympics saw the orthodox Japanese breast-stroker, Detsuo Hamuro, win in the time of 2 minutes, 42.5 seconds. The best a butterfly swimmer, John Higgins, could finish was fourth, but he had recorded a time of 2:41.1 in a preliminary heat.

During the period between 1933, when the butterfly stroke was introduced, until after the 1952 Olympics, when the breaststroke and butterfly were separated (effective with the 1956 Games), it was not uncommon to see butterfly being swum by some swimmers and breaststroke by others in the same race. Swimmers often switched back and forth between the two strokes in the same event. In 1942, the senior author of this book won the National AAU outdoor 200-meter butterfly-breaststroke, swimming the first 100 meters butterfly, the next 50 meters orthodox breaststroke, and the last 50 meters butterfly. The male butterflyers so overwhelmed the orthodox breaststrokers in the 1948 and 1952 Olympic Games that it became obvious the strokes should either be separated and the dolphin kick legalized or the orthodox breaststroke be abandoned entirely.

The breaststroke continued to undergo experimentation in an attempt to increase its speed. The focus of change has always been the same: how to minimize the profound deceleration that occurs during the recovery of the legs and to enhance the propulsive forces created by the kick and pull. Notable among the adaptations was an underwater stroke in which the swimmer submerged and took several strokes underwater. The arms were pulled in a long sweeping pull, all the way back and down to the sides. Underwater swimming was permitted, not only for one stroke after the start and turn, as the rules presently allow, but at any point in the race. The kick and pull were performed together, not alternately. The stroke helped swimmers with a poor kick, who relied on the arm pull for most of their propulsion. In the outdoor Nationals of 1957, which was one of the first to be televised, the senior author, from the vantage point provided by an overhead television camera, watched swimmers remain underwater for nearly the entire first length of the event (50 meters). It was the realization that, sooner or later, someone would push this practice too far, and injury or death would result, which led to a rule change prohibiting it. In the 1956 Olympic Games, the breaststroke event had been won by Masura Furukawa in a time of 2:34.7.

The rules were amended prior to the 1960 Games to exclude underwater swimming except for one long pull and kick after the dive and each turn, and to require that the head break the surface of the water at all other times during the race. Using this style, the Australian Terry Gathercole set the world record at 2:36.5, nearly two seconds slower than the stroke dominated by underwater swimming. (Furukawa's record had been disallowed when the rule was changed.) Gathercole's technique featured holding the head in a hyperextended position throughout the stroke cycle. While he had an excellent kick, his pull was relatively weak. He was said to receive 80 percent of his propulsion from his kick and only 20 percent from his arms.

In the summer of 1961 a new style of breaststroke was introduced by Chet Jastremski, who dramatically lowered all world records. He dropped the 100-meter event from 1:11 to 1:07.5, and the 200-meters from 2:36.5 to 2:29.6. Jastremski's relatively poor kick made it necessary to customize his stroke by streamlining his body and maximizing his arm propulsion. His stroke featured a faster turnover, a greater emphasis on the arm pull, a relatively narrow whip kick, and an up-and-down motion of the head to breathe. The senior author learned a valuable lesson in dealing with Jastremski's limitations. While a great many breaststrokers imitated Jastremski's stroke with success, it must be kept in mind that each swimmer should exploit his abilities and aptitudes to their best advantage and not slavishly follow each new trend without regard for how it works for him. For example, a swimmer with a strongly propulsive kick should employ a longer glide up front than the one used by Jastremski who was an *arms* swimmer. He pulled 100 meters breaststroke with his legs in a tube in 1:19, but could only kick the same distance on a kick board in 1:29.

In the 1970s, a new development occurred with the introduction of the "pop-up" (or "high rise," as it is termed in Europe) breaststroke, so termed because of the extreme elevation of the head and front part of the torso when the breath is taken. This radical departure from the flat style of the traditional breaststroke has created a sharp division between those two styles in competitive races. Some use the traditional style, others the more undulating pop-up style, still others a variation of the undulating style, which features arm recovery over the water and a forward lunging action just as the kick is occurring. This version has been termed the "wave-action" breaststroke by its proponents.

At this point in its continuing evolution, it is obvious there is little commonality of opinion as to how the stroke should be swum, but it is interesting to note that most of what is different about the various styles happens out of water, making it more noteworthy because it is so visible. Underwater, the differences are more subtle. However, it is possible that the undulating style presents a more streamlined body position during the kicking phase. Examination of Figure 5–1–A and B may help one form an opinion as to which style creates the most frontal resistance. In the undulating style, the power surge of the kick comes at a time when the head and upper part of the torso are out of water. It may be that the swimmer's body presents less drag at this point in the stroke than does the flat style even though the legs appear to present more frontal resistance. But in the flat style, certainly the head, shoulders, and upper torso also present a formidable frontal resistance at this point.

The focus of the traditional style has always been to minimize drag by keeping the body relatively flat and without much up-and-down movement, whereas that of the pop-up stroke has succeeded in reducing drag by lifting the front part of the torso high out of the water. The point of contention is whether or not the undulating movement which is introduced when the torso inevitably drops back into the water is actually propulsive. The authors believe it is more likely that it facilitates the kicking phase, bringing into operation the powerful back flexors and extensors.

FIGURE 5–1   COMPARING THE UNDERWATER VIEW OF THE LOWER PART OF THE
BODY OF AN UNDULATING STYLIST AND A TRADITIONAL STYLIST IN THE BREAST-
STROKE.
   A. The Undulating (or Pop-up) Style
   B. The Traditional (or Flat) Style

To explain the undulating style in terms of action-reaction, we need to
examine what happens when the erector spinae and other extensors contract to
hyperextend the back and raise the upper body out of the water. The reaction is
a contraction of the gluteus maximus and other hip extensors to raise the hips
and the lower extremities. This elevation produces a U shaped torso with the
midsection at the bottom of the U, thus reducing the frontal and eddy resistance
that would otherwise occur as a result of raising the upper body (see Figure
5–1–A). This action requires a supple back and may account for women being
more successful at this style than men. Although there is little movement between
individual vertebrae, seemingly the combined effect of the entire column of
vertebrae provides a great deal of flexibility particularly among young women
whose bones are small and who are more flexible. This is not to imply that either

FIGURE 5–2 A COMPARISON OF THE OUT-OF-WATER BODY POSITION IN TWO STYLES OF BREASTSTROKE.
  A. The Undulating Style
  B. The Traditional Style

style is totally exclusive to one or the other sex. These writers believe that the style which brings the best result to the individual swimmer should be the style of choice. Figure 5–2–A and B is composed of out-of-water shots of two great swimmers performing the stroke they and their coaches have settled on as best for them.

The rules have changed to accommodate the various developments of the last two decades. They are listed below in their entirety as they are stated in the U.S. Swimming rule book:

1. Start—The forward start shall be used.

2. Stroke—From the beginning of the first armstroke after the start and after each turn, the body shall be kept on the breast and both shoulders shall be in line with the water surface. The arms shall move simultaneously and in the same horizontal plane without any alternating movement. The hands shall be pushed forward together from the breast, on, under, or over the water and shall be brought back on or under the surface of the water. The hands shall not be brought beyond the hipline, except during the first stroke after the start and each turn. Some part of the swimmer's head shall break the surface of the water at least once during each complete cycle of one arm stroke and one leg kick, in that order, except after the start and each turn the swimmer may take one arm stroke completely back to the legs and one leg kick, while wholly submerged. The head must break the surface of the water before the hands turn inward at the widest part of the second stroke.

3. Kick—All vertical and lateral movements of the legs shall be simultaneous. The feet must be turned outward during the propulsive part of the kick movement. A scissors, flutter, or downward butterfly kick is not permitted. Breaking the surface with the feet shall not merit disqualification unless followed by a downward butterfly kick.

4. Turns—At each turn, the touch shall be made with both hands simultaneously at, above, or below the water surface, and the shoulders shall be in line with the water surface. The head may be submerged after the last arm pull prior to the touch, provided it breaks the surface of the water at some point during any part of the last complete or incomplete cycle preceding the touch. Once a touch has been made, the swimmer may turn in any manner desired. The shoulders must be at or past the vertical toward the breast when the feet leave the wall and the form prescribed in (2) above must be attained from the beginning of the first arm stroke.

5. Finish—At the finish the touch shall be made with both hands simultaneously at, above, or below the water surface. The body shall be on the breast and the shoulders in line with the water surface. The head may be submerged after the last arm pull prior to the touch, provided it breaks the surface of the water at some point during any part of the last complete or incomplete stroke cycle preceding the touch.[5]

BODY POSITION

As with all the competitive strokes, the body should be as streamlined or horizontal as possible, while still permitting the arms and legs to perform their function of creating propulsion. Underwater photographs of beginning swimmers and poor competitive breaststroke swimmers reveal that they swim with their bodies at a sharp angle, thereby creating a lot of frontal and eddy resistance (see Chapter 1, Figure 1–4, illustration C).

THE KICK

The old controversy which centered around the source of propulsion in the breaststroke kick has been revived by those who believe the formerly discredited wedge action plays a propulsive role in the undulating style of breaststroke. Those who disagree believe that the propulsive phase of the kick is over by the time the wedge action occurs at the end of the kick.

The preparatory phase of the wedge kick features drawing up the feet towards the buttocks through abduction of the thighs and flexion of the knees and hips, followed by full extension of the legs. Propulsion is believed to result from squeezing the fully extended legs together forcefully, an action which was believed to compress the water and force it backward, thus pushing the body forward. In 1907, Davis Dalton said about the wedge kick that the swimmer must draw up the legs, [then] "the legs, [having been] straightened out [in a wedge] bring them together . . . the water thus compressed between the legs pushes the body forward."[6]

The problem with this theory is that water is a yielding substance, and the swimmer cannot selectively determine the direction of its flow. He may want it to move backward, but, compared to the amount pushed backward by the whip action, relatively little will move backward when the wedge action is used. Most of the water squeezed between the legs will swirl randomly around them with little of the total amount moving backward. To test this hypothesis, coaches and swimmers may want to try an experiment wherein each kick is evaluated by pouring colored water between the legs of the swimmer as he holds onto the wall and observing the flow pattern of the water between his legs when each style of the kick is performed. The whip kick will be found consistently to move more water backward.

We now know—although we did not know it at the time this and similar experiments were first tried—it is the sculling action of the whip kick, featuring an advantageous angle of attack and the ability to move a high volume of water a short distance at fast speed, that causes this superior result.

Advocates of the whip kick further believe that the greater strength and speed of the backward thrust of the feet is due to increased hip flexion along with the involvement of the extensor muscles of the knees and hips (see Figure 5–3). Everyone would like to find a method of increasing propulsion without increasing drag. If a swimmer flexes his hips too much in the recovery phase of the kick, he will inevitably create more drag. If, on the other hand, he does not flex them enough, he will be unable to create as much force when he kicks.

The wedge action also does not permit the swimmer to develop as much acceleration as the whip action because it features a pause just after the knees are extended and before the squeeze begins, thus diminishing the opportunity for the development of great acceleration.

The lift effect produced by the sculling action of the whip kick follows the principle of action-reaction. Both drag and lift are action-reaction forces. Newton's Third Law is a factor in all movement in air and water, including that produced via lift and that produced by squeezing a wedge of water between the extended

FIGURE 5–3 KNEE FLEXION IN
THE BREASTSTROKE WHIP KICK
DRILL OF AN OLYMPIC CHAMPION
AND WORLD-RECORD HOLDER

legs. It is a matter of the relative effectiveness of the two styles of kick, and in
that respect the whip kick dominates easily. More important to this discussion,
however, is the concept that, as the swimmer moves forward through the water,
he needs to move a high volume of water a short distance in order to be constantly
encountering water that is not already moving backwards. The whip kick is far
better suited to do that than the wedge.

Recently, this issue has been further complicated by the idea that it is a
change in the whip kick, featuring less flexion of the hips that is responsible for
the effectiveness of the undulating style of breaststroke. Proponents of this belief
think this change reintroduces a wedge action, creating a combination whip-
wedge kick. They believe this change effectively reduces the frontal resistance
encountered by the upper legs as they are drawn up in preparation for the
propulsive phase of the kick.

Others believe that less flexion of the hips would translate into a less advantageous mechanical presentation, but that, in any event, less flexion is not occurring.
Rather they believe the reaction to the elevation of the trunk is an upward
movement of the lower legs, the consequence of which is to trade great frontal
resistance for a combination of reduced frontal resistance and laminar flow. In
the mechanics of swimming, these trade-offs present constant dilemmas to the
coach.

In an effort to decide what is operating in both the traditional style and the
undulating style, it is first necessary to know whether or not hip flexion is actually
less pronounced among good performers of the undulating style of breaststroke,
and, if it is, how this affects the balance between the amount of frontal resistance
and the power of the thrust phase of the kick. Presented here in Figures 5–4 and
5–5 are photo sequences of the kicks of two prominent breaststrokers: one an
undulating stylist, the other traditional.

The writers do not intend to imply that the undulating stroke has no merit,
rather that a whip-wedge combination kick is not responsible for its success. If
the undulating style of breaststroke is indeed equal or superior to the traditional
style, the writers believe it is due to decreased resistance (drag) at a crucial point
after the pull and during the backward thrust of the legs when the body is the
most streamlined and the kick is the most powerful.

If advocates of the whip-action concept believe that the power derived from

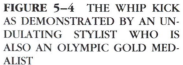

FIGURE 5–4 THE WHIP KICK AS DEMONSTRATED BY AN UNDULATING STYLIST WHO IS ALSO AN OLYMPIC GOLD MEDALIST

A. The legs are fully extended, and the feet are plantar-flexed. The pull is just beginning with the hands at shoulder width.

B. The recovery of the legs begins with flexion of the knees. Meanwhile the arms continue to spread, and the pull is half completed.

C. The legs continue to recover slowly as the hip and knee flexion increases. The arms scull inwardly.

D. The knees have flexed maximally, and the knees have been drawn up toward the buttocks. The pull is now complete, and the arms are extended forward in recovery.

E. The feet thrust out and backward by extension of the hips and knees in the power phase of the kick. The feet are dorsiflexed and present a good angle for sculling. The swimmer should concentrate on achieving a high rate of acceleration at this phase of the kick.

F. The legs have reached full extension, but have not come together. Very little, if any, propulsion is obtainable from this point onward to the last part of the squeeze. The arms are fully extended, and a short glide is taking place.

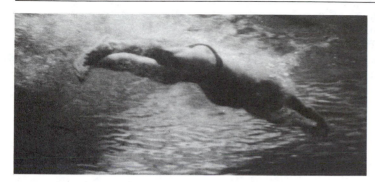

G. The body is streamlined with the face submerged, and the glide is held for a period of time which depends on the effectiveness of the kick: the better the kick, the longer the glide.

the wedge is negligible, coming exclusively from pushing water backward with the soles of the feet, how exactly do they reach that conclusion?

The preparatory phase of the kick in which the heels are brought up to the buttocks is achieved through hip rotation and medial rotation of the thighs. In the whip kick there is usually greater hip flexion (around 105 degrees) than in the wedge (around 125 degrees), while the wedge utilizes little or no medial rotation of the thighs. Reduced hip flexion and lack of hip rotation produce greater separation of the knees and feet.

Between the preparatory phase and the thrust of the legs backward, there is a brief sub-phase in the whip kick in the course of which the knees are brought inward and the feet are thrust outward (see Figure 5–5–E). This action is achieved by increased medial rotation of the femur, a movement not apparent in the wedge kick. It is also during this pre-thrust phase that the most profound changes in foot positioning occur.

The thrust phase features lateral rotation of the thighs and complete extension of the hips and knees. The knees do not reach full extension until the kick is nearly three-quarters finished. The feet finish the kick by pressing backward with a slight upsweep. The power of this kick is derived primarily from the extensor muscles of the hips and knees. The adductor muscles enter into the action, but their function is not as important as that of the hip and knee extensors. With stop action photography or video the sculling action of both the undulating and the traditional stylist is readily apparent at the end of the kick (Figures 5–5–E and 5–6–F).

Ideally, a good position of the legs immediately prior to the thrust, insofar as streamlining the body is concerned, would be an angle of hip flexion of about 130 degrees. But such an angle would not place the legs in a strong position to drive backward. The legs are relatively weak at this point and the drive of the feet backward would be accomplished primarily by the extensor muscles of the knees (the quadriceps extensor group). If the hips are flexed at an angle of 105 to 115 degrees, additional drag may be created, but this will be more than compensated for by the greater strength of the kick, which in turn can be accounted for by the increased involvement of the hip and leg extensor muscles, primarily the gluteus maximus and quadriceps extensors.

Were the legs to be flexed at an angle of 90 degrees, the increased drag would be so great that the effect would be the reverse: The drag would overcom-

FIGURE 5–5 THE WHIP KICK AS DEMONSTRATED BY A TRADITIONAL BREASTSTROKER IN A DRILL ON A KICK BOARD.

A. The knees begin to bend as the leg recovery begins.

B. The knees spread as the heels are drawn up to the hips.

C. The ankles flex as the feet get ready for the backward thrust.

D. The backward thrust begins with extension of the knees and the legs are squeezed together.

E. As the legs begin to come together, the knees are fully extended, and the propulsive phase of the kick has ended.

F. The final phase of the kick is made as the legs come together, thus streamlining the body.

pensate for the increased leg drive. Hip flexion of this extent has an additional disadvantage. It is accompanied by a sudden rise of the hips out of the water and a consequent drop during the backward thrust of the legs. Evidence of this type of stroke defect is an up-and-down motion of the hips. The optimum desirable angle of hip flexion appears to be somewhere between 105 and 115 degrees.

In the undulating style, as the legs are thrust diagonally down and backward, the reaction pushes the hips upward toward the surface and the body is thrust forward in a streamlined position. In the traditional style, since the head does not rise as high out of the water, the body remains flatter, so the swimmer must guard against allowing the thrust of the kick to finish too deep. This can be remedied by kicking in a semicircular pattern which finishes on an upward rise, thus achieving a flat and streamlined body position.

An important aspect of the whip kick is the progressive acceleration of the speed of movement of the feet during the thrust phase. The beginning of the kick should be made with a firm but not fast motion that will enable the swimmer to feel the water pressure on the soles of the feet. As the legs thrust around and backward in a circular motion, he should increase the speed of the feet to the point that maximum speed is reached during the last quarter of the propulsive phase. It is a serious mistake to accelerate the early part of the kick and then allow acceleration to trail off so quickly that the feet drift together during the last third of the kick. The speed of the thrust is directly associated with the extension of the knees. This is another reason the knees should not reach full extension until the kick is about two-thirds complete.

Ankle Flexibility

Ankle action is very important in the breaststroke kick. These movements require superior ankle flexibility, especially dorsiflexion (in which the top of the feet are brought up toward the shins). Good dorsiflexion aids the sculling action of the kick. As the feet are drawn upward in the prethrust phase, the ankles are relaxed and the feet merely trail the knees upward. As the feet start to spread, ankle dorsiflexion begins. By the time the sculling action starts, the ankles should have achieved maximum flexion. This ankle dorsiflexion is maintained until the kick is almost complete. As the kick nears completion, the ankles plantar-flex and supinate to enable the bottom of the feet either to face upward or to face each other.

A simple test to measure dorsiflexion is to have the swimmer stand erect with hands grasped in back of the neck. The feet should be held directly together with heels and toes touching. Without raising his heels, he should try to do a complete squat, letting his buttocks touch his heels. If he can't get all the way down, or if he raises his heels or falls backward, he has poor ankle dorsiflexibility and needs ankle stretching exercises. These exercises are discussed in Chapter 10.

Knee Injuries

A number of breaststroke swimmers complain of pain in the knees, and in some cases the pain becomes so great that those swimmers must switch to another stroke or stop swimming. This pain can be due to muscle injury but is most frequently due to injury of the ligaments or the muscle tendons. Such injuries can be avoided in three ways: (1) by stretching the legs with appropriate exercises before entering the water (The authors' experience is that dry land exercises, which strengthen and stretch the adductor muscles of the legs and the knee extensors, help prevent injuries to the knee ligaments and tendons.); (2) by kicking with only moderate effort at the beginning of practice, thus allowing the kicking muscles to be well warmed up; and (3) by eliminating the early extension of the knees during the backward thrust of the feet. This wedge action causes strain on the medial ligaments of the knees along with possible injury to the adductor muscles of the thighs, which squeeze the legs together.

While some swimmers have reported sore knees due to the whip kick, these writers have not had this problem with their swimmers. It is our belief that this is because we had developed a special technique for teaching the whip kick. Mechanics of the whip kick can be learned more easily by practicing the kick while lying on the back in the water with the arms held overhead. The knees should be brought up until they are about 4 to 6 inches above the surface of the water. This drill simulates the proper angle of flexion of the knees and is a useful teaching tool because it allows the coach to be aware of possible problems. During our career, we began every season with about half of our breaststroke kicking drills being done in this position.

THE ARM STROKE

It bears repeating that no stroke is more subject to misunderstanding than the breaststroke, and the arm stroke is a case in point. People talk of the pop-up style, the two-wave style, the undulating style with a lunge, and other vague terms, yet, underwater, where propulsion occurs, it is hard to find the evidence to document these opinions.

If everyone expressing opinions and writing articles on the breaststroke had to document those opinions with film, there might be less confusion concerning the mechanics of the stroke. Admittedly, even photographic proof is suspect: We are, after all, using a two-dimensional image to explain a three-dimensional action. Even computer imaging has a shortcoming: the human error that can result from less than accurate measurements. The best that can be done is to photograph from several angles in an effort to minimize error.

The Elbow Bend

The pull begins with the arms fully extended in front of the body, hands touching. The hands should be at a depth of 6 to 10 inches, not near the surface as many swimmers tend to place them, and pitched so the palms are facing diagonally outward at about a 40-degree angle (Figure 5–6–B). When the pull begins, the hands push almost directly sidewards with the elbows straight. After the hands have moved as wide as or a little wider than shoulder width, the elbows start to bend. In many respects the early part of the breaststroke pull and that of the butterfly are similar: the direction of the press, the pitch of the hands, and the amount of elbow bend being nearly the same. A comparison of the light-tracing

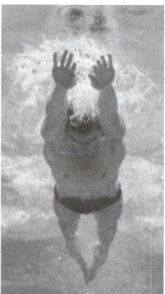

FIGURE 5–6 THE TOTAL STROKE OF AN OLYMPIAN, WHO IS AN UNDULATING STYLIST, AS SEEN FROM A DIAGONALLY, HEAD-ON VIEW.

The sequence of these pictures is identical with that of Figure 5–4, and the swimmer depicted is the same.

FIGURE 5–6
(continued)

FIGURE 5–6
(continued)

studies of each stroke reveals the similarity (see Figure 1–10–A and C). It can be seen that the arm positions are almost identical, which is not unexpected in view of their common ancestry.

High-Elbow Position

As the arms pull out, back, and down, the elbow bend increases. This elbow bend, combined with the inward or medial rotation of the upper arms, causes the arms to be pulled in a high-elbow position, as shown in Figure 5–6–D and E. High elbows place the arms in a good position for a proper application of the sculling action of the hands that accounts for most of the propulsion in the breaststroke. Some swimmers pull their elbows into their ribs in the mistaken belief that this action generates greater propulsion. The authors believe this technique is comparable to swimming the crawl stroke or butterfly with a dropped elbow, and should be avoided. Figure 5–10 at the end of this chapter shows this stroke defect (see p. 130).

Arm-Pull Pattern

In relation to the position of the body, the pull pattern of the hands should describe the shape of an inverted heart. This pattern is shown in Chapter 1, Figure 1–9–C. In relation to their path through water, the pull pattern is revealed by the flashing light pattern in Figure 1–10–C.

At the beginning of the pull, the palms are facing down and outward. The angle of attack permits the palms to apply a lift force as the hands scull out and then downward. At the end of the outward sweep the pitch of the hands reverses so the palms are facing down and in, an angle of attack best suited to scull inward.

A good way to communicate this idea is to tell the swimmers to form a V with their hands on the outward sweep and an A on the inward sweep, thus graphically representing a difficult idea. Figure 5–6–B and E shows this reverse of the angle of attack.

The fastest movement of the hands in any of the four competitive strokes occurs during the breaststroke pull. It behooves the coach and swimmer never to forget this important fact and to work on building hand speed. The authors believe the ability to accelerate and achieve high speeds at a point in the pull at which the sculling action is the most effective is the key to exploiting lift to the best advantage in the breaststroke.

BREATHING AND HEAD ACTION

The only out-of-water action in the breaststroke is that of the head and, among some breaststrokers, the recovery of the arms. The rule states that the head must break the surface of the water at least once during each complete stroke cycle.

In all styles of the breaststroke the head lift and air inhalation should be timed to occur when the shoulders are at their highest point. The arms press diagonally down and back during the pull. The downward press causes the shoulders to rise; consequently the highest elevation of the shoulders occurs at the end of the arm pull.

In the traditional style the head lift is achieved by extension of the neck (posterior flexion of the cervical vertebrae). This action is initiated shortly after the pull begins and continues throughout the pull. Once the inhalation is complete, the head should be dropped slightly by forward flexion of the neck. This action becomes clearer when out-of-water and underwater pictures are examined. A complete sequence from a head-on, diagonal angle is presented in this chapter to make these movements clear (Figure 5–8).

In the traditional style of the breaststroke, it is important to keep the amount of flexion and extension of the neck minimal, that is, to raise the head just enough to keep the mouth clear of the water during inhalation, but not so much as to cause the shoulders to bob. A suggestion that helps most swimmers obtain the proper amount of head movement is to use the line of sight as a guide. When the swimmer lifts his head to breathe, he should be able to look straight forward and see the end of the pool, and his chin should be just above the bow wave. When he lowers his head after inhalation, the line of sight should be diagonally downward so he is looking a little below the level of his hands. The breath is taken at the top of the climbing action. The head then drops below the surface of the water, becoming completely submerged as the hands rise slightly to the catch.

Among undulating stylists, a full range of head actions can be seen, ranging from little or none in the early variants of the pop-up style (see Figure 5–2–A) to the often excessive and unnecessary head action of later versions. In the case of the wave-action style, head action serves a different purpose from that of the traditional or flat breaststroke as described in the preceding paragraph. In the wave-action style, head action is said by its proponents to be for the purpose of preventing a large vertical drop of the head (and upper body) between the insweep phase and the thrust phase. This head action has been described as a *wavelike* movement of the head; hence its title. The benefits to be gained from preventing a more vertical drop of the head are unclear. Some contend that the wavelike head movement creates a lunging action that "throws" the body forward. This lunge has been compared to a body moving downhill or jumping off a platform. Others claim that the head action minimizes the deceleration of body velocity that is taking place in the phase of the stroke.

The theory that a lunging action is achieved by the wavelike action of the head is improbable because it is in violation of Newton's Third Law of Motion. One cannot move the body forward by applying force in the same direction. The second theory is based on the fact that the downward head movement occurs between the pre-thrust phase and the thrust phase of the stroke. It is at this point that the greatest deceleration of body velocity per stroke cycle is taking place. This deceleration is precipitated by hip flexion during the preparatory phase of the kick and not by the vertical drop of the head and torso. It is unlikely that the wavelike movement of the head has any influence to prevent or minimize deceleration.

COORDINATION OF THE KICK AND PULL

The timing of the kick and pull varies slightly from one swimmer to the next, and also varies depending on the distance of the race, but the timing in the two major styles does not vary radically. The main difference is in the arching of the back in the undulating style and in the relative flatness of the entire trunk at the same phase of the stroke in the traditional style. When the swimmer sprints, there is an overlap of the end of the propulsive phase of the arm pull and the beginning of the propulsive phase of the kick. In the longer (200-yard/meter) event many swimmers resort to a slight glide when the arms are fully extended forward. This occurs after the kick and just before the pull begins. Breaststrokers with a strong kick will prolong the glide even more.

In the undulating style of breaststroke the swimmer's heels are pulled up by the action of the hamstring muscles until they nearly touch the buttocks. The head is at the peak of its rise at this point. Some proponents of the undulating style say there should not be as much flexion of the hips as the pictures in Figure 5–6–G and H and Figure 5–7–E and F reveal; but the writers have photographed many elite breaststrokers and it is their conviction that the angle of hip flexion, regardless of style, is nearly the same. In Figure 5–7–E, F, and G the arms have become almost fully extended forward and the dorsiflexion of the feet show they are ready for their backward thrust. The thrust is backward, but has a downward and inward component. At the end of the kick the body is almost perfectly horizontal. In this position it creates minimal resistance. The same is true of the traditional breaststroke at this stage in the stroke cycle. It appears that the undulating style creates less resistance at certain points of the stroke and more at others. The prowlike presentation seen in Figure 5–7 may cause less frontal and eddy resistance at that point, but the flat style appears to present less total resistance because of its generally superior streamlining throughout the stroke (see Figure 5–8).

FIGURE 5–7 THE TOTAL STROKE OF AN OLYMPIAN, WHO IS AN UNDULATING BREASTSTROKER, AS VIEWED FROM THE SIDE

A. The swimmer has finished the glide portion of her stroke and is beginning her outward scull. Notice her head is facing straight forward. She will not flex her neck at any time during the stroke.

B. The arms scull down and outward. Notice the hand pitch of 40 degrees in relation to their path through the water. Medial rotation of the upper arms causes the high elbow position which permits the hands to scull from this advantageous angle.

C. The head, neck, and shoulders rise high out of the water as the swimmer sculls downward to facilitate the elevation of the upper torso—hence the term "pop-up." The

FIGURE 5–7 *(continued)*

hips consequently drop, and the resultant bowing of the trunk may tend to reduce frontal resistance.

D. The hands scull inwardly, helping to support the upper body as they also finish the propulsive phase of the arm pull. Inhalation takes place at this point.

E. The pull is now complete, and the upper body begins to drop back into the water. The backward thrust of the feet has begun. Note the dorsiflexion of the feet as they scull out in the first half of the circular motion which characterizes the whip kick.

F. The circular sweep continues with the swimmer simultaneously extending her legs. The head is still in the process of dropping back into the water.

G. The stroke cycle is now complete with the exception of the legs which have not become fully extended.

THE LONG PULL AFTER THE DIVE AND TURN

The rules of the breaststroke permit one complete arm pull, a kick, and one-half of a second pull underwater after the dive and each turn. The swimmer can take best advantage of this underwater stroke by using a long arm pull. The pull should be similar to the hourglass pull of the butterfly except that the body is completely submerged. The time period from the gun to completion of the long stroke when the head breaks the water should be from 4.5 to 6.0 seconds, as measured at the National Championships in the men's events. Women should emerge five-tenths of a second earlier due to their less powerful dive and long pull and smaller mass. When performing the turn the amount of time required from hand touch to head break after the long pull and kick is approximately the same as for the starting dive, long pull, and kick.

Swimmers frequently err by holding the pull too long, sometimes as long as six seconds or more. The younger and smaller the swimmer, the less time he should remain underwater. Any time a swimmer decelerates after the long pull to the point that velocity drops below swimming speed, he has held the long pull too long. Coaches should time their breaststrokers frequently in meets and in practice to make certain they do not stay down too long or come up too soon. This is also a good time to remind them of hand acceleration, since a swimmer can easily gain or lose one- to two-tenths of a second on each turn on this consideration alone. Figure 5–9 depicts this underwater pull.

FIGURE 5–8 THE TOTAL STROKE OF A TRADITIONAL BREASTSTROKER AS SEEN FROM THE DIAGONAL.

A. The stroke begins as the hands pull outward and downward.

B. The hands are pitched diagonally down and outward so as to gain propulsion through their sculling action. The body remains flat.

FIGURE 5–8   *(continued)*

C. The hands continue to scull down and outward. Exhalation begins.

D. The elbows flex and the upper arms rotate medially, providing a desirable high-elbow position from which to scull. The hands are at their widest spread, but are changing pitch to begin the inward scull. The neck flexes in preparation for the inhalation. The swimmer tries to maintain a flat body position. Contrary to the pop-up style, the flat breaststroker depends on flexion and extension of the neck to keep his shoulders low in the water and to minimize up and down movements.

E. The hands scull inward, and exhalation continues.

F. The hands finish their inward scull, coming close to the chin. The palms are almost facing upward. This latter action is merely an unintentional follow-through and provides no propulsion. To stop sculling earlier, and prevent this unnecessary action, would reduce the acceleration of the inward scull and thus be undesirable. The knees are beginning to bend as leg recovery starts.

G. The heels are drawn up towards the buttocks, and the arms assume a praying attitude, preparing to extend.

H. The elbows extend, pushing the hands forward. The feet are ready to sweep out and backwards in the circular action of the whip kick.

I. The arms are in a glide position, as the legs finish the propulsive phase of the kick. The kick will be over when the legs are squeezed together. The length of the time the glide can be advantageously held depends on the efficiency of the kick.

FIGURE 5–9 THE LONG PULL AFTER THE TURN IN THE BREASTSTROKE.

A. The swimmer pushes vigorously off the wall, maintaining his body in a streamlined position.

B. His hands have begun their long, keyhole (or hourglass) pull, pressing down and backwards with elbows starting to bend.

C. The hands scull inward towards the midline of the body, nearly touching. The swimmer should be concentrating on accelerating the movement of his hands.

D. The swimmer's hands finish the long pull by pushing back and finishing with the palms up. He avoids throwing water onto his upper legs as he pushes back. Such an action would tend to hold back his progress.

E. The swimmer recovers his arms close to his body, so as to not create excessive drag. He begins to recover his legs in preparation for the kick.

F. The swimmer pushes his arms forward, and he kicks in order to drive his body to the surface. According to the rules, his head must break the surface before the kick is half completed.

FIGURE 5–10 A STROKE DEFECT IN WHICH THE ELBOWS ARE DROPPED AND PULLED INTO THE RIBS AS THE INWARD SCULL BEGINS

COMMON MISTAKES IN THE BREASTSTROKE

1. Pressing too long during the pull with no bend in the elbows.

2. Allowing the palms to remain facing each other and angled slightly upward at the end of the pull. This appears to be a normal follow-through action which can be compared to the follow-through of the golf swing. Once the head of the club hits the ball, the golfer must dissipate the momentum of his swing by following through, although the follow-through plays no role in how far the ball travels. Similarly, as the hands finish the pull and begin the recovery, they are creating no propulsive force, and it would be a mistake to turn the palms up deliberately. This action pushes water directly upward, and the reaction is to lower the shoulders at a point in the stroke when the swimmer is striving for a streamlined body position. Supination of the palms has been recommended by some coaches, but in order to turn the hands over, the swimmer has to sacrifice the end of scull.

3. Pulling the legs up too late in the stroke. The legs should start their recovery during the last half of the pull (see Figure 5–6–E and F). Swimmers often fail to start the leg recovery until the arm pull has been completed.

4. Pausing during the arm action, thus failing to keep the arm pull and recovery motion one continuous action. This happens when the swimmer drops his elbows, as shown in Figure 5–10, at the same point as shown in the photograph. Dropping the elbows at this point breaks the continuity of the stroke and causes the swimmer to sink lower in the water. To correct the defect the swimmer should start to exhale sooner, that is, while his face is still underwater, thus permitting him to inhale during all the time his face is out of water. Most swimmers must make a conscious effort to avoid pausing at

this point in their stroke. The reason they pause is to prolong inhalation. Some coaches believe that the over-the-water recovery, used by some undulating stylists, is effective because it makes a pause difficult at this point and forces the swimmer to accelerate hand speed continuously.

FOOTNOTES

1. Melchisedech Thevenot, *The Art of Swimming*, 3rd ed., trans. (Moorsfield: John Lever, 1699), pp. 18–19.

2. *Kleines Lehrbuch der Schwimmkunst zum Selbstunterrichte*, cited in Ralph Thomas, *Swimming* (London: Sampson, Low, Marston & Co., Ltd., 1904), p. 99.

3. Ralph Thomas, *Swimming*, pp. 98–99.

4. Personal correspondence between James E. Counsilman and Henry Myers, December 4, 1957.

CHAPTER 6

Starts, Turns, Relay Exchanges, and Pace

As anyone who has watched a swimming meet can attest, races are often won or lost in the start, push-off, turn, or finish. Assuredly, this is enough reason to devote some attention to them. It is also common to see swimmers lose a foot or more on each turn and push-off due to faulty technique. Some swimmers begin each of their races at a disadvantage because of poor starting mechanics. There are also factors other than technique which can affect these skills, such as lack of leg strength or power. Still, nearly every swimmer can improve her skill within the parameters of her inherent abilities and sometimes beyond them, inasmuch as leg strength and power can be improved significantly through exercise (see Chapter 10). The best way to perfect technique is to work each of these skills in practice as though it were part of a race with a close rival. This is because people tend to do in a race what they do in practice. If a swimmer cheats on her start in practice by jumping the gun, if she fails to touch the wall with both hands at the same time as she turns in the breast or butterfly in training, or if she rolls onto her front too soon when practicing the backstroke, she will probably do the same in competition.

Any members of our teams who committed those transgressions had to stay after practice and do twenty starts or turns for each infraction. We have had a lot of swimmers say, "Oh, I would never do that in a race." And we would say back to them, "You're not kidding anyone but yourself if you believe that."

STARTS

Before attempting any start, the swimmer should be aware of the depth of the pool. If it is shallower than 5 feet, there is a danger of catastrophic injury should the dive be at too steep an angle.

It isn't necessary to this discussion to list the starting rules of each of the governing bodies in competitive swimming. It's enough to say that the preparatory command after the referee's whistle is "take your mark," to which the swimmers must respond immediately by assuming a starting position. When the swimmers are deemed by the starter to be still, he fires a starting pistol or sounds a starting horn. For the freestyler, butterflyer, and breaststroker the start is out of water from a front standing position on a starting platform.

The starts for these strokes are almost identical, being either a grab start or another version of the grab start called the track start. The wind-up or arm-swing start is now confined almost exclusively to relay take-offs. The angle of entry for the crawl is flatter than for the breaststroke, while that for the butterfly in somewhere in between. Breaststrokers dive deeper in order to facilitate the long underwater pull before surfacing.

The advantages of the grab start over the wind-up start are that the swimmer commits fewer false starts and gets off the starting block faster after the gun fires. He may not dive out as far as he would with the wind-up start, but, if the grab start is done correctly, the result will be faster than when he uses the wind-up start. Figure 6–1–A shows the starting position of the grab start, while Figure 6–1–B shows the variation of the grab start referred to as the track start.

The only other difference among the starts of the different strokes is that the breaststroke rule permits a long pull after the start and each turn. The long pull may consist of a pull-down and kick, and half of an arm stroke to the point where the hands turn inward before the head must emerge from the water. A swimmer with an effective underwater stroke has an advantage over one who comes to the surface too quickly and begins his surface stroke immediately.

It is important for breaststrokers to make full use of this advantage, extending the underwater stroke for as long as it remains faster than they can swim at the surface. Age-groupers will find this time to be about 4.2 seconds; for older, stronger swimmers it is about 5.2 seconds. The average time for senior men at a recent national competition was 5.4 seconds, while for senior women it was 4.8 seconds.

The wind-up start (see Figure 6–1–C) is better for relay exchanges than the grab start because it permits the outgoing swimmer to develop momentum before he leaves the block, while the grab start does not. Since the take-off swimmer wants to compensate for the caution he must exercise to avoid diqualification, it is important that he get as much distance and speed as possible from his start. Swimmers should practice the grab start and the arm-swing start because they will probably be called upon to use both.

FIGURE 6–1 STARTING POSITIONS FOR THE TRADITIONAL GRAB START, THE TRACK START, AND THE ARM-SWING START

A. Traditional Grab Start
B. Track Start
C. Arm-Swing Start

The Grab Start

Figure 6–2 is a sequence of photographs of an Olympic champion and Masters champion performing the grab start. Notable in his start is his explosive ability, but in comparison with other sprinters, all of whom are explosive, it is his streamlining in the water phase of his start that enables him to be ahead of other great swimmers when his head surfaces.

The start is an easy skill to learn, but not every swimmer can be a good starter. The reason is that two of the qualities needed for a superior start are largely inherent. The two are fast reaction time and overall quickness. The technique is similar to jumping for a basketball, requiring not only explosiveness, but also the proper sequence of coordinated action between the arms and legs.

Although most swimmers cannot improve their ability to react more quickly to the sound of the gun, they can be trained to get off the mark faster and out further. Despite deficiencies in reaction time and overall quickness, they can enhance the requisite speed-strength characteristics. Strength is the ability of the muscle to create tension. Speed-strength (power) differs from absolute strength in that it also involves *time rate* of work, that is, the expression of explosive strength and speed of muscular contraction.

A person with superior explosive power and poor mechanics often outdives one with the opposite combination. A person with good reaction time, quickness, and explosiveness who lacks good mechanics might get out faster and further than anyone on his team, but he would do even better if he took the trouble to improve his mechanics as well. Speed-strength can be improved—within limitations—through special strength training designed specifically to enhance explosive strength and speed of muscular contraction (see Chapter 10 and Appendix 2).

The Wind-up Start

Figure 6–3 is a sequence of photos depicting the wind-up (or arm-swing) start, as performed by the same swimmer who demonstrated the grab start in Figure 6–2. As mentioned previously, it is used primarily for relay exchanges. See Chapter 1, p. 30, the section on transfer of momentum for its application in the wind-up start.

A variation of the wind-up start has begun to be seen in relay exchanges in what is termed the "step-up" start. The outgoing swimmer stands at the back of the block and, as the incoming swimmer approaches the finish line, steps forward and dives in a single movement. The procedure must be perfectly timed or a disqualification will result due to the high percentage possibility of error. Only time will tell if the step-up start is actually faster than the traditional wind-up start and is therefore worth the added risk.

The Backstroke Start

The rules for the backstroke start have been stated in the chapter devoted to that stroke. These rules are more complicated than those for the other three strokes because placement of the feet with relation to the gutter before the

FIGURE 6–2   AN ANALYSIS OF THE GRAB START.

A. After the referee's whistle, the starter instructs the swimmers and directs them to "take your marks," to which they must immediately respond by assuming a starting position by moving at least one foot to the front of the starting block or platform. Sufficient time should follow "take your mark" to enable swimmers to assume starting positions, but no swimmer shall be in motion immediately before the starting signal is given. (Taken from Technical Rule 102.14.2 of the U.S. Swimming Rules and Regulations, 1992.)

FIGURE 6–2 *(continued)*

B. The swimmer has moved forward at the command "take your mark" and has grasped the leading edge of the starting block with his hands between his feet, awaiting the signal to start. Some swimmers choose to grasp the block from outside the feet, but they are among the minority.

C. At the sound of the gun (or horn), the swimmer pulls upward and his body starts to roll forward.

D. As he rolls forward, the swimmer bends his knees and hips, swings his arms forward, and starts to raise his head.

E. He extends his body, pushes backward against the block with his feet, continues to raise his head as if to look at the other end of the pool. His arms stop their movement when they are pointed diagnally downward.

F. The arms enter the water first; the body follows at the same angle.

G. The final entry is made with the body streamlined. The swimmer will hold the glide until his body has slowed to swimming speed.

FIGURE 6–3   AN ANALYSIS OF THE WIND-UP START

A. This start is used primarily in relay exchanges. As the incoming swimmer approaches the end of the pool, the outgoing swimmer steps to the front of the block, wraps his toes around its leading edge, and tries to time his take-off so his feet are still in contact with the block when the incoming swimmer touches.

B. The swimmer's arms begin to describe a circle, swinging up and backward in a counterclockwise direction, and his knees begin to bend in preparation for pushing against the block.

C. His arms continuing their circular action, the swimmer concentrates on accelerating this movement so as to gain momentum for the flight phase.

D. The center of gravity is now in front of the swimmer's feet, and he is falling forward. His heels raise and his arms continue their circular swing. The neck flexes backward, contributing forward inertia to the body.

E. Extension of the body begins and the head raises, looking toward the end of the pool.

F. The arms stop momentarily in a diagonally downward position, their forward and upward momentum transferring to the whole body and helping it achieve greater velocity and distance.

G. The hands enter the water first, followed by the rest of the body, which enters at the same angle. The swimmer concentrates on keeping his body streamlined. He begins to stroke when his body slows to swimming speed.

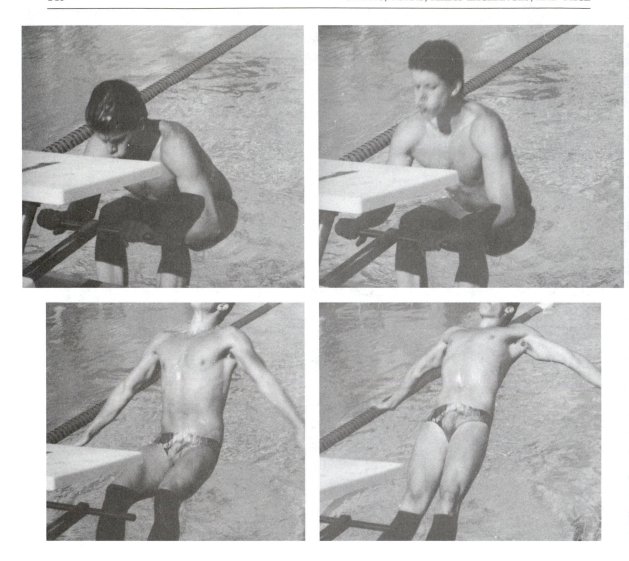

FIGURE 6–4 AN ANALYSIS OF THE BACKSTROKE START

A. The starting position.

B. At the sound of the gun (or horn) the swimmer pushes away from the starting block.

C. The arms begin to swing sidewards in a low, semicircular arc, the knees extend vigorously, and the head is pulled back by flexion of the neck.

command and starting signal is strictly regulated and because dolphining after the start and each turn is also subject to specific regulation. The start is depicted in Figure 6–4, while Figure 3–3 in Chapter 3 shows the dolphining action of the submerged kick.

D. The arms have momentarily stopped their low, backward swing over the water. This enables a transfer of momentum from the arms to the rest of the body. The legs are fully extended and are pushing vigorously against the starting end of the pool. (Notice the contraction of the quadriceps extensor muscles of the knees.)

E. The arms resume their swing over the water with the back arched. The legs continue to drive the body backward.

F. The hands nearly touch over the head and the arch of back increases. The hands are entering the water ahead of the rest of the body. The swimmer concentrates on stretching and streamlining his body in an effort to minimize resistance.

G. The swimmer enters the water, continuing to concentrate on streamlining. He will hold the glide until he slows to kicking speed. Many swimmers take advantage of the rule permitting them to remain underwater and to use a dolphin (fishtail) kick for as far as 15 meters (16.4 yards) off the start and each turn.

Common Mistakes in Starting

1. Holding the head too high, as though looking at the far end of the pool, or too low, as though looking at the feet. The head should be held somewhere between the two extremes; see Figure 6–2–B for the correct position.

2. Starting to swim too soon. Some swimmers begin to swim as soon as they hit the water; some even begin to kick while still in the flight phase. Swimmers should wait until they slow down to swimming speed before beginning to swim. It takes time and practice to learn this technique. Occasional stopwatch trials on short dashes of 12½ yards will help the swimmer evaluate his progress.

3. Piking upon entry and piking at the height of the flight phase. In the late 1970s a start was introduced which has variously been called the pike start, the scoop start, the arc start, the hole-in-the-water start, the sailor dive, and so on (Figure 6–5). From the beginning this start was of doubtful merit because it was dangerous and no faster than the traditional entry. No research conducted since its introduction has shown otherwise.

   The purported advantages are that its high vertical take-off increases the distance of the flight phase, and that the steeper angle of entry associated with piking during the flight phase allows the swimmer to enter the water with greater velocity and less drag than in the traditional (or flat) entry. The reduction in drag is predicated on the idea that the swimmer's body is literally entering the water through a hole created by his steep entry, while the traditional entry is said to expose a greater surface area of the body to drag.

   Proponents of the pike start also recommend that the chin be tucked into the chest in an effort to further reduce drag.

   The combination of these factors is said to increase horizontal velocity during the glide phase prior to actual stroking.

   These beliefs are, however, based on speculation, not on the results of corroborating studies. Research conducted to compare the different styles of grab start, that is, the standard start, the scoop start, the track start, and so on, have shown that none possesses a clear-cut advantage over the others. The study determined that, while a swimmer enters the water at greater velocity when using the pike start, he achieves excessive and undesired depth in the initial phase of the glide and then must abruptly adjust body position in order to surface. This action results in profound deceleration during the return to the surface and the net result is a considerable loss of horizontal velocity.[1]

   General observation of swimmers using the grab start and incorporating a pike reveals that piking may occur at one of two points in the start: (1) at the peak of the upward path of the flight phase, in which case the swimmer streamlines his body prior to entry into the water; or (2) just prior to entry, in which case he jackknifes and enters the water in a piked position. Neither type is recommended by these authors. In the first case, the axis of rotation around the center of mass is reduced, often resulting in excessive

FIGURE 6–5   THE PIKE START

torquing and a steep angle of entry. The second case creates excessive drag, which results from poor body position upon entry.

In addition to its technical shortcomings, the use of the pike or scoop start has been directly responsible for a large number of serious head and spinal cord injuries, resulting in paralysis and at least one known fatality. These accidents typically occur when the starting blocks are installed at the shallow end of a multipurpose pool in which the depth is 4 feet or less at that point.

4. Additional movements, such as kicking out the legs, pumping the arms, and extra head movements during the flight phase will not achieve greater distance. Once the feet lose contact with the starting block, any attempt to gain distance with any of these techniques will be unproductive.

TURNS

The Butterfly and Breaststroke Turn

The rules which regulate butterfly and breaststroke turns are similar. The swimmer must touch the wall with both hands at the same level and simultaneously, and the shoulders must be in line with the water's surface.[2] He may then turn off his chest and complete his turn. When he has pushed off the wall, he must once again be on his chest. Figure 6–6 depicts that turn.

In almost every respect this turn is identical to the one used in the butterfly except that breaststrokers use a deeper foot plant on the wall. The heels of the breaststroker should be set on the wall about 2 to 2½ feet below the surface, while those of the butterflyer should be planted at a depth of about 1½ to 2 feet deep on the turn.

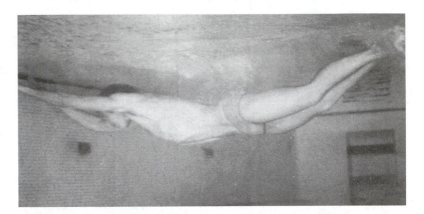

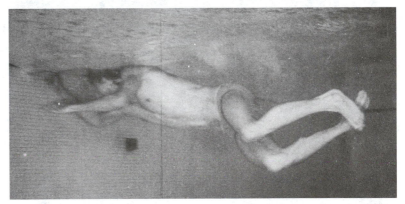

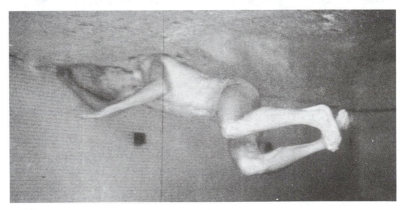

FIGURE 6–6 AN ANALYSIS OF THE BUTTERFLY AND BREASTSTROKE TURN

  A. The hands touch the wall simultaneously and at the same level.

  B. After the touch, the left arm pulls backward and the right arm pushes against the wall to initiate the turn. The knees begin to tuck, and one foot crosses over the other. The latter action decreases resistance by reducing surface area.

  C. The swimmer tucks his body by pulling his knees toward his chest. The tighter the tuck, the faster the swimmer rotates.

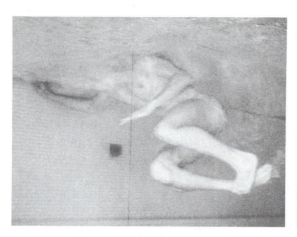 

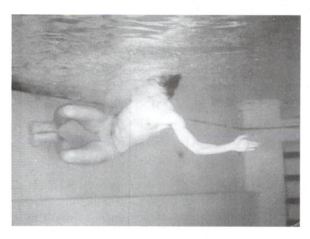

D. The tuck-and-push action continues as the feet are pulled under the body. The swimmer inhales.

E. The turning action continues. Note that the swimmer is in a tightly tucked position with the feet still crossed.

F. The feet have uncrossed and are planted sidewise against the wall in preparation for the push-off. The left arm is under water and the right arm is recovering over the water. As the swimmer pushes off he will extend both arms overhead and will concentrate on streamlining until the speed of the glide has dissipated. He will begin to stroke when the glide slows to swimming speed.

The Backstroke Turn

The rules for the backstroke turn were set out in the chapter devoted to the stroke. Figure 6–7 depicts the turn currently being used by most backstrokers.

The Freestyle Turn

The rules governing the freestyle turn merely state that the swimmer must touch the wall when turning. Most swimmers comply with the rule by touching with their feet as they push off. The standard flip turn is shown in a sequence of drawings in Figure 6–8.

RELAY EXCHANGES

Coaches tend to forget about relay exchanges until the competitive season is at hand. As the championship phase draws near, they are reminded of the crucial nature of quick yet safe take-offs. The key is practice—not just practice at the end of the season, but practice from the beginning of the season onward. The main emphasis should be on the proper timing of the exchange and the mechanics of the finish and take-off. The outgoing swimmer must, above all, learn to judge the appropriate distance and rhythm of the stroke of the incoming swimmer, while the incoming swimmer has the responsibility to perform a consistent and forceful touch.

PACE

The following discussion of pace applies to races in all four competitive strokes, but not to the individual medley events. Pace becomes significant only when the event exceeds 50 yards/meters. All-out 50s are swum just as the term implies: all out. Any distance longer than 50 yards/meters must necessarily involve the distribution of effort over the entire course of the race.

Pacing the 100-Yard/Meter Distance

In the 100-yards/meters it is wise to swim the first 50 within five-tenths to one second of the time the swimmer is capable of doing in a maximum effort 50. Since the swimmer is completing the 50 on the way to a 100 and is not driving in to the wall to touch the finish, the first 50 will necessarily be slower than an all-out effort. Swimmers in less than top condition may have to swim the first 50 more slowly than the recommended time or risk too great a drop-off in the last 50.

Occasionally, on the other hand, a swimmer will achieve a better time on the first 50 on the way to a 100 than on an all-out 50 effort. This is usually a signal to his coach that he is trying too hard on the all-out 50 and is literally "spinning his wheels." Such a swimmer can profit from time trials in practice sessions in which he is instructed to keep his stroke long and to slow his tempo to the point that he feels he is swimming slightly slower than all-out.

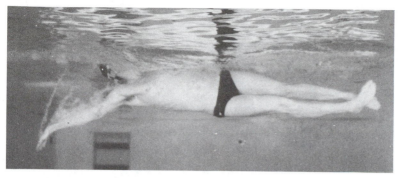

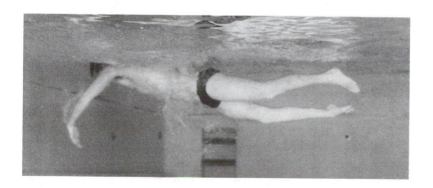

FIGURE 6–7 AN ANALYSIS OF THE BACKSTROKE TURN

A. The swimmer approaches the wall on his back.

B. Approximately one body length from the wall, he begins to roll onto his right side through the combined push-and-pull action of his arms with his left leg acting as a rudder.

C. He continues to roll until he is face down and nearly on his stomach. He accomplishes this movement by using his feet as a rudder, combining with the pushing action of his right arm and pulling action of his left arm.

D. The swimmer's left arm and right leg have now almost completely stabilized his body on its front as he prepares to turn.

FIGURE 6–7 *(continued)*

E. The swimmer drops his head, thus increasing frontal resistance on his head and shoulders. This resistance slows down the front part of his body and allows the lower body to conserve its forward momentum, resulting in a forward somersault.

F. He tucks his body by bending his knees and pulling his chin into his chest, thus reducing his radius of rotation.

G. The somersault has been completed, and the feet are on the wall ready to push off. The upper body has come out of its tuck and is in a streamlined position.

H. The swimmer's legs and ankles have fully extended in a vigorous push-off. When his body slows to kicking speed, he will begin an underwater dolphin kick which he is permitted to maintain for 15 meters (or 16.4 yards). Some backstrokers do not profit from the underwater dolphining action. These swimmers surface after the glide and begin the whole stroke.

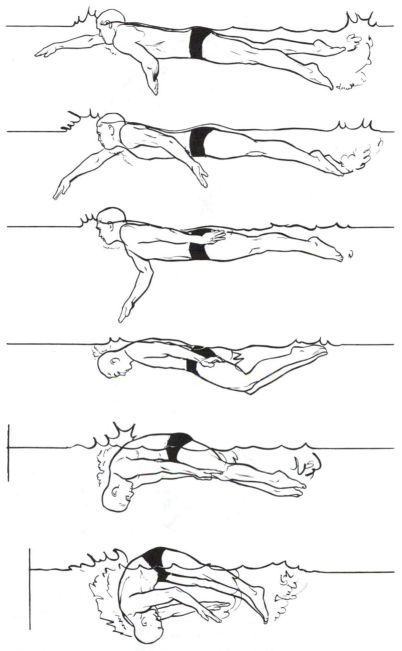

FIGURE 6–8 AN ANALYSIS OF THE CRAWL STROKE FLIP TURN

FIGURE 6–8 *(continued)*

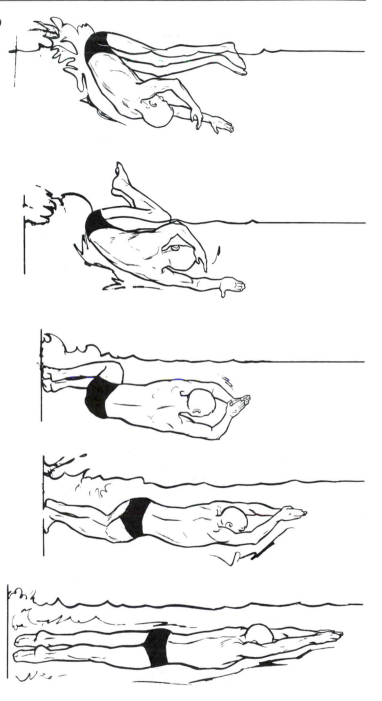

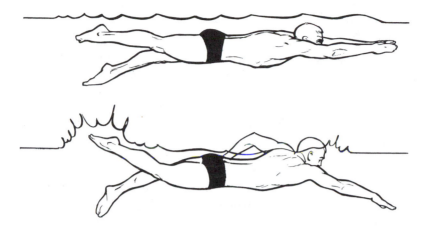

FIGURE 6–8 *(continued)*

A. When the swimmer's head is about 4 to 7 feet from the end of the pool, depending on his size and the effectiveness of his arm pull, he begins his last pull with his left hand. His right hand continues to push back as he looks forward at the wall.

B. The swimmer looks at the wall. He must make a decision to turn at this time or wait until the next stroke.

C. At this point the decision to turn has been made. Instead of recovering the left hand, the swimmer stops it at his side and continues to pull back with the right hand. His legs start to lift in preparation for making a small dolphin kick.

D. The head is thrown downward by flexion of the neck. The palms turn to face downward, the legs and feet remain together, and the knees bend.

E. The body is thrown out of straight alignment as the head continues down and the body flexes at the trunk. Simultaneously, both hands, palms down, push downward as if preparing for a surface dive. The feet kick downward in a fishtail kick in order to help drive the hips upward.

F. The body continues to bend forward at the hips. The resistance created by the head and body at this point tends to stop the inertia of the top part of the body. The forward inertia of the lower trunk and legs is not affected as much by this resistance, so the lower trunk and legs continue to move forward and over the upper trunk. If the swimmer is going fast enough, as in the sprints, this source of turning may be virtually all he needs to turn himself around. In this illustration the left hand is starting to bend at the elbow and pull toward the head.

G. As the hips pass over the head, the left hand continues to push water toward the head. This action helps accomplish the flip. The right hand, palm facing inward, sculls in a slight circular motion to turn the swimmer's body on its longitudinal axis. The feet are not brought directly over the head, but slightly to the right of the midline of the body.

H. The feet are completely out of the water. The legs are tucked and thrown backward to the wall as the hands finish their sculling action. The swimmer should consciously turn his head and shoulders and try to turn over on his side without breaking the rhythm of his movement.

I. The swimmer's turn is completed and he must get his body in position for the push-off. His hands are almost touching as they start forward. He continues to rotate his body in order to be on his side.

Pacing the Middle and Longer Distances (200 and Over)

Three principles involved in swimming distances of 200 yards/meters or longer demonstrate the need for pacing these events. One is the need to delay the onset of fatigue as long as possible. If the swimmer starts out too fast, he uses up energy so quickly that an imbalance between energy production and energy needs begins to occur early in the race, resulting in an almost immediate drop-off in efficiency and speed.

The second and third principles involve the disproportionately high rate of energy expenditure at faster speeds.

The second principle is that the theoretical square law governing air and water resistance is operating in swimming. See Chapter 1, p. 30, for a discussion of this principle.

The third principle states that energy costs of a muscle contraction vary with the cube of the speed of contraction. If the swimmer doubles his speed, he has to contract his muscles twice as fast; and he does not merely increase his energy expenditure and oxygen consumption by double or even four times, but by eight times in the process.

The following is an application of these two principles: A swimmer who swims his 200-meter event in two minutes by swimming his first 100 in 53 seconds and his last 100 in 67 seconds creates more total resistance, uses more energy, consumes more oxygen, and is more fatigued than a swimmer who paces his race more evenly, swimming his first 100 yards in 58 seconds and his last 100 in 62 seconds for the same total time.

Factors Affecting Pace and Split Times

While a fairly even pace throughout the race is desirable, it is not the authors' intention to advocate that each individual should pace his race just like everyone else. Factors other than mechanical and physiological principles enter into swimming a race. There is no constant pattern or rigid blueprint for pace that a swimmer must follow to achieve his best time. Individual differences may change a swimmer's strategy and, consequently, the pacing plan.

Some so-called agonistic swimmers seem to enjoy the pain of physical exertion. Such people can take a race out hard and retain intensity the entire distance. Others who are perhaps more timid physically must swim well within their pain threshold. They are willing to hurt themselves only during the last part of the race. Everything else being equal, the former will become the greater distance swimmer of the two.

Some swimmers perform better when they are in the lead. They seem to be able to relax and maintain the integrity of their strokes better when not being stressed by someone racing alongside them. Others are incapable of sustaining a constant pace unless someone is there with them, either pushing or pulling them along. Although some swimmers perform one way on one occasion and the reverse on another, most are consistent in the pattern they prefer. Inconsistency is probably due more to psychological than to physiological factors.

Swimmers who begin their race at faster than an ideal pace often want to get out in front of the pack and avoid the turbulence. As pools and lane lines become better designed, less turbulence will be transmitted from one lane to another and this strategy will diminish in importance.

There are swimmers who are strategists and, in some cases, have won National and Olympic titles by varying pace to suit the circumstances. Notable among these is Artur Wojdat, the great Polish Olympian, whose strategy has been to stay close enough to the leader to run him down and pass him near the end of the race but not to extend himself maximally until then. Such swimmers almost seem to disregard pace. They swim their adversaries in a race not necessarily planned to produce a good time but to win. Depending on the personality of the swimmer and the circumstances of his other events, this type of race may have merit; but it is unlikely to produce a great performance or break a record.

The Steady Pace Chart. The steady pace chart (Table 6–1) is a helpful guide in calculating a given pace in seconds per 50 yards or 50 meters. Simply locate the desired time for a given distance and work backward to find the pace for a given segment of that distance.

If a swimmer wants to swim the 1650-yard freestyle in 15:36, he locates that time under 1650 on the chart and works backward to the pace column to find that he should average 28.5 seconds for each 50-yard segment. If he wants to swim a 1500-meter race in 15:26, he locates that time under 1500 on the metric chart and works backward to the pace column to find that he should average 31 seconds for each 50-meter segment.

In middle-distance or distance races the swimmer should be on pace after the first 100 yards/meters and should try to hold that speed as constant as possible from that point onward. Vladimir Salnikov, two-time Olympic champion and world-record holder in the 1500-meter event, preferred to go out hard and thereafter maintain a steady pace throughout the race. He had a seemingly uncanny ability to stay precisely on pace, but he was not alone in this skill. Except for those who choose to split their races negatively, most great distance swimmers exhibit this ability, doubtless developed over years of training for these events.

Learning Pace

A swimmer learns pace both in practice and in competitive events by forming an association between cause and effect. The cause is the amount of effort put into swimming a given distance and the effect is the resulting speed, or the time it takes to cover the distance. In fact, the swimmer must learn to recognize her *perceived exertion* well enough to be able to apply it when she desires that speed again. She does so by memorizing the sensations that result from the application of a given amount of effort. These sensations arise from the accumulation of fatigue products in the muscles and the strain upon the metabolic system. The water pressure upon her hands and legs as they pull and kick, and the other sensations of the movement of her body through the water, also serve as guides to help the swimmer determine her speed. It is not unusual for a well-trained

TABLE 6-1-A   STEADY PACE CHART* (Split Times for 25- and 50-Yard Pools)

Pace per 50 Yards in Seconds	Distance: 50	100	150	200	250	300	350	400	450	500	1000	1500	1650
43	:40	1:22	2:05	2:48	3:31	4:14	4:57	5:40	6:23	7:06	14:16	21:26	23:35
42	:39	1:20	2:02	2:44	3:26	4:08	4:50	5:32	6:14	6:56	13:56	20:56	23:02
41	:38	1:18	1:59	2:40	3:21	4:02	4:43	5:24	6:05	6:46	13:36	20:26	22:29
40	:37	1:16	1:56	2:36	3:16	3:56	4:36	5:16	5:56	6:36	13:16	19:56	21:56
39	:36	1:14	1:53	2:32	3:11	3:50	4:29	5:08	5:47	6:26	12:56	19:26	21:23
38	:35	1:12	1:50	2:28	3:06	3:44	4:22	5:00	5:38	6:16	12:36	18:56	20:50
37	:34	1:10	1:47	2:24	3:01	3:38	4:15	4:52	5:29	6:06	12:16	18:26	20:17
36	:33	1:08	1:44	2:20	2:56	3:32	4:08	4:44	5:20	5:56	11:56	17:56	19:44
35	:32	1:06	1:41	2:16	2:51	3:26	4:01	4:36	5:11	5:46	11:36	17:26	19:11
34.5	:31.5	1:05	1:39.5	2:14	2:48.5	3:23	3:57.5	4:32	5:06.5	5:41	11:26	17:11	18:54.5
34	:31	1:04	1:38	2:12	2:46	3:20	3:54	4:28	5:02	5:36	11:16	16:56	18:38
33.5	:30.5	1:03	1:36.5	2:10	2:43.5	3:17	3:50.5	4:24	4:57.5	5:31	11:06	16:41	18:21.5
33	:30	1:02	1:35	2:08	2:41	3:14	3:47	4:20	4:53	5:26	10:56	16:26	18:05
32.5	:29.5	1:01	1:33.5	2:06	2:38.5	3:11	3:43.5	4:16	4:48.5	5:21	10:46	16:11	17:48.5
32	:29	1:00	1:32	2:04	2:36	3:08	3:40	4:12	4:44	5:16	10:36	15:56	17:32
31.5	:28.5	:59	1:30.5	2:02	2:33.5	3:05	3:36.5	4:08	4:39.5	5:11	10:26	15:41	17:15.5
31	:28	:58	1:29	2:00	2:31	3:02	3:33	4:04	4:35	5:06	10:16	15:26	16:59
30.5	:27.5	:57	1:27.5	1:58	2:28.5	2:59	3:29.5	4:00	4:30.5	5:01	10:06	15:11	16:42.5
30	:27	:56	1:26	1:56	2:26	2:56	3:26	3:56	4:26	4:56	9:56	14:56	16:26
29.5	:26.5	:55	1:24.5	1:54	2:23.5	2:53	3:22.5	3:52	4:21.5	4:51	9:46	14:41	16:09.5
29	:26	:54	1:23	1:52	2:21	2:50	3:19	3:48	4:17	4:46	9:36	14:26	15:53
28.5	:25.5	:53	1:21.5	1:50	2:18.5	2:47	3:15.5	3:44	4:12.5	4:41	9:26	14:11	15:36.5
28	:25	:52	1:20	1:48	2:16	2:44	3:12	3:40	4:08	4:36	9:16	13:56	15:20
27.5	:24.5	:51	1:18.5	1:46	2:13.5	2:41	3:08.5	3:36	4:03.5	4:31	9:06	13:41	15:03.5
27	:24	:50	1:17	1:44	2:11	2:38	3:05	3:32	3:59	4:26	8:56	13:26	14:47
26.5	:23.5	:49	1:15.5	1:42	2:08.5	2:35	3:01.5	3:28	3:54.5	4:21	8:46	13:11	14:30.5
26	:23	:48	1:14	1:40	2:06	2:32	2:58	3:24	3:50	4:16	8:36	12:56	14:14

*The first 50 is listed as 3 seconds faster and the second 50 as 1 second faster than the pace or time for each 50 thereafter.

TABLE 6-1–B STEADY PACE CHART* (Split Times for 25- and 50-Meter Pools)

Pace per 50 Meters in Seconds	Distance: 50	100	150	200	250	300	350	400	800	1200	1500
50	:47	1:36	2:26	3:16	4:06	4:56	5:46	6:36	13:16	19:56	24:56
49	:46	1:34	2:23	3:12	4:01	4:50	5:39	6:28	13:00	19:32	24:26
48	:45	1:32	2:20	3:08	3:56	4:44	5:32	6:20	12:44	19:08	23:56
47	:44	1:30	2:17	3:04	3:51	4:38	5:25	6:12	12:28	18:44	23:26
46	:43	1:28	2:14	3:00	3:46	4:32	5:18	6:04	12:12	18:20	22:56
45	:42	1:26	2:11	2:56	3:41	4:26	5:11	5:56	11:56	17:56	22:26
44	:41	1:24	2:08	2:52	3:36	4:20	5:04	5:48	11:40	17:32	21:56
43	:40	1:22	2:05	2:48	3:31	4:14	4:57	5:40	11:24	17:08	21:26
42	:39	1:20	2:02	2:44	3:26	4:08	4:50	5:32	11:08	16:44	20:56
41	:38	1:18	1:59	2:40	3:21	4:02	4:43	5:24	10:52	16:20	20:26
40	:37	1:16	1:56	2:36	3:16	3:56	4:36	5:16	10:36	15:56	19:56
39	:36	1:14	1:53	2:32	3:11	3:50	4:29	5:08	10:20	15:32	19:26
38	:35	1:12	1:50	2:28	3:06	3:44	4:22	5:00	10:04	15:08	18:56
37	:34	1:10	1:47	2:24	3:01	3:38	4:15	4:52	9:48	14:44	18:26
36.5	:33.5	1:09	1:45.5	2:22	2:58.5	3:35	4:11.5	4:48	9:40	14:32	18:11
36	:33	1:08	1:44	2:20	2:56	3:32	4:08	4:44	9:32	14:20	17:56
35.5	:32.5	1:07	1:42.5	2:18	2:53.5	3:29	4:04.5	4:40	9:24	14:08	17:41
35	:32	1:06	1:41	2:16	2:51	3:26	4:01	4:36	9:16	13:56	17:26
34.5	:31.5	1:05	1:39.5	2:14	2:48.5	3:23	3:57.5	4:32	9:08	13:44	17:11
34	:31	1:04	1:38	2:12	2:46	3:20	3:54	4:28	9:00	13:32	16:56
33.5	:30.5	1:03	1:36.5	2:10	2:43.5	3:17	3:50.5	4:24	8:52	13:20	16:41
33	:30	1:02	1:35	2:08	2:41	3:14	3:47	4:20	8:44	13:08	16:26
32.5	:29.5	1:01	1:33.5	2:06	2:38.5	3:11	3:43.5	4:16	8:36	12:56	16:11
32	:29	1:00	1:32	2:04	2:36	3:08	3:40	4:12	8:28	12:44	15:56
31.5	:28.5	:59	1:30.5	2:02	2:33.5	3:05	3:36.5	4:08	8:20	12:32	15:41
31	:28	:58	1:29	2:00	2:31	3:02	3:33	4:04	8:12	12:20	15:26
30.5	:27.5	:57	1:27.5	1:58	2:28.5	2:59	3:29.5	4:00	8:04	12:08	15:11
30	:27	:56	1:26	1:56	2:26	2:56	3:26	3:56	7:56	11:56	14:56
29.5	:26.5	:55	1:24.5	1:54	2:23.5	2:53	3:22.5	3:52	7:48	11:44	14:41
29	:26	:54	1:23	1:52	2:21	2:50	3:19	3:48	7:40	11:32	14:26

*The first 50 is listed as 3 seconds faster and the second 50 as 1 second faster than the pace or time for each 50 thereafter.

The steady pace chart can be used for either long- or short-course pools. Locate the desired time for a given distance, then work backward to find the pace for a given segment of that distance.

swimmer to be able to maintain an assigned pace to within 1 or 2 percent, and it is commonplace for good pacers to swim 100 yards and state their time within a few tenths of a second. Such drills are effective and should be a continuing part of the training process throughout the season. When a swimmer is tapered, theoretically, she is able to swim a race at a faster pace than she could in her hardest training phase. If she is aware of her times as she swims in the interval training, repetition training, and time trial phases of her seasonal program, she will be more likely to grasp intuitively the level of effort required for the championship phase. This knowledge serves the dual purpose of conditioning her and of teaching her pace.

Mechanical pacing devices and pace clocks, as well as times taken by the coach, all help the swimmer evaluate her speed and, consequently, develop a better sense of how fast she is swimming.

Races and all-out time trials are a necessity during this process. In training for races of 100- and 200-yard/meter distances, she should swim eight to twelve such races or time trials during the last two months of the season. These will reinforce learning. In training for the longer races, she may want to swim fewer all-out efforts over the racing distance because they will tend to disrupt her training schedule unduly, but she should do four to six such efforts. Pace for the 1650-yard or 1500-meter race can also be learned by swimming shorter races such as 1000-yard or 800-meter swims.

Various methods of teaching pace by breaking the race into segments are discussed in Chapter 11. These techniques, whether they be *broken swims* or *simulators*, all contribute to the swimmer's complete understanding of how the race is swum most effectively.

A swimmer may go to a championship meet and improve his best time in a 200-yard freestyle event by as much as five seconds, say from 1:45 to 1:40. He swims a well-paced race, yet has never been near 1:40 before. It is hard to understand how he trained for this pace without having previously swum that fast. The fact is that the swimmer, when working on pace, has learned *how much effort to exert*. He has been training hard all season long and he is nearly always tired, even on meet days. The amount of effort he exerts on these occasions gives him enough speed to swim the 200-yard distance in times that hover around 1:45. As he approaches the championship season, having tapered for three or more weeks, he becomes rested. Under these conditions the same amount of effort now produces a time of 1:40. It is this phenomenon which illustrates so well the importance of another phenomenon: *perceived exertion*. To the extent that he is able to acquire this perception, he will be able to take advantage of his physiological capabilities.

Pacing the Individual Medley

The individual medley is the most variable of the competitive races insofar as pace is concerned. The relative positions of the various swimmers usually changes after the leg of each stroke, making it nearly impossible to devise a theoretical pace that is perfect for all swimmers. This is because each swimmer excels over some other swimmers in one or more strokes. In this event the swimmer must truly swim his own race and try to disregard the race patterns of his opponents.

The individual medley swimmer needs to study his split times in order to avoid making crucial errors. By working constantly to improve his ability to switch from one stroke to the other, while maintaining about the same amount of effort, he may achieve mastery of his pacing technique, even though his rate of speed may vary in each leg of the race. Experimentation with different race patterns both in training sessions and in competition is the key to learning this *perceived exertion*, and is the best way to learn to swim this event with maximum effectiveness.

FOOTNOTES

1. James E. Counsilman, and others, "Three Types of Grab Start for Competitive Swimming," *Swimming Five*, Proceedings of the Fifth International Symposium on the Biomechanics of Swimming, Bielefeld, Germany, Bodo Ungerechts, ed., (Baltimore: University Park Press, 1987), pp. 81–91.
2. U.S. Swimming, Inc., *1992 Rules and Regulations*. Colorado Springs, CO: 1992.

CHAPTER 7

The Physiological Basis for Training Swimmers

The physical preparation of the swimmer is based on a theoretical knowledge of the physiological aspects of training. Sports training physiology is the study of changes in the organic capacity of the athlete as a result of the stress of training and the adaptations to that stress.

To exist as a distinct biological organism, all living things, from single cell protozoans to humans, must be able to carry out certain life functions. To do so requires a continual metabolic exchange with the external environment. A state of homeostasis is said to exist when a balance is achieved between the external environment and the internal life functions. When changes occur in the external environment, homeostasis is disrupted, and changes must occur within the organism to restore balance. The factors in the external environment that produce these changes are referred to as stresses (or stimuli). The organism's responses to the stress are referred to as adaptations.

Complex multicellular animals, such as humans, possess two different mechanisms of adaptation: short and long term. Short-term adaptations are reactions to stress in which the mechanism for response is ever-present and ready-made. They include thermal responses to heat and cold, ventilatory and cardiovascular responses to shortages of oxygen or build-up of carbon dioxide, and so on.

These responses are mediated neurally, are to a great extent autonomic, and may incorporate hormonal effects as well. Once the stress is removed, the organism recovers and is essentially the same as before the stress was applied.

Prolonged or repeated exposure to stress produces biochemical changes that stimulate the cells to increase synthesis of nucleic acids and proteins, which, in turn, lead to structural changes within the cells. This usually results in the growth or hypertrophy of the cells, and an increase in the size or number of organelles and enzymes, leading to an increase in the level or rate of body chemical processes that sustain essential cell functions.

Stress may take the form of physical, chemical, or physical-chemical agents which cause changes in the environment and to which the organism must adapt. Physical preparation for sports involves the use of *physical loads*. The term physical loads is the expression of stress through increased physical activity which results in increases in the level of physiological work. The key effect of physical loads in influencing the various mechanisms which cause structural changes in the cell is the effect on the metabolic functions of creating energy.

Although we derive energy from the breakdown of complex nutrients, all energy for fueling the biochemical processes is provided by a molecule known as adenosine triphosphate (ATP). Energy liberated for work by breaking the chemical bond between ATP and its phosphate atoms occurs through a process known as hydrolysis.

$$ATP \longrightarrow ADP + P(1) + Energy$$

When ATP is broken down to ADP, the process is referred to as ATP turnover. The metabolic functions are involved principally in recombining ADP and a phosphate atom: The process is known as ATP resynthesis. This involves the use of proteins in the cells known as enzymes, which break down nutrients into molecular intermediates directly or indirectly involved in the synthesis of ATP.

THE THREE ENERGY SYSTEMS

The turnover and resynthesis of ATP involves three energy systems, each of which employs one or both of two means of energy production. The means of energy production are categorized by whether or not oxygen is an important molecular requirement in the biochemical process. The two means are *anaerobic* (without oxygen)/*non-robic* (oxygen independent) and *aerobic* (with oxygen). These systems are:

The Phosphocreatine or ATP—PCr
System of Energy (Anaerobic/Non-robic)

This is the first hand energy provider for the muscle in the initial seconds of work. As ATP breaks down to ADP with the release of energy, phosphocreatine is available in the muscle to resynthesize ATP from ADP (PCr + ADP = Creatine + ATP). Theoretically, this activity can go on until the supply of phosphocreatine is exhausted.

Lactic-Acid-ATP, Glycolytic System
(Anaerobic/Non-robic)

The resynthesis of ATP from ADP occurs through the biochemical process known as glycolysis. This process consists in breaking down muscle glycogen or blood glucose in the presence of certain enzymes in the cell cytoplasm. The end result is the resynthesis of ATP and a by-product known as *pyruvate*. When the rate of glycolysis is high, certain cofactors become limited and the build-up of pyruvic acid can result. The pyruvate may be converted to lactic acid.

The Oxidative or Steady-State System
(Aerobic)

In this system ATP is resynthesized by a complex biochemical process known as *oxidative phosphorylization*. This takes place via enzymes located in a specialized organelle in the cells known as mitochondria.* The biochemical pathways within the mitochondria include the Krebs citric-acid cycle and electron transport chain. The enzymes combine ADP and phosphate through biochemical intermediates in the presence of oxygen to synthesize large quantities of ATP with carbon dioxide and water as by-products.

The three systems must not be treated as though they operate independent of each other. Each is a part of an energy continuum in which each contributes to resynthesizing ATP in a different way, depending on the nature of the physiological work.

The function of the phosphocreatine system is to provide immediately available stores of energy for the initial onset of work. The PCr and intramuscular stores of ATP in the muscle can supply the energy demands of all-out sprinting for a short period of time—approximately five to ten seconds. Since the swimmer can swim only a 25-yard all-out effort in that time, his muscles must regenerate their ATP from another source, if he is to continue swimming hard for the next 25, 50, or 75 yards/meters.

It is possible that the level of PCr in the muscle can be increased by sprint training. Resting levels of ATP have been reported to double, while creatine phosphate has been shown to increase by about 40 percent. Such efforts as 10 × 25 with a minute of rest between each 25 qualifies as sprint training.

The source of much of the ATP for distances beyond 25 yards/meters is via the lactic-acid-ATP system (also termed the glycolytic system). Like the ATP-PCr system, it does not require oxygen to generate ATP from the combustion of glucose, and it is also limited insofar as the length of time it can function as the primary source of energy. The highest levels of lactate accumulation occur during exercise that lasts between approximately two and three minutes. This system operates, depending on the individual, long enough to swim 50, 100, even up to 200 yards/meters. At this point, if the exercise intensity is maintained, levels of lactate begin to rise precipitously and, with only the non-robic systems supplying the energy to do work, ATP becomes limited. The exercise intensity at which lactic acid begins to accumulate within the blood used to be termed the *anaerobic*

---

*Mitochondria are energy-generating cellules in the muscle fibers, as many as 100 to 1000 per muscle fiber. They contain a system of enzymes, coenzymes, and activators which carry on the oxidation of foodstuffs and release the ATP used during aerobic work.

threshold. This was in the belief that either the supply of oxygen or its delivery system could not meet the oxygen demand. It is now believed that the level of oxygen on both sides of the threshold remains adequate, and that lack of oxygen is not the sole reason that the levels of lactate begin to rise. Instead, it is theorized that rate limiting steps in the glycolytic process, converting glucose to ATP are more important than the presence or lack of oxygen in the muscle cells at any given stage (the lactate threshold). When demand for ATP and available stores have been exhausted, lactate formation is a convenient *side step* in metabolism, which allows additional ATP to be generated. Although oxygen does not take part directly in the creation of lactic acid and then ATP, if oxygen were absent, *without* lactate formation the process of glycolysis would come to a halt. The fact that has training ramifications for the coach is that there is a definite threshold at which the production of lactic acid becomes elevated. The goal of training is to raise the point at which this uptake-versus-production imbalance occurs, and to perform at or below it.

Much of the ATP produced past this threshold comes from the breakdown of muscle glycogen or glucose in the presence of enzymes in the cytoplasm of the muscle. It is true that one result of this kind of energy release can be the production of lactic acid. (Glycogen breaks down into pyruvic acid and, by doing so, provides energy which is available to change ADP back into ATP. Pyruvic acid is then changed into lactic acid by picking up a hydrogen ion.) It is believed by some researchers that the next stage of glycolysis is getting the glycolytic end product into the mitochondria for further metabolism and that this stage is the *bottle-neck that upsets the balance and causes pyruvate to accumulate, requiring lactate formation.*

Recent studies indicate that, due to a lack of a needed cofactor (NAD, a hydrogen acceptor whose supply is limited), the formation of lactic acid allows additional glycolysis to occur. Once the lactic acid has been formed, the NAD, having lost the hydrogen ion to the lactic acid formation process, is again available to accept another hydrogen ion, and the glycolytic cycle can continue.

Since lactic acid is freely metabolized *without loss of energy*, and the vast majority of lactic acid is now thought to be oxidized both during and following the exercise, it appears it cannot be a build-up of lactic acid that causes discomfort and loss of performance capacity. More likely it is the state of acidosis created by the accumulation of hydrogen ions ($H+$). It could be theorized that one positive effect of training may be to increase the alkaline reserve in the blood and tissues, thus enhancing the body's capacity to sustain activity in the presence of lactic acid and free hydrogen in the muscle tissue through its ability to neutralize (buffer) them. Theoretically, all types of training improve the buffering capacity, but those which most stress the non-robic systems are the most effective. The methods used here are referred to as *intensive training methods*. These include *intensive interval and repetition training methods*, which can be defined as all-out efforts of short to moderate duration. High levels of heart rate are achieved in such efforts—170 beats per minute and over. This is how pulse rate may be used as a determinant of intensity of effort.

Bicarbonate loading has been reported to be successful in buffering the high state of acidosis created (theoretically) by the presence of hydrogen build-up in the tissues. Ordinary bicarbonate of soda is used to counteract acidity, while not altering it. This apparently enables work to continue, meanwhile allowing the glycolytic process also to continue unabated to meet energy demands.[1]

When the intensity of effort is not sufficiently great to reach the lactate threshold, theoretically, the athlete can sustain that intensity indefinitely (or at least as long as glycogen levels remain adequate). This is because he can resynthesize ATP as fast as it is depleted, in what can best be described as a closed circuit. This type of exercise is exemplified by the 1500-meter race or the four-mile event, both of which are now on the national program for Masters and senior swimmers. In such efforts the oxygen supply in the muscles is sufficient and lactic acid is being consumed at a rate sufficient to keep it free from building up, with the release of carbon dioxide, water, and energy, the final products. When the body works at this level, it is said to be in a *steady state* (or steady rate). Of the primary fuel sources available to do work—glucose, fats, and proteins—one added effect of training is to shift towards fats as the main fuel source during steady-state work. Fats are metabolized aerobically, primarily within the mitochondria.

One of the most important areas of progress in sports science since the mid-1970s has been the recognition of glucose as a work-limiting substance and an ergogenic aid. Much work in this area was spurred by the popularity of marathon running and the commercial development of sport drinks. However, transfer of this knowledge towards the benefit of swimmers has been only recent. Carbohydrates in the diet are crucial for sustained performance. It has been shown that muscle glycogen levels deteriorate throughout a week of training such that by the end of the week glycogen levels are significantly lower prior to a workout than they were at the beginning of the week. This may be a critical aspect of the fatigue that is observed in some swimmers as the week progresses. Current knowledge suggests that replenishing glycogen by ingestion of glucose is critical and most effective if begun as soon as possible following the exercise bout. For additional information, the reader may want to read an article by Sherman cited in the references at the end of the chapter.[2]

Most swimming races involve at least two of the systems described previously, and some use all three, as in a 200/400 yard/meter swim. Table 7-1 summarizes the forms of energy release as they are represented in the different types of training and estimates the relative contribution of the aerobic and anaerobic systems at the various distances.

In events under two minutes' duration (approximately 200 yards/meters) the work can be sustained at high intensity with little increase of lactate. After that, the ability to sustain moderate to high levels of work for longer periods reflects a level of conditioning that has successfully raised the lactate threshold. For untrained individuals the threshold occurs at or around 65 to 70 percent of their maximal ability to do work. It is, therefore, difficult for these individuals to sustain muscular work above 70 percent for very long. For highly trained endurance athletes the threshold may not occur until well above 90 percent of their maximal effort. Thus, these athletes are capable of sustaining very intense efforts, sometimes for hours. In the 1500-meter (1650-yard) event, most of the energy used is developed via the aerobic system. Obviously a person training for this

TABLE 7-1   TYPES OF TRAINING AND THEIR EFFECTS

	Over Distance	Interval Training	Repetition Training	Sprint Training
Definition and Description	Training distances greater than race distance for which swimmer is training, usually at moderate and constant speed: 70% to 80% effort.	A series of moderate effort repeat swims, such as 20 × 100, swum with a controlled *short interval* of rest of 5 to 45 sec. between efforts: 80% to 90% effort.	A series of near-maximum efforts, such as 6 × 100, swum with a relatively *long interval of rest* of 1 to 5 min. between efforts: 95% to 100% effort.	A series of 100% efforts of short duration, such as 8 × 25 all-out effort with 1 to 2 min. rest interval between efforts.
Examples	5000-yard continuous swim, constituting over distance for a 1500-meter swimmer. 500 yards continuous swim, constituting over distance for a sprinter.	30 × 50 with 10 sec. rest interval. In practice, most swimmers leave on controlled departure times: :35 for free, :40 for back and fly, :45 for breast. 10 × 200, leaving on 3 min. or 5 × 400, leaving on 5 min.	8 to 20 × 50 from a dive, leaving every 2 min. 4 × 200, leaving every 6 to 8 min. These sets are called *goal sets* and are used weekly to measure progress, as well as for conditioning.	10 to 20 × 25 all-out sprints with 1 min. rest between efforts. 20 × 20 on 60 sec.
Pulse Rate	140–170. This P.R. will remain relatively constant, depending on percentage of effort.	P.R. will fluctuate, going as high as 170–180 and dropping as low as 160–130, following each effort, depending on the interval of rest.	P.R. will rise to terminal rate of 180–190 following each effort and will drop as low as 110–100 during the rest interval and before the next effort begins.	P.R. will rise as high as 170–180 following each effort, but will drop to 110–100 or lower, depending on the duration of the rest interval.
Effect on Performance	Improved endurance and some sustained speed. Little, no, or perhaps detrimental effect on explosive speed.	Improved ability to swim middle distances at fast speed; little effect on explosive speed.	Improved sustained speed and somewhat improved explosive speed.	Improved explosive speed only, as in a sprint 50.
Form of Energy	Aerobic (Steady-State) System—99% Anaerobic—1%	Aerobic—50% to 80% Anaerobic—20% to 50%, depending on intensity of effort. The higher the intensity, the more anaerobic the effort.	Primarily anaerobic—50% to 80% Aerobic—20% to 50%, depending on intensity of effort.	ATP-PCr System, phasing to anaerobic, depending on duration and intensity of effort.
Adaptation	Improved cardiovascular efficiency.	Improved ability to tolerate moderately high levels of lactate. Improved cardiovascular endurance without overstressing.	Improved ability to tolerate high levels of lactate.	Improved speed and power-strengthening through muscle hypertrophy. May raise capacity to buffer acidosis state. Probably increases levels of actomyosin in connective tissue.

event should stress the systems which improve his ability to transport oxygen and to use the oxygen at the cellular level. The best methods of endurance training for this purpose are referred to as *extensive training methods*. These methods include *overdistance training* (also referred to as *constant* or *duration methods*) and *extensive interval training*.

THE NEURO-MOTOR SYSTEM

In the specialized study of human muscle fatigue, Edwards[3] has implied that impaired muscle function cannot be attributed to either simple energy depletion or metabolite accumulation alone. This reinforces the idea that work output is determined by the apparatus of locomotion, in particular, by its central innervation link, and that fatigue is due primarily to impaired nervous system function. In the course of study of nervous system fatigue, it is necessary to distinguish *central* from *peripheral* fatigue.

CENTRAL FATIGUE	*PERIPHERAL FATIGUE*
Failure (voluntary or involuntary) of neural drive, resulting in: reduction in the number of functioning motor units and reduction in motor unit firing frequency.	Failure of force generation of the whole muscle, resulting in: impaired neuro-muscular transmission and impaired excitation contraction coupling.

The mechanisms for fatigue at this level are obviously physiological, but they also involve electrophysiological as well as metabolic adaptations. These constitute neurophysiological adaptation, which cannot be assessed by metabolic methods. It is this neurophysiological adaptation, combined with psychological factors, that constitutes the *volitional capabilities* of the athlete. This is considered a *psychophysiological phenomenon*, a combination of central nervous system resistance to fatigue and athletic will power. In athletics, the nature of this psychophysiological control is assumed in the nature of being able to sustain or even *increase* locomotor function, even when a state of *organic exhaustion* has been reached.

It has been observed that athletes are able to draw on what have been called *endurance reserves* to achieve heightened performance results. The so-called endurance reserves are explained more precisely as compensating mechanisms for exercise-induced fatigue.[4] As the athlete progresses further into intense work and becomes fatigued, volitional effort combined with proprioceptor input from the muscles elicits intense affector input into the higher cortical centers. This boosts synaptic inflow into the lower neuronal pools and activates previously dormant higher threshold motor units. The weakening lower threshold elements are replaced by highly functioning motor elements, which theoretically could result in the actual increase in work output by the muscles. It is this phenomenon of compensatory mechanisms at work that can explain why some athletes appear to increase work effort as they fatigue.

The implications of training to increase neurophysiological capability justify the high training demand that exists today. Such training often conflicts with the ideas of physiologists to train merely enough to increase metabolic potential. Training to increase central nervous system resistance to fatigue is not mentioned in most physiology research, but is well documented in sports training research literature.

PHYSIOLOGICAL ADAPTATIONS TO SPECIFIC MEANS AND METHODS OF TRAINING

Different types of adaptations are made to the different means and methods of training. As an example, in sprint training, the muscles are being loaded in terms of intensity—somewhat as they would be in lifting heavy weights. In endurance training, the muscles are being loaded in terms of duration. Endurance performance and sprint performance are neither enhanced nor limited by the same factors. Much of sports training science involves identifying the limiting factors, and a lot is known about what appears to be important.

The means and methods of each type of training exemplify the stress and adaptation syndrome in the concept of *the specificity of training*. The concept states that a specific stress brings about a specific physiological change or adaptation. A good example is training for maximal strength. Strength training can enhance the muscle's ability to generate high levels of muscle tension, but such training does not enhance the endurance of the muscle or its speed of contraction. The principle of specificity can also be applied in competitive specialization. Swimmers training for long-distances train differently from those preparing for short events. The former concentrate on the types of training that promote endurance, while the latter concentrate on the types of training more characterized by high intensity. The fact that all swimmers should integrate all the different means and methods of training may seem to contradict the idea of specificity, but it is more a reflection of the nature of swimming events, plus the fact that few swimmers compete in only the short sprints or very long distances.

Exercise researchers define adaptations into two categories: *systemic* and *local*. As an example, any endurance activity, whether it be swimming, running, or bicycling, will have the systemic effect of increasing cardiovascular endurance. Bicycling or running will not, however, enhance the local effects of neuromuscular endurance specific to the demands of competitive swimming. Sports training scientists often define systemic and local adaptations as *general* and *specialized* levels of preparation. These are divided into general and specialized preparation for strength, endurance, and speed. Endurance preparation includes training for aerobic-endurance, lactate-endurance, and alactate-endurance (maximal speed). Strength preparation includes training for absolute/maximal strength, strength-endurance, and speed-strength/explosive strength (power).

Physiological Adaptations to Endurance Training

In competitive swimming, the best understanding of the principle of specificity involves determining the physiological effects of the different methods of endurance training. The different methods and their specific effects are often defined by the percentage of aerobic/anaerobic productivity and the long-term cumulative training effects of such methods. From this point onward the term "anaerobic" will be used in preference to "anaerobic/non-robic." This is because the latter term is not accepted in sports training science parlance.

Over Distance Training.   Definition: Continuous swimming of long distance, such as 400 meters, 500 yards, 1650 yards, 1500 meters, or even longer distances.

Percentages aerobic and anaerobic: 70 to 95 percent aerobic; 30 to 5 percent anaerobic.

Physiological changes: This type of training places a great demand on the oxygen-transport system, resulting in the following adaptations: increased cardiac output and greater stroke volume of the heart; slower resting pulse rate; improved ability of the lungs to extract oxygen from the air; advantageous changes in blood chemistry, enabling it to carry more oxygen; increased ability to store glycogen in the liver and muscles; increased number of functional capillaries in the muscle; increased number, size, and composition of mitochondria in the muscle fibers.

Extensive Interval Training.   Definition: Efforts at low to moderate intensity with short rest intervals, such as 15×100 with ten-second rest intervals.

Percentages aerobic and anaerobic: 55 to 85 percent aerobic; 45 to 15 percent anaerobic.

Physiological changes: The changes manifested here are similar to those mentioned above in over distance training, with the addition of, but to a lesser extent, those mentioned later under repetition training. One advantage of this method when compared to over distance training is that during the short rest period some of the ATP-PCr resources are partially replenished and available for use in the next repeat swim, due to an increased ability to oxidize lactate. The ability to *clear* lactate prevents its accumulation. This has ramifications for improving work tolerance. The lactate threshold (OBLA—Onset of Blood Lactic Acid, previously known as the anaerobic threshold) serves as a function of the ability to consume lactic acid. The oxidation of lactic acid is proportional to workload and/or VO(2). The result is that extremely high levels of lactic acid are not accumulated even though the work is more intense than in over distance training. During the rest interval, post-exercise oxygen supplies may help normalize body temperature, stabilize catecholamine levels, aid in fatty acid oxidation, partially restore heart and respiratory oxygen volumes, re-oxygenate myoglobin, and so on. The former idea that the distress caused by a low level of oxygen and a high level of carbon dioxide was a stimulus for the changes that improve aerobic and anaerobic capacity has largely been abandoned due to the fact that there appears to be adequate oxygen to perform the above functions and less production of carbon dioxide than expected.

Intensive Interval and Repetition Training.   Definition: Efforts of submaximal to maximal intensity with long rest intervals, such as 4×150 at near top speed with five- to ten-minute rest intervals.

Percentage aerobic and anaerobic: 30 to 50 percent aerobic; 70 to 50 percent anaerobic.

Physiological changes: During this type of training most of the ATP comes from anaerobic breakdown of glucose in the cytoplasm. The enzymes required for the breakdown are also found in the cytoplasm of the muscle cell. With training, there is an apparent increase in both the glycogen and catalyst stored in the muscles. This is perhaps the main adaptation that results from repetition training.

There is speculation that high levels of lactic acid incurred during this type of training might be the stimulus for changes that cause more efficient binding and transportation of oxygen, that is, increased number of functional capillaries, increased number and quality of mitochondria, advantageous changes in blood chemistry, and so on.

Sprint Training. Definition: All-out sprinting for short distances, such as 10 × 25 yards/meters, with rest intervals ranging from twenty seconds to two to five minutes each. Approximately 80 to 90 percent of the ATP-PCr used during a short sprint is replaced during this rest interval.

Percentages aerobic and anaerobic: 85 percent anaerobic; 15 percent aerobic.

Physiological changes: This type of training improves the muscles' ability to contract quickly, due to improved neuromuscular coordination. There is probably also an increase in the ATP-PCr level in the muscle, resulting in the increased ability of the swimmer to sustain sprinting tempo for a longer period of time.

The separate classification of the four methods of training does not imply that they should not be used in a variety of combinations. Such sets as moderate rest interval training (15 × 100 with 30 second rest intervals) is more anaerobic than the type mentioned under extensive interval training, but not as anaerobic as that mentioned under repetition training.

The four methods and their variations and combinations are all based on the idea that the body has the ability to adapt itself to maintain a high level of ATP in the muscle. Insofar as endurance is concerned, the more of the ATP in the muscle that can be produced aerobically the better, since fuel sources other than glucose can be utilized to provide this energy. Glucose is generally considered a limited substrate. It appears that any adaptations that bring about better transportation and absorption of oxygen and metabolic tolerance to high levels of acidity will benefit the athlete.

Physiological Adaptations to Strength Training

The physiological adaptations that result from strength training are associated not so much with changes in intermediary metabolism, but with musculoskeletal and neural adaptations.

Musculoskeletal Adaptations. The main beneficial changes induced by strength training are the enhancement of the contractile properties of the muscle proteins (the actin and myosin). This is accomplished by increasing the quantity of the contractile proteins, which leads to hypertrophy of the muscle cell and, in turn, to hypertrophy of individual muscle fibers, resulting in an increase in the *cross-sectional area* of the individual muscle. All other factors being equal, the level of maximal force or tension exerted by a muscle is proportional to its cross-sectional area. In addition, strength training increases the amount of connective tissue in the muscle, thereby increasing the size and toughness of the muscles and their attachments, as well as increasing the density of bones at the sites of the muscles' origins and insertions.

Strength training that emphasizes the development of explosive-strength (speed-strength training) has its greatest influence on the non-contractile or elastic element of the muscle. This includes the tendons, the investing membrane of the muscle fibers, and other non-contractile elements of the muscle cell. Such training increases the quantity of elastic tissue in the muscle. This results in an increase in the size, toughness, and suppleness of the tendons and other elastic elements. Increasing the elasticity of the muscle is essential for three reasons: the elastic element absorbs force from high mechanical stresses encountered in sports movement, serving as a buffer between the contractile element of the muscle and the external load; it smooths out rapid transitions in different phases of movement and accumulates mechanical energy as contraction continues; and it allows the utilization of absorbed kinetic energy to produce a movement velocity faster than achieved by the maximal rate of fiber shortening of the contractile proteins.

Neural Adaptations. The changes that occur in the nervous system from strength training are those concerned with the *central nervous system* (CNS): that part of the nervous system involved in voluntary control of movement. The peripheral nerves of the CNS, known as motor nerves, consist of neural cells called motor neurons or alpha fibers, which branch out to innervate individual muscle fibers. The combination of a single alpha fiber and the number of muscle fibers it innervates is called a *motor unit.* The main adaptation from strength loads is the effect it has on individual motor units during muscular work to overcome high resistance. They include increasing the rate or frequency of motor unit stimulation, which raises the level or force of contraction of muscle fibers through a process known as *summation*; increasing the number of functioning motor units during muscle contraction; and recruiting the stimulation of muscle units to fire in a *synchronous* manner.

Strength training that develops speed-strength or explosive-strength has its greatest effect on the *reactive properties* of the nervous system. This involves an interrelationship between involuntary components of the nervous system, including certain types of reflex actions and their direct effect on voluntary movement. When effectively utilized, the nervous system is trained to increase both speed of muscle tension development and speed of muscle contraction. This is accomplished through training the rapid recruitment of a high number of motor units, as well as a quick transition to high frequency stimulation of individual motor units, especially during the beginning of the active phase of the movement.

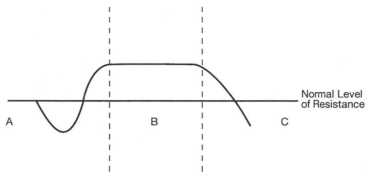

FIGURE 7–1   THE THREE PHASES OF THE GENERAL ADAPTION SYNDROME

A. Alarm Reaction. The body shows the changes characteristic of the first exposure to a stressor. At the same time, its resistance is diminished, and, if the stressor is sufficiently strong—severe burns, extremes of temperature, death may result.

B. Stage of Resistance. Resistance ensues, if continued exposure to the stressor is compatible with adaptation. The bodily signs characteristic of the alarm reaction have virtually disappeared, and the level of resistance rises above normal.

C. Stage of Exhaustion. Following long-term exposure to the same stressor, to which the body has become adjusted, eventually adaptation is exhausted. The signs of the alarm reaction reappear, but now they are irreversible, and the individual dies.

THE CHRONOBIOLOGY OF STRESS AND ADAPTATION

It is not enough to acknowledge that stress and adaptation are taking place from the utilization of different means and methods of training. Just as important is the knowledge of how stress and adaptation to training are realized *over time*. The science or study of the effect of time on life systems is referred to as *chronobiology*. The term first came into usage in the study of circadian periodicity (internal clocks, the diurnal sleeping/waking rhythms, jet lag, and so on). The idea of chronobiology now plays a crucial role in training in that the training process must be programmed to produce optimal adaptation to physical loads at the appropriate time, relative to training and competitive priorities.

Many of the current ideas about how stress and adaptation to physical loads occur over time were developed from the theoretical groundwork of Hans Selye.[5] On the basis of experiments in which animals were exposed to stress, Selye determined that the reaction to stress occurs as a predictable syndrome which lends itself to be described as a model. It subsequently became known as the *general adaptation syndrome (GAS)*. It is characterized as being triphasic, that is, as having three steps which typify the reaction to stress. The GAS model and the three stages of reaction are shown in Figure 7-1.

Models of Adaptation

Current models of adaptation to physical loads are still based on the GAS model. The initial models include the cycle of overcompensation proposed by

Yakovlev in 1967[6] (Figure 7-2) and the cycle of super adaptation proposed by Counsilman in 1968[7] (Figure 7-3). Both models possess fundamental similarities in relation to the Selye model, but the theoretical beliefs as to how adaptations are actually achieved differ on the basis of how the training loads are implemented in the actual training process. The differences have given rise to two theoretical proposals as to how stress should be implemented: recovery following stress and stress superimposed on stress.

Both the Yakovlev and the Counsilman models agree on fundamental aspects of stress and adaptation derived from the Selye model. Both agree that the central reaction to physical loads is equivalent to the alarm reaction in the form of decreased work capacity or fatigue. But unlike the Selye and Counsilman models, the Yakovlev model proposes that adaptation to the loading (or increase in resistance) can take place *only* after the loading or stress has been removed. The body recovers from the fatigue and this recovery is followed by a brief period of overcompensation in which work capacity rises above initial levels. Yakovlev has proposed that increased loading be implemented during this period of overcompensation and that, otherwise, involution will ensue and adaptation will be re-

FIGURE 7–2 THE YAKOVLEV MODEL OF STRESS AND ADAPTATION TO PHYSICAL LOADS

A. Phases of alternating performance level during effort and rest.

B. Alternating functional potentialities in the execution of work during the phases of varying performance levels: a. if repeats are carried out when the traces of previous loading are no longer recognizable, the functional level will remain unchanged; b. if repeats take place when the "remains" of the preceding effort have disappeared, there will be no change in the functional level.

C. If repeats take place before the organism has fully recovered, there will be a drop in the functional level.

D. If every consecutive effort takes place during the phase of "enhanced recovery" and with a gradually rising load level, the functional potentialities will increase accordingly.

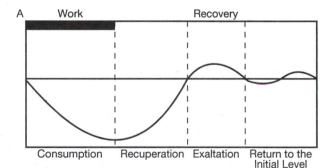

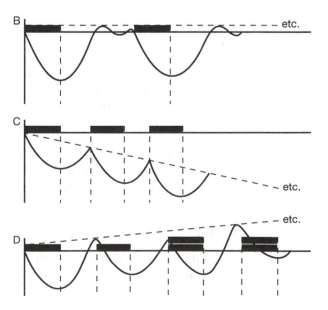

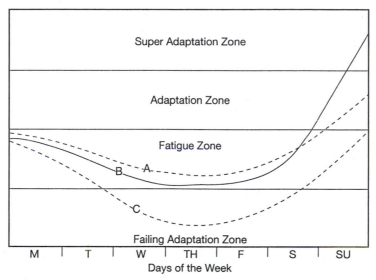

FIGURE 7–3 THE COUNSILMAN MODEL OF STRESS AND ADAPTATION TO PHYSICAL LOADS

How hard should an athlete work, and how much fatigue should he condition himself to endure in order to build maximum endurance? Should he work hard, and, when he becomes fatigued, rest in order to be fresh for the next practice? Or should he impose another workload which is so great that he will not recover completely from one practice session to the next? Should he always feel slightly fatigued? Can he push himself too hard?

These are questions asked by most coaches of such sports as middle or distance running, walking, swimming, and bicycling. This chart is a non scientific attempt to present a concept.

"A" represents the progress of a swimmer who has worked moderately hard from Monday through Friday. With reduced work on Saturday and Sunday, he began to recover from the previous five days of work, and his level of adaptation went above normal.

"B" represents the progress of a swimmer who worked hard enough to bring himself close to the edge of the failing adaptation zone. With reduced work he was able to achieve superadaptation.

"C" represents the progress of a swimmer who has worked so hard that he has fallen into the failing adaptation zone. Even with rest or reduced work he did not return to the normal level.

To achieve superadaptation, athletes must work very hard, pushing themselves to the verge of failing adaptation ("B") before they reduce their workload.

versed. This has brought about the theory that adaptation occurs in a sequential, cyclic manner, which has led to the resolution of training into cyclic patterns of increased loading and unloading to establish a regular pattern of recovery from training. Although the Yakovlev model tends to oversimplify the entire training process and is subject to frequent misinterpretation, it has established the importance of rest or recovery as a means of eliciting adaptation to physical work.

The Yakovlev cycle of overcompensation is the model most frequently cited in overseas sports training literature. Due to its frequent misinterpretation, the means by which the model was created require some clarification. Yakovlev derived the model based on research that made use of *uniform workloads.*

Uniform workloads are training sessions or units (workouts) devoted to the development or training of a *single* physical ability. It was research like this that confirmed the specificity of training. That is, training to stress one physical ability diminished or fatigued that capacity, but did not affect other physical capacities (for example, a workout which stresses the anaerobic processes diminishes anaerobic capacity temporarily, but does not diminish aerobic capacity). The means of actually implementing training loads based on uniform workloads has given rise to the *multimethod system* of training, which advises that only one physical ability should be stressed in a given training session.

The system normally used in competitive swimming is that of *integrated training*, which suggests that several physical abilities can be stressed in a single training session. In this case, stress is imposed as cumulative (that is, the superimposition of stress upon stress, resulting in prolonged periods of incomplete recovery). The Counsilman model of the cycle of superadaptation is based on the theoretical approach of stress superimposed on stress. Two important variables are considered in this model. The first is that the magnitude of accumulated stress determines the level of superadaptation, with work capacity diminished beyond a threshold of *failing adaptation*. The second consideration is that superadaptation requires an extended period of at least one week of incomplete recovery to provide the necessary training stimulus for adaptation to take place before the cycle begins again. The Counsilman model considers the necessity of determining accumulative load demand of successive training sessions to prevent failing adaptation. Yakovlev acknowledges the potential for failed adaptation, but cites this phenomenon as the result of executing successive workloads before recovery. Counsilman has proposed that, up to a certain point, adaptation can take place while the body is undergoing stress and is not undergoing enhanced recovery, but does not acknowledge the need for complete recovery by diminishing the workload.

The model proposed by Matveyev[8] (Figure 7–4) combines the Yakovlev and Counsilman models, depicting more accurately than either of them how stress and adaptation manifest themselves over the course of a training cycle. It notes both the need for extended periods of incomplete recovery and the need for

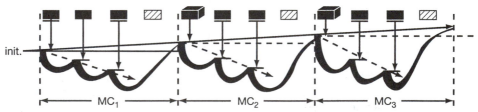

FIGURE 7–4 THE MATVEYEV MODEL OF STRESS AND ADAPTATION TO PHYSICAL LOADS

This chart diagrams one of the variants of the summation of the effects of several training sessions.

MC—microcycles: dark rectangles are training sessions, the effect of which is intensified by rigid rest intervals; hatched rectangles are sessions of a primarily rehabilitative nature; wavy curve conditionally shows the work capacity dynamics (unit—initial level).

enhanced recovery at the end of the cycle. This is to be achieved through reduction of the demand of the training loads towards the end of the training cycle.

The period of restoration or rehabilitation compensates for the loss of work capacity caused by the fatigue of the physical load and allows adaptation to take place. Because of this phenomenon the training cycle is often referred to as the *cycle of overcompensation* and the resulting adaptation is referred to as *compensatory adaptation*, as illustrated in Figure 7–4.

The Heterochronicity of Adaptation

In addition to the cyclic nature of adaptation, there is variability in the rate of improvement of specific physical abilities within the biological systems. This is known as the *heterochronicity of adaptation*. These different rates of improvement determine the duration and interaction of different physical loads to ensure that compensatory adaptation of the holistic athletic state is achieved at the time of major competition. This phenomenon is one of the crucial determinants in the *periodization* of training. The periodization determines the organizational structure of the training process in terms of the emphasis and succession of different tasks throughout the time period allocated to training prior to major competition.

The heterochronicity of adaptation of specific physical abilities is stated by Volkov:

> The adaptive changes that are connected with aerobic capacity take place slowly and require a long training period. Adaptations in the synthesis system of specific proteins which provide high contractile capability in muscles is just as slow. But, when developed as a result of training, these changes are maintained at a given level for a long time.
>
> Biochemical changes associated with the glycolytic anaerobic process develop much faster under the influence of physical loads. But they are lost just as fast after the cessation of training. This peculiar feature of biochemical adaptation to physical loads should be studied from the standpoint of the "dosage" of the training loads and its distribution throughout the different stages of training.[9]

The Effects of Training

Compensatory adaptation and the heterochronicity of adaptation are two of the major factors within the phenomenon of the effects of training. The different effects of training include the following categories:

The Partial Effects of Training. These are changes that occur as a result of different types of physical loads. They include: the training effects of endurance loads, which include aerobic-endurance loads, lactate-endurance or anaerobic-endurance loads, and alactate-endurance or cyclic speed loads; and the training effects of strength loads, which include maximal, absolute strength loads, strength-endurance loads, and speed-strength/explosive-strength loads.

The Immediate Effects of Training. These are changes that occur as a result of the partial training effects of physical loads in one training session. They include *urgent training effects*, that is, the changes which take place during the loading, and the *lagging training effects*, that is, the changes which occur immediately after the loading has taken place.

The Delayed Effects of Training.   These are changes that lag in time after the execution of the loading.

The Cumulative Effects of Training.   These are changes that occur from the partial training effects of physical loads as the result of many training sessions.

Negative and Positive Effects of Training.   These are productive or counter-productive effects of the partial training effects of different physical loads *within* each type of physical preparation, such as the negative or positive effects of different endurance loads on one another.

Transfers of Training Effects.   These are productive or counterproductive effects of the partial training effects of different physical loads *between* each type of physical preparation, such as the negative or positive effects of strength preparation on speed preparation.

The Residual Effects of Training.   These are changes from partial training effects which remain after loading has been discontinued and the time period for possible delayed adaptation has elapsed.

The Role of Certain Training Effects in Adaptation

While the perspective of national exercise physiology understands the immediate and cumulative training effects of partial loads, there are crucial aspects of other training effects that have been identified by international sports training science. These give greater clarity to current theoretical ideas about stress and adaption in the sports training process. They include delayed training effects, positive and negative training effects, transfers of training, and residual training effects.

Short- and Long-Term Delayed Training Effects.   Compensatory adaptation is possible because all training effects are of a delayed nature, that is, adaptation to physical loads is realized some time after the loading has taken place. To understand the true nature of delayed training effects, it is necessary to understand the nature of work *and* rest. The immediate effects of training result in fatigue-lowering work capacity below initial levels. The raising or lowering of work capacity over time is known as change in work capacity dynamics; and this constitutes the nature of delayed training effects.

There are two forms of delayed training effects: short-term, manifested by changes in work capacity dynamics from training session to training session, and long-term, also called long-lasting training effects, which are the result of organizing a succession of training sessions to achieve a cumulative/delayed training effect. Long-lasting and cumulative training effects are often the same thing, although they can vary in their ultimate manifestation.

There are three types of short-term delayed training effects. The means by which they are achieved depends on changes in the demand of the physical loading from session to session and the nature of the rest or recovery between individual training sessions.

Short-term delayed training effects of the first type are manifested by incomplete recovery of work capacity between training sessions, achieved primarily through the use of short rest periods between training sessions and an increase in the demand of loading with each successive training session.

Short-term delayed training effects of the second type are characterized by full restoration of work capacity to initial levels, which is achieved through the use of physical loads that do not change or increase in their demand from session to session, and in which use is made of longer rest periods between training sessions.

Short-term delayed training effects of the third type are exemplified by the overcompensation or superadaptation of work capacity. They are achieved through the use of a maximized rest interval and/or reduced loading following the previous training session. The state of overcompensation allows the subsequent execution of training loads at high demand to cause more profound disturbances in work capacity dynamics.

The organization of training sessions makes use of all three delayed training effects. The delayed training effects of the second type are useful in allowing the athlete to repeat certain types of physical loads in order to consolidate or maintain their effect. They do not, however, permit considerable increases in volume and intensity of the physical load. The achievement of compensatory adaptation usually calls for the use of delayed training effects of the first and third type to achieve the effects of a true cycle of training. The Matveyev model demonstrates this effect (see Figure 7–4).

Long-term (or long lasting) training effects have been resolved into recurrent patterns of adaptation as short as weekly cycles of training by both Counsilman and Yakovlev. It has been discovered that cycles of training periods of incomplete recovery and loss of work capacity can be extended for months, even years, before the benefits are realized. For example, it has been shown that the concentrated variant of strength loading causes drops in speed-strength capabilities during the execution of strength loading. Once the strength loading is discontinued, speed-strength eventually increases and surpasses initial levels (see Figure 7–5).[10,11]

As another example, training at altitude has been shown to cause profound disturbances and loss of work capacity, which eventually are restored and increased above initial levels once the swimmers have returned to sea level (see Figure 7–6).[12] Increases in the anaerobic threshold during the competitive period of the training season are attributed to the execution of a high volume of aerobic and strength loads in the preparatory period. The competitive period is marked by a reduction in both total volume of work and changes in the content of training. This provides the necessary stimulus for the delayed training effect, which raises the anaerobic threshold. The types of delayed effect selected in the organization

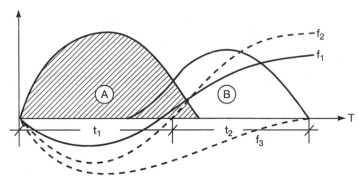

FIGURE 7–5 LONG-LASTING TRAINING EFFECTS OF DIFFERENT VARIANTS
OF STRENGTH LOADS

A. *Principal model of the long-lasting training effects of concentrated strength training*
(taken from Verkoshansky, 1983)
A scheme of the long-lasting effects of concentrated strength loading:
A—concentrated strength loads
B—general developmental work
f1 and f3—changes in dynamics of speed-strength over the course of training
f1 and f2—optimal ranges of strength loading
f3—excessive level of strength loading

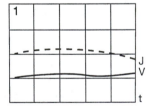 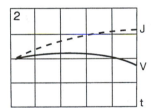 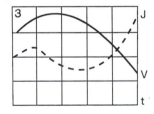

B. *Different strength loading variants and their effect on speed-strength* (taken from
Levchenko, 1984)
1. With a steady load volume (5%-8% of the yearly volume per month), the level of
speed-strength preparation is maintained at the achieved level. Thus, this specialized
strength preparatory regime is for maintenance.
2. With mean volume strength loads (12%-18% per month), the level of speed-strength
preparation increases gradually together with the loads executed. This regime, in strength
preparation of the sprinter, is developmental.
3. In execution of a large volume of strength loads (greater than 20% per month), a
drop in speed-strength preparation is observed. After decreasing the load volume, there
is an intense increase in speed-strength. This specialized strength preparation regime is
developmental, with a delay in the training effect.

of training depend on the level of trainedness of the athlete. As the athlete
increases his level of sports mastery, smaller cycles of recurrent compensating
adaptation are less likely, and the training must be geared to achieve more prolonged cumulative delayed training effects, often referred to as delayed or lagging
transformation.

Positive and Negative Training Effects. Although each type of training load
is said to elicit a narrowly specific training effect, it has been discovered that the

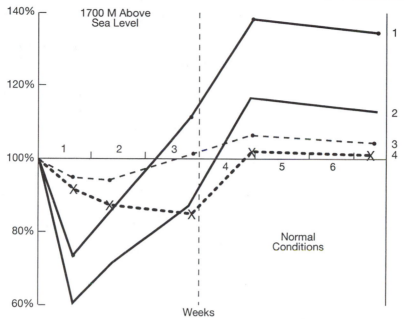

FIGURE 7–6 DYNAMICS OF THE FUNCTIONAL INDICATORS OF SWIMMERS
(taken from S. M. Vaitsckhovsky and others, 1974)
1. Summed volume of work at level of critical power
2. Maximum aerobic capacity
3. Alactate portion of the oxygen debt
4. Maximum oxygen consumption (MOC)

different types of training loads within each type of training (endurance, speed, and strength training) have a strong interdependence with one another as to how they affect the total level of physical preparation over time. Cumulative training effects of each type of training load can have both positive and negative effects on one another. Training loads should never be viewed as always having a completely beneficial effect on training.

Positive and negative training are said to occur when *subsequent* training loads of a specific type of partial training effects are superimposed over the training effects achieved by the preceding work. If the preceding work creates favorable conditions for the subsequent work, there will be a positive accumulation of their training effects; if the preceding work creates unfavorable conditions for subsequent work, there will be a negative accumulation of their training effects.

In the use of training loads that affect endurance (aerobic and lactate endurance) and cyclic speed loads (anaerobic alactate), of prime consideration in determining possible positive or negative training effects is the restoration of energy resources and disturbances in neuroendocrine equilibrium. Examples of prime consideration are the effects of aerobic and anaerobic endurance loading on cyclic speed loads. The training effects of anaerobic alactate loads are positive only when full restoration is achieved after the previous loading.

The presence of positive or negative training effects is considered in both short-term and long-term training plans, the latter in particular with the multiyear and yearly plans.

In experimental data analyzing the partial training effects of endurance loads within successive training sessions, the conditions of previous loading that created favorable conditions for the execution of the subsequent loads include the following: aerobic endurance loading after the execution of anaerobic alactate work, aerobic endurance loading after a small volume of anaerobic lactate work, and anaerobic lactate work after anaerobic alactate work.

Some conditions create a negative interaction with endurance loads: Anaerobic alactate work after a high volume of anaerobic lactate work and anaerobic lactate work after high volumes of aerobic work are examples.

In securing long-term, cumulative training effects, it is the main objective of training to achieve positive cumulative training effects. In endurance and cyclic speed training, such an effect can be secured through the initial development of aerobic endurance, then lactate endurance, then alactate endurance.

AEROBIC ENDURANCE	LACTATE ENDURANCE	ALACTATE ENDURANCE
(initial stages of endurance training)	(later stages of endurance training)	(final stages of endurance training)

The establishment of an aerobic base creates favorable conditions for the training effects of anaerobic work. Excessive use of anaerobic endurance and cyclic speed work in the presence of insufficient aerobic capacity can lead to negative training effects.

In strength training, a positive training effect is achieved when speed-strength/explosive strength training is preceded by the partial cumulative training effects of voluminous strength loading of maximal to submaximal intensity to develop the level of absolute strength.

Absolute Strength (initial stages of training)	Speed-Strength/Explosive Strength (later stages of training)

In special-strength training for endurance, a positive training effect is achieved by the initial development of the required level of absolute strength, followed by the development of strength-endurance, then speed-strength endurance.

Maximal Strength (initial stages of special-strength training)	Strength Endurance (later stages of special-strength training)	Speed-Strength Endurance (final stages of special-strength training)

The reverse in either situation in strength training would result in a negative training effect.

The practical achievement of these positive cumulative training effects is brought about not through a singular, sequential development, but through a complex increase in the utilization of all partial training effects through all phases of training, along with a sequential shift in their emphasis. This results in changes in the content of training as the swimmer progresses from general to specialized physical preparation.

Transfers of Training. In addition to positive and negative training effects *within* each type of physical preparation, there exist positive and negative training effects *between* the different types of physical preparation. These are known as transfers of training, or interconnections between motor abilities. There are many different types of transfers of training, but the ones most frequently encountered are negative and positive transfers of training. In physical preparation the most commonly cited transfer of training is the effect of strength training on endurance and/or cyclic speed training, the most frequently studied being the effect of strength gains on speed. Research has established that, while a positive transfer exists between strength and speed gains, the development of excessive levels of absolute strength has eventual negative effects on speed. This is a case in which certain types of transfers of training might have initial benefits, but can produce counterproductive effects later on.

Strength training has been shown to have positive effects on endurance. But, like speed, excessive strength can have eventual negative effects on endurance. The prevention of such effects calls for the proper rationing of all partial training effects throughout the long- and short-term training plan, to prevent inordinate volumes of partial training effects from interfering with the desired growth of all physical abilities. As an example, in long-range or multiyear plans the level of strength preparation is reduced when the required levels of strength needed for current or future specialized preparation has been reached, anticipating that further gains in strength will result in potential loss of performance capacity. In yearly or seasonal training programs, the volume of strength work is reduced during those stages of training when greater emphasis is placed on cyclic speed development. The reason for this is that high volumes of strength work cause profound disturbances in the neural system, which must function at optimal levels during training. This places greater emphasis on speed development. Although most coaches perceive parallel gains in strength, endurance, and speed through the athlete's career, the growth of a particular physical ability should never be accelerated to the point that it limits or impedes the holistic development of the physical abilities required by the athlete's performance potential or the demands of the competitive events for which the athlete is preparing.

There are also theoretical approaches to training in which direct negative training effects or negative transfers of training are seen as having beneficial effects. Athletes predisposed to making large genetic gains in physical abilities that might disrupt total performance capability can employ negative training effects or negative transfers of training to disrupt or retard unwanted or counterproductive gains in physical abilities. For example, athletes predisposed to making high strength gains that could have long-term detrimental effects on speed could resort to chronic endurance training to neutralize this effect or could resort to other conditions, such as changes in dietary habits, to retard excessive hypertrophy of muscle fibers. This requires careful, long-term analysis of the total integral preparation of the athlete throughout his career, resulting in the development of some esoteric approaches to theoretical preparation.

Residual Effects of Training.   High-level athletes are often able to reduce their training for long periods of time and still make competitive performance gains. In addition, mature athletes who have discontinued training for years are able to achieve a high level of trainedness after only a brief period of retraining. This is because the changes due to adaptation to physical loads can be maintained for long periods of time or can be recalled quickly once training has restarted. This phenomenon is called *the residual effect of training*.

Residual effects have different levels or rates of retention and recall in the different biological systems. In addition, the interactivity of the biological systems affects the magnitude of the residual training effects of different physical abilities or motor qualities. The level of the residual training effect is affected by such factors as the athlete's training background, level of trainedness, genetic predisposition for retaining residual training effects, and perhaps even performance capability.

The most fundamental residual training effects are intracellular adaptations for peak metabolic productivity, which occur from aerobic or anaerobic loading. The adaptations to anaerobic loads occur rapidly but, once training has ceased, are often lost just as quickly, indicating that adaptations to anaerobic loads are relatively transitory and do not have long-lasting residual effects. Although adaptations to aerobic loads to achieve peak aerobic metabolic productivity take longer to develop, they possess a higher degree of stability and are retained for longer periods of time once training has ceased. This indicates a longer-lasting training effect. In addition, the rate of loss of peak metabolic productivity in cells is not equivalent to the rate of loss of other intracellular changes which have led to major adaptational restructuring of the entire biological systems. Many of these have even greater residual training effects.

Fig. 7-7 is a model that proposes the different types of residual training effects and their different rates of loss or retention once training has discontinued.

Residual training effects are used as part of seasonal or long-term training to allow necessary changes in training without fear of loss of trainedness. By programming rates of loss it is possible to allow for the holistic development of the physical qualities needed for optimum competitive performance capability. For example, maximum strength loads are executed early in the season and may result in strength gains that exceed the needs of the athlete for optimum performance. Strength loading is thus discontinued in the later phases of the season. This is done for two reasons: to prevent strength loading from interfering with the development of other physical abilities, such as speed development, and to program the rate of loss so the required level of strength is achieved during major competition. In the Olympic training (or quadrennial) plan, the first year

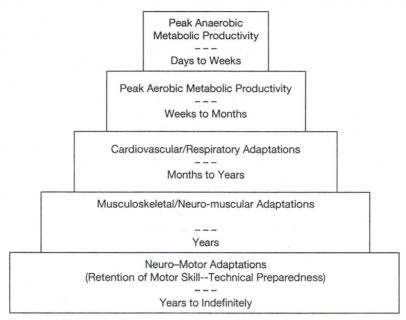

FIGURE 7–7 THEORETICAL REPRESENTATION OF THE RESIDUAL EFFECTS OF TRAINING AND THEIR SUGGESTED LONGEVITY

is often devoted to endurance training that exceeds the endurance demands of the athlete's chosen event or events. As the plan progresses, endurance training is reduced and more time is spent on strength and speed training, the long-term retention having been planned to achieve the required level of trainedness at the end of the Olympic cycle.

Failure to Adapt

Implicit in the concept of the stress and adaptation syndrome is *failing adaptation*. Failing adaptation takes different forms: *training staleness* and *overloading*. Training staleness occurs when the athlete's trainedness plateaus and no further adaptation occurs. This is usually the result of a training program in which the overall demand has leveled off and is no longer capable of disrupting the athlete's physical homeostasis. Overloading is a case of failing adaptation in which the athlete's work capacity has actually diminished over the course of training. Overloading usually occurs when the training demands of conditioning programs far exceed the athlete's ability to adapt. Both staleness and overloading can usually be resolved by correcting either of the two training circumstances that lead to these conditions.

Failing adaptation depends upon the individual capabilities of the athlete. This can be determined in part by such factors as the age of the athlete (including not only chronological but also biological and training age), the level of trainedness and sports mastery, the physical resiliency of the athlete, and other factors.

Adaptation is also subject to external stresses, which may have nothing to do with the sports training. Stress from whatever source tends to be cumulative. Such factors are collectively termed *exogenous* and are involved in athletic hygiene. They include medical, nutritional, and environmental factors. Psychological factors also affect the ability to adapt. This includes not only psychological preparation for sport, but also the psychological hygiene of the athlete (see Chapter 9).

Coaches must often rely on subjective observation to alert them to the approach of failing adaptation. Observant coaches learn to recognize the most common signals and then take steps to change the training before failing adaptation becomes established. The typical signals for overloading include unusual and unexplained irritability and anxiety, insomnia, loss of appetite, loss of weight, loss of enthusiasm for training, and an increased incidence of upper respiratory illnesses. The coach must not only control training, but must also attempt to identify and control the hygienic factors that have contributed to the state of failing adaptation. This can include advice on nutrition, the use of restorative therapy, and even psychological counseling.

MUSCLE FIBER TYPING

Another of the major variables affecting stress and adaptation is *fiber-type distribution* in human skeletal muscle. It is one of the factors that has been identified with the innate predisposition of the athlete and is a limiting factor in setting both competitive and training performance goals.

While physiologists have identified four distinct types of muscle fiber in human skeletal muscle, most sports training literature considers only three types, based on different biochemical and contractile properties. Table 7–2 charts the differences in fiber-type characteristics.

The functional and structural characteristics of the different fiber types determine their classification: White Type 2b fibers have a faster rate of contraction and a higher glycolytic capacity. This is the reason they are termed *fast-twitch glycolytic* (or FG) fibers. While Type 1 fibers' speed of contraction is slower, their properties of higher capillary density, higher myoglobin content, and higher oxidative potential define them as *slow-twitch oxidative* (or SO)

TABLE 7-2 DIFFERENCES IN THE FUNCTIONAL CHARACTERISTICS OF SKELETAL MUSCLE FIBER

	Type I SO Fibers	Type IIa FOG Fibers	Type IIb FG Fibers
Primary source of ATP production	Oxidative phosphorylization	Oxidative phosphorylization	Anaerobic glycolysis
Myosin-ATPase activity	Low	High	High
Glycolytic enzyme activity	Low	Intermediate	High
Glycogen content	Low	Intermediate	High
Number of mitochondria	High	High	Low
Myoglobin content	High	Intermediate	Low
Capillary density	High	Intermediate	Low
Speed of contraction	Slow	Fast	Fast
Rate of fatigue	Slow	Intermediate	Fast

fibers. Intermediate fibers are called *fast-twitch oxidative/glycolytic* (or FOG) fibers, also termed Type 2a.

The fast-twitch fibers are adapted to contract quickly, but they also tire easily; the red, slow-twitch fibers contract more slowly but are capable of greater endurance. The most important difference between the two types is the level of *myoglobin*. Myoglobin is a protein material in the muscle that has a strong affinity for oxygen. It is also the source of the redness in the slow-twitch muscle fibers. The slow-twitch fibers, having considerably more myoglobin than the fast-twitch fibers, obviously display the difference in color. The myoglobin in the red fibers facilitates the passage of oxygen from the capillaries to the mitochondria. Oxygen consumption is a function of mitochondrial mass: the greater its mass, the greater the muscles' capacity to metabolize nutrients and generate ATP. Slow-twitch fibers also have a high capacity for oxidation of lactic acid. Fast-twitch fibers lack these properties, which allow slow-twitch fibers to do sustained endurance efforts.

In humans, as well as the various species of animals, both Type 1 and Type 2 muscle fibers are found in nearly every muscle. However, there are variations in the percentage proportion of slow- to fast-twitch fibers in their muscles from one individual to the next. This is known as *relative fiber-type distribution*. These variations in fiber-type distribution are apparently inherent, being established shortly after birth. It is believed that evolution has played a role in this proportionality, with function dictating fiber type. For example, within the human species, it is possible to generalize about certain muscles and muscle groups. The muscles that support the back have mostly red slow-twitch fibers, while the muscles that blink the eyes contain primarily white fast-twitch fibers. Yet, the prime movers of the limbs differ widely in their percentage distribution from one person to another. The best means of determining muscle fiber type distribution in individual athletes is through the use of muscle biopsy techniques. A device known as a muscle biopsy needle is used to extract a sample of muscle tissue from deep within the belly of the muscle. In exercise research, the most common muscles used are the large knee extensors, such as the quadriceps femoris. The deltoid muscle of the shoulder is often selected to determine fiber type distribution in the musculature of the upper extremities. Figure 7–8–A and 7–8–B show the muscle sample being taken from the deltoidus of an athlete and then being processed for microscopic examination. Figure 7–8–C is a typical microscopic slide example.

The best non-invasive means of determining fiber type distribution is through the use of specially selected performance tests. These tests normally measure speed-strength/explosive strength or strength-endurance indices. The most common test is the Sargent Standing Vertical Jump Test. Table 10-1 in Chapter 10 provides norms for ages 10 through 17 for both sexes.

The use of muscle biopsies and non-invasive measures have been combined with cross-sectional studies of athletes who are divided into different groups based on the sports they excel in and the types of events within the sport in which they are best suited to compete. These are often distinguished on the basis of duration or distance. Such studies show that there is a significant relationship between fiber type distribution and the propensity to excel in events requiring significant speed and power, or to excel in events requiring great endurance. This

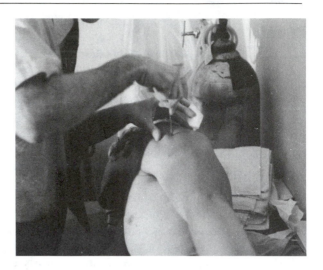

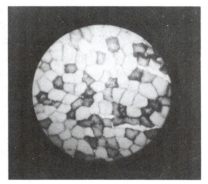

FIGURE 7–8   MUSCLE FIBER TYPING
A. Taking the specimen from the deltoidus of a swimmer.
B. Preparing the specimen of muscle tissue for staining, freezing, and slicing.
C. Microscopic slide showing cross-section of muscle tissue. The stain causes the Type 1, slow-twitch fibers to appear the darkest, the Type 2a fast-twitch fibers to be the lightest, and the Type 2b intermediate fibers to be in between.

is especially the case with competitive swimming. Swimmers who possess a higher percentage of fast-twitch fibers are more likely to excel in shorter events, such as the 50, 100, or 200 yards/meters events. Swimmers who possess a higher percentage of slow-twitch fibers will be more likely to excel in events requiring greater endurance, such as the 400–500, 800–1000, and 1500–1650 yards/meters events.

What are the implications for training of fiber-type distribution? Prins'[13] research, involving the effects of isokinetic training at different speeds on fiber type, showed that slow speed exercise caused hypertrophy of the slow twitch fibers, while high speed exercise had its greatest effect on fast twitch fibers. This finding emphasized the importance of speed in exercise, disputing the long held belief that *strength is speed*.

There is a controversy about the effects of training on the relative muscle fiber composition. It concerns whether or not changes occur in the percentage of the three muscle fiber types in mixed skeletal muscle. Some researchers suggest that chronic endurance training converts fast-twitch fibers to slow-twitch fibers, but most studies confirm that the only change taking place is a modification of the Type 2 fibers.[14] It has been established that the percentage of existing slow-twitch fibers cannot change. Research in sports training has shown that training programs that emphasize endurance work modify a limited number of Type 2b fibers to become Type 2a fibers, while speed and speed-strength training cause a reverse effect, although not to the same degree that endurance training effects conversion to Type 2a fibers.[15]

Other more theoretical proposals suggest that chronic endurance training causes the destruction of fast-twitch fibers. The mechanism is said to involve a biochemical breakdown of the fast-twitch fibers by the lysosomes of the muscle cells, stimulated by the execution of chronic endurance loading. Once the fiber is destroyed, hyperplasia (or fiber splitting) of adjoining slow-twitch fibers is believed to replace the lost fibers and to cause an actual change in relative fiber distribution. This theory remains speculative.

How is fiber-type information useful to a coach? Is it useful only for selection purposes? Theoretically, coaches could administer muscle biopsies and, based on the proportionality of fast- to slow-twitch fibers, assign their athletes either to sprints, middle-distance, or distance events. This topic presents an interesting area of discussion, which the authors hesitate to include because of its potential for affecting the work habits of so-called "drop dead" sprinters and causing a stampede to the sprinters' lane. The prime movers of most humans appear to fall somewhere near the midline of possible fiber types—50 percent slow-twitch and 50 percent fast-twitch. These individuals—most of us—can be successfully coached to perform well in either sprint or distance events. However, it is unlikely that any of these athletes will become outstanding or elite in either endurance or sprint activities. The closer to one or the other end of the fiber continuum a person is, the greater the potential for elite endurance or elite sprint performance. This is not to minimize the importance of the many other factors, but to emphasize the potential significance of just this one. For the coach, the dilemma is that from this perspective it may be more difficult to train a true sprinter than it is to train a true endurance athlete. Fiber fatigue early in the season may preclude or limit cardiovascular adaptation. Later, cardiovascular fatigue may limit optimal local adaptations, and so on.

FOOTNOTES

1. C. A. Horswill and others, "Influence of Sodium bicarbonate on Sprint Performance: Relationship to Dosage," *Medical Science, Sports Exercise*, 20, 1988, 566.

2. W. M. Sherman, "Carbohydrates, Muscle Glycogen, and Improved Perfromance," *Physician and Sportsmedicine*, 15 (2), 1987, 157–161, 164.

3. R. H. T. Edwards, "Human Muscle Function and Fatigue," *Human Muscle Fatigue: Physiological Mechanisms* (London: Pitman Medical, [CIBA Foundation Symposium 82], 1981) pp. 1–18.

4. D. D. Monogarov, "Developing and Compensating for Intense Exercise Induced Fatigue," *Teoriya i Praktika Fizicheskoi Kultury*, 4, 1990, 43–46.

5. Hans Selye, *The Stress of Life* (New York: McGraw-Hill Book Co., 1956), p. 277.

6. Manfred Scholich, *Circuit Training* (Berlin: Sport Verlag, 1986), pp. 62–63.

7. James E. Counsilman, *The Science of Swimming* (Englewood Cliffs, NJ: Prentice-Hall, Inc., 1968), p. 236.

8. Leonid Matveyev, *Fundamentals of Sports Training* (Moscow: Progress Publishers, English translation of the revised Russian edition, 1981), p. 56.

9. N. Volkov, "The Logic of Sports Training," *Legkaya Atletika*, 10, 1974, 22–23; sec. ref. *The Soviet Sports Review*, M. Yessis, ed., 10(2), 1975, 29–34.

10. Yuri Verkoshansky, "The Long-Lasting Training Effect of Concentrated Strength Loads," *Teoriya i Praktika Fizicheskoi Kultury*, 5, 1983, 5–8.

11. A. Levchenko, "The Sprint," *Legkaya Atletika*, 3, 1984, 6–8; sec. ref., *The Soviet Sports Review*, M. Yessis, ed., 25 (2), 1990, 78–83.

12. S. M. Vaitsckhovsky and others, 1974; sec. ref., Yuri Verkoshansky, *Programming and Organization of Training* (Moscow: Fizikultura i Spovt, 1986), p. 116; trans. (Livonia, MI: Sportivny Press).

13. Jan Prins, "A Physiological Review of Leg Extensor Power and Jumping Ability," *Biokinetic Strength Training*," Vol. I, Application Notes, compiled and annotated by Evan Flavell (Albany, California: Isokinetics, Inc., 1980–81), pp. 109–113.

14. Dirk Pette, "Activity-Induced Fast to Slow Transitions in Mammalian Muscle," *Medicine and Science in Sports and Exercise*, 16(6), 1984, 517–528.

15. Yazvikov, V. V., "The Effect of Sports Training (Endurance and Speed-Strength) on the Muscle-Fiber Composition of Skeletal Muscles in Man," *Teoriya i Praktika Fizicheskoi Kultury*, 2, 1988, 48–50.

CHAPTER 8

International Sports Training Theory

This chapter presents theoretical and methodological information derived largely from European and Eurasian sources. Since the 1960s, a number of countries in these regions, notably the former Soviet Union and the former East Germany, have enjoyed great success at the highest levels of international sports competition. Although some of this success may have stemmed from the financial support of the political system, that fact does not diminish its impact.

Scientific documentation and supportive data for the theories presented here have been available to the scientific community in this country since the 1960s. The two main sources have been *The Soviet Sports Review* (now the *Fitness and Sports Review*), published by Dr. Michael Yessis,[1] eminent sports training scientist and the United States' top expert in international sports theory, and the sports textbooks, translated and distributed by Progress Publishers (Moscow) and *Sport Verlag* (Berlin). These publications are the end result of sports training science, with the research controlled by the needs of the sports preparation system. Up to now, our scientific community has been largely unaware of or has discounted the findings of this research, primarily due to the belief that sports training research does not adhere to the narrow strictures of academic research protocol. In addition, the ultimate use of this research is decided not by the researchers themselves, but by the sports theorists, who decide on its practical application within the actual sports environment. But the continued athletic success among the East European programs and the unique opportunities provided for significant discovery within a centralized sports organization has prompted many other countries to imitate those programs.

The information presented here attempts to cover the fundamentals of training, based on both *general sports theory* and on theory that is *specialized to the demands of competitive swimming.*

FUNDAMENTALS OF SPORTS TRAINING THEORY

Sports training is an organized and systematic process of preparation that develops the necessary physical and mental qualities for improving competitive performance. The level of sports results achieved depends upon the *total integral preparation* of the athlete. This refers to the successful unification of all five levels of preparation: *physical, technical, tactical, psychological,* and *theoretical.*

Theoretical preparation controls all the other levels. It involves a scientific search that determines the logic of the sports preparation system. Figure 8–1, taken from Matveyev,[2] outlines the scientific methodological process in the development of sports theory.

The Principles of Sports Training

The evolution of training theory has given rise to the development of fundamental principles that control sports training. They have emerged from the formation of training concepts and theories. In sports theory, concepts are ideas or opinions that result from the observation of regularly occurring phenomena during the training process, while theories are beliefs that are used to guide a given course of action in training. Principles are concepts or theories that have achieved universal acceptance. They are not scientific absolutes because they are subject to theoretical contingencies. For example, it is generally agreed that there should be a progressive increase in the demand of training, as dictated by the principle of overload, but there are many different approaches to achieving overload.

Some training principles reflect moral and educational doctrine derived from the science of sports pedagogy. Others give direction to the application of methodology within the sports preparation system. Still others deal strictly with physical preparation, based on existing knowledge of the physiological effects of training. It can be seen that many principles are either interrelated or simply derive from other principles. In addition, many sports principles are reflective of general sports theory. They must be adapted to the unique demands of a particular sport or be subject to misapplication. Others are unique to the nature of the particular sport, such as the principle of all-sided preparation in competitive swimming.

The following principles are taken from the published works of Leonid Matveyev, N. P. Ozolin, Dietrich Harre, and others.

The Principle of Consciousness. This principle states that the athlete must develop the proper conscious attitude and disciplined behavior to display correct conduct in training, competition, and private life.

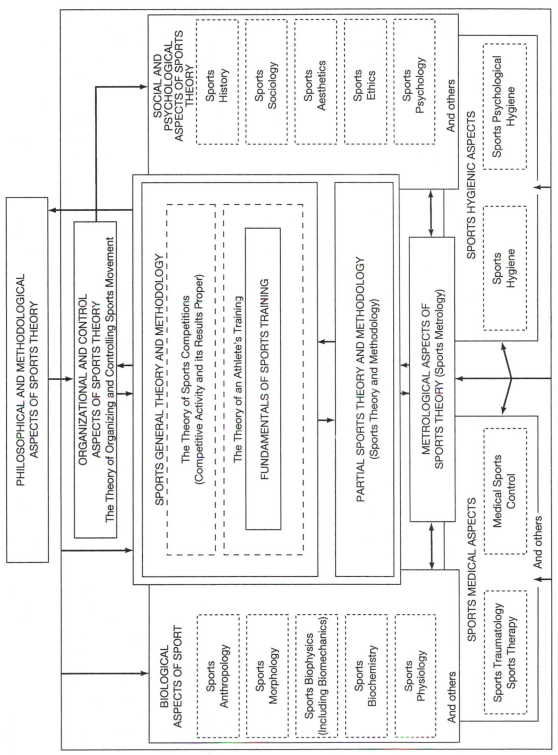

FIGURE 8–1 THE MAIN SECTIONS AND ASPECTS OF SPORTS THEORY

The Principle of Health Promotion.   This principle states that training must center on developing long-term health and a sense of well-being. The rigors of training can be implemented in such a way as to promote destructive effects on health: the effects of over-training and poor training hygiene, for example.

The Principle of Versatility.   This principle requires that training should develop a balance between the mental and physical qualities needed to cope with a variety of tasks. It is seen as both general versatility, which is proficiency in several sports, and versatility within a selected sport, which is thought of as both training and competitive versatility.

The Principle of Systemization.   This principle merely recognizes that training must follow a systematic process, in both the short and long term. Principles that are related to the systemization of training include the principles of the cyclic nature of training, the periodization of training, and the modeling of the training process.

The Principle of Repetition.   This principle recognizes that fundamental to the execution of physical exercises is the methodical *repetition* of the selected and formed movements. By progressively increasing the number of repetitions, movement becomes automatic. Exercises to increase the physical abilities of endurance, strength, and speed have limitations set by the number of repetitions. The quantitative expression of repetitions takes the form of *physical loads*.

The Principle of Specialization.   Also known as the *utility principle*, this principle simply states that the means, methods, and exercises used in training for a selected sport must relate to the demands of that sport as closely as possible. The exercises used must be of either an integral or an ancillary nature to the specifics of the competitive exercise.

The Principle of Unity of General and Specialized Preparation.   Also known as the principle of *comprehensiveness*, this principle states that while training should relate to the specifics of the competitive activity, training should also ensure the comprehensive motor development of the athlete. General physical preparation refers to the development of physical and mental abilities that are nonspecific to the demands of the sport. Based on a foundational approach to training, general physical preparation serves as the *training base* upon which more specialized work is built. The long-term development of the athlete requires that general physical preparation dominate the initial stages of the athlete's career. Gains in the level of trainedness and sports mastery over time will require a progressive shift toward more specialized work in the later stages of the athlete's career. In these later stages, general physical preparation will continue to serve as a contrast activity, providing recovery from intensive specialized work.

The Principles of Load.   These principles quantify the means and methods of training as physical loads, both as *training loads* or external load factors and as *physiological loads* or the internal load response. Different principles are associated with the main principle. They include the dynamics of the training load, which are identified as volume, intensity, and density.

The next is the principle of *load demand*, which is the volume/intensity ratio of individual training loads. Third is the principle of *load structure*, which identifies changes in load demand both between successive work loads and between individual training units or even training sessions. Fourth is the principle of *load degree*, which is the variable level of the internal load response at the moment of loading. Fifth is the principle of *load process*, which identifies the methods of loading. Interrelated to these principles are the principles of *overload, specificity*, and *reversibility*.

The Interval Principle.   This principle emphasizes the importance of rest as well as work in the training process. It stresses the recuperative process and establishes the structure of loading and recovery, sometimes known as the *loading rhythm*. Its quantitative character is expressed as the load dynamic of *density*.

The Principle of Gradualness.   This principle is also known as the principle of intensification of the training process or progressive increase in the training load. Whichever defining terminology is selected, the principle states that the total training load must be gradually and progressively increased as the athlete gains in maturity and levels of trainedness.

The Principle of Individualization.   This principle states that training must be structured to suit the needs of the individual athlete. A principle that is interrelated to the individualization is that of age-dependence. This principle states that there are age considerations to be made in the training process. This involves not only the chronological age, but also the biological age and the training age of the athlete.

The Principle of All-Sided Preparation.   This principle is also known as the principle of *universalism*. Unique to the demands of competitive swimming, this principle states that the specialized preparation must center around training for a wide variety of events and distances.

On the basis of these principles of training and other theoretical conceptions, Ozolin has elaborated on the different levels of preparation, dividing each level into its various *components* (see Figure 8–2).[3]

The components of sports preparation exist at various levels within the athlete, and their presence is determined by two criteria: the innate predisposition of the athlete and the level of trainedness of the athlete. As an example, when determining in what distances a swimmer should compete, it is especially important to consider the components of the first type, such as muscle fiber type distribution.

The components interact and affect other components of different levels of preparation. An athlete may possess the necessary coordinative capability for effective movement skill, but lack the strength and flexibility to make good stroke mechanics possible. Improper stroke mechanics can set limitations on the development of higher levels of special endurance preparedness. Flexibility training

FIGURE 8–2. SPORTS PREPARATION FACTORS AND SOME OF THEIR COMPONENTS (adapted from N. P. Ozolin, 1986)

#	Type of Preparation	Components			
1	Theoretical preparation	Scientific world outlook	Knowledge of basic anatomy, physiology, biology, biomechanics, hygiene, self-control & others	Knowledge of the general bases of the sports preparatory system	Theoretical & methodological knowledge in the area of sports specialization
2	Technical preparation in competitive exercise	Stability in motor skills	Absence of extra tension in movements	Correct & biomechanical effectiveness of different movements, elements & relationships	Muscular effort & relaxation in separate movements
3	Ability to construct & coordinate movements	Ability to remember tasks & to construct different actions from accustomed movements	Ability to coordinate complex technical movements	Ability to coordinate movement in difficult conditions (dexterity, accuracy & others)	Ability to redo & improve motor skills
4	Ability to learn	Physical preparation for learning	Psychological preparation for learning	Memory, its views & essentials of mastery	Motor presentation & verbal delineation of the learner
5	Adaptational Capabilities	Level of allowable loads in different work	Time of restoration after different loads	Percent of increase in different physical qualities	Percent of overloads in moderate & large cycles of preparation
6	Physical preparation	General physical	Preliminary specialized ("specialized foundation")	Specialized	Physical preparedness in separate exercises
7	General physical preparation	General development of the musculature & ability to display strength	Ability for fast movement	Endurance in different work	Mobility in the joints in execution of various movements

#				
8	General functional preparation	General state of health according to anthropomorphological, physiological & medical indices	Ability to withstand general increases in loads according to physiological & medical indices	Restoration after general loads (according to medical tests)	Reaction to execution of exercises of general physical preparation according to biochemical indices
9	Specialized physical preparation	Development of the musculature & ability to show strength in chosen sports events	Speed (quickness) of movement in the chosen sports events	Endurance in the chosen sports events	Mobility in the joints in execution of movements in the chosen sports events
10	Specialized functional preparation	Specialized preparation of the "leading" organs & systems according to physiological, biochemical, morphological & medical indices of the competitive exercise	Restorative & adaptational reactions after competitive exercise according to physiological, biochemical & medical indices	Reaction to execution of specialized exercises & tests according to physiological, morphological & medical indices	Restorative function of separate organs & systems after execution of specialized exercises & tests according to physiological, morphological & medical indices
11	Preliminary specialized preparation ("specialized foundation")	Ability to execute the competitive exercise with slow & moderate intensity for long periods	Ability to execute the competitive exercise in different regimes & with different methods for long periods	Level of the preparatory components & their relationship to long work of slow to moderate intensity	Ability to show volition in overcoming the difficulties in long-term work
12	Specialized muscular strength	Strength of the main muscle groups in execution of the competitive exercise	Strength of absolute & separate muscle groups in execution of the main movements of the competitive exercise	Muscle strength in their different work regimes: dynamic, isometric, isotonic, ballistic & mixed	Condition & preparedness of separate muscle groups (volume, length, structure of tissues, excitability, elasticity & others)
13	Specialized speed (quickness of movement)	Speed of the "leading" movements in the competitive exercise	Speed of motor reactions, undertaken resolution, execution, changes, inhibition	Speed & acceleration of movement in different regimes of muscle work: dynamic, isotonic, ballistic	Relationship between fast & slow muscle fibers. Elasticity & resiliency of the muscles

FIGURE 8–2. *(continued)*

#	Type of Preparation	Components			
14	Specialized endurance	Endurance in competitive exercises	Endurance in different regimes of executing the competitive exercise	Physiological & biochemical "ceilings" & indices of work restoration in the function of the "leading" organs & systems	Relationship between fast & slow muscle fibers. Elasticity & resiliency of the muscles.
15	Tactical preparation	Sum total evaluation of all components of tactics in the competitive exercise	Recall & execution of the tactical variant	Ability to select & execute tactical resolutions in different situations	Tactical thought & fast realization
16	Psychological preparation	Preparation for "field of combat" conditions	Psychological steadiness in competitive exercise in usual, more difficult & complex conditions	Force of motivation in striving toward the goal	Reaction to positive & negative influences, to failure & losing in competitions
17	Volitional qualities	Ability to show volitional strength for success, to overcome record "ceilings" & to open up the potential strength	Ability to concentrate attention, to show courage, resolution, cold-bloodedness & others in execution of the sports exercise	Reaction to extreme conditions, courage, instantaneous actions & others	Love for work, steadiness in overcoming difficulties, in striving toward the goals.
18	Specialized mobility in the joints	Amplitude of movements in the competitive exercise	"Reserve" in amplitude of movement in the competitive exercise	Amplitude of movement in specialized exercises	Level of tension of the antagonist muscles. Elasticity of the muscles & ligaments in the competitive exercise movements
19	Integral preparation	Sports results in the competitive exercise	Sum total evaluation of all components comprising the integral preparation	Steadiness, stability in execution of the competitive exercise in usual, more difficult, more complex & easier conditions	Precision of ideo-motor execution of the competitive exercise

not only serves to increase joint mobility, it also acts as a means of psychic relaxation needed in psychological preparation. The sheer number of potential interactions demonstrates the complexity of sports preparation.

Understanding and analyzing the components of preparation is an essential aspect of planning the training process. It involves a factor analysis of the individual athlete to determine training priorities: the components needing work and development, those requiring only maintenance, and those requiring no further training.

In physical preparation, distinctions must be made between general and special preparation. Physical preparation is divided into different levels on the basis of the physical abilities, each of which has its own levels of general and special preparation. Strength, speed, and flexibility training are divided into general and specialized preparation, while endurance training is divided into general, preliminary-specialized, specialized, and competitive-specific preparation.

Preliminary-specialized preparation involves over distance swimming, which establishes the endurance or aerobic base upon which more specialized swim training is built. This is the reason preliminary-specialized preparation is also referred to as specialized-foundation preparation. Competitive-specific preparation involves the training that is gained from the use of *competitive loads*.

Physical Abilities of Athletic Performance

The purpose of physical preparation is to develop the abilities of endurance, strength, speed, and mobility. These abilities are interrelated in total performance and have been resolved into *complex abilities*. Figure 8–3 illustrates these abilities and their relation to and interaction with other abilities.[4]

Each of these complex abilities contributes differently to the demands of the selected sport and events within that sport. Figure 8–4 shows the relative contribution of complex endurance abilities to long-distance, middle-distance, and short-distance events.[5]

Methodology of Training

The methodology of training constitutes its practical realization. The methodological approach is defined by the *means and methods* of training. The means of training are physical exercises, which are specially selected, organized and formed movements; methods refer to the manner of repetition of the means of training. In training, exercises are divided into two categories: *training* and *competitive*. Training exercises are further subdivided into *general preparatory, special preparatory, exercises from other sports*, and *supplemental exercises*; competitive exercises are subdivided into *competitive, integral competitive*, and *certain forms of special preparatory exercises*.

General physical preparation makes use of general preparatory exercises and exercises from other sports, while specialized physical preparation makes use of special preparatory and integral-competitive exercises.

Figure 8–5 outlines the different training methods. The interval method can be subdivided into extensive-interval, intensive-interval, and repetition methods.

FIGURE 8–3 SCHEMATIC REP-
RESENTATION OF THE RELA-
TIONSHIP OF BASIC FITNESS
CHARACTERISTICS AND THEIR
INVOLVEMENT IN THE SPECIAL
FITNESS REQUIRED OF INDIVID-
UAL DISCIPLINES

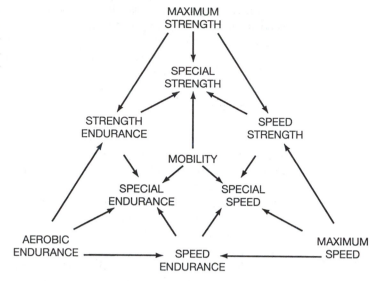

Competitive methods include simulated or actual competitions and training forms
that are known as *model training methods.*

The principal form of implementing the means and methods of training is
the individual training session. The composition of individual training sessions is
broken down into what are known as *training units.* A training unit is defined as
a practice session in pursuit of a single training objective. An individual training
session or workout can be composed of either a single training unit or groups of
training units. When a training unit pursues the development of one physical
ability, but uses different methods and exercises to fulfill the training task, it is
referred to as a *training complex.* An individual training session can be composed
of either one or several training complexes. This is often determined by the
system of training. The best known include the multimethod, complex, and
integrated systems of training.

FIGURE 8–4 INTERRELATION-
SHIPS OF VARIOUS AREAS OF EN-
DURANCE

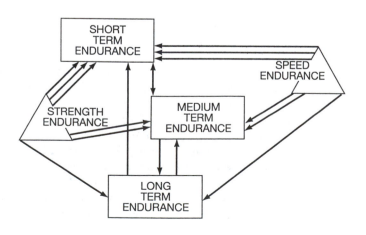

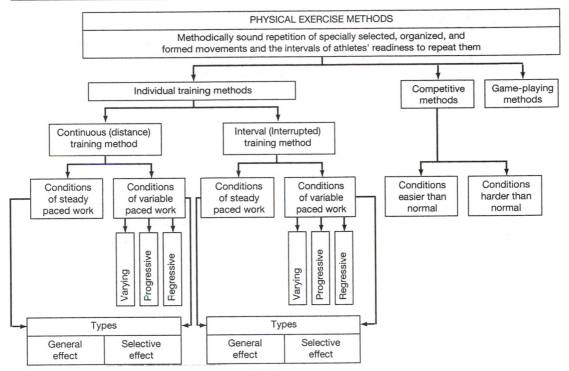

FIGURE 8–5 METHODS OF SPORTS TRAINING

The long-term planning of training organizes individual training sessions into *cycles of training*. The most fundamental of these is the *microcycle* (or weekly cycle of training). Microcycles form the components of monthly, yearly, and multiyear training cycles.

FUNDAMENTALS IN THE DEVELOPMENT OF ENDURANCE ABILITIES

In modern sports classification schemes, competitive swimming is defined as an endurance sport. The quality of endurance alone, without regard to a particular activity or sport, is defined as

1. the ability to resist physical stress over a given time period,
2. the ability to resist fatigue, and
3. the onset of fatigue or time to fatigue.

Fatigue due to the execution of motor action is defined as constituting impaired mental-motor performance and force production, resulting in the reduction of desired performance results. The quality of fatigue, as perceived by the athlete, includes increased effort of maintaining force production, discomfort and pain associated with muscular activity, and perceived impairment of force production.

THE CLASSIFICATION OF ENDURANCE ABILITIES

In sports training science the theoretical notion has evolved that there are different types of endurance abilities. The other physical abilities of strength and speed are obviously interrelated with endurance efforts in the total performance. These different types of endurance are classified on the basis of how much strength and speed contribute to performance.

Aerobic Endurance

Aerobic endurance is seen as an endurance ability to sustain prolonged, continuous effort. It is defined as an endurance ability that makes relatively low demands on strength and speed, with the primary stress being placed on the respiratory and cardiovascular systems. How low or how high the stress is placed on strength or speed depends on the intensity which is controlled by either the duration of the competitive event or the total volume of the training load.

Strength-Endurance

This is a crossover ability, considered as much a quality of strength as a quality of endurance. In strength training, it is the ability to resist fatigue when executing repeated or sustained strength exercises. In endurance training, strength-endurance is defined as the capacity to produce higher muscle tensions or strength efforts under endurance conditions of extreme fatigue.

In a sport like competitive swimming, locomotion through water creates higher factors of resistance than in other endurance sports. It has been found that only minor increases in speed lead to high increases in water resistance, thus, sports endurance is a prime quality in competitive swimming. Competitive swimming is often defined as a strength-endurance sport. In longer- and middle-distance efforts, performance is often rated on a strength-endurance index, while higher intensity efforts of shorter duration (50 and 100 yard/meter efforts) are rated on a speed-strength endurance index. In many cases the term speed-strength endurance is used to describe maximal speed or sprint-endurance efforts. The term is more appropriately used when defining strength training methods used to increase swimming strength.

Speed-Endurance

Also known as sustained speed or anaerobic endurance (or lactate endurance), speed-endurance is defined as the ability to sustain high speed levels or high quality performance efforts under endurance conditions of extreme fatigue. As the term implies, it is the ability to combine the factors of speed and endurance. The duration of effort is sufficiently prolonged that it should not be confused with the execution of maximal speed in sprint-type efforts. The nature of fatigue in speed-endurance efforts is tied to the predominance of energy acquisition under anaerobic/non-robic conditions.

Sprint-Endurance

Sprint-endurance is also known as maximal speed or speed-strength endurance. It is associated with endurance efforts of extremely short duration, requiring the highest expression of frequency of motor actions. The means of energy acquisition is almost entirely anaerobic/non-robic, but differs from speed-endurance efforts in that the immediately available energy stores are utilized throughout the effort without the onset of glycolysis that would normally occur in more sustained efforts. Fatigue due to metabolic conditions is not the prime cause of impaired performance. The loss of maximal speed output is due to the impairment of the neuromotor system.

THE DIFFERENT LEVELS OF ENDURANCE PREPARATION

There are four levels of endurance preparation. They are defined by the principles of general and specialized preparation: *general endurance preparation, preliminary-specialized* (or specialized foundation endurance preparation), *specialized-endurance preparation*, and *competitive-specific endurance preparation*.

General Endurance

The first type of endurance developed is the process of general endurance. It is defined as the endurance capacity that is non-specific to the demands of the competition and is reflective of other endurance activities not directly associated with the sport. General endurance is developed through the use of general preparatory exercises. The only similarity between these exercises and the competitive exercise is that they should involve the use of cyclic/endurance regimes of work. The aim is to increase the comprehensive physical development, harden the body, and improve the overall health and restorative capacity of the athlete.

Preliminary Specialized or Specialized Foundation Endurance Preparation

This level of endurance preparation involves the execution of the *competitive exercise* (that is, the actual swimming) and is expressed in the ability to do sustained, prolonged efforts of low to moderate intensity. Its main function is to increase the aerobic capacity of the swimmer. Preliminary specialized endurance preparation forms the foundation or training base that ensures the maximal realization of more specialized endurance preparation.

Specialized Endurance Preparation

This type of endurance preparation denotes the ability to execute what are referred to as more *specialized* or *specific* training loads. This comprises endurance loads demanding higher work outputs that nearly approximate competitive intensity, but show deviations in load characteristics that derive internal load responses resulting in adaptations that directly or indirectly ensure the progressive development of specialized endurance.

Competitive-Specific Endurance Preparation

This level of endurance preparation requires the execution of the competitive exercise to achieve near ultimate results under load conditions that are directly specific to the demands of competition. This type of preparation is demonstrated during training sessions that simulate competitive conditions or the actual competitive events themselves that are repeated consistently throughout the competitive season prior to peaking for major competition.

MEANS AND METHODS OF ENDURANCE PREPARATION

The different levels of endurance preparation only establish limited considerations, when determining the types of means and methods used in endurance training. The means and methods used, and how they are used, are controlled by many other theoretical and practical considerations in training.

Basic Load Characteristics of Endurance Methods

Before actual methods are explained, the basic characteristics of endurance training loads must be distinguished. There are two types of loads: *extensive* and *intensive*. Extensive loads are training loads executed at the lower ranges of intensity. To elicit a training effect, high volumes of such loading must be executed. The conditioning qualities developed from extensive loads require a longer training period because the rate of adaptation is very slow. Once these qualities are developed as a result of extensive training, they achieve a high level of stability and potential rate of loss is very low.

Intensive loads are those executed at higher ranges of intensity and in relatively low volumes. The qualities developed from intensive loads are acquired very rapidly, but are unstable and are lost just as quickly as they were developed. One often sees rapid development in performance results from intensive loads, but how these improvements are maintained or stabilized depends on the magnitude of development achieved from extensive loads.

The use of extensive and intensive loads is guided by certain methodological principles: extensive loads by the *constant load principle*, making use of *over distance methods*, the *interval principle*, or the use of *extensive interval methods*. Intensive loads are dictated by the interval principle, involving the use of *intensive interval methods* and *repetition methods*.

Over Distance Methods

These extensive training loads are prolonged, sustained efforts and are not considered to be interval work, which is always characterized by periodic breaks between work bouts. The distance swum is usually in excess of 800 yards/meters, with distances or duration determined by the individual swimmer's tolerance level for sustained effort. *Continuous loads* are over distance loads of extremely high duration, usually in excess of 30 minutes to several hours, reaching the upper limits of very long distance events, such as marathon swimming. *Duration loads* are also over distance loads, but of shorter distance than continuous loads, usually between 800 to 1500 meters.

The intensity of over distance training can be changed to suit various training objectives. In preparatory and compensatory efforts, such as warm-ups, loosen-downs, and so on, the intensity is sufficiently low so that no fatigue develops, and the physical stimulus acts as a means of facilitating recovery. In actual training efforts, the intensity is high enough to increase the intake of oxygen over time, providing the stimulus to increase aerobic capacity. Long-term improvement of aerobic capacity is accomplished by performing increasingly longer loads under aerobic conditions or by using over distance loads that emphasize predetermined increases or variations in intensity over time of workload. With the second form of work, aerobic capacity is increased because the work bout occasionally draws upon anaerobic/non-robic metabolism for its energy requirements. This provides a strong training stimulus to tax the body's capability to acquire oxygen.

Interval Methods

This type of endurance training includes all those endurance methods which follow the interval principle. These methods of swimming involve a series of repeated efforts at a given distance with a controlled amount of rest between efforts. When considering how the intervals should work, the fundamental guiding rule is that the interval be long enough to permit partial, but not complete, recovery between work bouts.

The initial concept of the use of interval training in swimming called for the use of repeat efforts, which were never to be longer than the event for which the swimmer was preparing and which were to be worked at a pace that was either lower than, equivalent to, or greater than the speed of the competitive event. The concept of interval methods as a sequence of very short phases of hard work interrupted by pauses is too narrow a requirement and prevents the full utilization of various workloads arranged in intervals. The external load factors (volume, intensity, and density) can be used within the framework of interval methods to create a variety of approaches in which each interval method is classified on the basis of different criteria.

Interval Methods Based on Duration of a Single Workload   (subdivision of load duration often referred to as a *repeat*). Short distance interval methods utilize single workloads that range from about fifteen seconds to two minutes in duration. Middle-distance methods utilize single workloads that are two to eight minutes in duration. Long-distance interval methods utilize single workloads that are eight to fifteen minutes in duration.

Interval Methods Based on Speed Executed During a Single Workload.   Slow interval training is characterized by slow to medium speeds applied at any duration. Fast interval training is characterized by speeds of moderate to submaximal intensity.

Interval Methods Based on Duration of Interval.   Short rest interval methods make use of five to twenty second rest intervals, usually in association with interval workloads of high duration and low intensity. Long rest interval methods utilize rest intervals from twenty to thirty seconds or longer in association with interval workloads of low duration and high intensity.

Other Variants in the Interval Methods.   There are other conditions that can be introduced when using interval methods. They in turn introduce other methodological approaches. These include: the arrangement of successive workloads, determined by the number of repetitions used and the arrangement of repetitions into sets or series within sets; type of interval used in the interval method, which includes flat or ordinary intervals, such as fifteen seconds' rest between each repeat, and fixed or rigid intervals, such as those which designate departure times rather than a fixed amount of rest (15×100 on 1:15). Both flat and fixed intervals can be constant or varied, and the nature of recovery can be passive or active.

Both constant and extensive interval methods can utilize other variants that can change the nature of the endurance work. These include conditions of both steady and variable pace work. Variable pace work includes progressive, regressive, and varying conditions.

REPETITION METHODS

Repetition methods consist of swimming a series of workloads at a distance that is either equivalent to or less than the competitive event. The main difference between repetition methods and interval methods is that the rest interval is long enough to permit almost complete recovery between workloads.

Repetition training pushes the swimmer closer to the execution of intensive load qualities requiring maximal effort. The intensity of effort depends upon the competitive speed range of the event for which the repetition methods are preparing the athlete. This method definitely pushes the quality of effort into anaerobic/non-robic energy expenditure. It is the main means of inducing high lactic acid accumulation, which, in turn, provides the stress for adaptation to improve anaerobic/lactate endurance (speed-endurance).

In addition, repetition training may also be one of the best methods of improving the special strength qualities of the swimmer's muscles. The increased resistance caused by the greater speed of movement serves as the primary stimulus for strength development while swimming. In repetition training using short workloads, there is a high expression of the speed-strength endurance qualities of muscular effort in swimming. Longer workloads of high intensity place higher demands on strength-endurance qualities.

The interval of rest should be long enough for the swimmer to feel no great discomfort from the previous workload. It should be at least three times longer than it takes to swim the distance of the workload. This holds true particularly on shorter repeat swims, such as 50 to 200 yards/meters, but not necessarily on longer repeats, such as 400 meters or 500 yards or longer. As the swimmer becomes progressively fatigued, a longer rest interval may have to be allowed.

SPECIAL ENDURANCE METHODS: THEIR LOAD FACTORS AND THE THEORETICAL APPROACH TO THEIR EFFECT

In the organizational approach to training, endurance loads and their methodological implementation are categorized on how they fall into a given level of endurance preparation (general or specialized). This is often based on the ability of the endurance loads to elicit a specific physiological effect. Endurance loads are frequently classified into work *zones of intensity*. There are many different zones of intensity schemes. The following is the most universal.

Zone I—Low intensity aerobic (as seen as preparatory and compensatory efforts)

Zone II—High intensity aerobic (including constant efforts below the anaerobic/lactate threshold and efforts at the anaerobic/lactate threshold)

Zone III—Mixed loads (including aerobic-anaerobic/lactate work and anaerobic/lactate-aerobic work)

Zone IV—Anaerobic lactate or glycolytic loads (speed-endurance or anaerobic/lactate endurance)

Zone V—Anaerobic alactate (maximal speed or sprint endurance)

The use of endurance methods to induce selective physiological effects constitutes only one of the theoretical approaches. The other approaches include structuring methods according to the particular needs of the athlete, based on his competitive specialization. General endurance preparation involves the use of training exercises used outside the realm of swimming and is beyond the scope of this book.

Preliminary-Specialized Endurance Training

Preliminary-specialized endurance training uses methods that influence the development of aerobic endurance (work regimes within Zones 1 and 2).

Constant or Over Distance Loads

CONTINUOUS LOADS.   These involve continuous swimming of long distances with durations over ten to thirty minutes for the young swimmer and one to two hours for the mature swimmer.

DURATION LOADS.   Duration loads require over distance interval training in which duration depends on the events under preparation:

long distance—1500 meters or more
middle distance—800 meters or more
sprint distance—400 meters or more

The *percent of aerobic/anaerobic* results from duration loads are 80 to 95 percent aerobic and 20 to 5 percent anaerobic/non-robic. The *target heart rate* for such training is 120 to 140 beats per minute.

Specialized Endurance Training

Specialized endurance training includes several training methods. These include: interval methods that influence the aerobic and anaerobic/non-robic mechanisms in a selective manner; and transitive methods and model training methods.

Interval Training that Affects the Aerobic and Anaerobic/Non-Robic Systems in a Selective Manner. Interval training in the anaerobic/lactate threshold regime involves constant efforts at the threshold of anaerobic/lactate metabolism (second variable of work at Zone 2) and short rest interval training based on the procedures for the establishment of cruise intervals, as described in Chapter 11.

Interval Training in the Anaerobic-Aerobic/Aerobic-Anaerobic Regime (mixed loads: work regimes in Zone 3). This training is of special importance in the preparation of middle-distance and long-distance swimmers. It constitutes much of the specialized training that creates a wide functional shift between the aerobic and anaerobic/non-robic regimes of work. The shift is normally of a progressive nature in either direction, but there may also be an abrupt change in work regime or a widely variational shift between the aerobic and anaerobic/non-robic systems.

The methods used here incorporate both extensive and intensive interval training elements with emphasis on executing them in a variational manner. In sets of repeats in which single work bouts are of long- and middle-distance duration, use is normally made of variational efforts within the single work bout. The work bout can utilize:

1. Gradual variational efforts within individual work bouts.
   a. Progressive build-up: gradual increase from slow to fast (for example, 400 meters—first 100 slow, second 100 moderate, third 100 submaximal, fourth 100 maximal)
   b. Regressive build-down: gradual decrease from fast to slow (for example, 400 meters—first 100 hard, second 100 moderate, third 100 medium, fourth 100 easy)
2. Sudden variational efforts within individual work bouts.
   a. Negative split: easy to hard (for example, 400 meters—first 200 easy, second 200 hard)
   b. Positive split: hard to easy (for example, 400 meters—first 200 hard, second 200 moderate)
   c. Varying conditions: non-uniform shifts (for example, 500 yards—first, third, and last 100 hard, second and fourth easy)

In interval training sets in which the single work bout or repeats are of smaller duration (for example, 50–100 or 200), use is normally made of gradual or sudden variational shifts within the set:

1. Gradual variational efforts within sets of work bouts.
   a. Descend sets, in which each successive repeat is faster than the previous repeat: within an entire set (for example, 4 × 100 descend on 1:10—first 100 easy, second 100 medium, third 100 moderate, fourth 100 hard) or descend series within sets (for example, 9 × 100, descend each 3 × 100)
   b. Ascend sets, in which each successive repeat is slower than the previous repeat: within an entire set or descend series within sets
   c. Varying conditions, in which there are nonuniform shifts within sets (for example, 9 × 100, every other 100 fast, and so on)

Interval Training in the Anaerobic Lactate/Glycolytic Regime   (work regimes in Zone 4: speed-endurance or anaerobic/non-robic-endurance). This specialized endurance approach incorporates the procedure of intensive interval/repetition training methods. Training is connected to the progressive formation of a high oxygen debt and accumulation of excessive lactic acid. This type of work is not used to develop maximal speed or explosive power, but to develop speed endurance or sustained speed in the 50-, 100-, and 200-meter events.

The fundamental load condition is at work in the zone of maximal intensity, constituting primary anaerobic energy acquisition. Intensity should be at 90 percent or above, eliciting heart rates of 170–180 beats per minute or higher.

The duration of the single work bout or repeat is sufficient to introduce endurance factors. The duration of the work bout must be long enough to deplete ATP-PCr stores and initiate onset of glycolysis, but short enough to prevent extreme loss of anaerobic/non-robic work capacity. The work bout should not make use of over distance durations (over 200 meters). Longer-duration workloads prescribed for middle-distance and long-distance swimmers in repetition training or goal sets constitute greater components of aerobic work, but they are still executed at high intensities to create conditions of high lactic acid accumulation.

In certain training theory, anaerobic lactate/lactate endurance training limits the duration of repeats from 50 to 100 or 200 yards/meters, and no more. Thus, repetition training or goal sets for sprinters constitute anaerobic lactate/lactate endurance training, but anaerobic lactate endurance training does not constitute repetition training or goal sets for middle distance and long distance swimmers. In other sports theory, any duration can be used so long as the work is done at an intensity that elicits high lactic acid accumulation. In this case, the work is not so much anaerobic lactate/lactate endurance work as it is *lactate tolerance* work. Such an effect could classify any duration executed under repetition training conditions as anaerobic/non-robic work. In some training literature, lactate tolerance work is the same as anaerobic/lactate threshold work, involving more sustained efforts to produce a more progressive high lactate profile. In either case, the basic rule for the prescribed duration depends on the competitive needs of the swimmer, that is, nearly always at or under race distance.

The interval of rest is usually two, three, or four times longer than the duration of effort. The long period of rest between each repeat swim should permit the heart rate to return to normal, or at least below 100 beats per minute. This depends on the basal heart rate of the individual.

The total number of repetitions depends on the prescribed volume or total distance of anaerobic lactate/lactate endurance work executed in a single training session. This is determined by exemplary load distribution schemes in the periodization of training, which is controlled by the age and/or training capacity of the swimmer. Periodization of training is explained in Chapter 9.

Collegiate and senior level swimmers and well-trained age-group swimmers can go up to 1000 yards/meters in this regime of work. Anaerobic lactate/lactate endurance work of 1500 yards/meters can prove too stressful. Goal sets or repetition training for middle distance and distance swimmers can exceed 2000 yards/meters, but are not as intense and can be classified as more aerobic than anaerobic/non-robic endurance.

Progressive loading in anaerobic lactate/lactate endurance training is often called for. The following rules apply:

1. Conditions for increased loading: increase in duration of repeats (for example, 8 × 50—6 × 100); increase in total number of repetitions (for example, 6 × 100—10 × 100); determining an average intensity of the swim over a given distance (for example, 10 × 100 in 50 seconds per effort on an interval of 3 minutes); or a gradual increase in intensity over the average (for example, 10 × 100 in 48 seconds on 3 minutes).
2. Conditions for unloading: gradual increase in interval of rest and decrease in density (for example, 8 × 100 at 48 seconds on 4 minutes); reduction of total number of repetitions (for example, 10 × 100 to 8 × 100).

The main task of progressive loading is to increase duration and number of repetitions; in unloading, to decrease number of repetitions and density (increase the amount of rest).

Other variations can be introduced in anaerobic lactate work, such as the following:

1. Sets in which distances are mixed.
   a. 2 × 200 meters on 3 to 6 minutes, 3 × 100 on 2:30 to 4 minutes, 6 × 50 meters on 1:30 or 2:30).
   b. 3 × 100 meters on 2:30 to 3:30 minutes, 4 × 75 meters on 2 to 3 minutes, 8 × 50 meters on 1:30 to 2:30 minutes.
   c. 2 × 150 meters on 3 to 4 minutes, 4 × 75 meters on 2 to 3 minutes, 8 × 50 meters on 1:30 to 2:30 minutes.
2. Breaking up sets in which repeats do not have to be consecutive. Sets can be broken into sections and dispersed at various points in the training

session, depending on how complex or demanding the other sets in the training sessions are.

Interval Training in the Anaerobic-Alactate/Alactate Endurance Regime (maximal speed or sprint endurance).   This is a specialized endurance method that incorporates the general approach of intensive interval and repetition training methods. Training is connected to the display of efforts of maximal intensity and of brief duration with prolonged recovery between single work bouts.

The duration of a single workload is no longer than six to ten seconds. In swimming, this normally involves distances of 25 yards or less.

Rest intervals are of such duration as to allow complete recovery between workloads. Prolonged rest periods are advised.

Use should normally be made of series within sets, with interseries intervals of longer duration than rest intervals between repeats within a series. Use can be made of passive or active recovery in interseries intervals.

Number of repetitions within sets is limited to the maximal number beyond which profound loss of maximal speed is experienced. This depends on the work capacity of the individual. The usual number of repetitions within series is three or four and up to six.

Interval Training Aimed at Improving the Strength Component of Special Endurance.   These endurance methods are derivatives of special strength preparation. They involve the use of in-water strength training exercises for the development of strength-endurance and speed-strength endurance. These methods are considered more of an integral part of endurance training than of strength training because the in-water exercises use *free swimming conditions*, and they also make use of strength work delineated by endurance load factors associated with endurance training methods.

This training is connected with the use of additional external resistance (extra weight, extra drag). The main consideration is to rate or gauge the resistance to allow the strength overload to be achieved without loss of swimming technique. The magnitude of the resistance used will be affected by the regime of work utilized. The two main regimes include strength-endurance and speed-strength endurance work. Strength-endurance work will require additional loads of low to moderate magnitude, while speed-strength endurance regimes must be executed with submaximal to maximal loading.

Methods utilized for the development of strength endurance make use of constant loads and extensive interval methods with load conditions equivalent to those used for preliminary-specialized preparation. A variation on this approach in the development of reserve-strength endurance is to execute medium-distance interval work at moderate to submaximal intensities until exhaustion. Methods for the development of speed-strength endurance will make use of intensive interval or repetition training methods. The main emphasis in this type of work is to achieve high intensity efforts of short duration, as in those conditions that are used to develop maximal speed, as in the anaerobic-alactate regime.

Transitive Training.   These special endurance methods, elaborated by Matveyev[6], make use of the general approach of intensive interval and repetition training methods, with two main variants of structuring loads to achieve a selective theoretical effect.

The first variant of transitive methods makes use of the cumulative effects of repeat efforts, that is, each effort is shorter than the duration of the competitive event, but the total sum of repeats considerably exceeds the competitive distance (cumulative overload, sometimes called the summation of discrete loads).

The intensity of effort is equivalent to the speed of the competitive event (within 5 to 10 percent of maximal speed).

The duration of the single work bout depends on the distance of the competitive event. Under-distance repeats are normally used, but the duration must not become too small, especially for longer-duration events.

Rest intervals must be established to maintain quality of effort, while still maintaining the desired cardiovascular output level over the entire course of the exercise.

The total amount of work must be considerably greater than the competitive event, but the excess can vary.

Progressive loading as training capacity increases is accomplished mainly through the shortening of intervals, increasing the duration of each repeat (or discrete load), increasing the number of repeats, and so on (see Figure 8–6).

The second variant of transitive methods makes use of the general approach of intensive interval and repetition training methods. Training work is more prolonged than the competitive distance or duration.

The intensity of effort must be maintained within the related or required work zone, although loss of speed can be expected, depending on duration of training load.

Progressive loading in the second variant is achieved by designating the volume of work that exceeds the duration of competition, then, as the athlete gains in level of trainedness, eventually achieving the intensity parameters equivalent to the competitive event.

Use is normally made of variational efforts within the training work, alternating competitive intensity pace work with work at reduced intensity (mixed loads). Progressive loading in this variant is achieved by gradually increasing the number of laps worked at competitive pace (see Fig. 8–7).

Model Training. Also known as model competition, the full scientific term for model training is *integral-approximated modeling*. This mode of training is so termed because the main theoretical approach is to achieve the closest possible modeling of the competitive event during training. It has been felt for some time that most training never simulates the physiological stress encountered by the swimmer during an actual competitive event. The repetitive use of isolated time trial efforts disrupts the continuity of training, can often prove too exhausting, and can affect the athlete psychologically.

There are several theoretical approaches to model training; the choice depending on the particular demands of the sport. In competitive swimming and other cyclic sports, use is commonly made of a method called *simulators*. The idea is to execute a training load equivalent to the competitive distance, which

---

FIGURE 8–6   EXAMPLES OF TRANSITIVE METHODS THAT USE THE EFFECT OF THE SUMMATION OF DISCRETE LOADS

100/200 events 8 to 10 × 50 at competitive speed range, with 10 to 30 secs. rest; or 6 to 8 × 100 at 90%–95% competition speed range, with 30 to 60 secs. rest.

400/500 events 5 to 8 × 150 to 200 at 95%–100% competitive speed range, with 1 to 2 mins. rest;
4 to 6 × 300 at 90%–95% competitive speed range, with 1 to 3 mins. rest

800/1000 events 4 to 6 × 400 at 90%–95% competitive speed range, with 1 to 3 mins. rest

1500/1650 events 3 to 5 × 800 at 90–100% competitive speed range, with 2 to 5 mins. rest

---

FIGURE 8–7   EXAMPLES OF TRANSITIVE METHODS CONNECTED WITH EXCEEDING THE DURATION OF THE COMPETITIVE EVENT

100/200 events 3 to 4 × 1.5 times 2.0 competitive distance near competitive speed range, with 2 to 6 mins. rest.

400/500 events 800 to 1000 with certain laps or segments of work bout at near competitive speed.

800/1000 events 1000 to 1500 with certain laps or segments of work bout at near competitive speed.

1500/1650 events 2000 or more with certain laps or segments of work bout at near competitive speed.

---

is broken up into smaller work bouts. Each work bout is to be executed at a strictly defined speed that falls within the range required during actual competition. The rest pauses between work bouts are very small: the intervals are rated within five- to fifteen-second limits, depending on the length of the distance covered. Without these pauses it would be difficult to maintain the desired speed, but the use of longer intervals would cause considerable shifts in the functional state of the athlete and approximate modeling of the activity would not be achieved. The duration of each work bout can be the same (that is, all work bouts are the same distance); however, work bouts of varying duration normally are used, with a tendency for the initial work bouts to be of longer duration, tapering to those of shorter duration towards the finish of the total load. The duration of either the longest or shortest work bout and where each falls within the entire structure of the training load depends both on the duration of the competitive distance and how the load is organized to account for regular strengths and deficits within the athlete's performance during initial competition.

Typical examples of simulators based on varying competitive events are listed in Figure 8–8.

If, in a practice situation, the swimmer's heart rate can be elevated to the level it will reach in a race and he can then rest just long enough to allow his heart rate to recover slightly (perhaps from 180 to 170) before continuing the swim, the swimmer will be nearly duplicating the stress encountered in a race, yet the method will not be as exhausting as an all-out time trial. An example of this type of swim for a butterflyer, whose goal for the 200-yard butterfly is 1:51,

FIGURE 8–8.   EXAMPLES OF SIMULATORS SETS

Simulator Total Distance	1st Seg.	R.I.	2nd Seg.	R.I.	3rd Seg.	R.I.	4th Seg.	R.I.	5th Seg.
100	50	5 sec.	25	5 sec.	25				
100	75	5 sec.	25						
200	100	5 sec.	50	5 sec.	25	5 sec.	25		
200	125	5 sec.	50	5 sec.	25				
400	200	10 sec.	100	5 sec.	50	5 sec.	50		
400	250	10 sec.	100	5 sec.	50				
500	200	10 sec.	100	5 sec.	100	5 sec.	50	5 sec.	50
500	250	10 sec.	100	5 sec.	100	5 sec.	50		
800	400	15 sec.	200	10 sec.	100	5 sec.	100		
800	300	15 sec.	200	10 sec.	150	10 sec.	100	5 sec.	50
1500	600	15 sec.	400	10 sec.	200	10 sec.	200	10 sec.	100
1500	500	15 sec.	400	10 sec.	300	10 sec.	200	5 sec.	100

might be as follows: swim 100 yards from a dive in the time the swimmer wants to go out in a race (:53.0 seconds), rest 5 seconds, then swim a 50 yard butterfly in 29 seconds, rest 5 seconds, then swim a 25 in :13.5, rest 5 seconds, then swim another 25 in :13.5. The total swimming time would be 1:49.0, with a total elapsed time of 2:04. If there are pace clocks on both ends of the pool, the swimmer can time himself. By starting when the second hand is on 45, he can cancel out his resting time and read his total swimming time directly from the clock. In this respect this effort is like a broken swim set of repeats (see Chapter 11).

The important considerations in using simulators follow:

1. The rest interval should not be so long enough as to let the pulse rate drop more than fifteen beats. That is, it should adhere to the rule that the rest interval should fall within the five- to fifteen-second limitation.

2. The distance of each succeeding segment of the simulator should be shorter than or the same as the preceding segment.

3. In races of 400 meters or less, the first segment of the simulator should be approximately half the total distance of the race. In longer races, a smaller segment might be used; for example, for a 1500-meter simulator, the first segment might be 500.

4. The total elapsed swimming time should be close to or better than the best the swimmer can swim this event in a race.

Near the end of the simulator the swimmer may have to swim 25s, because this distance accommodates to a short-course pool. Simulators may be used in a 50-meter pool by eliminating the 25s or by directing the swimmer to stop in the middle of the pool, rest five seconds, and then push off the bottom to swim the next 25.

Mistakes made by swimmers in pacing their races are most commonly made in the first half of the race. If a butterflyer wants to learn how to pace a 53 second time for the first 100 yards on the way to his 200-yard race, he can practice swimming isolated 100s in this time. Experience has shown that this type of practice helps somewhat, but an isolated 100 is not the same as a 100 on the way to a longer race.

Through the use of simulators in which the swimmer knows he will get only a short rest before he must continue, he can come closer to creating the same mental as well as physical (or physiological) approach he will want to have in the race. *Except for the race itself, simulators are the best method of teaching pace to swimmers.* In this respect they are even superior to practice time trials. Similar precautions are necessary in using simulators as in all-out time trials, that is, they should be used sparingly. There is the possibility that their excessive use will cause undue fatigue. They should be introduced into the training program after the swimmer has had some basic conditioning; therefore, they best fit into the hard-training and tapering phases of the training schedule.

Competitive-Specific Training. This training involves the rationale that competitions themselves constitute a necessary training stimulus in the total preparatory process. No matter how intensive training becomes, or how training loads themselves are modeled to approximate competitive conditions, the special competitive endurance of the athlete is realized or developed only under competitive conditions—actual or simulated.

There are essentially two different theoretical ideas in the functioning of the structure of competitive-specific training. The first approach, which is based on general sports theory, concludes that competitions should not be treated as isolated events that exist outside the training process and involve the disruption of the continuity of training. Instead, competitive-specific training involves the development of special endurance through an aggregate of training approaches centering around the use of *competitive loads*. Competitive loads must be viewed as to how they affect the total level of trainedness and performance capacity of the athlete.

The second approach concludes that competitions should be treated as isolated events that exist outside the realm of training proper. This view is quite common because competitions themselves do indeed often disrupt the regular day-to-day continuity of training. Many swimmers, even elite swimmers who prepare themselves to excel in major competitions, view previous lower priority competitions as an impediment to achieving ultimate performance gains at the end of a major training plan. But without regular competitions elite performers or athletes with a high training status cannot expect to attain a degree of technical or tactical stimulus high enough to attack competitions with consistent proficiency. In such cases, competitive loads contribute more to competitive experience than they do to a physical stimulus.

The effect of competitive loads upon special endurance training is influenced by a number of factors. These factors include the following:

1. The number of competitions within a training plan—both short term and long term

2. The amount of time between competitions
3. The ratio of training loads to competitive loads
4. The conditions of the competitions themselves, which include:
   a. The importance of the competitions in terms of training or performance goals
   b. The number of events competed in during the competition
   c. The amount of time between competitive events
   d. The amount of time taken for the competition (hours, a day, several days)
   e. Additional factors introduced by the coach during competitions

Number of Competitions within a Training Plan.   There are a number of theoretical approaches to consider when deciding the number of competitions that should be undertaken to enhance competitive-specific endurance. The general theoretical approach dictates that, on a long-term basis, the number and/or frequency of competitions should increase as the state of trainedness of the athlete improves. This is based on the notion that, as the total volume of training loads performed by the swimmer stabilizes and levels off, the total volume of competitive loads should become more of a factor for further development of the training and performance level.

The number of competitions required to enhance competitive-specific endurance is also affected by the length of the season, or, more specifically, by the length of the competitive period or that part of the season in which competitions dominate.

Absolute numbers or frequency are also affected by the specific demands of the sport, the demand placed on the individual athlete in individual competitions, and the number of major competitions for which the athlete prepares in a season. In some team sports, athletes may participate in up to one hundred competitions in a season because the competitions themselves do not constitute an ultimate physical performance demand and actually are the main form of training. In sports like swimming that place great demands on endurance and strength endurance, the number of competitions should be limited and should be planned around the *major* competitions for which the swimmer will have to rest and peak, if optimal performance is to be attained. The optimum number of competitions the swimmer requires should be the number needed to optimally develop and stabilize competitive-specific endurance, but no more.

With too high an incidence of competitions, there is the danger that the general and specialized endurance state will not develop according to plan. It is generally agreed that only after years of carefully regulated preparatory work can an athlete use competitions or competitive loads as a main means of improving results.

Amount of Time between Competitions.   If competitions are viewed as *competitive loads*, with training effects that further enhance special endurance, the time periods between competitions should be gauged to allow a *cumulative* effect of training. Too long an interval between competitions may well result in losing the training effects of previous competitions. The nature of the training effect of competitive loads and how long they last depend on the demands of the competition: the more exhaustive the competition, the greater the time period allotted or needed for the realization of training benefits. In sports or particular competitions in which the demand is not excessively high and recovery occurs quickly, it has been found that the ideal interval between competitions, allowing the best cumulative training effect of competitive loads, is seven to nine days. Beyond nine days the effect of competitive loads may be lost. Shorter intervals between competitions performed over time periods of three weeks or longer may ensure a high degree of execution of competitive loads, but this can still disrupt the level of the training state and result in loss of work capacity. Work capacity can diminish through the combined factors of disruption of training loads, cumulative fatigue, and competitive staleness.

Ratio of Training Loads to Competitive Loads. The ratio of training loads to competitive loads varies in accordance with an aggregate of training factors that are figured into the organizational training scheme dictated by the periodization of training. How training is periodized, that is, how training quantitatively expresses changes in load distribution or how training loads are altered to meet specific competitive needs, is affected by the age, training level, and competitive performance level of the athlete. This not only includes consideration of physical preparedness, but also the psychological state of the athlete to accept changes in the training loads during phases in the organization scheme in which competitions are frequent. If the laws of periodization are adhered to, it is obvious that the ratio of training loads to competitive loads will shift in different phases of the seasonal plan. Of critical importance is the determination of this ratio in the phases of the season in which competitions are frequent, or when the athlete approaches and prepares for major competition. The main function of determining this ratio is to ensure that the training level is maintained during competition without the training loads themselves lowering work capacity to the point of adversely affecting competitive results.

Conditions of the Competitions Themselves. How the conditions of the competitions themselves will influence the effect of competitive loads upon competitive-specific endurance is first assessed by declaring the degree of difficulty of the competitions. They are classified as main (or peak) competitions, preparatory competitions, and training (or controlled) competitions. The next variable involves determining the overall volume and demand that is encountered in each competition regardless of its classification, such as the number of individual events to be swum in each, the time between events, the amount of time taken for competition, and any additional factors the coach may introduce during competition.

The general approach in the use of competitive loads calls for a rational and systematic distribution of training, preparatory, and main competitions throughout the season. The distribution of training and preparatory competitions must be such as to allow their cumulative effect to help the athlete achieve peak competitive-specific endurance during main competitions. In competitive swimming there should be only a few main or peak competitions per year. Championship meets, qualifying meets to participate in championship meets, and national or international competitions qualify as main or ultimate competitions. The general rule, when applied to structuring the effects of competitive loads, is to progressively increase the volume or the overall demand (degree of difficulty) of competitions or both in order to achieve an increased cumulative training effect as the swimmer's trainedness increases.

The yearly plan should be such that competitive loads increase in their training effect as the season progresses. Main competitions should themselves also increase in difficulty in order to increase the effect of competitive loads. How increased demand in competitive loads is structured depends on factors already mentioned (number and distribution), and factors introduced within each individual competition.

It is obvious that volume or the demand of competition is increased if *the number of individual events* is greater than in the past. Younger swimmers compete in numerous events, but normally such events are of relatively small demand due to the prevalent use of short-duration events. As the swimmer matures and the events involve greater distances and higher competitive demands, the coach must resort to different schemes of structuring increases in the volume of competitive loads, which also consider the increased level of specialized preparedness of the swimmer. The duration of each individual event is of prime importance. One cannot expect even a well-trained swimmer to execute a high frequency of long-duration events, since the energy expenditure would be too high and would require longer periods of recovery between events than the competition would allow.

Increasing the amount of time between events (decreasing the density of competitive events) also has the effect of increasing the training stimulus of competitive loads. The duration or overall demand of each particular event must first be considered, then the time proximity between individual events should be assessed. Determining the effects of participation in numerous events and the close proximity of events not only allows the coach to assess the effects of competitive loads, but also allows him to evaluate the overall training endurance of the swimmer. If work capacity and performance diminish too rapidly, training or the competitive loads themselves must be reassessed to ascertain whether or not the demands are unreasonable.

Successive days of competition offer the best conditions for evaluating the effects of high volumes of competitive loads. In such competitions, swimmers are often required to execute the same events several times a day. Recovery from initial efforts and approximating or excelling previous efforts offers the best training effects of competitive loads and ensures a high volume of execution. Two to three successive days of competition require that the overall endurance state be carefully monitored, since such competition can disrupt training and lead to the necessity for considerable periods of recovery.

To heighten the effect of competitive loads, *coaches may introduce additional factors* that increase the overall volume of competitive loads or increase the degree of difficulty in competition, when scheduling or rules of competition prohibit further attempts to increase competitive loading. Coaches may increase the number of training competitions or deepen training effects by other means.

In training competitions, the coach may want to restructure or control variants of competitive conditions that increase the volume of difficulty of competitive training efforts. This may include frequent repetition of competitive events or changing the duration of events to achieve an increase or partial modeling of actual competitive events.

During actual competitions, coaches may deepen training effects through different means. These include the introduction of training loads on the same day or the day following competitions, or swimming alternative events at intensity levels approximating those of other events with the emphasis of achieving either increased or partial modeling of competitive efforts of those other events.

It is important to remember that the effects of competitive loads must be brought into question if the competitive loads themselves are executed at efforts that fall short of minimal performance expectations. This is especially problematic in endurance efforts. The rational use of competitive loads must seriously consider the individual needs of the swimmer.

FUNDAMENTALS IN THE DEVELOPMENT OF SPEED ABILITIES

Defining Speed Abilities

The term *speed*, as used in sport, has assumed special connotations, depending on both the particular sport and the different types of events within that sport. In recent sports training theory it has become prevalent to define separate speed abilities that can be seen as involved directly or indirectly with a particular sports activity or event. These speed abilities include:

1. *The speed of motor reaction.* This can involve the speed of reaction to either simple or complex motor stimuli normally encountered in sport. In competitive swimming, the situation most typically encountered is the reaction to the starter's signal at the beginning of a race.

2. *The speed of separate motor actions.* This ability is essential in sports that depend on the speed of execution of a single movement (acyclic sports). It is also an ability that is gauged within each individual cycle of movement that is repeated frequently within cyclic or endurance sports. It is measured by speed or acceleration indices within either the entire action or components within the entire sequence of the whole movement.

3. *The speed or frequency of motor actions.* This ability is essential in cyclic sports that require the execution of repetitive motor actions. It is often measured on the basis of tempo or frequency of motor actions per unit of time, such as stroke rate. This is the ability required most in competitive swimming for the development of speed.

Specialized Speed Preparation

This level of preparation involves the use of special motor (special-preparatory), integral-competitive, and competitive exercises. These exercises are selected with the idea of allowing partial or whole bodily movement to achieve movement speed, which approximates or exceeds the movement's speed achieved in competition. Such exercises, however, are few and rarely implemented effectively in competitive swimming. Of special consideration in the use of partial or complete competitive exercises are the required load factors that allow the acquisition of maximal or near-maximal speeds throughout the training load deployed for speed development. Such training loads require work bouts of extremely short duration with long periods of recovery between work bouts. These recovery periods help to maintain near-optimal work capacity without the onset of progressive fatigue. In addition to this variant, use is made of special apparatus, which allows the swimmer to exceed ultimate speed levels during the execution of the competitive exercise. These will be described later in this chapter in the section on nonconventional means and methods used in speed training.

Traditional or Conventional Methods

Traditional or conventional methods most commonly employed in speed training are sprint training (maximal speed) or anaerobic alactate training. This type of training consists of maximal or near-maximal efforts of short distance, and, as the term anaerobic alactate implies, without oxygen and without a build-up of lactate in the blood. The energy requirements for such work depend entirely upon the immediately available stores of energy (phosphocreatine and intramuscular stores of ATP). Such energy is available for maximal efforts of anywhere from six to ten seconds. Beyond this duration the anaerobic mechanism of glycolysis furnishes the energy for high-intensity work and lactic acid begins to accumulate.

This sets a limitation on what distance can be considered a sprint. The distance chosen depends on the maximal speed the swimmer can achieve, which is normally age-dependent. Young swimmers in initial training should be limited to sprints of 10 yards/meters. As the athlete matures and his level of trainedness improves, sprint distances should be expanded to 20 or 25 yards/meters. Greater distances exceed sprint-endurance capacity and make greater demands on speed-endurance.

The variants of sprint training include the following: straight goal sprints, alternating sprints, and alternate sprints.

Straight Goal Sprints. These are sprints of maximal or ultimate speed, based on the repetition method of endurance training, normally performed with a racing start, and with or without a turn. They feature long periods of rest between repeats (for example, 6 × 15 to 25 yards/meters with racing start; maximal speed; two to five minutes between repeats) and a low frequency of repeats, the total number determined by eventual loss of quality of performance. Progressive overloading is achieved mainly through the acquisition of faster performance times while setting limitations on the total volume of work and rest between workloads.

Alternating Sprints. These are sprints at maximal or near-maximal effort based on either the intensive interval or repetition method, while making use of the variational approach. They can be done with a high frequency of repeats (20 to

30 × 25 yards/meters or more) and can be executed as a straight set or in a series (5 × 4 × 25 yards/meters). With the execution of a high frequency of repeats, the amount of rest interval designated is limited to 30 to 60 seconds. The intensity is varied within each repeat for a number of theoretical training efforts. (For example, a training base may require 20 × 25 yards/meters done in a series of 4 × 25 yards/meters in which a designated sequence follows this pattern: first 25—12½yards/meters at all-out speed, 12½yards/meters of easy swimming; second 25—12½yards/meters easy swimming, 12½yards/meters all-out sprint; third 25—progressive swims in which the pace is built up gradually until the swimmer is going all-out; fourth 25—entire length is swum at maximal speed.) Other variations in the use of variable sprints, that is, how they are distributed or structured within the series or set, can be established. Variable sprints in which the first 12½yards/meters are executed at top speed are effective for developing speed strength in the push-off, initiating high locomotor velocity, and helping to develop the accelerative capacity of the swimmer. Variable sprints in which the second 12½yards/meters are executed at top speed train the swimmer to change the tempo and rhythm of cyclic activity quickly. They also serve as an important training base for enhancing both the speed and speed-strength characteristics of the movement. The execution of higher workloads with shorter rest does not usually result in significant blood lactate increase, and overload can be achieved by increasing the number of repeat swims with only marginal decreases in the level of rest.

Alternate Sprints. These are sprints at maximum speed with 15 to 25 yards/meters of easy swimming, utilizing the intensive interval or repetition approach with active recovery between work bouts (for example, 20 × 25 yards/meters in which swimmers sprint the first 25 maximum effort and swim back slowly, starting the fast 25 on total intervals of sixty seconds to two minutes.) Active recovery serves as an effective means of eliciting faster recovery between workloads. There is very little build-up of blood lactate, unless attempts to achieve overload expand sets to 40 × 25 or more. In this case sets should be broken down into series, such as 2 × 20 × 25 yards/meters with 100, 200, or more yards/meters of easy swimming between series.

In addition to whole technique competitive exercises, partial exercises such as kicking or pulling, or combinations of both whole and partial technique exercises can be utilized within these types of maximal speed work.

Nonconventional Method Techniques to Enhance Maximal Speed

In addition to traditional sprint-endurance techniques, other methods have been developed in a further attempt to provide different training stimuli to enhance maximal speed capability. Some of the proposed methods are described here.

The Leading Method. This method involves the use of a visual object that *leads* the swimmer to achieve the necessary speed. The swimmer is required to follow or keep pace with some object that establishes the required speed and/or establishes conditions which help reduce the conditions of resistance normally encountered in the activity. For example, a boat or other object can create tail suction, which helps reduce frontal water resistance and pulls the swimmer along at greater speeds than he can swim. This method has a variety of uses in other sports, but its use is limited in competitive swimming. Underwater light pulse tracking devices have been developed but have seen limited use in swimming. They have a more likely utility in pace work for distance events than for the development of maximal speed.

In general, the method establishes certain speed parameters through the use of special devices such as sound pacers, light pacers, object pacers, and so on. Devices such as these have been developed for swimming, but have seen limited application.

Variable Resistance Method.   This method is based on the notion that movement speed may temporarily increase under *lightened* conditions, that is, after having previously executed the same exercise with additional weight. This is due in part to a residual activation of the nervous system. In swimming, this can mean executing a sprint or a given repetition of sprints, following an execution of sprints while wearing a dry suit or weight belt. The variable resistance approach also advises the execution of sprints following the use of a given number of repeated sprints under lightened conditions in which the methods of speed-assisted training are utilized. Additional research in the variable resistance method advises the use of a complex of all conditions within one session, the best combination not having been precisely determined in competitive swimming. Experience in application suggests a different variety of regimes can be utilized. The authors consider the following two to be the best combinations:

Additional Resistance Conditions	———	Normal Conditions	———	Speed Assisted Conditions
Additional Resistance	———	Speed Assisted Conditions	———	Normal Conditions

The precise execution in terms of the number of repetitions, the degree of loading under additional resistance, and other factors under consideration must be experimented with in practice and individualized to the needs of each swimmer.

Additional Acceleration Method.   This method attempts to impose a higher level of acceleration during the acceleration phase of sprinting. The acceleration phase of sprinting has been studied extensively in track and field, but its existence in competitive swimming is unlikely. Instead of actually accelerating into maximal speed, the swimmer is required to attempt to maintain the speed of the momentum of the racing start into the actual swimming. This involves the proper execution of starting technique as the swimmer enters the glide phase going into the water following the flight phase of the start. The swimmer can, however, create conditions in which additional momentum and speed are imparted to the glide phase. This is accomplished through the use of additional movement, such as the use of a *running* start before entering the water.

The Speed Barrier and Speed-Assisted Training Method.   The use of speed-assisted training is associated with attempts to utilize training to help the athlete break the so-called *speed barrier*. The speed barrier must not be viewed as an absolute that sets limitations on high level performance, but as a barrier that limits the development of a swimmer's basic speed abilities.

The limiting factor is usually associated with the development of *movement stereotypes*. Movement stereotypes can occur as a result of improper training which disrupts the normal or desired course of preparation. This includes the development of proper movement skill. In competitive swimming poor stroke mechanics or counter-productive additional movement, the ability to achieve the desired pattern of hand acceleration may contribute to this phenomenon. In addition to poor technical preparation, other factors contributing to the speed barrier are oversprinting the young swimmer or neglecting the speed-strength preparation of the older athlete.

The use of speed-assisted training in swimming focuses on the idea that lightened or *overspeed* conditions allow swimmers to achieve swimming velocities that cannot be achieved under normal or unaided conditions. Experiencing greater swimming speed, it is hoped, will provide different sensory input into the nervous system, which will allow the swimmer to adjust the required movement patterns and movement speed and break out of the movement stereotype.

Speed-assisted training requires the use of special apparatus or special swimming environments in order to achieve greater than normal speeds. In competitive swimming such apparatuses include:

1. Swimming under more buoyant conditions, such as swimming in salt water
2. Swimming with, not against, moving water, such as swimming a river or sea current, or in a wave-generating pool, or in tail suction under *leading* conditions
3. Swimming under forced conditions, such as against the current of a flume while being held stationary in a harness
4. Swimming with the use of swim fins, hand paddles, or both
5. Swimming while being towed by a boat or by a special device which pulls the swimmer through the water at greater than normal speeds, such as a Sprint Master, an electric winch, a specially modified commercial electric fishing reel, or a reel with a hand crank

In research concerned with the use of speed-assisted training, it has been discovered that there exists a critical *speed range* above the normal swimming speed that must be adhered to in order to achieve a training effect or transfer of training effect. Achieving excessively high speeds above the critical speed range usually results in loss of technique and the hydrodynamic conditions not normally encountered in competitive swimming, such as an unusually high bow wave. The authors' research indicates that speeds beyond 6 to 8 percent above maximal speed no longer possess any major training benefit for increasing maximal speed.

Regardless of the level of speed preparation and the means and methods used, all speed exercises that play a role in the more selective development of speed abilities must be viewed as strictly *rationed* exercises within the total preparatory process.

Speed exercises place great demands on the neuromuscular system, and the amount of speed work within either the single training session or yearly training plan must be kept at a relatively low level. Training to enhance speed must take place when work capacity is optimum and must not follow training that places great demands on the body, such as training loads to develop speed-endurance or changes in training loads that place greater demands on other physical abilities. It must also be remembered that maximal speed plays a limited role in competitive swimming. Even though events like the 50- and 100-yard/meter are called "sprint" events, in competitive swimming such events place more demands on the speed-endurance capability of the swimmer than on maximal speed. The role of maximal speed or speed abilities proper will always play a subordinate role to the development of endurance abilities in this sport.

PSYCHOLOGICAL PREPARATION

Psychological preparation involves training the mental volitional aspects of the athlete's personality. This is to achieve an optimal psychic state needed for both competition and training. Most of the methodology concentrates on immediate psychological preparation for competition, but total psychological preparation is a training process that is integral to the principles of all other levels of preparation.

Immediate psychological preparation is divided into three areas: *ideomotor, psychoemotional*, and *volitional* preparedness. Although they are treated as separate psychic entities, their interaction is high, the relative proportion being determined by the individual's sports character.

Ideomotor preparedness pertains to control of sports technique by an idea. Ermolaeva[7] divides ideomotor preparedness into two psychological categories: *motor image* and *motor orientation*. Motor image is the sum of notions in the athlete's mind about the structure of the sports activity: the technique of the sports movement, the competitive event, and the environment in which it takes place. Motor orientation is the inner readiness to carry out a trained skill in a strictly defined way. The ability of motor imagery and motor orientation is partially consolidated in both technical and physical preparation. This does not guarantee the development of concentration and the fixed attention that is required. Special psychological training, known as ideomotor training as well as *hypnoideomotor* training, is often required to enhance these psychic faculties. Such training is referred to as *mental imagery* or *mental rehearsal*.

While an athlete's level of ideomotor preparedness can be high, training and competitive performance can be enhanced or disrupted by the athlete's emotional state. This is a collective mental state that is determined by the presence of *negative* or *positive* emotions (also known as sthenic or asthenic emotions), as well as by the magnitude of the emotional state, often referred to as the level of *excitation* or *arousal*. The quantity and quality of emotions have a direct effect on both the general feelings of the athlete and the specific sports emotions that relate directly to competition. The training used to achieve what is considered an optimal emotional state is referred to as *autogenic training*, which uses methods of *self-regulation*.

Volitional preparedness depends on the demands of the sport. In an endurance sport such as competitive swimming, the psychological qualities of persistence, self-control, force of will, and mental buoyancy are factored as the primary characteristics of volitional preparedness. In addition to being a psychological quality, volitional preparedness has also been found to be a psycho-physiological quality. Monogarov[8] cites volitional capability as a prime factor in the compensating mechanisms for exercise-induced fatigue. This allows for the neuromuscular capability of replacing fatigued, weakly functioning motor elements with higher threshold, stronger functioning motor elements. This permits the athlete to sustain or increase work output, even under conditions of increasing fatigue. This is the true nature of *endurance reserves* so commonly cited in exceptional sports performance. In many cases, the large training demands placed on competitive swimmers in high level programs are conducted more for training volitional capability than to increase organic capacity.

Assessment of Psychic Qualities

To assess ideomotor capability in an individual, scientific techniques that measure concentration and fixed attention are utilized. The most sophisticated is the use of electro-encephalographic techniques to measure the activity of certain cortical centers in the brain. Their examination is based on the *principle of dominance*, which stipulates that concentration is enhanced when certain cortical nerve centers are able to increase their levels of stimulation and dominate other centers in order to filter out minor random external stimuli and create a focal point of excitement or stimulation in the cerebral cortex.

Assessment of psychoemotional preparedness is done primarily through the use of personality tests and scientific techniques that measure the electrical activity in the skin. A vast array of personality tests to determine an athlete's emotional state is available. The most interesting is one offered by Mazurov and Korneev[9] that combines the use of questionnaires and methods to assess psychological tension, using indices of physiological functions, such as heart rate, reflex time, reaction time, and so on. They determined three psychoemotional indices: *psychological tonus*, which refers to the activeness or passiveness of the athlete's attitude toward his performed activities; *emotional tone*, which refers to the intensity of the athlete's positive and negative experiences; and *psychological tension*, which refers to the athlete's emotional excitement level.

Assessment of volitional capability is done mainly through performance tests in training and also through electromyographic studies to measure the strength of increased electrical activity in the muscles during exercise-induced fatigue.

The tests of ideomotor and volitional capability can offer some objective indices. Psychoemotional assessment still tends to offer relative interpretations of what constitutes the optimal emotional state for immediate psychological preparation. It is often referred to in loaded terms that stress the *positive* aspect of personality traits. Such terms as high-spiritedness, no gloominess, always being cheerful, having an elevated mood, a happy, joyful frame of mind, and always ready for action are typical. The factors that are considered to give rise to negative emotions include negative personality and character traits, poor self-assessment, too low a level of self-presence, poor motivation, and an unstable mentality that produces extreme physical and neuropsychological tension during competition. The level of psychological tension displayed at the moment of competition is often referred to as *start fever* or *start apathy*.

Hierarchy of Psychological Preparation

To achieve the desired levels of ideomotor, psychoemotional, and volitional preparedness, the athlete must ascend a hierarchical structure of total physical preparation. This hierarchy has been adapted from Maslow's Hierarchy of Needs[10] and incorporates methods of both general and sports psychology. The succession of the different levels of psychological preparation include:

1. the psychological hygiene of the athlete/member of society,
2. the general psychological preparation of the athlete,
3. special psychological preparation for training and competition,
4. psychological preparation for certain competitions,
5. psychological readiness for competition, and
6. mobilizational readiness for a specific competitive event.

Psychological preparation is a long educational process, while psychological readiness is a relatively brief period of adjusting the psychic state prior to competition. Mobilizational readiness refers to the level of psychological readiness in one competitive instance. The ultimate goal of psychological preparation is to optimize mobilizational readiness. It is felt that this cannot be achieved until the athlete has successfully fulfilled total psychological preparation, beginning with the base of the hierarchy.

Psychological Hygiene

In the discussion of overtraining, Harre[11] cites psychological hygiene as being the main factor in *failing adaptation*. This acknowledges the cumulative effect of both physical and mental stress factors, which interfere with the training process of the athlete. Factors of psychological hygiene are categorically listed as *way of life* and *environment*. Fig. 8–9 lists these hygienic factors.

In many cases, the athlete's psychological hygiene represents the greatest impediment in the total psychological preparation. In these instances, additional psychological consultation is required, which makes use of various strategies developed by general psychology. A complex program utilizing both behavioral and humanistic psychological strategies is the best approach.

General and Special
Psychological Preparation

General psychological preparation involves the development of *athletic character*. This includes the establishment of proper long-term motivation, appropriate sport-ethics behavior, and comprehensive educational and intellectual development for sport. Special psychological preparation involves volitional, ideomotor, and autogenic training.

Volitional Training

As mentioned earlier, the methods of training to increase volitional capability depend on the qualities of will that are needed for the sport, as well as the individual needs of the athlete. Training to increase courage or precision are subordinate to the role of methods of increasing psychological endurance and self-control in competitive swimming.

Increasing volitional capability is strongly interrelated with psychological hygiene and general psychological preparation. The ability to adhere to the strictures of a proper lifestyle and to follow the code of sports ethics is in itself a powerful volitional capability.

The three specialized methods of volitional training include: educating the athlete to fulfill the demands of the training program, introducing additional difficulties in the training process, and increasing the demands of competitive situations.

The first method is simple and obvious. The athlete must be taught to carry out training without hesitation or vacillation. The athlete must finish the assigned training. The athlete must finish the sets and repeats without quitting. The athlete must put forth the required effort in sets and repeats without giving in to discomfort and fatigue. The fulfillment of training requirements not only enhances will, but prevents the development of psychological barriers in training.

Often the coach will introduce unusually difficult training tasks as a means of disrupting the psychological equilibrium that has developed from routine training by making exceptional demands on volitional capabilities. These methods include: unusually prolonged training sessions; introduction of unannounced sets and repeats during the training session, especially at the end of the session; introduction of sets with difficult training tasks (i.e., 1000 yard/meter butterfly or sets with difficult or near-impossible departure intervals), use of strength-endurance methods in creating difficult endurance loading conditions, and introduction of regular motivational situations in training (i.e., goal setting for training loads, times to beat, competitive situations in practice sessions, and so forth).

Competitions must be scheduled and implemented in such a way as to make regular demands on volitional capability. The athlete must be exposed to regular competitive loading in order to become accustomed to the demands of competition. The long-term growth of volitional effort must be accompanied by increased numbers of competitions and increased demands placed on the athletes in the competitions. In addition, the coach should introduce unusually difficult impedi-

FIGURE 8–9. PSYCHOLOGICAL HYGIENIC FACTORS AFFECTING TOTAL PSYCHOLOGICAL PREPARATION (adapted from Harre, 1981)

Living habits	Environmental influences	Material conditions
Sufficient sleep	Untroubled family life	High-standard training facilities
Regular daily schedule	Family members, teachers and colleagues at work have a positive attitude to sports and encourage participation	High-standard training equipment (athletic clothing, footwear)
Optimum diet		High-standard training apparatus
Avoiding stimulating drugs (alcohol, nicotine, caffeine)	Comradely team-mates	
Normal, regular sex life	Stable relations of mutual confidence between athletes, between athletes and coach, between sports physician and athlete	
Regular body hygiene		
Sensible, relaxing leisure activities	Job satisfaction, success at work, in studies or at school, clear career prospects	
Proper living conditions in quiet neighborhood with clean air	Coordinated occupation through training, job, school	
	Short commuting distances to job and training facility	
	Certain territorial and climatic conditions	

Factors reducing performance

Way of life	Environment	Health problems
Insufficient sleep; irregular daily routine; loose conduct; consumption of alcohol and nicotine; excessive consumption of caffeine; poor housing conditions (noise, overcrowded rooms, inadequate lighting and other factors); disturbed communal life; lack of leisure time or unfitness for leisure time (no relaxation); deficient nutrition (lack of vitamins), rushing things; frequent 'gaining of weight'	Family responsibilities; tensions in the family (parents, husband/wife), unhappy love affair, jealousy; unsatisfactory job; irritation and quarrels with superiors and colleagues; too much to cope with in profession, study, school; bad appraisals and marks at school, university, etc., continuous struggle against others hostile to sport (family, superiors and others); subjection to external stimuli (TV, cinema)	Feverish colds; gastrointestinal complaints; chronic suppuration (tonsils, jaws, ovaries, frontal sinus); aftereffects of infectious diseases (angina, scarlet fever and others)

FIGURE 8–9. *(continued)*

Signs of overloading

Psychological signs	Performance symptoms	Somatic-functional symptoms
Increased irritability; tendency towards hysteria, grumbling, defiance; increased quarrelsomeness; lack of contact with coach and fellow athletes; oversensitivity about criticism *or* growing inertia; weak driving force; listlessness; obsessions; anxiety; depressions; melancholy; insecurity	*Coordination of movement:* increased susceptibility to disturbances in movement (appearance of errors that seemed to have been overcome, spasms, inhibitions, insecurity); disturbances in the rhythm and flow of movement; loss in powers of concentration; diminishing ability of differentiation and correction *Condition:* lowering of endurance, strength and speed abilities, recovery periods become longer; loss of 'sprightliness' *Competing qualities:* decreasing enthusiasm for competition; fear of competition; failure in difficult situations, especially in a finish; panic in competing, abandoning own tactical skill; strong susceptibility to demoralising influences before and during competitions; growing tendency to give up competing	Insomnia; anorexia; loss of weight; disturbance of the gastro-intestinal functions; frequent dizziness; slight perspiration; increased susceptibility to injuries and infectious diseases; lowering of vital capacity; prolonged pulse recovery etc.

ments in both training and actual competitions. The designation of nonspecialized events, the assignment of high numbers of competitive events within the competition, and partial competitive goals within competitive events—these factors and others can be used to increase volitional capability.

Ideomotor Training

Ideomotor preparation is considered an integral part of technical preparation. Ozolin[12] has recommended a variety of techniques and exercises that can be classified as ideomotor exercises in that they provide significant or relevant *feedback* to the athlete toward the enhancement of mental imagery. Most methods in technical training involve producing the movement, then evaluating and correcting it. Ideomotor training involves a reverse approach, in which a mental image of the movement forms in the brain, then the movement is carried out.

The success of ideomotor training depends on the completeness of the athletes' conceptualization of their actions. They must receive preliminary education in sports technique and be exposed regularly to visual media in the form of photographs, films, and videos. In the actual ideomotor training, the athlete is often placed in a dark room in which distracting sensory input is limited. The athletes are exposed to the proper visual media and then shown films or videos of themselves while executing the sports exercise and/or engaging in actual crucial competitions. Deficiencies and strengths are pointed out at such times.

During such sessions, the athletes are instructed to form mental images of themselves executing perfect technique or peak sports form. The crucial ideomotor training, as pointed out by Alekseev,[13] begins when the athlete is able to break down the ideal motor images into a sequence of elements and to assign *verbal formula* to each element. The verbal formula are repeated habitually to ensure the reinforcement of the mental image. Verbal formula discipline thinking and help achieve highly focused attention. The success of the entire training process is determined by whether the athlete can achieve greater levels of motor orientation, changing the neuromotor input to the muscles to physically realize the movement that has been programmed in the brain. Progress is made when the athlete can decrease the number of verbal formula and condense them into verbal *blocks* that are inclusive of greater numbers of motor elements. This indicates the refinement of concentration as the primary or important motor elements come into greater mental focus, and the smaller, supportive motor elements are trained to function optimally at an almost *subconscious* level.

Omelyanenko and Molonosov[14] have determined that hypnoideomotor training is more effective than ideomotor training. Under the hypnotic state, athletes have been found to achieve a more profound thought concentration and, therefore, vivid figurative thinking as well. The athletes were able to memorize a larger number of maneuvers and technical drills through multiple repetition in hypnotic sleep without the hazard of overworking them. Russian swimmers have been noted to have made regular use of hypnotic training.

Autogenic Training

There are a variety of methods used to help the athlete control his emotional state. Some are very similar to ideomotor training in that they involve forms of autoregulation or self-induced mental strategies that allow them to alter their moods or states of mind. Other forms of autogenic training introduce training and nutritional hygienic factors to help bring about alterations in moods and feelings.

Some methods of autogenic training are interrelated with general psychological preparation. These are often referred to as voluntary situational methods.

This includes voluntary, goal-oriented changes in the athletes' outward expressions which reflect the athletes' emotions, control the orientation of the athletes' attention, switch from negative to positive emotional stimuli, and alter images and thoughts.

The next methods are referred to as *self-suggestion* methods. These are special ways of affecting emotions through second-signal stimuli in the form of self-encouragement, self-calming, and self-commands. The most common usage of such methods is to initiate a calming action to remove excessive psychological tension, then to remobilize and switch to a cheerful and active state.

The next methods involve the use of special training regimes and exercises which have been shown to help the athletes control their emotions. They include exercises that have a calming effect or ideomotor exercises which help to redirect the focus of the athlete. Flexibility training has also been shown to relax the muscles and dissipate physiological tension. Special breathing exercises are also used for the same purpose.

The last methods used in autogenic training involve changing the hygienic conditions of training and competition. Restorative methods, such as massage, self-massage, air ionization, reflexive therapy, acupressure, hydro treatment, sauna, and others fall into this category. In addition, environmental hygiene must be observed. Comfortable living conditions and the use of music to enhance environment are typical examples of environmental hygiene.

Nutritional hygiene is a factor in autogenic training. Foods, such as meat, eggs, and other dairy products, which have an acidifying effect, are used to treat athletes who are said to be in an *addisonoid* state (state of training apathy). Foods with an alkalinizing effect—vegetables, fruits, and so on—are used to treat athletes who have achieved a *basedowoid* state (state of agitation).

When proper use is made of special psychological training, the athlete should be able to mobilize both ideomotor and psychoemotional readiness in a timely and expedient manner. The initial process involves achieving psychic relaxation, then mentally rehearsing both the perfect technical execution of the sports skill and the optimal emotional state. This is collectively termed *visualization*, uniting all psychic processes to achieve the highest state of *mobilizational readiness* for competition.

FOOTNOTES

1. Michael Yessis, Ph.D., prominent sports training scientist and publisher of *The Soviet Sports Review*. Dr. Yessis presently resides in Escondido, California.

2. Leonid Matveyev, *Fundamentals of Sports Training* (Moscow: Progress Publishers, English translators of the revised Russian edition, 1981), p. 24.

3. N. G. Ozolin, "The Components of Sports Preparation," *Teoriya i Praktika Fizicheskoi Kultury*, 1986, 4, 46–49, sec. ref. *The Soviet Sports Review*, 22(4), 1987, 157–161.

4. Frank Dick, *Sports Training Principles* (London: Lepus Books, Harry Kimpton Publishers, Ltd., 1980), p. 170.

5. Dick, *Sports Training Principles*, p. 209.

6. Leonid Matveyev, *Fundamentals of Sports Training*, p. 233–237.

7. M. Ermolaeva, "Psychology in Training," *Legkaya Atletika*, 11, 1988, 10–12.

8. V. D. Monogarov, "Developing and Compensating for Intense Exercise Induced Fatigue," *Teoriya i Praktika Fizicheskoi Kultury*, 4, 1990, 43–46.

9. O. N. Mazurov, and A. S. Korneev, "An Operative Method of Assessing Athletes' Psychological States," *Teoriya i Praktika Fizicheskoi Kultury*, 1, 1984, 5–7.

10. Benjamin Maslow, *Motivation and Personality*, 2nd ed. (New York: Harper & Row Publishers, Inc., 1954.

11. Dietrich Harre, *Principles of Sports Training* (Berlin: Sport Verlag, 1982), pp. 21 and 70.

12. N. G. Ozolin, "Feedback in Training," *Legkaya Atletika*, 12, 1984, 7–9.

13. A. Alekseev, "A Word about Ideomotorics," *Fizkultura i Spovt*, 9, 1988, 24–25.

14. V. I. Omalyanenko and A. S. Molonosov, "Hypnoideomotor Training for Athletes," *Teoriya i Praktika Fizicheskoi Kultury*, 11, 1988, 52–54.

CHAPTER 9

Advanced Theories in the Planning of Training

Nearly everyone agrees that effective training for sports should follow a systematic and organized plan. The term *training plan* can be defined as a logically conceived strategy that controls the process of training to allow the swimmer to achieve predesignated competitive performance objectives. This includes short-term performance goals as well as long-term ones, which extend well into the future of the swimmer's career.

Despite minor variations in their theoretical approach, nearly all training plans have these essential components:

1. *The Plan Period or Time Course of the Training Plan*
   This can be either the entire season or stages within the season. These time periods are nearly always regulated on the basis of the calendar in days, weeks, months, and years and are controlled by the schedule of competitions.

2. *Performance Objectives of the Training Plan*
   Training plans are organized on the basis of performance objectives. They may be (1) *partial* objectives within the total performance requirement of the athlete (for example, achieving a certain time split on a segment of a competitive event); (2) *intermediate*, after certain training goals have been

accomplished (for example, improving a 100-meter freestyle time following a training phase devoted to speed-endurance development), or (3) *ultimate* (for example, winning a national collegiate event, a national or international championship, or an Olympic medal in some or all of the athlete's designated events).

3. *Profile of the Training Plan*

Training plans outline the training objectives, the tasks that will have to be completed, and the time periods within which they must be completed. They define the different training methods and types of training to be employed for each training objective and task, and they determine the proportion of the different types of training which will occur within the different stages within the plan period. These proportions may then be expressed in methodological indices which clarify the distribution of loading in the training plan.

Training plans are based on fundamental concepts, theories, and principles. To understand the plan, it is necessary to understand the logic which underpins the need to control the training process. Verkoshansky[1] has organized the logic of controlling training into three main areas: programming, organization, and management. Figure 9–1 illustrates the observed phenomenon that emerges from the controlling process.

The process of programming, organization, and management is a complex and interrelated one. To illustrate this point, Figure 9–2 demonstrates the logical process involved in the organization of training. What emerges from the process is training theory, which, when considered in relation to other, divergent training concepts, theories, and principles, resolves into the general theory of planning training or, as Verkoshansky terms it, training construction.

TRAINING THEORIES INVOLVED IN THE PLANNING PROCESS

The following sections list the main theoretical approaches used in the planning of training that have come into use in international sports training circles. These theoretical approaches include: *the periodization of training, the cyclic nature of training, and the modeling and systemization of training*.

The Periodization of Training

The modern theory of periodization was first advanced by Matveyev[2] in 1965. This approach divides the training plan into major stages and periods of training to give an organizational structure to the time-course of the training plan. It includes multiyear and annual plans. Multiyear plans direct the training needs of the athletes throughout their training and competitive careers. The multiyear plan is composed of an aggregate of yearly plans, which change in accordance with the level of trainedness and performance capability of the athlete as he progresses through the major stages of the long-term training plan. Within each training year, periodization breaks down the annual plan into major periods of training, which are further broken down into smaller stages of training. The

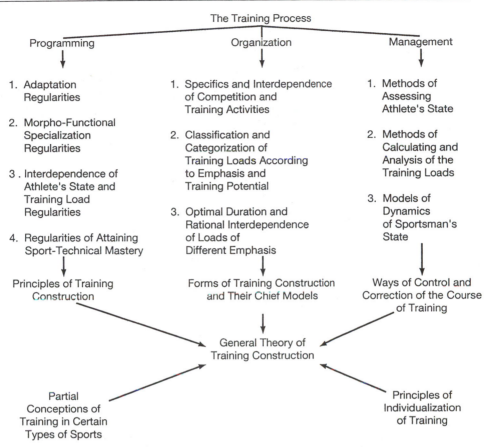

FIGURE 9–1 SCHEME OF A GENERAL THEORY OF TRAINING CONSTRUCTION

objective of annual periodization is to guide the athletes toward achieving peak sports form during major competitions and to ensure their continued growth toward sports mastery.

The Periodization of Multiyear Training Plans. Multiyear plans attempt to regulate the training tasks throughout the swimmers' training and competitive careers. An essential guideline in multiyear plans is the determination of the age ranges in which training should begin, the ages at which athletes should begin specialized training, and the ages at which the highest swimming performance should be achieved. Surveys of elite swimmers have raised the possibility that early specialization in competitive swimming is detrimental to the development and longevity of the swimmers' final career stages.[3]

The data gained from extensive studies of major competitions has lead to a notion of "the age of highest achievement." Separate age brackets have been identified for men and women, with men achieving ultimate sports performance at ages eighteen to nineteen and women achieving ultimate sports performance at ages sixteen to nineteen.

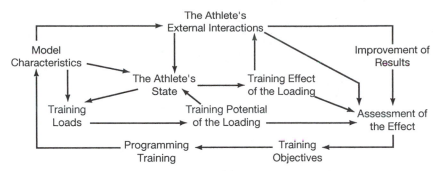

FIGURE 9–2   A LOGICAL SCHEME OF TRAINING ORGANIZATION

On the basis of this data, multiyear training plans have been divided into different major stages of training. Matveyev[4] has divided multiyear training plans into two major stages: (1) the preliminary training stage or Stage 1 and (2) the years of extensive specialization, Stages 2 through 5. Stages 2 through 5 are defined as follows:

Stage 2. Stage of initial specialization

Stage 3. Stage of advanced specialization

Stage 4. Stage of event-specific preparation and sports perfection

Stage 5. Stage of highest mastery

The preliminary training stage apparently runs from age seven through eleven. This stage emphasizes general physical preparedness, which is marked by participation in a wide variety of other sports and movement education, the objective being the promotion of health and harmonious bodily development. Rudiments of aquatic activities are stressed in this stage, with minimal participation in competitive efforts.

Stage 2 marks the beginning of the first stage of training in the base period of the years of extensive specialization. The age range is usually from eleven to twelve. The swimmer should display relative proficiency in all four competitive strokes. Aquatic activities for recreation should continue to be implemented, but the rudiments of structured training should be introduced at this point. The number and frequency of competitions should continue to grow, but should not exceed the athletes' volitional level.

It is during the third stage that the athletes experience rapid growth and maturation. Training must be conducted in such a manner that favorable adaptive restructuring of the biological systems is ensured. This is important because the maturation process can actually lead to performance detriments in competitive swimming. This is especially true in the sports hygiene of the female swimmer.[5] Training in Stage 3 is similar to that of the second stage in that it is marked by increased expansion in both the quality and quantity of training, with a progressive shift to more specialized preparation. In-water training should be of an *all-sided* nature, in which the swimmers prepare for a wide variety of competitive events and distances. The number, frequency, and demands of competition should continue to increase. Competitive results should continue to improve, and it is at this stage that the swimmers should be experiencing their first big successes.

Stage 4 establishes different goals within the preparatory process. Training is entirely specialized, and it is at this point that a leveling-off in the total extent of training should begin to occur. Specialized preparation becomes less all-sided and more event-specific as the swimmers reduce the number and variety of competitive events in favor of those in which they excel. It is usually at this stage that the athletes begin to approximate their highest performance levels and to plan the training process around major competitions.

It is at Stage 5 that the athletes reach the final phase of their careers. The purpose of this stage is to elevate the swimmers to their ultimate performance level, attempting to maintain that level as long as possible. The total volume of training levels off at this stage, but the training demand increases by boosting the volume of high intensity work and reducing the volume of nonspecific, low intensity work. Because sports form has achieved a high level of stability at this stage, the swimmers are able to prepare almost exclusively for major lead-up or ultimate competitions.

When swimmers enter Stage 4 or 5 of the multiyear plan, their probable level of competitive aspiration has been determined. Multiyear training programs are then structured to suit the demands of the calendar of ultimate competitions. For elite athletes this usually takes the form of a two-year cycle, or, more commonly, a four-year training cycle, as in an *Olympic cycle* or *quadrennial plan*. The Olympic cycle is based on the theory of *macrotapering*. This theory establishes a succession of training years in which each year places primary emphasis on the development of one principal physical ability. The succession of years shifts training emphasis to different annual priorities in the development of other physical abilities. The first three years of training attempt a long-term positive, cumulative training effect, while the fourth year culminates with the integral development of these physical abilities toward optimal tapering and peaking for ultimate competition. Some elite athletes, once the ultimate competition has finished, will reinitiate the Olympic cycle.

Figure 9–3 illustrates the fundamentals of quadrennial planning.

The Periodization of the Yearly Training Plan. Multiyear training plans designate only fundamental training tasks within each training year. It is the periodization of the annual plan that begins to establish the specifics of training organization. Periodization breaks down training years or seasons into *plan periods*. There are three main plan periods of training. These include the preparatory period, the competitive period, and the transitional period.

The preparatory period initiates the training plan and constitutes the period of training in which most of the physical preparation of the swimmer is realized. It can be broken down into the general-preparatory and the special-preparatory stages. Traditional periodization alternates these two stages, while other training approaches argue that they should run concurrently. The competitive period is divided into a precompetitive and a competitive stage. Each of these different stages identifies changes in the proportion of training devoted to general and specialized physical preparation.

FIGURE 9–3.   THE FUNDAMENTALS OF QUADRENNIAL PLANNING
(adapted by P. Bergen, 1991, with theory from Hickson, 1980 and
Balyi, 1985)

First year	Second year	Third year	Fourth year
Stamina Skill	Strength Skill	Speed Skill	Full Integration of
(Skill development is limited due to RELATIVE lack of strength and speed,	Endurance Maintenance (will improve!) and Speed	Strength and Endurance Maintenance	Former Years Tapering and Peaking
BUT			Tschiene's Model might be used
to develop strength and speed, endurance is a PRECONDITION			
Thus,			
first year priority is ENDURANCE, secondary is skill, then strength and speed)			

The priority in the preparatory period is the *volume* of training, up to 80 percent of the total training load is executed in this period. The general-preparatory stage promotes the comprehensive development of the swimmers, providing a training foundation upon which more specialized work can be built. Training exercises such as whole body exercise and exercise from other sports dominate this stage. While this promotes the attainment of physical readiness, the special-preparatory stage places emphasis on the development of sports form. The main forms of exercise used in this stage are special-preparatory and integral-competitive exercises. These exercises are executed at high volume and low to moderate intensity for the development of the swimmers' preliminary-specialized preparation.

The competitive period starts with the beginning of the competitive schedule, or that part of the schedule which contains the important lead-up competitions and ends with major competitions. The priority is *intensity*; the total amount of training drops significantly, but the quality of work is higher. In the precompetitive stage, training is strictly specialized as the combination of the training structure and minor competitions perfects the swimmers' level of competitive-specific preparation. In the competitive stage, much of the training prior to major competition is changed to allow extended periods of restoration of work capacity. Often referred to as the taper period, it provides a period of enhanced recovery to achieve superadaptation for peak sports form at the moment of major competition.

The transitional period is the post-competition period of rest and recovery. Training is not discontinued, but the quantity and quality is cut back to maintenance levels. This period is intended to prevent the loss of trainedness detrimental to the next major period of training.

Traditional approaches to periodization base the duration of the major periods and stages on the structure of a single (annual) or double (semiannual) periodized plan, as well as the approach that alternates the stages of general and specialized preparation. Based on this criteria, the preparatory period should last

FIGURE 9–4 VARIANTS OF PERIODIZATION (taken from Bondarchuk, 1986)

VARIANTS	Months											
	10	11	12	1	2	3	4	5	6	7	8	9
1	Preparatory / GPP stage		SP stage		Comp.	Preparatory / GPP stage		SP stage		Comp.		
2	Preparatory / GPP stage		SP stage		Preparatory / GPP stage		SP stage	Competitive				///
3	///	Preparatory			///	Preparatory		Competitive				
4	///	Preparatory		Preparatory				Competitive				
5	Preparatory / GPP stage		SP stage		Comp.	Preparatory / GPP stage		SP stage		Comp.		///
6	///	Preparatory		Comp.	///	Preparatory		Competitive				
7	///	Preparatory		Comp.	Preparatory					Comp.		
8	///	Preparatory / GPP stage				SP stage			Competitive			
9	///	Preparatory			///	Preparatory			Competitive			
10	///	Preparatory			Preparatory					Comp.		
11	///	Preparatory			///	Comp.	Preparatory			Comp.		
12	///	Preparatory / GPP stage				SP stage				Comp.		
13	///	Preparatory			Preparatory							Comp.
14	Preparatory				///	Preparatory				Comp.		///
15	///	Preparatory						Competitive				
16	///	Preparatory						Competitive				
17	///	Preparatory						Competitive				
18	///	Preparatory						Comp.				

The dynamics of biological and pedagogical indices related to the development of sports form.

Note: SP—special preparation; GPP—general physical preparation; Comp—competitive.

from three to four months in a semiannual plan and five to seven months on an annual plan. The competitive period should last from one-and-a-half to two months in double periodization and four to five months in single periodization. The transitional period can last from three to six weeks.

The length of the general-preparatory and special-preparatory stages depends on the age or level of trainedness of the swimmer. For beginning swimmers the general-preparatory stage is much longer than the special-preparatory stage, usually in a ratio of three to one. As the swimmer matures there is a progressive shift that decreases the length of the general-preparatory stage and increases the special-preparatory stage. If the two stages coincide, the proportion of general and special physical preparation relies on plan changes in load distribution. Load distribution will be discussed in a later section.

More recent findings have established new criteria for the length of the yearly plan periods. Bondarchuk[6] has found that periodization should not be determined by the narrow strictures of a one-cycle or two-cycle annual plan. He questions the benefits to be gained from general physical preparation leading to a positive transfer in the development of sports form. Instead, he proposes that the periods be determined by the length of time it takes to achieve peak sports form, arranging the plan periods to suit the individual needs of the athlete and determining whether the general and special physical preparation should alternate or run concurrently in the athletes' training. This approach has resulted in the formation of eighteen variants of periodization over the course of the training year. Figure 9–4 depicts the possible variants of periodization and the variants selected on the basis of the length of time needed to achieve sports form.

As can be seen, the diversity of the plan periods diminishes as the time it takes to achieve sports form increases. In variants 1, 2, 5, 8, and 10, the preparatory periods are based on traditional designs that subdivide the preparatory period into alternating stages of general and special preparation. The other variants are not subdivided into stages because general and special preparation occur simultaneously. If the traditional design is used, the preparatory period should be twice as long, when compared to variants in which general and special preparation coincide.

The Cyclic Nature of Training

Another term that is used to describe the periodization of training is *cycling*. Because of the nature of stress and adaptation, physical preparation tends to assume a recurrent pattern that can be resolved into cycles of training. Many training plans are referred to as either *operative* or *cyclic* plans, based on a succession of training cycles which define the plan period and its stages. Training cycles can be repetitions of previous cycles, but usually they are structured to allow for changes in accordance with training and competitive needs, dictated by the periodization of training. Periodization is necessary to ensure that the program of cycles is synchronized with competitive goals.

There are three types of training cycles. The shortest is the *microcycle*, defined as an aggregate of training sessions. It can be as short as two days, but is usually a week in duration, being referred to as a *weekly cycle*. A longer type of training cycle is the *mesocycle*, which is an average or intermediate cycle. Mesocycles can be as short as two weeks, but are usually a month in duration, and contain a finalized number of microcycles. The longest type of cycle is the *macrocycle*. Macrocycles include annual or semiannual training cycles, also referred to as one-cycle or two-cycle plans within a training year. They also include multiyear training cycles, such as the Olympic quadrennial cycle used by elite athletes.

Macrocycles and Periodization.   Macrocycles simply designate the number and duration of the main periods within each training year. A one-cycle yearly plan consists of one preparatory, one competitive, and one transitional period, while a two-cycle yearly plan consists of two preparatory, two competitive, and one or two transitional periods. Current theory requires a year-long intensification of training which will change the organization of subsequent macrocycles within the yearly plan.

Mesocycles and Periodization.   Most of the literature reveals that mesocycles are themselves the separate stages of periodization in annual or semiannual plan periods. In accordance with prevailing training theory, there are different types of mesocycles with different training tasks that must be resolved within them. Once the periodization of the yearly plan is established, then the sequence and duration of the different mesocycles is set within the preparatory and competitive periods. Figure 9–5 from Harre[7] shows the different types of mesocycles.

FIGURE 9–5. TYPES OF MESOCYCLES FOR THE SUPERVISION OF TRAINING DURING PREPARATORY AND COMPETITIVE PERIODS
(taken from D. Harre, based on Matveyev)

Types (working terms)	Main tasks	Contents
Introductory meso-cycle	Revising and establishing general athletic education	Chiefly or predominantly general training methods; intensity not very high
Basic meso-cycle	Improving the functional level of individual performance factors by stressing selected skills and abilities; learning and improving training	Predominantly special training methods; optimally high load parameters relating to volume and intensity
Preparatory and control meso-cycles	Transforming the individual performance factors which were developed at a higher level, into a new, higher and more complex standard of performance; controlling the performance level	Special training methods, control tests; reinforced measures for rapid recovery
Supplementary meso-cycle	Elimination of known weaknesses, correction of faults, stabilisation of newly acquired skills and abilities	Predominantly special training methods (special exercises); optimum load parameters
Competitive meso-cycle	Putting special emphasis on the build-up of performance; working for flexible and standardised tactics under competitive conditions	High proportion of competitive related load forms; frequent competitions, series of competitions; intensive total load; therefore reinforced measures for a rapid restoration
Intermediate meso-cycle, type A	Further build-up of foundations determining the performance following a series of competitions; eliminating weaknesses	Special exercises for further increase of the level of individual performance factors; little competition; optimum load parameters (extensive, less intensive)
Type B	Restoring and stabilising the standard of performance during a relatively long competitive period	Reinforced application of methods contributing to active recovery (general exercises among others); substantial reduction of demands
Pre-competitive meso-cycle	Optimum expression of the performance and of all performance factors and their stabilisation; preparation for the competitive peak	Sequence of contents according to the kind of introductory, basic and preparatory meso-cycles; highest possible load parameters depending on the main tasks

Among the variants of mesocycles, some remain intact over entire periods or stages of the training process, while others are typical only in certain substages of the different stages of periodization. The latter include control-preparatory mesocycles, intermediate mesocycles, and rehabilitative mesocycles.

In addition, different mesocycles are characterized by the type of training tasks over the course of a plan stage or plan period. They can either be *stimulating*, in which case the training load progressively increases over the course of the stage or cycle, or *stabilizing*, in which case the training load remains relatively uniform. The stimulating cycles usually occur in the initial stages of the plan period, while the stabilizing cycles occur in the final stages prior to major competition.

The arrangement of mesocycles in the following examples is based on the variants of periodization proposed by Bondarchuk (see Figure 9–4). The first arrangement is suitable for a one-cycle, annual plan with a lengthy preparatory period which consists of alternating general- and special-preparatory periods (variants 8 and 12).

Introductory———Base (general-preparatory, stimulating)———Base (general-preparatory, stabilizing)———Base (special-preparatory, stimulating)———Base (special-preparatory, stabilizing)———Precompetitive———Competitive———Transitional.

The following variants occur in an annual plan with a lengthy preparatory period in which general and special preparation coincide (variants 4, 13, and 15 through 18).

Introductory———Base (stimulating)———Base (stabilizing)———Precompetitive———Competitive———Transitional.

The following variants of mesocycles are proposed for a semiannual plan with alternating general and special preparatory stages.

Introductory———Base (general-preparatory)———Base (special-preparatory)———Precompetitive———Competitive———Transitional.

The following arrangement proposes the introduction of substages, precipitated by a lengthy competitive schedule which includes competitions in the preparatory period.

Introductory———Base———Control-preparatory———Base——— Precompetitive———Competitive———Intermediate——— Competitive———Transitional.

The number of possible variants is endless. The sequence of mesocycles selected depends on many training and competitive factors, and the division of the main mesocycles into substages of periodization is the most challenging and creative aspect in the planning of training.

A variation in the arrangement of mesocycles has been proposed by the Russians in resolving the unique requirements of competitive swimming. They frequently use five macrocycles per year, each of eight to eleven weeks' duration, with major competition at the end of each macrocycle and each composed of five mesocycles of one to two weeks' duration. Koshkin identifies these unique types of mesocycles and resolves their training tasks as follows:

1. Entry Mesocycle—the entry mesocycle is devoted to the problems of technique, speed, versatility of complex preparation in the water, and dryland preparation.

2. Starting-in Mesocycle—this mesocycle solves the problems of specific strength preparation of the main style, increase in power without loss of speed or technique.

3. Attack Mesocycle—this mesocycle solves the problems of: maximum development of functional possibilities without loss of technique, speed, or power.

4. Precompetition Mesocycle—this mesocycle solves the problems of meeting all the previously developed qualities into the swimming result (i.e., the creation of supercompensation).

5. Competition and the Rest Cycle.[8]

This arrangement of short macrocycles and mesocycles attempts to modify traditional approaches to periodization in an effort to accommodate the unique demands of the calendar of international competitive swimming.

Microcycles and Periodization. There are two basic categories of microcycles: The first is based on the criteria of training tasks to be accomplished within the periodized plan. These are *training and competitive microcycles*. The second category of microcycles is based on the training load. These are *loading and recovery microcycles*.

Training and competitive microcycles are broken down into other variants which depend upon the different types of mesocycles or stages of training. Figure 9–6 represents the different variants.

Ordinary microcycles are of average training demand, while *shock microcycles* are of much higher training demand, pushing adaptational capacity to the limit. These microcycles are normally used in the base mesocycles. Competitive microcycles include introductory, control-competition, and competition microcycles, used within precompetitive and competitive mesocycles. Both introductory and control-competition microcycles introduce training forms that attempt to simulate competitive conditions which prepare the swimmer for the competition microcycles in which actual competition takes place. Regardless of the type of mesocycle, it usually contains a rehabilitative microcycle to allow recovery from training and competitive demands. This establishes the recurrent pattern of stress and adaptation.

These microcycles are classified by the type of training and competitive tasks they contain, but this categorization does not express the true nature of

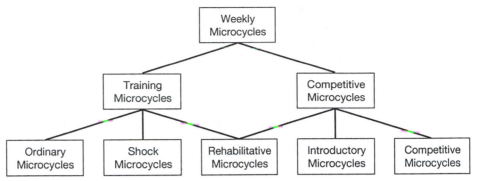

FIGURE 9–6 VARIANTS OF WEEKLY MICROCYCLES

training cycles. The cyclic character of training implies that work and rest must alternate in a given rhythm. As training efforts progressively increase to peak or threshold levels, the training load must be reduced to permit recovery and superadaptation. In accordance with this approach, the microcycle is structured to (1) vary in its training demand to alternate periods of work and recovery and (2) change the training demand between microcycles.

On the basis of these criteria, training microcycles are defined either by their loading *or* recovery characteristics. Mesocycles are usually a finalized number of loading and recovery microcycles expressed as load/recovery ratio. Some of the common load/recovery ratios are 1/1, 2/1, 3/1, and 4/1, in which the first number represents the load factor. Figure 9–7 depicts some of these training cycles.

The significance of expressing training cycles in the major stages of the

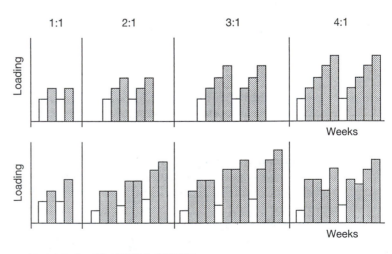

FIGURE 9–7 TRAINING CYCLES

periodized year in terms of loading and recovery microcycles is illustrated in the training model shown in Figure 9–8. The model expresses load-recovery ratios within each mesocycle and training stage, as well as the total load-recovery ratio for the total annual plan. This can change, based on the requirements of the competitive calendar.

The Modeling and Systemization of Training

In recent years, most training plans have been resolved into *training models*. The process of modeling allows for clarification of the structure of training, giving it a quantitative character. It is usually expressed in graphic diagrams, such as flow charts and bar graphs. These graphs represent specific training indices that allow the coach and athlete to understand the relation and interaction of the basic components of training. The most common indices in training models include changes in the external load factors or training loads of different primary emphasis. The most typical of these are changes of training loads of different intensities. Plotted against these indices are such factors as changes in performance results and, more commonly, changes in the work capacity dynamics of the athlete. This allows the sports scientist to assess the influence of training loads upon the athlete's state of trainedness. These comparisons are part of the management of the training process and have enabled sports scientists to evaluate the beneficial or detrimental effects of different approaches to training organization.

Multiyear Training Models.   Multiyear training models express essential data in the form of yearly *maximal loads*. They designate the total volume of loading of certain types of training loads over the course of the annual training plan. In endurance training for swimming, these are expressed as miles or kilometers per year, while strength training is expressed in tons lifted or total number of lifts, or in the amount of hours spent in strength training.

A multiyear training model has been proposed by Guzhalovsky and Mantevich.[9] The model, shown in Figure 9–9, plots the changes in yearly maximal loads for swimmers from age twelve to nineteen. It also breaks down the content of the yearly maximal loading into two indices, based on the five zones of training intensity in the aerobic zones (Zones 1 and 2) and the content of loading in the mixed/anaerobic zones (Zones 3 through 5). Also plotted in the model are changes in the quantity devoted to strength training (expressed in hours per year).

The model not only demonstrates an increase in the total volume of endurance loading from year to year, but also a progressive increase in the overall training demand, with intensive loads assuming a greater proportion of the work. Models for athletes beyond the age of nineteen recommend yearly maximal loads on the basis of event specialization.

Suggested loads for sprinters—2000 to 2400 kilometers

Suggested loads for middle-distance swimmers—2800 to 3000 kilometers

Suggested loads for distance swimmers—3000 to 3500 kilometers

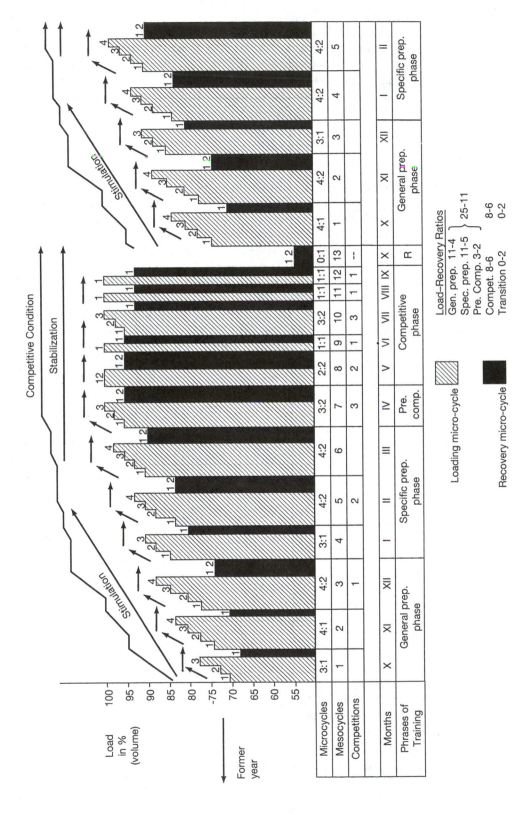

FIGURE 9–8 RATIO OF LOADING AND RECOVERY CYCLES OF AN ANNUAL PLAN

242

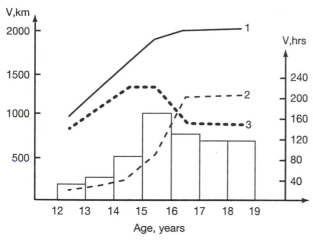

FIGURE 9–9 MULTI-YEAR TRAINING MODEL

(taken from Guzhalovsky & Mantevich)

1 - Total volume of swimming preparation
2 - Volume of swimming in I-II zones of intensity
3 - Volume of swimming in III-IV zones of intensity
right angles - Volumes of strength preparation on land

In multiyear strength training, Mantevich and Petrovich[10] studied long-term specialized strength training and its relationships to individual maturation. They established that the ages of twelve to sixteen for girls and twelve to seventeen for boys were the ranges between which any increased strength in the stroke-executing muscles is usually accompanied by increased stroking power and swimming speed. The recommended yearly maximal strength loading, depending on age, falls within the following ranges:

Twelve to thirteen years—boys: 25–30 hours; girls: 40–50 hours
Thirteen to fourteen years—boys: 40–50 hours; girls: 70–80 hours
Fourteen to fifteen years—boys: 70–80 hours; girls: 140–160 hours
Fifteen to seventeen years—boys: 120–160 hours; no values for girls

The noteworthy increase in the volume of strength training among fourteen- to fifteen-year-old girls and fifteen- to seventeen-year-old boys reveals that these age ranges are the most favorable periods for specialized strength training because the rate of increase in the development of strength, leading to favorable gains in power and speed, is highest in these age brackets. Past this range, reducing the volume of strength loading is recommended because further gains in strength may lead to decreases in swimming power and speed. The studies of long-term strength account for differences in individual rates of strength development; thus, the maxim "strength training where it is needed" applies here.

Annual Training Models

Once the multiyear model has designated the required maximal loads, the next task is to establish training models for the annual plan. Annual training

FIGURE 9–10   DISTRIBUTION OF TRAINING LOAD OVER THREE MESOCYCLES IN YOUNG CYCLICAL-ENDURANCE ATHELETES

   (taken from Filin & Rubin, 1988)
   The relationship between the total training volume over the three mesocycles (the solid line) and the training volume of the individual mesocycles (the broken line) and the age and qualification levels of the young athletes.

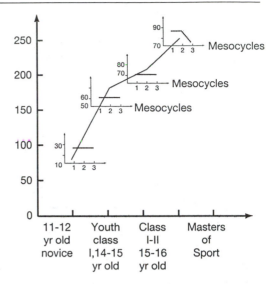

models determine the proportion of different types of training loads throughout the different stages and cycles of the plan periods. This is known as *training load distribution.*

Principal Training Models.   Principal models of load distribution are utilized in the initial stages of guiding the athlete's entry into the training process. The most innovative feature of principal training models has been the discovery that different levels of performance qualifications not only require different training in terms of quantity and quality of loads, but also require different distribution of these loads to achieve desired training effects. Filin and Rubin[11] determined that changes in load distribution, based on traditional approaches to periodization, do not emerge until the athlete becomes involved in the stages of deep specialization, usually at about age fourteen to sixteen for endurance athletes (see Figure 9–10).

   The first principal training model was proposed by Matveyev in 1966 (see Footnote 2). This model takes the general training load and expresses changes in loading, based on a volume/intensity training ratio determined by the traditional periodization of training. Figure 9–11 represents these changes in both one-cycle and two-cycle yearly plans.

   The volume/intensity ratio in principal training models is the result of studies to determine the appropriate means of intensifying the training process in order to achieve the desired load and recovery rhythms for compensatory adaptation during the time of major competition. The traditional training model increases the load in the initial stages, primarily by increasing the volume of work, while increasing the intensity level only slightly. In the latter stages of a training plan, the intensity increases and it is necessary to decrease the volume of work, as is shown in Matveyev's model (Figure 9–11).

   Verkoshansky[12] has proposed different variations of principal models, based on the training needs of athletes of different levels of trainedness. He compares the traditional model with one he refers to as unidirectional (see Figure 9–12–A

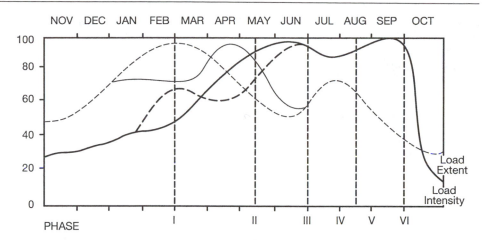

FIGURE 9–11 MATVEYEV'S PRINCIPAL MODEL OF TRADITIONAL PERIODIZATION
The suggested relationship between extent and intensity of loading in the annual cycle of single and double periodized years (1965).

and B). The main difference between the two is the organization of different types of training loads within the models, making a distinction between the *distributed* and the *concentrated* variants. The distributed variant stresses a relatively uniform distribution of loads throughout the plan period, based upon the complex system of training, which emphasizes the multilateral or parallel development of physical abilities. The concentrated variant concentrates physical loads at certain stages of the plan period, based on the *conjugate-successive* or *series development* of physical abilities. Figure 9–13 shows the conjugate-successive system of loading organization.

The use of either a traditional or more unidirectional training organization, along with more distributed or concentrated loading variants, is dictated by the level of trainedness of the athlete. Traditional periodization and distributed training loads are more suited for intermediate athletes, while unidirectional training with concentrated loads are more suited for elite athletes. This is because the latter training forms provide the necessary intensification of the training process which is needed for athletes of high levels of trainedness.

More recent principal training models show differences in the distribution of different types of training loads (i.e., strength and endurance loads of different intensities). Verkoshansky[13] has proposed different training models for endurance sports. The first model demonstrates training-load distribution for middle-distance endurance athletes (Figure 9–14). The distribution of endurance loads follows a traditional approach, while the strength loads are organized into "blocks" of concentrated strength work. This is based on findings that have determined that concentrated strength loads in the initial stages of training result in a long-lasting, delayed training effect which raises the level of speed and speed-strength capabilities after the work itself has been discontinued.

The model shown in Figure 9–14 is based on a two-cycle periodization of training. To ensure the continued intensification of the training process throughout the year, the first competitive period serves as a control period in which the

FIGURE 9–12A & B   VARIANTS OF TRAINING LOAD ORGANIZATION

A. Traditional
B. Unidirectional
(taken from Verkoshansky)

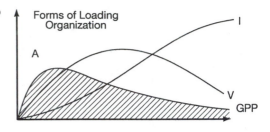

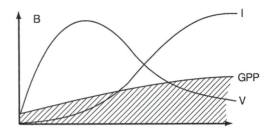

FIGURE 9–13   CONJUGATE-SUCCESSIVE ORGANIZATION OF TRAINING LOADS

Aerobic endurance loads
Mixed loads and strength loads
Anaerobic-alactate endurance loads
Anaerobic-lactate loads

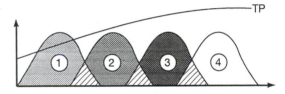

athlete competes in other events or distances that serve as estimates of aerobic and anaerobic capability. This is because the general strategy of load organization in the yearly cycle is based on the following unidirectional sequence of developing specific work capacity: general endurance———speed———speed endurance. The direction of strength loading is toward the systematic development of specialized endurance in the stage of important competitions.

The means of endurance training are broken down into special work in the mixed aerobic-anaerobic regime and anaerobic work in the glycolytic and alactate regime. The organization of endurance loads provides for a two-peak change in aerobic and anaerobic loading. The ratio of aerobic to anaerobic work changes during the yearly cycle. There is a predominance of aerobic loading in the first preparatory period and of anaerobic-threshold loading during the second preparatory period. Increases in speed and speed-endurance work occur during the competitive period.

The two blocks of concentrated strength loading are executed simultaneously with the mixed endurance loads. The first block emphasizes the development of explosive strength and local muscular endurance. The second block chiefly emphasizes local muscular endurance.

An examination of the dynamics of the athlete's state shows the results of the training distribution. There is a two-peak change in aerobic and anaerobic

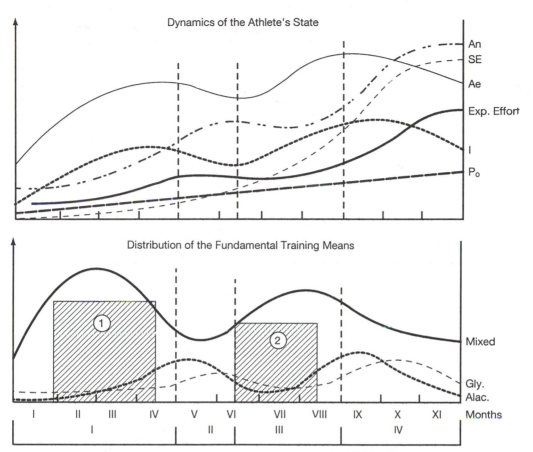

FIGURE 9–14 A Principal Model of Training Constuction for Middle Distance Endurance (taken from Verkoshansky)

Functional Indicators
Po—absolute strength
I—explosive strength
Exp. Effort—repetitive
display of explosive effort
(speed-strength endurance)
SE—strength-endurance
An—anaerobic capacity
Ae—aerobic capacity

Training Loads
Mixed—aerobic/anaerobic endurance loads
Gly—anaerobic glycolytic endurance loads
Alac—anaerobic alactate endurance loads

capability. The dynamics of special strength preparation show an accelerated growth in general strength-endurance and the special endurance for repetitive execution of explosive effort (speed-strength endurance) in the second competitive period. There is also a gradual rise in absolute strength. Explosive strength, as revealed in acyclic movements, reaches its maximum at the second competitive period, then decreases, due to the increase in intense cyclic work. The most important functional abilities, strength-endurance and speed-endurance, theoretically reach their highest levels during the period of major competition.

In preparation for long-distance events, Verkoshansky[14] proposes a one-cycle periodization of training. This is based on practice which shows that the predominance of low intensity work requires a long preparatory period of up to

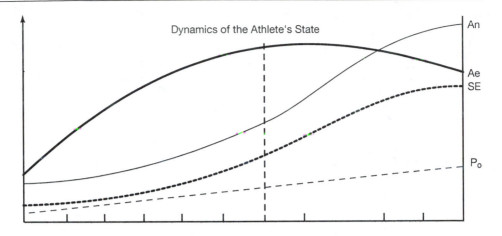

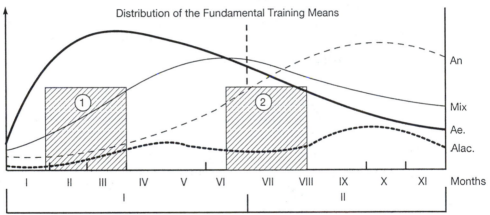

FIGURE 9–15 A PRINCIPAL MODEL OF TRAINING CONSTRUCTION FOR LONG-DISTANCE ENDURANCE

(taken from Verkoshansky, 1986)
I—preparatory period
II—competitive period

six months in order to stabilize special work capacity and preserve it during the four to five months of the competitive period (see Figure 9–15).

Endurance preparation takes a traditional approach in the use of aerobic, mixed, and anaerobic loads to ensure progressive intensification of the training process in developing special work capacity: aerobic endurance————anaerobic threshold endurance————anaerobic lactate endurance. Two stages of strength loading occur in the one-cycle plan. The first block contains strength work of a general formative nature, while the second block emphasizes the development of local muscular endurance. Increases in the level of speed loading are timed to

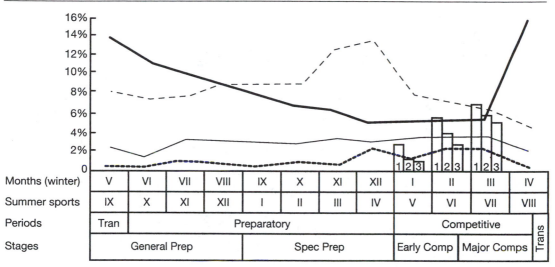

FIGURE 9-16 QUANTITATIVE TRAINING MODEL FOR CYCLICAL SPORTS

(taken from Topchiyan, 1983)

Key: Volume of cyclical loads, solid line
Volume in the I through III intensity zones, dashed line
General physical preparation (GPP), long dashed line
Volumes of intense loads 90% and higher, dot and dashed line
Sports results in skiing, 1
Sports results in ice skating, 2
Sports results in rowing, 3

take place during the realization of the long-lasting training effect of concentrated strength loading.

Changes in the functional indicators show an increase in the aerobic endurance at the beginning of the competitive period, with some decrease toward the end. There is a gradual rise in special strength-endurance and absolute strength during the stage of important competitions.

Quantitative Training Models. Principal models are used for the development of concrete, quantitative models for individuals or groups of athletes. The practical purpose of quantitative training models is to establish the quantity of training loads in the monthly cycles of preparation. Topchiyan[15] has devised training models for both speed-strength and cyclical-endurance sports (see Figure 9-16).

In speed-strength sports the monthly training load fluctuates from 3 to 13 percent of the total yearly volume. The distribution of loading in cyclical-endurance sports remains more evenly distributed throughout the entire year, with the possible exception of one major increase in the total training load prior to and going into the major competitions (see Figure 9-17).

Quantitative training models for highly qualified athletes designate changes in load distribution of all the different means of training.

While training models chart dynamic changes in load distribution, *load distribution schemes* break down training organization into simple numerical tables. Multiyear load distribution schemes divide the percentage of general,

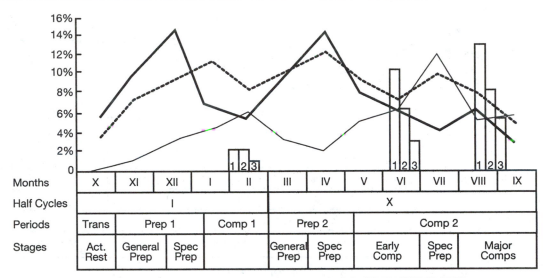

FIGURE 9–17 QUANTITATIVE TRAINING MODELS FOR SPEED-STRENGTH SPORTS

(taken from Topchiyan, 1983)

Key: Total training load volume, dashed line
General physical preparation (GPP), heavy solid line
Volume of intense loads 90% and higher, light solid line
Results in the throws, 1
Results in the jumps, 2
Results in the sprints, 3

preliminary specialized, and specialized preparation within the different training stages of each training year of the athlete's career (see Figure 9–18).

Figure 9–19 shows two important considerations of load distribution in a quadrennial plan. The first table shows three variants of incrementing the total training load, based on the total load for the training year prior to the four-year cycle. The first two variants are for athletes of lower performance ranking, while the third variant is for higher-ranked, record-holding athletes. The second table shows the distribution of the different levels of physical preparation over the course of four years.

Modeling and Partial Systemization of Weekly Cycles. Once the distribution of training loads in the monthly cycles of training has been established, the distribution of loading over weekly cycles should be arranged. The current ideas of modeling cycles are based on several approaches. The first to be considered is the establishment of weekly cycles in relation to the multiyear preparation of the athlete. These considerations include the number of training days per week, individual training sessions, and hours spent training per week. The second consideration is changes in the load structure of weekly cycles (that is, the volume/intensity ratio) over the course of the week, as well as changes in the total training load from week to week within the monthly cycle. The third consideration is the

FIGURE 9-18.   MULTI-YEAR LOAD DISTRIBUTION SCHEME

Age in Years	General Preparatory G-PS-S	Special Preparatory G-PS-S	Precompetitive G-PS-S	Competitive G-PS-S	Transitional G-PS-S
8–10	70-20-10	60-30-10	40-40-20	30-40-30	80-10-10
11–12	60-30-10	40-40-20	20-50-30	10-40-50	70-20-10
13–14	40-50-10	20-60-20	10-40-50	0-30-70	50-40-10
15–16	30-60-10	10-70-20	0-50-50	0-30-70	40-50-10
17–18	20-70-10	0-60-40	0-40-60	0-20-80	30-60-10
19–20+	10-70-20	0-70-30	0-30-70	0-10-90	20-70-10

Percentage distribution of general (G), preliminary specialized (PS), and specialized preparation (S) with each stage of the periodized year.

succession of training tasks over the course of the week. This is not only determined by the load structure, but also by the *training system*. The training system designates the organization of individual training sessions into training units or complexes and determines their succession or interaction.

As the swimmer matures, the quantity and quality of maximal loading increases. Obviously the time devoted to training will necessarily increase. The following chart lists the suggested number of training days and sessions per week in accordance with the training level of the athlete.

FIGURE 9-19.   LOAD DISTRIBUTION IN A QUADRENNIAL PLAN
(As taken from Matveyev)

A.	First Year	Second Year	Third Year	Fourth Year
1st Variant	0.45	0.35	0.15	0.05
2nd Variant	0.25	0.35	0.20	0.20
3rd Variant	0	0.50	0.20	0.30

General increment of the total training load, based on the loading from the previous year.

B. Means of Preparation	First Year	Second Year	Third Year	Fourth Year
Aerobic Endurance Preparation	75	55	60	50
Anaerobic Endurance Preparation	5	8	10	15
Cyclic-Speed Preparation	10	12	20	15
Specialized-Strength Preparation	10	25	15	20

Distribution of training load volume, according to yearly cycles in percent of the total volume.

TRAINING LEVEL	TRAINING DAYS PER WEEK	TRAINING SESSIONS PER WEEK
Novice	3–4	3–4
Intermediate	5–6	5–9
Advanced	5–6	10–12

The total training load of the weekly cycle will depend on the monthly training load and the manner in which the weekly cycles are arranged as loading and recovery cycles within the training month. In the introductory and base mesocycles, the most frequently used load/recovery ratio is 3/1. Percentage values of the total monthly training load are then prescribed to each weekly cycle. In training mesocycles that involve the use of two ordinary, one shock, and one rehabilitative microcycle, the typical percentages of load distribution are shown below. These weekly percentage distributions are typical in the stimulatory stage of training.

VARIANTS	FIRST WEEK	SECOND WEEK	THIRD WEEK	FOURTH WEEK
1	22%	28%	35%	15%
2	28%	22%	35%	15%
3	25%	25%	35%	15%

Weekly percentage distributions will differ in the stabilizing stage.

VARIANTS	FIRST WEEK	SECOND WEEK	THIRD WEEK	FOURTH WEEK
1	22%	25%	28%	25%
2	25%	25%	30%	20%
3	30%	25%	30%	15%
4	22%	28%	30%	20%

In the precompetitive and competitive stages, changes in the *load recovery ratio* will result in different weekly percentage distributions. Depending on the frequency and priority of competitions, the common load recovery ratios seen are 1/1, 2/2, and for important competitions 1/3. The following table depicts the possible variance of weekly percentage distributions in the stages of the competitive period.

VARIANTS	FIRST WEEK	SECOND WEEK	THIRD WEEK	FOURTH WEEK
1	35%	28%	22%	15%
2	28%	35%	22%	15%
3	28%	22%	35%	15%
4	35%	15%	28%	22%

Current training theory establishes a load structure within the weekly cycle. This designates changes in the volume/intensity ratio from day to day and even session to session. Changes in the load structure establish an alternating rhythm of loading and recovery within the weekly cycle, in the form of alternating either load demands or training tasks.[16] Figure 9-20 illustrates a typical weekly load structure. The rationale behind this load structure requires that the development of certain physical abilities must take place when the level of work capacity is high. As an example, training that emphasizes the development of speed, speed-strength, or technique should never follow training sessions of high-intensity demand, such as those devoted to the development of speed-endurance. Sessions devoted to considerable anaerobic loading should be followed by training loads of aerobic emphasis, not only to increase the level of aerobic capacity, but also to allow for recovery from high-intensity work. Interviews by Peter Daland and Ernie Maglischo[17] with European coaches reveal samples of weekly training content based on this theoretical approach to load structure. Most coaches seemed to make use of a training cycle in which considerable anaerobic loading takes place twice a week. The training sessions to develop anaerobic endurance were usually separated by two to three days of lower intensity work. The use of a *two-peak* microcycle is consistent with the practice of *cruise interval* and *goal set* usage as recommended by the authors in Chapter 11. In theories advocating unidirectional training, a three-peak microcycle has been suggested; but the majority opinion appears to hold with the two-peak cycle.

Kindermann[18] has formulated weekly training cycles which demonstrate his opinions concerning appropriate and inappropriate successions of training tasks (see Figure 9–21). Platonov[19] determined the succession of workloads within microcycles based on the recuperation of work capacity, using both heterogeneous and uniform workloads. Such formulations help clarify the concept of load structure between individual training sessions.

The structure of weekly cycles changes with the different stages of training. A weekly structure of loading which emphasizes two training days of speed-endurance work has no place in the general-preparatory stage. Kubelin[20] differentiates weekly micro-cycles of aerobic and anaerobic emphasis (see Figure 9–22). In traditional periodization, weekly cycles of aerobic emphasis should be used in the initial stages of the preparatory period, while those of anaerobic emphasis should be used in the final stages of periodization. In forms of periodization based on *helix* (or spiral) models, there exists the alternating use of aerobic and anaerobic weekly cycles to achieve what is known as *the "pendulum" effect* of frequent swings of recurrent stress and adaptation.

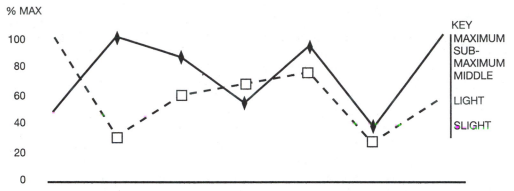

FIGURE 9–20   THE STRUCTURE OF LOADING

(taken from Carl, 1967)

	Day 1	Day 2	Day 3	Day 4	Day 5	Day 6	Day 7
Correct	Low INT. Aerobic 90 - 120'	Recovery 45 - 60'	Recovery 45 - 60'	Aerobic 90 - 120'	Recovery 45 - 60'	Low INT. Aerobic 90 - 120'	Interval or Fartlek
		Anaerobic	High INT. Aerobic 45 - 60'		Anaerobic		

		Day 2	Day 3	Day 4	Day 5	Day 6	Day 7
Incorrect		Anaerobic	Interval or Fartlek	Anaerobic		Low INT. Aerobic 90 - 120'	Low INT. Aerobic 90 - 120'
		Recovery 45 - 60'	Low INT. Aerobic 90 - 120'			High INT. Aerobic 45 - 60'	

FIGURE 9–21   CORRECT AND INCORRECT VARIANTS OF STRUCTURING MICRO-CYCLES

(taken from Kindermann, 1978)

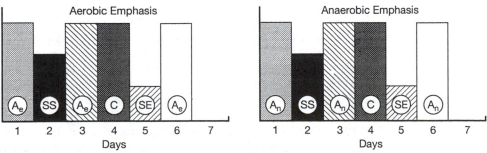

FIGURE 9–22   MICROCYCLES OF PRIMARY TRAINING EMPHASIS

(taken from Kubelin, 1980)

FOOTNOTES

1. Yuri Verkoshansky, *Programming and Organization of Training* (Moscow: Fizkultura i Spovt, 1986), p. 12.

2. L.P. Matveyev, *Periodization of Sports Training* (Moscow: Fizkultura i Spovt, 1966).

3. I. I. Barynina and S. M. Vaitsekhovskii, "The Aftermath of Early Sports Specialization for Highly Qualified Swimmers," *Teoriya i Praktica Fizicheskoi Kultury*, 6, 1989, 21–23.

4. L.P. Matveyev, *Fundamentals of Sports Training* (Moscow: Fizkultura i Spovt, 1977); sec. ref. Progress Publishers, English translation, 1981.

5. Christina Wells, *Women, Sport, & Performance* (Champaign, IL: Human Kinetics, Inc., 1985).

6. A. Bondarchuk, "Periodization of Sports Training," *Legkaya Atletika*, 12, 1986, 8–9.

7. Dietrich Harre, Team Editor, *Principles of Sports Training* (Berlin: Sports Verlag, 1983), p. 84.

8. Igor Koshkin, "The Training Program of Vladimir Salnikov," *Swim 86 Yearbook*, Australian Amateur Swimming Association, Rothman's National Sport Foundation, 1986, p. 21.

9. A.A. Guzhalovsky, and D.E. Mantevich, "Long-Term Dynamics of Absolute Strength (Dry Land & Water) in Crawl Stroke Swimmers," *Teoriya i Praktika Fizicheskoi Kultury*, 10, 1986, 25.

10. D.E. Mantevich, and G.I. Petrovich, "Scientific Methodical Aspects of Long-Term Strength Training in Swimmers," *Teoriya i Praktika Fizicheskoi Kultury*, 12, 1987, 26–28.

11. V.P. Filin, and V. S. Rubin, "Loads and Periodization of the Training Process of Young Athletes during Individual Phases of Multi-Year Preparation in Cyclical-Endurance Sports," *Teoriya i Praktika Fizicheskoi Kultury*, 12, 1988, 22–24; sec. ref., *The Soviet Sports Review*, September, 1990, 133–135.

12. Verkoshansky, *Programming and Organization*, p. 141.

13. Verkoshansky, *Programming and Organization*, p. 159.

14. Verkoshansky, *Programming and Organization*, p. 162.

15. Y.S. Topchiyan, and others, "Training Young Athletes in the Yearly Cycle in Speed-Strength in Cyclical-type Sports, *Teoriya i Praktika Fizicheskoi Kultury*, 11, 1983, 47–50.

16. G. Carl, *Gewichtheben* (Berlin: Sport Verlag, 1967); sec. ref., Frank Dick, *Sports Training Principles* (London: Lepus Books, Harry Kimpton Publishers, Ltd., 1980).

17. Peter Daland, and Ernie Maglischo, "Summary of Interviews with the Coaches from Europe," *American Swimming Coaches Association Magazine*, February 1988.

18. W. Kindermann, "Regeneration und Trainings Prozess in deu Ausdawer—sportarten aus Medizinischer Sicht," *Leistungssport*, 4, 1978, 357–84; sec. ref., Gullstrand, *Swim 86 Yearbook*, Australian Amateur Swimming Association, 1986.

19. V.N. Platonov, "Concerning the Use of Large Work Loads in Modern Swimming," *Plavanie*, 1, 1977, 15–18; sec. ref., Verkoshansky, *Programming and Organization*, p. 150.

20. A.B Kubelin, sec. ref., Verkoshansky, *Programming and Organization*, p. 150.

CHAPTER 10

Fundamentals in the Development of Strength Abilities and Flexibility in Swimmers

THE NATURE OF STRENGTH

Strength is defined as the ability of a muscle or group of muscles to create tension. Tension is produced by the phenomenon of muscle contraction. Without getting into exact physiological mechanisms, tension development or muscle contraction is caused by the interaction of contractile proteins within individual muscle fibers. This interaction is based on the sliding filament theory. Interaction occurs when the muscle fiber is stimulated by the neuromuscular system. The degree of muscle tension which can be developed within an individual muscle depends on how many individual fibers are stimulated during contraction as well as the cross-sectional area of the muscle. The level of tension a muscle can develop is referred to as the force capacity of the muscle. The skeleton acts as the leverage system that converts the force capacity of muscle tension into force application and allows the realization of joint movement. Single joint movements are the individual links in the chain of partial body movements which unite into patterns or sequences to form the whole body movement.

Force application within the human body is described by the various types of muscle action and joint movements. The technical terminology used to describe the various roles of muscular activity follows:

1. *Prime Mover or Agonistic:* The muscle that bears the principal responsibility for a specific joint action.
2. *Antagonistic:* The muscle that works in opposition to the specific joint movement of the prime mover.
3. *Synergistic:* Any muscle that contributes to the activity of the prime mover but cannot itself be classified as a prime mover.
    a. *Assistant Mover:* A muscle which aids the prime mover to effect joint action.
    b. *Stabilizer:* A muscle which anchors, steadies, or supports a bone or body part to allow the primary mover a firm base upon which to contract.
    c. *Neutralizer:* A muscle which contracts in order to counteract or neutralize an undesired action from another contracting muscle.

Technical terms are also used to describe basic joint actions:

1. *Flexion:* Decreasing the angle between two segments of the body (also known as bending).
2. *Extension:* Increasing the angle between two segments of the body.
3. *Abduction:* Moving body segments away from the midline of the body.
4. *Adduction:* Moving body segments towards the midline of the body.
5. *Rotation:* The muscular movement of a body segment about its longitudinal axis.

IDENTIFYING THE DIFFERENT STRENGTH ABILITIES

In athletic movement, strength is obviously interrelated with speed and endurance. Because different sports and different events within those sports make varying demands on all these physical abilities, the identification of distinct and separate *strength abilities* emerges. Identifying the main forms of strength abilities developed by the athlete's movement depends on the nature of resistance encountered. Resistance may take the form of weights or sports apparatus, the athlete's own body weight, air resistance, or, in the case of competitive swimming, the resistance of water and the resistive and buoyant forces of the swimmer's body.

There are essentially three main strength abilities. They are defined as maximal (or absolute) strength, speed-strength (or explosive strength), and strength-endurance. Though most coaches and athletes are familiar with maximal or absolute strength, the latter two are the ones needed most in the majority of sports.

Maximal/Absolute Strength

In most sports literature, maximal and absolute strength are considered to be different manifestations of strength. Absolute strength is defined as the greatest level of tension that can be developed by a muscle in the isometric regime. Maximal strength is defined as the greatest level of force that can be developed in a single maximal, voluntary contraction. In a sport such as weight lifting, maximal or absolute strength can determine performance. In other sports, it is the point in a given phase of the movement at which the greatest strength display occurs.

Speed-Strength/Explosive Strength

Variously referred to as power or fast strength, the term *speed-strength* or *explosive strength* is used to describe a number of different strength manifestations in movements which depend on a high speed of muscular contraction to overcome resistance. In its strictest sense, *speed-strength* is the ability to execute an unloaded movement or a movement of low resistance quickly, and it is assessed relative to the absolute speed of muscular contraction. In contrast, *explosive strength* is the ability to express significant muscular tension in a minimal period of time. This differentiation permits a distinction to be made between the *speed of contraction* as opposed to *speed of muscular tension development.*

Although competitive swimming is defined as an endurance sport, as differentiated from speed-strength sports such as field events or Olympic-style weight lifting, all sports movements are measured and assessed by their speed-strength characteristics, that is, in force/time patterns.

Strength-Endurance

Strength-endurance refers to the ability to maintain effective muscular function under conditions of relatively long duration. It determines performance, particularly in endurance events in which significant resistance must be overcome. Competitive swimming is considered to be a strength-endurance sport in which long- or middle-distance efforts of low to moderate intensity are called strength-endurance efforts, and shorter duration efforts of high intensity are referred to as speed-strength endurance efforts. In the use of specific resistance modes for the development of swimming strength, the regimes of strength work are differentiated as strength-endurance and speed-strength endurance efforts.

SPECIAL STRENGTH TRAINING FOR SPORT

Special strength training for sport is broken down into two levels of preparation. These include general and specialized strength training.

General Strength Training

In the theoretical approach to general physical preparation, general strength focuses on the development of balanced, comprehensive strength. It is important because it serves as the base upon which more specialized strength is developed by enhancing the level of *supportive* and *secondary*, as opposed to *primary*, strength. General strength promotes better intermuscular coordination, helping to reinforce the dynamic balance of supportive musculature and prevent overuse injuries.

General strength training has its most dominant role in the strength training of young athletes who are in the early stages of training. As an athlete matures, and the level of special physical preparedness increases, general strength training decreases and more specialized strength methods are substituted. In the mature or elite athlete, general strength training is often equated with strength training for absolute strength, while training for speed-strength and strength-endurance constitute the focus of specialized strength preparation. Other more appropriate strength training approaches differentiate between the development of general versus special complex strength abilities, such as general versus special strength-endurance.

Specialized Strength Training

When conducting specialized strength preparation, the selection of means, methods, and exercises are dictated by the principle of *dynamic correspondence*. This principle states that the dynamic characteristics of the strength training exercise must conform to the competitive exercise as closely as possible.

In specialized strength training for competitive swimming, a distinction is made between the use of traditional resistance modes—such as free weights, barbells, dumbbells, and pulleys—and those of specific resistance (that is, apparatus that is especially designed for the task of enhancing swimming strength). Specific resistance modes for training swimming strength are divided into two categories: dry land strength training exercises and in-water strength training exercises.

THE MEANS OF STRENGTH TRAINING

Without being categorized according to different levels of strength preparation, the *means* of strength training refers to the general approaches or procedures of strength training. Strength exercises, being the primary means of strength training, require greater levels of muscle tension than are achieved in the normal sports movement. This may be accomplished by several means: increased external resistance, kinetic energy, volitional effort, and electrostimulation.

Increased External Resistance

Most strength exercises make use of external resistance as the main means of stimulating the display of greater muscle tension. The most common forms of resistance used in strength exercises include: (1) additional weight; (2) the athlete's own body weight; (3) counteractive exercise with another partner; (4) mechanical resistance modes, such as mechanical frictional, hydraulic, pneumatic, electrical, and elastic; and (5) other natural external media, such as water, snow, sand, and hills.

Most strength exercises make use of extra weight to increase resistance and elicit greater muscular tension. Extra weight is the preferred resistance mode in strength training because it can be rated on an incremental basis, permitting some control to more precisely determine the dosage or volume of the strength stimulus.

Kinetic Energy

This means of muscle tension stimulation centers around the absorption of energy caused by the athlete's falling body or by a training apparatus. The basis of this utilization of kinetic energy lies in the ability of the muscle to contract with more power after a sharp, preliminary stretch (forced extension). The state of the neuromuscular system during forced extension instantaneously elicits high muscle tension and contraction speed (the stretch reflex).

Preliminary stretching is achieved with specially modified strength exercises, which implement certain resistance modes. They are referred to as *shock* exercises (or pliometrics, as they are known in the United States).

Volitional Effort (Isometric)

When use is made of isometric contractions as a means of strength training, the idea is to create muscle tension against a fixed resistance without a change in the length of the muscle. The nature of the strength stimulus is to display and sustain a given magnitude of volitional effort. Being able to slowly increase isometric tension and sustain it for long periods of time involves an adaptive response in the neuromuscular system that is best suited for eliciting increases in absolute strength. On the other hand, when the emphasis is on the speed of developing isometric tension, the use of isometrics is seen not only as a suitable means, but probably the best means, of developing explosive strength, especially in movements which require explosive effort against considerable resistances or loads. The difference between the two can be seen in the following example. When performing a dead lift, tension is developed slowly and gradually with peak tension levels of 80 to 90 percent of maximum effort over six to eight seconds or more. In an explosive isometric effort, muscular tension levels of up to 60 to 70 percent are developed as rapidly as possible in a total duration of three to four seconds.

Electrostimulation

Enough research has been conducted to show that electrostimulation of the muscle can serve as an adequate training stimulus for the enhancement of strength. Direct electrical stimulation at the point of the muscle innervation has been shown to elicit levels of muscle tension substantially higher than those achieved from voluntary effort. This allows a greater expression of the *latent strength reserves* unachievable by more conventional strength training means. In addition to enhancing strength potential, electrostimulation can also play a greater role in the technical preparation of the athlete. Multichannel electrostimulation integrated with electromyographic data can be used to stimulate entire muscle groups in accordance with desired electromuscular patterns, simulating the entire coordinative structure of partial or even whole body movement at the neuromuscular level. This use of *simulatory electrostimulation* allows the potential realization of greater special strength training in highly qualified athletes.

THE METHODS OF STRENGTH TRAINING

The methods of strength training involve the systemization of the means of strength training into procedures for the development of specific strength abilities. These include the development of maximal strength, speed-strength, explosive strength and reactive ability, and strength-endurance. In competitive swimming it is deemed necessary to differentiate between methods that use *traditional* resistance modes for the development of strength abilities and those that use *specific* resistance modes for developing strength abilities.[1]

All the methods used to develop strength abilities are defined by two subcategories: the *methodological approach* to the use of the exercise and the required or suggested *load procedures* in the use of the strength exercise.

The methodological approach involves the classification of the unique approaches of various strength training exercises. Such categories as the *repetitive* method, *variable resistance* method, *shock* method, and so on are in this subcategory. These variables designate how to execute the exercise, the speed and tempo of work, and the use of special apparatus.

Load procedure denotes the external load factors of intensity, volume, and density. In strength exercises *intensity* is determined by magnitude of resistance, *volume* is expressed in repetitions and sets, and *density* is the quantity of rest between sets. *Repetitions* refer to the number of times a strength exercise is repeated in series and *sets* refer to the number of separate series.

Intensity is often expressed as a percentage of maximal performance (maximal load, maximal effort, or maximal single voluntary contraction). This is determined by the *repetition maximum* method in which a strength load is repeatedly lifted until failure. The relationship between the number of repetitions to percentage of maximal performance is listed in the following chart:

INTENSITY	PERCENTAGE OF MAXIMAL PERFORMANCE	NUMBER OF REPETITIONS IN A SINGLE APPROACH (RM = REPETITION MAXIMUM)
Maximum	100	1 RM
Submaximum	99–90	2–3 RM
Big (1st Subzone)	89–80	4–6 RM
Big (2nd Subzone)	79–70	7–10 RM
Moderate (1st Subzone)	69–60	11–15 RM
Moderate (2nd Subzone)	59–50	16–20 RM
Small (1st Subzone)	49–40	21–30 RM
Small (2nd Subzone)	39–30	31 or more RM

In other strength exercises in which the intensity or resistance can only be approximated or in which other load conditions exist, the volume versus extent of loading must be based on other criteria, such as the tempo of work or quality of performance, the duration or distance covered in the execution of the exercise, or performance of the exercise until failure, and so on.

When the external load factors are precisely rated and executed in repetitions and sets, the required or suggested load procedure for developing different strength abilities is based on the DeLorme Principles of progressive resistance:

> Strength is built by the use of high-resistance–low-repetition exercises.
> Endurance is built by the use of low-resistance–high-repetition exercises.[2]

The DeLorme Principles do not take into account the speed of executing strength exercises, an important consideration in special strength training. It is understood that the execution of strength exercises at higher speeds requires the use of lower resistance. Any increase or decrease in resistance will result in reciprocal variations in the demands placed on strength and speed of movement.

Traditional Resistance Methods for Developing Strength Abilities

Methods of Developing Maximal/Absolute Strength. The development of maximal/absolute strength requires load conditions which elicit large to maximal muscle tension. The traditional resistance modes, such as weight lifting (barbells, dumbbells, pulleys, and so on), auxiliary gymnastic exercises (pullups and bar-dips), and isometric exercises, are best suited for the development of absolute strength. The exercises are differentiated as to how they develop general versus specialized maximal strength. The methodological approach most commonly used to develop maximal strength is stationary training using the method of repetitive effort.

REPETITIVE EFFORT. The best approach to developing maximal strength is the method of repetitive effort. This involves performing a set of repetitions in which the resistance remains the same within the set. A variation of the repetitive method, sometimes called the progressive resistance method, changes the resistance from set to set (different variations include *DeLorme Method, McCloy Method, Oxford Method*. In competitive swimming, it has been found that moving from lighter to heavier resistances avoids the development of excessive muscle bulk, an undesirable effect.[3] The number of sets and repetitions in the use of the repetitive method have been studied extensively, but the research has ultimately concluded that there is no standard load procedure ideally suited to every athlete, and that load conditions should accommodate to different needs. Advanced swimmers must use maximal to submaximal loads to increase maximal strength, but use big and moderate-strength loads when they are tired (see the chart on page 261). Most research indicates that three to five sets with repetition of anywhere between two RM and ten RM weights are required. Beginning or younger swimmers can make substantial strength gains using moderate or small resistances and more repetitions because the strength exercise enhances the general physical preparedness, allows better execution of correct technique, and prevents injury.

ISOMETRIC EFFORTS. Isometric training is an effective means of increasing maximal strength without creating excessive muscle mass. In strength training, functional isometrics, which are isometric efforts at various joint angles throughout a given range of movement, are preferred. The suggested load procedure is three sets of five to six repetitions per exercise. Each repetition should develop tension levels of about 60 to 80 percent of maximum and last about five to six seconds once the desired tension level is reached. Isometric training is not normally used in strength training for competitive swimming because dynamic regimes of work are seen as more effective in producing strength.

GENERAL VERSUS SPECIALIZED MAXIMAL STRENGTH.   The selection of exercises is based on the development of either general or special maximal strength. General maximal strength makes use of both weight lifting and auxiliary gymnastic exercises. In weight lifting, exercises that work the large or main muscle groups are used, which include such exercises as the bench press, squats, bicep curls, power cleans, back hyperextensors, and so on.

Exercises to develop specialized maximal strength are strength exercises whose movements duplicate parts or components of movements seen in competitive swimming and place high strength demands on those muscles that serve as the primary movers in swimming movements (for example, the arm depressors, upper arm rotators, elbow extensors, and forearm rotators).

Methods of Developing Speed-Strength.   The development of speed-strength focuses on improving the speed of muscular contraction. Traditional resistance modes are utilized in an integral approach to improve speed-strength. These include strength exercises with smaller weights and variable resistance methods.

EXERCISES WITH SMALLER WEIGHTS (BALLISTIC EXERCISES) USING THE REPETITIVE METHOD.   Exercises which utilize small additional resistances are required in order to execute the strength exercises at higher movement speeds. The exercises are performed with the goal of accelerating the apparatus as rapidly as possible. In speed-strength training, it is recommended that different resistances be used in an integral approach to develop the ability to display strength movement with different combinations of strength *and* speed. To accomplish this, resistances as high as 70 percent of maximum or as low as 20 percent of maximum are used. The optimal number of repetitions depends on the level of resistance. Higher resistances have been rated in numbers of repetition (for instance, loads at 70 percent of maximal effort can be maintained at full speed of execution for about ten repetitions) or on the basis of duration (70 percent of maximal effort can be executed at full speed for about six seconds). For much smaller loads the speed of executing the exercise is determined by the tempo of work and is rated in terms of duration of work at a given tempo until performance declines.

VARIABLE RESISTANCE EFFORTS.   Unlike the repetitive method, the variable method makes use of lighter and heavier resistance and of changing resistance from repetition to repetition instead of from set to set. The best combination makes use of lighter weights, subsequently switching to heavier weights. The use of projectile objects, such as differently weighted medicine balls, is the best method for the development of movements requiring both strength and speed.

Methods of Developing Explosive Strength/Reactive Ability
SHOCK METHOD (PLIOMETRICS).   As previously described, shock exercises require that the muscle(s) be forcibly extended prior to the actual active phase of

the strength exercise. In most strength exercise utilizing resistance apparatus, the weight or resistance is *lowered* slowly back into the starting position before the next repetition begins. Shock exercises require that the weight be lowered rapidly under *free-fall-like* conditions. The kinetic energy developed during the descent, along with the rapid eccentric contraction of the muscles, results in the forced extension of the muscle. The kinetic energy absorbed by the elastic component of the muscle, and the stretch reflex elicited by the forced extension, causes the muscle to contract with greater force and higher contraction speed. Figures 10–30 and 10–31 later in this chapter provide some examples of shock exercises that can safely be employed by competitive swimmers.

The *free-fall* properties of resistance apparatus should not be overlooked. Furthermore, the recent development and use of *impulse unit resistance apparatus* have opened up new dimensions in the use of shock exercise, and their continued application and development will expand the possibility of developing explosive strength/reactive ability.

EXPLOSIVE ISOMETRIC EFFORTS.   Another method for developing explosive strength is known as *explosive isometric efforts*. Isometric efforts to develop explosive strength are different from isometric efforts to develop absolute strength. In developing absolute strength, the magnitude of tension developed is the primary objective, and the rate or speed of tension development is immaterial. In explosive isometric efforts, the magnitude of tension developed is not as important as the speed of tension development. In the execution of explosive isometric efforts, tension levels of 50 to 65 percent of maximum must be achieved with each effort, with the emphasis on achieving these tension levels as rapidly as possible. Each effort should be sustained no more than two to three seconds, with enough rest between efforts to sustain the quality of rapid tension development. Because starting strength is required in the initial phases of movement, the extremities must be positioned so the isometric effort takes place at the beginning of the active phase of the movement. In developing explosive strength for pulling in competitive swimming, the arms should be fully extended and elevated to the position known as *full circumduction*. The emphasis of isometric effort is on developing rapid tension in the upper arm depressors by pushing downward against fixed resistance. The number of efforts should be limited to the point at which the swimmer believes he can no longer develop tension rapidly. This usually occurs at about ten repetitions. As the athlete gains trainedness, that number should increase.

Methods of Developing Strength-Endurance.   Strength-endurance is often divided into two basic categories: general strength-endurance and special strength-endurance. Both can emphasize the development of dynamic and static strength-endurance. Static strength-endurance—or the ability to sustain isometric efforts for long periods of time—is used only as part of an integral approach in some training programs to help the swimmer develop tolerance to pain and fatigue, but it does little to help develop key motor qualities needed in the general physical preparation of swimmers. Dynamic strength-endurance is more essential to swimmers and tends to dominate strength-endurance development.

Traditional resistance modes are the best means of enhancing general strength-endurance. This not only includes strength exercises with equipment designed for strength development, but also the use of preparatory training exercises such as auxiliary gymnastic exercises and exercises used in other sports.

When determining load procedure for general strength-endurance training, the magnitude of resistance and number of repetitions are not the only considerations. The methodological approach in strength-endurance training also considers the same variables used in the development of endurance abilities. These include:

1. The tempo of work
2. The duration of the work
3. The rest interval between workloads
4. The frequency of workloads

The long-term development of strength-endurance must also consider such variables as the interval of rest between training sessions devoted to the development of strength-endurance, and the initial levels of strength-endurance of the swimmer.

In the development of general strength-endurance, strength exercises classified as general-preparatory and special-preparatory are used. General-preparatory strength exercises include exercises from other sports, auxiliary gymnastic exercises, and weight lifting. When making use of training exercises from other sports, it is appropriate to execute the work under more difficult (hardened) conditions. Examples include running while wearing a weight vest or ankle weights, cycling uphill in low gear, and so on. Auxiliary gymnastic exercises should work local muscle groups which do not necessarily bear the weight of the entire body; that is exercises which allow the athlete to execute multiple repetitions at a tempo of work similar to the regime of the special or competitive exercise.

When strength exercises are used with resistive apparatuses, multiple repetition exercise using various weights is the most fundamental method of developing strength endurance. The magnitude of resistance used depends on the magnitude of resistance encountered in the special or competitive exercise. In competitive swimming this varies with the duration of the event. In the shorter events, which require significant effort, large weights should be used in combination with light weights with tempos of work that approximate or exceed the regime of the sports activity. In middle-distance or long-distance events in which the special or competitive exercise is associated with prolonged efforts of moderate force display, it is recommended that use be made of light weights performed in repetitive series until fatigue or failure. The most common resistances are used within the first and second subzones of moderate intensity (69 to 60 percent and 59 to 50 percent of maximum repeats per minute respectively), and the first and second subzones of small intensity (light weights of 49 to 40 percent and 39 to 30 percent respectively). Repetitions performed in series will vary between eleven to twenty in the moderate zones and twenty-one to thirty-one in the small zones (see the chart on page 261).

Individual work bouts of strength-endurance work are rated on percentages of total work capacity. This takes the form of percentages of repetitions relative to the number of repetitions performed until fatigue or failure, or on the basis of percentage of total duration of work until failure. When rating individual workloads the tempo of work is of prime importance. Lighter loads at higher tempos of work have been shown to have similar training effects (in raising the level of strength endurance) to larger weights at slower tempos. When tempo of work is designated, it is initially desirable to use some form of audible or visual cues to establish tempo (a metronome or flashing strobe light, for example).

When the swimmer's strength-endurance level increases, overload is achieved by increasing the resistance or duration of the work, or both. The change in strength-endurance load must be carefully monitored to ensure that such changes do not result in the long-term loss of desired motor qualities. Such losses usually indicate too abrupt an increase in the load demand beyond the athlete's adaptational capability.

Specific Resistance Modes for Developing Strength Abilities

Specific resistance modes refer to strength exercises and apparatus which are developed to meet the requirements of special strength training based on the principle of *dynamic correspondence*. The principle states that the strength training implemented must match the kinematic or dynamic characteristics of the special or competitive exercise as closely as possible. Basically, there are two different types of specific resistance. The first type is dry land apparatus which attempts to replicate the more complex *phasic* nature of the swimming movement, along with increased resistance. The second type is in-water strength training, which involves strength-training forms of the competitive exercise.

Dry Land Specific Resistance. This type of resistance includes special preparatory exercises which utilize unique modes, such as isokinetic resistance. They includes accommodating (isokinetic) resistance and semiaccommodating (biokinetic) resistance, as well as some forms of variable resistance, as seen in cam systems such as Polaris or Nautilus systems. Included in this category are several brands of swim bench which allow the swimmer to duplicate as closely as possible the full direction and amplitude of the swimming movement. As of yet, none of these dry land resistance modes fulfills all the requirements of the principle of dynamic correspondence; at least no single mechanism of specific resistance does. The most effective use of such devices requires an integral approach along with other special preparatory exercises.

In-Water Strength Training. This training method was based initially on a single theoretical approach, entailing the use of small additional resistances during the execution of actual swimming. Now, a variety of different approaches, based on increasing the external resistance through different means, have proliferated. An example is the use of equipment that requires the hands to push a greater volume of water than before. Other approaches increase the physical effort of swimming. Following is a list of the basic approaches:

1. *Free Swimming Conditions*
   a. The use of devices which increase the resistance or weight of the swimmer's body or extremities, such as a drag suit, drag belt, or weight belt for the body, or weighted cuffs for the ankles or wrists.
   b. The use of devices which increase the physical effort of moving the extremities, such as hand paddles of various sizes, which allow an alternating resistance approach; buoyant wrist cuffs or buoyant gloves; swim fins in kicking; kick sticks to increase the physical effort of kicking; or swimming against moving water (*reverse hydrochannel method*).
2. *Tethered Swimming Conditions*
   a. The use of rope or elastic tether fastened to a fixed point with the swimmer harnessed to the other end and engaged in either stationary swimming or tension-rated swimming.
   b. The use of resistance apparatus fastened to a tether, such as weighted pulley systems or other resistance apparatus which allows the tether to be drawn out against increased resistances which can be precisely rated.
3. *Combined Conditions*

   The use of apparatuses which can be combined to allow different in-water strength-loading conditions. Following are listed the most commonly used combinations:
   (1) Drag suits or weight belts with hand paddles.
   (2) Hand paddles with swim fins (speed-assisted and explosive strength training).
   (3) Tether with hand paddles.
   (4) Tether with swim fins and/or kick sticks.
   (5) Swimming against moving water with hand paddles or other apparatus.

As can be seen the variations are many.

REGIMES OF WORK IN THE UTILIZATION OF SPECIFIC RESISTANCE

Many different types of work can be devised when making use of specific resistance modes, but there are essentially two approaches based on the types of specific strength abilities to be developed. They are the *speed-strength endurance* regime of work and the *strength-endurance* regime of work.

Speed-Strength Endurance

When specific resistance modes are used, this type of work centers on the development of speed-strength, as displayed in speed-cyclic movements. This is also referred to as the repetitive display of explosive effort. It requires that the strength exercise allow the swimmer to maintain the optimal level of *swimming strength* for a given period of time at a given work tempo. The primary consideration here is the speed of movement or the speed of muscular tension development. In speed-strength endurance work an *optimal* combination of resistance and duration of work must be selected in order to achieve a movement tempo that approximates or, in some cases, exceeds the speed of movement that is achieved during the competitive exercise.

Increases in resistance can reduce speed of movement and cause rapid onset of fatigue. The execution of work over long periods of time at slower movement tempos also reduces speed of movement.

Thus, careful consideration must be given to the level of resistance and duration of work in order to maintain the desired movement tempo and speed of movement. In the execution of speed-strength endurance work, when the speed-strength endurance of the swimmer increases, overload is achieved not necessarily by increasing the load, but by increasing the movement tempo and the duration of the work. Increases in resistance should occur as the athlete's special strength potential increases over the course of multiyear development but, in the later stages, should never exceed the optimal resistance at which optimal speed of movement can be maintained.

In the use of dry land apparatus, the execution of speed-strength endurance depends entirely on the mode of resistance adopted, but when differentiating speed-strength endurance work from strength-endurance work, speed-strength endurance work is executed at higher resistances and at high movement tempos (or higher power outputs) for short periods of time. This is equivalent to the type of physical effort executed during sprint-endurance/maximal-speed work. When making use of special dry land apparatus in which resistance can be rated in percentages of maximum, speed-strength endurance work is best executed at 70 to 80 percent of maximum with eight to ten repetitions, as in the case of the Mertens-Huttel exerciser.* In other apparatuses in which resistance can only be approximated, the workload is determined by selecting the optimal resistance at which the desired speed of movement can be maintained, then instructing the athlete to execute the work at an optimal movement tempo, and timing the duration of work until fatigue sets in and work tempo slows. The duration of the work at optimal mode tempo serves as the standard by which training efforts are gauged. In the use of semiaccommodating resistance (biokinetic) in which hand acceleration can be preserved even at high resistance, work tempo is not the guiding factor. Rather the level of work output with each individual movement cycle is the criterion. In this case an inverse relationship will exist wherein increases in resistance reduce the duration of work at which the desired work output can be maintained.

Work can be based on the number of repetitions of individual movement cycles or on time of the duration of work. The authors' experience with semiaccommodating apparatuses (biokinetic pull ergometers and swim benches) has produced the following approximations of setting and duration at which they believe speed-strength endurance work is best achieved:

SETTING	DURATION OF INDIVIDUAL WORK BOUT
1	6 to 10 seconds
2	12 to 15 seconds
3	15 to 18 seconds
4	19 to 21 seconds
5	22 to 25 seconds
6	25 to 30 seconds

*A resistance device of European origin, which is reported to achieve phasic replication of swimming movements, similar to the semiaccommodating resistance provided by some swim benches of American manufacture. Reference to the Merton-Huttel device is seen frequently in European studies. The spelling has not been consistent.

Insofar as the method of execution of speed-strength endurance work is concerned, when use of dry land apparatus is included, most apparatuses are designed to exploit the factor of repetitive effort. The practice of alternating resistance from set to set is an effective means of maintaining desired movement tempo and speed in many apparatuses.

Semiaccommodating resistance apparatuses, which change resistance over the course of the movement cycle, are already available. In the future, apparatuses will be designed which will change resistance from repetition to repetition (variational method), permitting new variations in the training of speed-strength endurance.

In-water strength training for the development of speed-strength endurance requires the swimmer to execute ultimate or near-ultimate efforts of short duration under considerable strength loading. Movement tempo (stroke rate) quality of swimming performance and swimming speed must be monitored under these conditions. Under tethered conditions, the same circumstances prevail in which movement tempo is the primary measure of the speed-strength endurance effort. The total volume of work and number of work bouts executed should be discontinued when quality of swimming performance cannot be maintained. As speed-strength endurance increases, duration of work and work output should also increase.

Strength Endurance

In the use of specific resistance modes the strength-endurance regime of work places emphasis not so much on the quality of the strength performance of the work, but simply on increasing resistance to fatigue. When differentiating strength-endurance work from speed-strength endurance work, use is made of a wide variety of resistances at slower work tempos for longer periods of time. The tempo of work or speed of movement is not of prime importance, although the ability to sustain continuous efforts at higher movement tempo is an essential indicator of an increase in special-strength endurance.

In the use of dry land apparatus, if the resistance cannot be changed or precisely rated, the swimmer should be instructed to execute the effort at lower intensities until failure. Individual work bouts based on a percentage of total work capacity to failure can be calibrated or based on the duration of the competitive event for which the swimmer is preparing, or simply in accordance with strength-endurance methods of training as seen in *circuit* or *round* training.

In-water strength training for strength-endurance follows the same basic approach. In free swimming conditions, endurance training methods (interval method, repetition method, variable method, and so on) should incorporate only small additional resistances. Swimming under tethered conditions should be executed at lower movement tempos (stroke rate) over longer periods of time.

STRENGTH EXERCISES

Strength exercises, or the specially selected and formed movements of strength training, are based on the following criteria: (1) the direction and amplitude of the movement, which can take the form of whole body movements or partial movements; and (2) the muscles or muscle groups involved in the movement. The strength exercises are then grouped and classified, based on their theoretical objective. There are two basic categories of strength exercises: general-preparatory and special-preparatory strength exercises.

General-Preparatory Strength Exercise

General-preparatory strength exercise aims for comprehensive strength development to achieve a proper balance of strength in all major muscle groups. It also strives to correct defects in body type and posture, attempting to prevent inordinate muscle gains or lack of muscle development, conditions which can result in the development of *strength imbalances* between muscles more actively involved with the sport and their antagonistic muscle groups. Strength imbalances are said to be the main cause of many pathomechanical problems among swimmers, especially overuse injuries in the shoulder joint.

Because the number of general-preparatory exercises is so large and diverse, we include here only the basic categories of exercise and a few examples. Many texts have been devoted entirely to recording the best complex of available means of strength training exercises, but that is far beyond the intention here.

Calisthenics.   When use is made of calisthenics, the exercises chosen should be based on their ability to bring the full brunt of the athlete's body weight to bear on the movements. Resistance can be further increased by combining the use of calisthenics with objects such as dumbbells, kettlebells, weighted balls, medicine balls, sandbags, weighted vests, weighted belts, weighted cuffs for ankles and feet, or leaden weights fitted to shoes. Figure 10–1 shows some common examples.

Auxiliary Gymnastic Exercise.   The strength exercises shown in Figure 10–2 are implemented on gymnastic apparatus, in particular, wall bars, parallel bars, beam, and bench. Common examples include leg lifts from wall bars, pulleys, and swinging exercises.

Combined Exercise.   Included are two variations: (1) exercises employing rope- or rope ladder-climbing combined with additional bending, twisting, and swinging movements or with use of such objects as medicine balls, sandbags, weighted apparel, and so on; and (2) auxiliary gymnastic exercises combined with the use of objects. Figures 10–3–A and B are examples.

Partner Exercise.   Strength exercises which require the involvement of a partner are (1) composed of *counteractive* or *combative* movements in either the dynamic or static regime, (2) those which require the support of one partner while the other engages in the exercise, or (3) those which require additional resistance or extra weight in the movement. Combined/partner exercises are those which also make use of objects such as medicine balls, sandbags, and gymnastic apparatus. Examples of the first two types are shown in Figure 10–4.

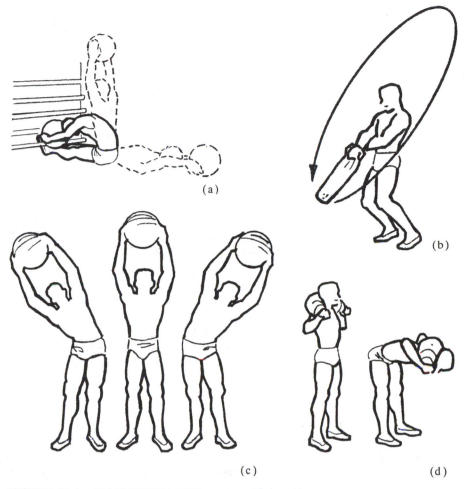

FIGURE 10-1 CALISTHENICS WITH AND WITHOUT LOADS
A. Sit-up with Medicine Ball, Using Wall Bar to Maintain the Legs in Position
B. Sandbag Swinging
C. Swinging Trunk Rotations with Medicine Ball
D. Trunk Bend with Weighted Neck Roll

Weightlifting. The use of barbells or other resistance apparatus in the formation of general-preparatory strength exercises involves two major theoretical
approaches: (1) the selection of exercise movement which involves sequences
of multiple joint movements to achieve whole body strength development, and/
or (2) in the use of single joint or partial movement strength exercise, the
selection of a sequence of strength exercises which results in a balanced strength
program involving all major muscle groups.

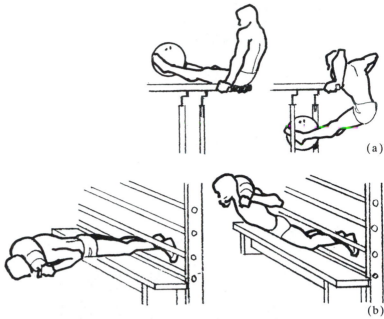

FIGURE 10-2 AUXILIARY GYMNASTIC EXERCISES
A. Body Lift from Parallel Bars with Medicine Ball
B. Upper Body Lift with Weighted Neck Roll, Using Wall Bar and Bench

Whole Body Strength Exercise. The best form of whole body strength exercise is barbell and dumbbell or kettlebell exercises derived from strength training in preparation for Olympic-style weight lifting. These include trunk curling, cleaning and jerking, and snatching exercises, plus their training derivations. Figure 10–5–A illustrates one of these.

Partial/Single Joint Strength Exercises. Most barbell or resistance apparatuses involve strength training exercises using only single joint or partial movement exercises. The use of such exercises for general-preparatory strength training requires the selection of successive exercises within the single training session if comprehensive strength development is to be guaranteed. The major muscle groups and/or basic movements should be factored out and appropriate weight lifting exercises selected. Many of them are considered *classic* exercises because they are the fundamental weight lifting exercises on which hundreds of other weight lifting movements are based. The following is a list of such successive strength exercises in common usage for the development of balanced strength:

1. Squats—to work leg, trunk, and back muscles.
2. Bench Press—to work chest, shoulder, and arm muscles.
3. Bicep Curls—to work arm flexor muscles.

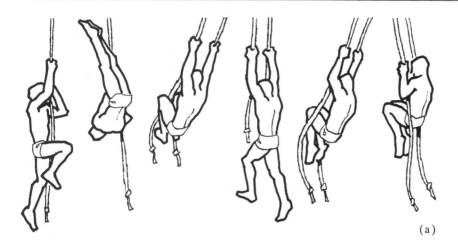

(a)

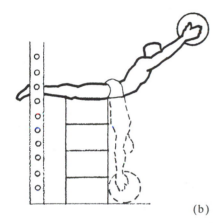

(b)

FIGURE 10-3 COMBINED EXERCISES

A. (Type 1) Rope and Ladder Climbs with Additional Twisting and Other Movements (Warning: Rope and ladder climbs are hazardous; a spotter should always be present when these climbs are attempted)

B. (Type 2) Rotated Grasp Swings from a Stack of Boxes, with Legs Maintained by Wall Rack, with or without Additional Load.

(a)   (b)

FIGURE 10-4 PARTNER EXERCISES

A. (Type 1) Counteractive or Combative Exercise

B. (Type 2) Push-up Supported by Partner—(this exercise exemplifies the partner type because the supporting partner must absorb the resistance of the active partner to sustain the supportive role)

FIGURE 10-5 WHOLE BODY STRENGTH EXERCISES

A. The Jerk (an example of an Olympic lift beging employed as a general-preparatory strength exercise)

B. Whole Body Twisting Exercise

4. **Elbow Extensors** (using a latissimus bar or triceps press)—to work arm extensors.

5. **Good Mornings** (or back hyperextensors)—to work back muscles.

6. **Lat Pulls** (using a lat bar)—to work arm depressors.

7. **Dead Lifts**—to work leg and trunk muscles.

8. **Knee Extensors**—to work leg muscles.

9. **Leg Curls**—to work hamstrings.

10. **Shoulder Press**—to work shoulders.

11. **Heel Raises**—to work calf muscles.

Special-Preparatory Strength Exercise

Nearly all special-preparatory exercises used in competitive swimming are strength exercises. Their selection and usage is explained by the fact that a *narrow* action can bring about a more significant change in separate parts of the body, acquiring greater strength in the primary musculature than is acquired during the execution of actual swimming.

The selection of special-preparatory strength exercises is based on the movement and musculature more actively involved in the swimming movements. Those basic action, prime mover muscles are described here, and most can be found on the muscle charts in Figures 10–6–A and B.

Arm Depressor and Scapular Rotators. The major arm depressor muscles include the latissimus dorsi, pectoralis major, teres major, and triceps. The primary musculature involved in scapular rotation includes the trapezius longus, the upper and lower serratus anterior, and the levator scapulae. These muscles are involved in the primary action of pulling the arm through the water, and they provide the main source of propulsion for the four competitive strokes.

Barbell Exercises 5, 8, 9, and 11 can be used to develop these muscles.

Other types of exercise which can be used to develop the arm depressors include the following:

1. *Lat Pulls*—classified either as lat pull-downs or lat pull-ins using a latissimus machine or adjustable wall pulley with different types of pulley attachments.
2. *Rows*—rowing type of exercise using wall pulleys or specially adapted rowing machines, rowing bars, or dumbbells.
3. *Pullovers*—pullover exercises using barbells or dumbbells or Nautilus or Polaris types of equipment.
4. *Chinning*—chinning exercises using a chinning bar with different chinning grip attachments.

Inward Rotators of the Upper Arm and Forearm. The primary musculature involved in inward rotation of the upper arm includes the teres major, subscapularis, latissimus dorsi, and pectoralis major. The primary musculature for forearm rotation includes pronator teres and pronator quadratus. These muscles are needed for inward rotation of the upper arm to achieve a high elbow position in the initial phase of the pulling action. Forearm rotation strength, especially the strength for pronation of the forearm, is essential for the maintenance of the desired hand-pitch needed to maximize lift propulsion in swimming.

Barbell Exercises 5, 8, and 9 develop these muscles.

Other types of exercise which may be used to develop the upper arm and forearm rotators are dumbbells or adjustable pulley apparatuses. Exercises to develop forearm rotator strength requires a special resistance apparatus which simulates the turning action of a water faucet or doorknob. A specially designed isometric apparatus to develop forearm rotator strength is also now available.

Wrist and Finger Flexors. These flexor muscles are the flexor carpi ulnaris and palmaris longus. Strength of the forearm is necessary to stabilize the wrist and hand when encountering the resistance of water. Lack of this strength usually results in extension of the wrist and fingers which disrupts the desired hand pitch, thus reducing the level of lift propulsion achieved during the pulling phase.

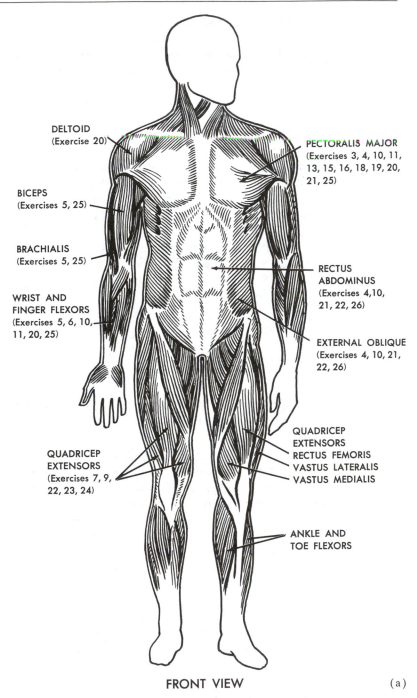

DELTOID
(Exercise 20)

PECTORALIS MAJOR
(Exercises 3, 4, 10, 11,
13, 15, 16, 18, 19, 20,
21, 25)

BICEPS
(Exercises 5, 25)

BRACHIALIS
(Exercises 5, 25)

RECTUS
ABDOMINUS
(Exercises 4, 10,
21, 22, 26)

WRIST AND
FINGER FLEXORS
(Exercises 5, 6, 10,
11, 20, 25)

EXTERNAL OBLIQUE
(Exercises 4, 10, 21,
22, 26)

QUADRICEP
EXTENSORS
RECTUS FEMORIS
VASTUS LATERALIS
VASTUS MEDIALIS

QUADRICEP
EXTENSORS
(Exercises 7, 9,
22, 23, 24)

ANKLE AND
TOE FLEXORS

FRONT VIEW   (a)

FIGURE 10-6   MUSCLE CHART
A. Front View

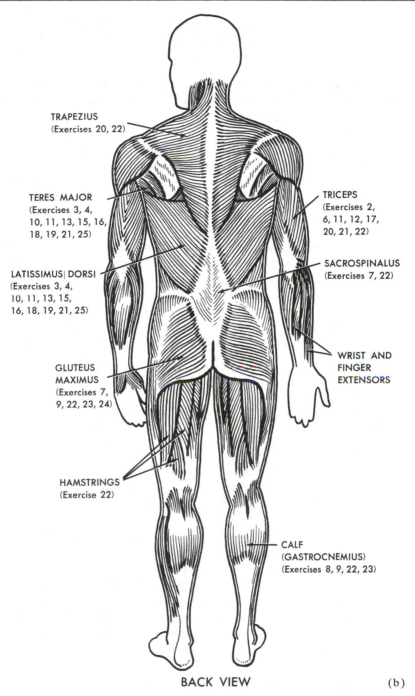

TRAPEZIUS
(Exercises 20, 22)

TERES MAJOR
(Exercises 3, 4,
10, 11, 13, 15, 16,
18, 19, 21, 25)

LATISSIMUS| DORSI
(Exercises 3, 4,
10, 11, 13, 15,
16, 18, 19, 21, 25)

**GLUTEUS
MAXIMUS**
(Exercises 7,
9, 22, 23, 24)

HAMSTRINGS
(Exercise 22)

TRICEPS
(Exercises 2,
6, 11, 12, 17,
20, 21, 22)

SACROSPINALUS
(Exercises 7, 22)

**WRIST AND
FINGER
EXTENSORS**

**CALF
(GASTROCNEMIUS)**
(Exercises 8, 9, 22, 23)

BACK VIEW

(b)

FIGURE 10-6 (*continued*)
B. Back View

Barbell Exercises 1 and 10–A develop these muscles.

Adjustable pulley systems can also be modified to exercise the wrist and finger flexors.

Elbow Extensors.   The triceps brachii is the elbow extensor. As the swimmer finishes the pull phase of the butterfly, crawl, and backstroke, this powerful extensor of the elbow is used to push the water backwards.

Barbell Exercises 2–A and B, 5, 7, and 11 develop this muscle.

In addition to the use of barbells, a lat bar or pulley system can be used. In these exercises the upper arm is placed alongside the rib cage and is stabilized. The lat bar or pulley cable and attachment is raised or lowered by flexion and extension of the elbow, moving the forearm only. Other effective exercises are kickbacks.

Hip, Knee, and Ankle Extensors and Flexors.   The leg extensors and flexors include the quadriceps extensors, gluteus maximus, and muscles of the hamstring complex. The ankle extensors include the soleus and gastrocnemius, while the ankle flexors include the tibialis anterior.

The leg extensors and flexors are essential for the start and push-off of all the strokes. Their strength in the kicking action is especially essential for the mechanics of the breaststroke kick. In order to position the feet properly for *plantar-flexion* (actually extension) in the crawl, back, and butterfly, the swimmer needs to strengthen the ankle extensors. The ankle flexors are also essential to achieve *dorsiflexion* in the breaststroke kick, which requires mobility in the ankle joint almost the reverse of that required in the other three strokes. Also essential to the breaststroke kick is the development of the tibialis posterior to aid in the inversion or supination of the feet. This essentiality occurs during the thrust phase of the whip kick, when it enables the swimmer to change the pitch of the feet to achieve the desired sculling action.

Barbell Exercises 13, 14–A, 15–B, 19–A, and 20 develop the leg extensors and flexors. Barbell Exercises 16–A and B and 20 develop the ankle extensors and flexors.

In many strength-training facilities apparatus is available to work hip and leg strength without barbells. This includes squat racks, leg-press machines, knee and hamstring extensor and flexor machines, and trunk curling machines. Heel-raise machines which effect extension of the ankles against resistance are the best devices to develop the gastrocnemius and soleus muscles for plantar-flexion strength. Toe-raise equipment is also available which effects toe-raising against resistance. Existing apparatus must be specially modified to meet the need for enhancing dorsiflexion of the tibialis inferior.

GENERAL AND SPECIAL STRENGTH EXERCISES FOR SWIMMERS, USING A BARBELL

In the case of barbell exercises, when the goal is maximum speed-strength and the number of repetitions is six to ten, the rule of thumb is to use the amount of weight that is 60 to 70 percent of the maximum the individual can lift for a given exercise. When endurance-strength is the goal, the number of repetitions is the deciding factor in selecting the amount of weight: the more repetitions, the less weight. The weight should be lighter than that used to develop speed-strength.

Some exercises are included here which develop the synergistic muscles that assist, but do not cause, the swimming movement. The trunk muscles, both the anterior group and the lateral and posterior group, are in this category. They act as links between the power applied in the front of the body by the arms and that applied in the back of the body by the legs. They stabilize the body and provide a streamlined position for the trunk.

Exercise 1. Bicep Curls

As the drawing indicates, the weight is lifted through the full range of motion. The weight should be lifted at a steady rate, not thrown upward. It should be lowered at the same rate because the muscles gain in strength and endurance as much from the stress of lowering the weight as they do from raising it.

Muscles Developed—biceps, brachialis, elbow flexors, wrist flexors, and forearm muscles.
All Strokes.

BICEP CURLS

Exercise 2A. Two-Arm Press

Muscles Developed—triceps and deltoids.
All Strokes.

TWO-ARM PRESS

Exercise 2B. Two-Arm Press Variation (from behind the neck; not pictured)

Muscles Developed—same as 2A, except it places more load on the elbow extensors (triceps) and less on the arm elevators (deltoids, etc.).

All Strokes.

Exercise 3. Horizontal Rowing

Muscles Developed—muscles of the upper back and upper arms: trapezius, rhomboids (not shown on muscle chart), deltoids, biceps, and brachialis.

All Strokes.

HORIZONTAL ROWING

Exercise 4. Upright Rowing

Muscles Developed—muscles of upper back, shoulders, and arms: trapezius, deltoids, and biceps.

All Strokes.

UPRIGHT ROWING

Exercise 5. Bench Press

Muscles Developed—muscles of the chest and arms: pectoralis major, triceps, and deltoids.
All Strokes.

BENCH PRESS

Exercise 6. Shoulder Shrug

Muscles Developed—muscles of the upper back and neck: trapezius and levator scapulae (not shown on muscle chart).
All Strokes.

SHOULDER SHRUG

Exercise 7. Elbow Extensor

Muscles Developed—triceps.
All Strokes.

ELBOW EXTENSOR

Exercise 8. Arm Rotator

Muscles Developed—the medial arm rotators: pectoralis major, subscapularis (not shown on muscle chart), latissimus dorsi, and teres major.

All Strokes.

ARM ROTATOR

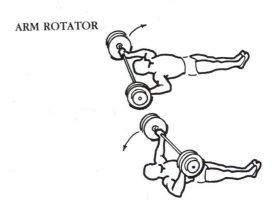

Exercise 9. Supine Straight Arm Pullover

Muscles Developed—the arm depressors: pectoralis major, latissimus dorsi, and teres major.

All Strokes.

SUPINE STRAIGHT ARM PULLOVER

Exercise 10A. Double Wrist Curl

Muscles Developed—Wrist flexors.
All Strokes.

DOUBLE WRIST CURL

Exercise 10B. Reverse Double Wrist Curl (not pictured)

This exercise is done in the same manner as 10A except that the bar is grasped with the palms facing downward. This brings the wrist extensor muscles instead of the flexors into action.

Muscles Developed—Wrist extensors.
All Strokes.

Exercise 11. Backward Arm Press

Muscles Developed—elbow extensors, triceps, and shoulder muscles: deltoids, teres major, latissimus dorsi, and rhomboids (not shown on muscle chart).
Freestyle and Butterfly.

BACKWARD ARM PRESS

Exercise 12. Forward Raise

Muscles Developed—shoulder muscles: deltoids and coracobrachialis (not shown on muscle chart).

All Strokes.

FORWARD RAISE

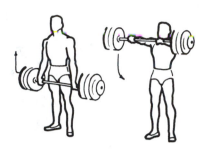

Exercise 13. Dead Lift

Muscles Developed—extensor muscles of the back: sacrospinalis; extensors of the thighs and knees: quadriceps extensors and gluteus maximus.

All Strokes.

DEAD LIFT

Exercise 14A. Half Squat

Muscles Developed—muscles of the legs and hips: quadriceps extensors, hamstrings, and gluteus maximus.

All Strokes.

HALF SQUAT

Exercise 14B. Full Squat

Caution is recommended in the use of this exercise; it can be hazardous if done with a heavy weight.

Muscles Developed—stretching of the Achilles tendon.

All Strokes.

FULL SQUAT

Exercise 15A. Straddle Lift with Full Squat

Muscles Developed—extensor muscles of the back: sacrospinalis; thigh and lower leg extensors: gluteus maximus and quadriceps extensors.

All Strokes.

STRADDLE LIFT WITH FULL SQUAT

Exercise 15B. Straddle Lift with Half Squat (not pictured)

Half squats are less dangerous than full squats and provide the same stress as full squats.

Muscles Developed—same as in Exercise 15–A.

Breaststroke.

Exercise 16A. Rise on Toes

Muscles Developed—calf muscles: gastrocnemius and soleus (not shown on muscle chart).

All Strokes.

RISE ON TOES

Exercise 16B. Rise on Toes with Toes Elevated

Muscles Developed—same as 16A, but it permits a greater amount of contraction and stretches the Achilles tendon.

All Strokes.

RISE ON TOES WITH TOES ELEVATED

Exercise 17. Side Bend

Muscles Developed—lateral muscles of the trunk: external and internal oblique (internal oblique not shown on muscle chart) and sacrospinalis.

All Strokes.

SIDE BEND

Exercise 18. Side Bend with Barbell on Neck

Muscles Developed—lateral muscles of trunk: external and internal obliques (internal oblique not shown on muscle chart) and sacrospinalis.

All Strokes.

SIDE BEND WITH BARBELL ON NECK

Exercise 19A. Forward Bend

Muscles Developed—back and hip extensors: sacrospinalis and gluteus maximus.

All Strokes.

FORWARD BEND

Exercise 19B. Forward Bend with a Twisting Motion

Muscles Developed—trunk rotator muscles.

All Strokes.

FORWARD BEND WITH A TWISTING MOTION

Exercise 20. Jumping Quarter Squat

Muscles Developed—speed and power in the hip and knee extensors; and plantar flexors of the ankles: gluteus maximus, quadriceps extensors, gastrocnemius, and soleus (not shown on muscle chart).

All Strokes.

JUMPING QUARTER SQUAT

Exercise 21. Sit-Up with Knees Bent
(bent-knee position is preferred)

Muscles Developed—hip flexors (as with plain sit-ups): psoas muscles, rectus femoris; and abdominal muscles: rectus abdominus.

All Strokes.

SIT-UP WITH KNEES BENT

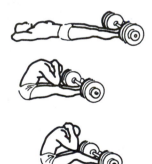

Exercise 22. Stationary Hi-Walking and Running

FIRST LEVEL	SECOND LEVEL	THIRD LEVEL	FOURTH LEVEL
Hi-Walking for 15 seconds	Hi-Walking for 10 seconds	Hi-Walking for 5 seconds	Running in place for 2 minutes continuously
Running in place for 5 seconds	Running in place for 10 seconds	Running in Place for 10 seconds	
Repeat for total of 2 minutes	Repeat for 2 minutes	Repeat for 2 minutes	

Stationary Hi-Walking and Running

Swing Arms Vigorously, Knees Up, Shoulders Back, Chest Out, Running in Place, Hi-Walking.

First Level
Hi-Walking for
15 seconds

Running in place
for 5 seconds

Repeat for Total
of 2 minutes
duration

Second Level
Hi-Walking for
10 seconds

Running in place
for 10 seconds

Repeat for
2 minutes

Third Level
Hi-Walking for
5 seconds

Running in Place
for 10 seconds

Repeat for
2 minutes

Fourth Level
Running in
place
for 2 minutes
continuously

STATIONARY HI-WALKING AND RUNNING

Exercise 23. Latissimus Device

Muscles Developed—the arm depressors, the medial rotators of the arms, and the elbow extensors.

All Strokes.

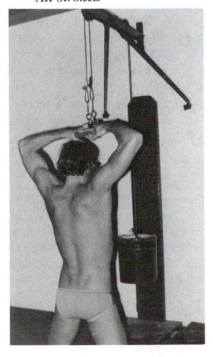

LATISSIMUS DEVICE

SHOCK EXERCISES/PLIOMETRICS

These exercises have been chosen for their ability to achieve a powerful extension of the muscle prior to the actual active work of the muscle or movement involved. The type of shock exercise selected also depends upon the maturity and level of trainedness of the athlete and the athlete's resiliency.

To develop the lower extremities, beginning swimmers should start with hopping and jumping calisthenics and rope jumping. As the athletes progress, exercises which consist of multiple hopping and jumping over benches or other obstacles may be added. In the final stages, depth jumps from a platform or jumping exercises with a barbell or other resistance may be used.

To develop the upper extremities, exercises with light medicine balls should be used with movements that do not place high mechanical stress on the shoulder joint. As the athlete gains in maturity and trainedness, heavier medicine balls with more vigorous movements may be introduced. For swimmers in particular, overhead throws with a medicine ball are an effective means of developing explosive strength in the arm depressors. In addition, swinging and throwing exercises with dumbbells and kettlebells or other projectile resistance apparatus may be added. Figure 10–7 shows examples of introductory shock exercises.

When resistance apparatuses other than free weights are used, such as pulley systems and lat machines, the speed of movement and *free fall* qualities of the apparatus should be considered. Many devices are designed to prevent rapid changes or transitions in the strength training movement. These have little use as shock exercises. Apparatuses collectively referred to as *impulse units* are now being designed to make use of kinetic energy or momentum in order to achieve the desired shock effect. Shock effect exercises have come into favor for their theoretical ability to develop explosive strength and reactive ability. Figure 10–8 shows examples of shock exercises.

It must be kept in mind that shock exercises have potential hazards. They should only be used by mature swimmers who possess the musculoskeletal integrity to withstand the mechanical stresses of such exercises. Young swimmers or those with weak bone joint integrity should not be encouraged to use these exercises. Even athletes at the top level should attempt such exercises only under the supervision of a well-qualified instructor or trainer.

THE VERTICAL JUMP AS A MEASURE OF EXPLOSIVE POWER AND SPEED

Use of the vertical jump to measure explosive power as a potential for speed in swimmers has been highly effective. Other factors being equal, those with a high score on the vertical jump make better sprinters; those with a low score make better distance swimmers. A rough estimate of the scores of adult males in the standing vertical jump reads something like this:

24 to 31 inches—sprinters

18 to 25 inches—middle-distance swimmers

11 to 22 inches—distance swimmers

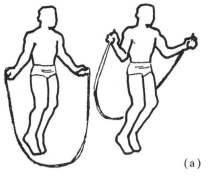

FIGURE 10-7   INTRODUCTORY SHOCK EXERCISES
   A. Rope Jumping
   B. Medicine Ball Throws

(a)

(b)

(a)

FIGURE 10-8   SHOCK EXERCISES
   A. Jumping from Stand
   B. Shock Exercises with External Resistance from Pulley Weights

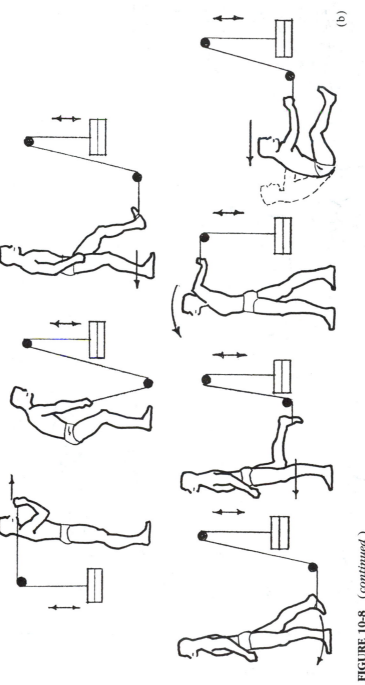

FIGURE 10-8 (*continued*)

The "other factors" alluded to are so many and varied that no coach would be so naive as to use the standing vertical jump as the sole criterion for assigning swimmers in their events. Yet its predictive value is so high that it can be helpful. Figure 10–9 shows how to do the vertical jump test and Table 10–1 is a list of norms for swimmers of various ages and both sexes.

FIGURE 10-9 VERTICAL JUMP
A. Reach
B. Jump

TABLE 10-1   NORMS FOR THE VERTICAL JUMP

	−2		−1		Mean		+1		+2

Distance

Sprinter

Long Sprinter

Middle Distance

Female Swimmers

Age	−2 Std. Dev.	−1 Std. Dev.	Mean	+1 Std. Dev.	+2 Std. Dev.
10	22.4	27.6	32.7	37.8	42.9
11	25.6	30.1	34.6	39.1	43.6
12	26.9	32.1	37.2	42.3	47.4
13	28.8	34.0	39.1	44.2	49.4
14	29.5	34.6	39.7	44.9	50.0
15	28.8	34.6	40.4	46.2	51.9
16	29.5	35.9	41.0	47.4	53.8
17	29.5	35.9	41.0	47.4	53.8

Male Swimmers

Age	−2 Std. Dev.	−1 Std. Dev.	Mean	+1 Std. Dev.	+2 Std. Dev.
10	25.6	30.1	34.6	39.1	43.6
11	26.9	31.4	35.9	40.4	44.9
12	26.3	32.7	39.1	45.5	51.9
13	30.8	37.2	43.6	50.0	56.4
14	35.3	41.7	48.1	54.5	60.9
15	37.8	44.2	50.6	57.1	63.5
16	40.4	46.8	53.2	59.6	66.0
17	42.3	48.7	55.1	61.5	67.9

Sample Size: Females (1800)   Males (2100)
Measurements in Centimeters

Procedure: The swimmers stand sideways next to a wall which has been marked in scale units and raises the dominant hand (reaching as far as possible without hyperextension of the shoulder). The text monitor records this height. The swimmer then moves slightly away from the wall. Without taking a step, the swimmer jumps upward and reaches as high as possible with the dominant hand. Maximum height attained is recorded and the difference between the reaching and jumping heights is the swimmer's vertical jump.

Computations by Ralph Richards, then doctoral student, Indiana University. Subjects were clinic participants of the Counsilman Swimming Stroke Analysis Program. Dr. Richards is currently a staff member at the National Sports Institute, Canberra, ACT, Australia.

FLEXIBILITY

Flexibility, as a term to describe human movement, is the degree or range of movement of a joint. The two limiting factors that determine flexibility are bone structure and the degree to which the muscles around a joint will permit it to move (the muscles' elasticity).

Bone Structure

People whose bones are large and have large protruberances are usually less flexible than their small-boned counterparts. Thus, it is most often the large-boned, adult male swimmer who finds he must stretch out before each practice session and before competition, if he is to perform his swimming movements optimally. People who are small-boned often possess unusually flexible joints and need little or no flexibility exercise during their competitive careers. It is unlikely that small-boned swimmers can be harmed by observing the stretching rituals seen at every meet, but they should avoid the *forced stretching* that was popular in the past and which sometimes resulted in strain or even serious injury to the athletes' joints, especially of the shoulder girdle.

Muscle Elasticity

In the past, it was common to believe that *long* muscles were an important asset for a swimmer. This, of course, was a misleading description. Muscles are only so long: They reach from the point of origin on one side of a joint to the point of attachment on the other side of that joint. The idea that the coaches of a half century ago meant to convey was that a person who builds too much bulk will not be able to move freely in all directions. A better way of describing the ideal state of suppleness is to say that the muscles, while strong, should possess the ability to allow the joint to move freely in the direction opposite from the one in which they pull the joint. To do this, the connective tissue which surrounds each muscle fiber and each bundle of fibers, and which forms the sheath of the entire muscle, may need to be stretched to achieve greater elasticity. It will then be capable of stretching and returning to its original shape, as the activity requires, and will be less likely to incur injury.

Every athlete needs flexibility in a specific joint or joints. The hurdler in track needs above-average flexibility in forward flexion of his upper leg in order to be able to go over the hurdles and still keep a low center of gravity. Swimmers can get by with only average flexibility of the hip joint, but they must have well above average flexibility in their ankles to kick effectively. Butterflyers, freestylers, and backstrokers must have flexible shoulder joints to be able to recover their arms easily over the water. Tight-shouldered crawl swimmers will be forced to overroll in order to recover their arms properly or will have to adopt a wide, flat arm recovery. Either of these practices will disturb body position and increase drag. Butterflyers who lack shoulder flexibility will either have to climb too high in the water to succeed in recovering their arms over the water or will skip them along the surface of the water, creating unwanted additional drag. On the other hand, breaststrokers need only average shoulder flexibility since their arms work within the normal range of movement.

In the course of the crawl, backstroke, and butterfly kick, the ankles should be plantar-flexed as much as possible in order to push the water backward and downward in the fly and crawl or backward and upward in the backstroke. Sitting on the heels while pointing the toes is helpful in improving plantar-flexion of the ankles.

Breaststrokers need to flex their feet in the opposite direction, that is, to dorsiflex them. Dorsiflexion permits the swimmer to apply the force of the kick in a more backward direction. Strengthening the soleus and gastrocnemius muscles and stretching the Achilles tendon, which is formed by the connective tissue surrounding the gastrocnemius, will improve dorsiflexion. The stretching exercises in this section include two methods of stretching the Achilles tendon (see Figures 10–17, 19, and 20).

Figures 10–10 through 10–15 demonstrate the tests of flexibility that are important to competitive swimmers. Figures 10–16 through 10–20 illustrate stretching exercises which can be used to improve flexibility of the specific joints that need to be flexible for swimming.

FOOTNOTES

1. A. P. Kiselev, "The Use of Specific Resistance in Highly Qualified Swimmers' Strength Training," *Teoriya i Praktica Fizicheskoi Kultury*, 5, 1990, 46–47.

2. Thomas L. DeLorme, "Restoration of Muscle Power by Heavy Resistance Exercises," The Journal of Bone and Joint Surgery, XXVII:4 (October 1945), 666.

3. William Heusner, "The Theory of Strength Development" (presentation, ASCA World Clinic, New Orleans, 1980).

FIGURE 10-10   SHOULDER FLEXIBILITY TEXT (HORIZONTAL)

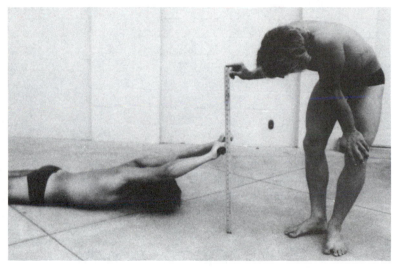

FIGURE 10-11   SHOULDER FLEXIBILITY TEST (VERTICAL)

FIGURE 10-12   FORWARD TRUNK FLEXION TEST

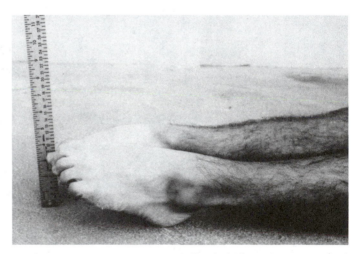

FIGURE 10-13   ANKLE FLEXIBILITY TEST (PLANTAR-FLEXION)

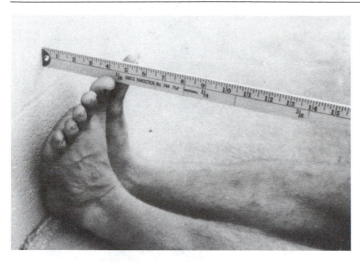

FIGURE 10-14 ANKLE FLEXIBILITY TEST (DORSIFLEXION)

FIGURE 10-15 BREASTSTROKER'S SIT-DOWN TEST

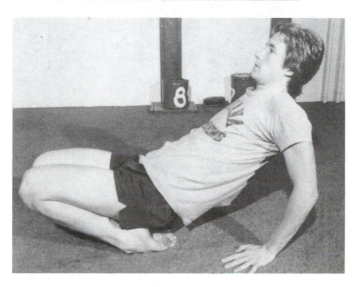

FIGURE 10-16 ANKLE STRETCHER EXERCISE TO INCREASE PLANTAR-FLEXION

FIGURE 10-17 ACHILLES TENDON STRETCHER
EXERCISE TO INCREASE DORSIFLEXION

FIGURE 10-18 ALLIGATOR SHOES

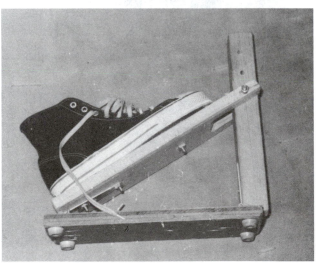

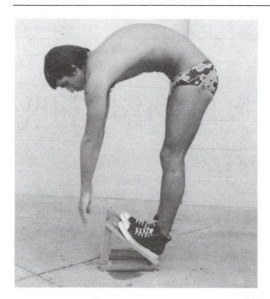

FIGURE 10-19 ACHILLES TENDON STRETCHER WITH ALLIGATOR SHOES

FIGURE 10-20 ANOTHER WAY TO STRETCH THE ACHILLES TENDON

CHAPTER 11

A Practical Guide to Organizing a Season's Program

Certain precepts have been developed which can guide the swim coach in planning a training program. Those precepts have their origins primarily in the physiological effects of training. The main thrust of this chapter will be the everyday decisions of managing the practicalities of training. This can range from the time allotted for a single training session to the time allotted for the long term development of an athlete.

The fundamental questions which must be answered when designing a training program are the following:

1. How far: 5000 yards/meters a day, 10,000, 12,000, or 20,000?
2. How often: once, twice, three times a day?
3. How hard: the level of intensity: all-out, moderate, easy?
4. How long: three months, ten months, or twelve months a year?
5. What methods: how should the emphasis be shifted among the methods as the season progresses?

There are no absolute answers to these questions because they depend on so many variables: the age and level of maturation of the swimmer, the level of trainedness of the swimmer, the intrinsic capacity of the individual athlete to absorb work. But, most important, is the event (or events) for which the athlete is preparing. The specificity of the training load to the events for which the swimmer is training should remain foremost in the mind of the coach, who should always be thinking of what it takes to improve the performance of the energy-producing and energy delivery systems, the neurologic system, and the musculo-skeletal system.

THE USE OF INTERMITTENT WORK AND ITS APPLICATION

Most physical activity is of an intermittent nature; very little can be characterized as continuous. Short bouts of activity are commonly interspersed by periods of light work or rest. This is as true of most sports activity—football, baseball, and tennis—as of general physical activity or of such vigorous physical work as digging a ditch or working on an air hammer. It could be said that intermittent physical activity is so common as to be considered an intrinsic pattern of human behavior.

An examination of the training regimes provided by the coaches listed in Chapter 12, *Train with the Experts*, will show that most of their swimmers' training is done in some form of intermittent work.

Swimmers use an intermittent form of training called *interval training*. The different forms of interval training include extensive interval, intensive interval, and repetition training. Extensive interval training is also known as slow and short-rest interval training. Intensive interval training is also known as fast and long-rest interval training. Sometimes *sprint training* is distinguished as a different method of training, but, in fact, it fits the same qualifications as for repetition training. They have already been discussed in Chapter 8.

When using interval training methods, decisions have to be made concerning four factors. They can be remembered easily by recalling the cue word *DIRT*:

D—distance to be swum

I—interval of rest between each repeat swim

R—repetitions (number of bouts of exercise or repeat swims)

T—time (average time assigned to each repeat swim)

The distinction between interval and repetition methods is as follows:

Distance:: Both methods may use the same distances (50, 100, 150, 200, 300 yards/meters and so on).

Interval of Rest: Interval training uses short rest intervals (5, 10, 15, 30 seconds), while repetition training uses long rest intervals (one, two, and three minutes).

Interval methods that make use of flat amounts of rest between each repeat effort are referred to as *flat intervals. Fixed intervals* designate *departure times* instead of flat intervals.

Repetitions: Interval training involves the use of many repeats, such as 30 × 50, 20 × 100, and 10 × 200, while repetition training uses fewer repeats, such as 10 × 50, 5 × 500, and 4 × 200.

Time: In interval training the assigned times should be much slower than those assigned to repetition efforts. Repetition training times should be five to fifteen percent faster than interval training times for the same distance. Pace clocks, the large, analog clocks equipped with a second and minute hand and visible from all parts of the pool, are an invaluable tool in maintaining the integrity of all types of intermittent training.

A coach might want to assign a set of repeats with a moderate amount of rest, for example, 10 × 100 with a forty-five seconds rest interval. Would this be interval training or repetition training? It qualifies more as intensive interval training, which falls between extensive interval and repetition methods.

The following rules are important to consider regarding repetition and interval training:

1. The shorter the rest interval between repeat swims, the greater the endurance effect and the lesser the effect on speed.

2. The longer the rest interval, the higher will be the intensity of the swim.

3. A swimmer can tolerate large volumes of low or moderate-intensity work, such as overdistance or interval training, but not large quantities of high-quality work such as repetition training or all-out time trials, which are extremely demanding and, if not used judiciously, can lead to failure to adapt.

TYPES OF SETS

This section describes the different ways of organizing interval and repetition training into what are known as *sets*. Sets are the most rudimentary form of implementing and realizing training methods as actual work loads. The different types of sets are arranged to achieve certain types of training effects, which are based on both training and competitive objectives.

Straight Sets

A straight set of repeat swims is one in which the swimmer holds the distance, the rest interval and the time of each repeat swim constant. For example, 30 × 50 meters; departure time 45 seconds; average time to swim the distance, twenty-eight seconds; average rest interval, seventeen seconds.

TYPICAL STRAIGHT SETS

10 × 50 or	10 × 100 or	8 × 200 or	5 × 400 or	3 × 800 or
20 × 50 or	15 × 100 or	10 × 200 or	8 × 400 or	5 × 800 or
30 × 50	20 × 100	14 × 200	10 × 400	8 × 800
(75s, 150s, 300s—in fact, any distance can be used)				

Descending-Time Sets

In a descending-time set the swimmer tries to swim each successive repeat faster than the preceding one.

For example: 6 × 400 meters, departure time six minutes.

	1	2	3	4	5	6
Time	4:40	4:38	4:34	4:30	4:28	4:22

This type of set is very popular with high-level performers. It enables the swimmer to impose various intensities of stress and it is physiologically sound. Typical descending-time sets are variations of straight sets because the departure time remains unchanged.

Out-Slow/Back-Hard Sets (Negative Split)

In this type of set the swimmer swims the first half of each repeat swim slower than the second half; that is, swim 8 × 200, departure time three minutes on each 200. Swim first 100 in 1:08 and second 100 in 1:06 or better for a total time of 2:14 or better. This type of swimming gives the athlete confidence that he can come back hard in the second half of his race, and it teaches him to pace himself.

TYPICAL OUT-SLOW/BACK-HARD SETS

4 × 200	3 × 400	3 × 800	3 × 1500
8 × 200	5 × 400	6 × 800	8 × 400

Decreasing Rest Interval Sets

The most popular variation of the standard sets is one in which the interval of rest is decreased as the set progresses.

For example: 20 × 100 meters.

1. The first 10 × 100 meters is swum with a departure time of 1:20 (this must be adapted to each swimmer—1:20 would be used for a world-class male freestyle, average time 1:10 or better, average rest interval 10 seconds).
2. The next 5 × 100 is swum with a departure time of 1:15 (average time 1:05 or better).
3. The last 5 × 100 is swum with a departure time of 1:10 (average time 1:05 or better).

This type of set varies the stress and is very challenging. As the season progresses and the condition of the swimmer improves, the departure time is gradually decreased. This type of set is particularly effective early in the workout because it gives the swimmer a chance to warm up before he really has to exert himself. He is also able to measure the improvement in his conditioning by realizing he is able to use a shorter departure time than he could manage formerly.

Increasing Rest Interval Sets

If the rest interval between sets is changed enough, it is possible to combine training methods into one set of repeats. For example, if a swimmer is assigned a set of 20 × 100-yard repeats, the first 5 × 100 can be done with a ten-second rest interval between each 100, the second 5 × 100 with a twenty-second rest interval, the third 5 × 100 with a thirty-second rest interval, and the last 5 × 100 with a one-minute rest interval. As the rest interval increases, the swimmer is expected to swim faster, thus the method changes from the first set of 100s, which is strictly interval training, to the last set, which, with one minute of rest, qualifies as repetition training. Again, in reality, the swimmers will not use precise rest intervals, but departure times.

TYPICAL INCREASING REST INTERVAL SETS
(Using Departure Times for Good Freestylers)

10 × 50 on 40	4 × 200 on 2:30	3 × 400 on 5:00
10 × 50 on 50	4 × 200 on 2:45	3 × 400 on 5:30
10 × 50 on 60	4 × 200 on 3:00	3 × 400 on 6:00

It is important to stress that each of the different strokes will require different take-off intervals. Even swimmers using the same stroke may require different take-off intervals, depending on their repeat times. To avoid the chaos that would result if every swimmer in the pool needed a different departure time, the coach must organize the lanes so swimmers who do similar repeat times, regardless of stroke, are using the same lane. This is the sort of challenge routinely placed on the organizational skills of a coach.

Varying-Distance Sets

A set of repeat swims that many swimmers find challenging is one in which the distance of each repeat swim is changed.

TYPICAL VARYING-DISTANCE SETS

Example A.
1. Swim 400, look at your 300.
2. Swim 300 faster than you were at the 300 on the way to the 400, look at your 200.
3. Swim 200 faster than the 200 on the way to the 300, look at your 100.
4. Swim 100 faster than the 100 on the way to the 200.

Example B.
1. Swim 4 × 400, thirty-second rest interval.
2. Swim 4 × 200, twenty-second rest interval.

     3. Swim 4 × 100, ten-second rest interval.

     4. Swim 4 × 50, ten-second rest interval.

Example C.

     1. Swim 100, allowing thirty seconds to one minute after each swim.

     2. Swim 200.

     3. Swim 300.

     4. Swim 400.

     5. Swim 300.

     6. Swim 200.

     7. Swim 100.

Example D.

     1. Swim 10 × 50, ten-second rest interval.

     2. Swim 4 × 100, fifteen-second rest interval.

     3. Swim 4 × 200, thirty-second rest interval.

A varying-distance set offers limitless opportunities for variety. The swimmer and coach must take care not to use these sets exclusive of the use of straight sets or broken sets. The authors used them two or three times a week during the one-workout per day level of training. They can be done in either interval or repetition training methods.

Broken Swims

This type of set should be used at least twice a week during the hard-training phase. They are called broken swims because they provide a means by which a swimmer who is training for a 200-meter race, for example, but who, at this stage of training cannot do a 200 at race pace, can sustain the desired pace by swimming 4 × 50 repeat swims—each 50 in 30 seconds with ten seconds rest between them. This pace can be maintained because the ten-second rest period between each 50 permits enough recovery to make that pace possible.

Broken 300s.   Broken 300s usually consist of 3 × 100 repeats with ten seconds rest between 100s. This gives the swimmer a total of two rest periods of ten seconds each, or a total elapsed rest interval of twenty seconds. If the swimmer is using a pace clock, he can start when the second hand hits forty, and his actual swimming time will be displayed on the pace clock.

Broken 400s.   Broken 400s can be swum as 4 × 100 with a ten-second rest interval between 100s for a total elapsed time of thirty seconds, once again canceling out the rest time interval by starting his broken swim when the second hand hits thirty.

Broken 400s can also be done as 8 × 50. If the swimmer is doing 400 with a ten second rest interval between 50s, he will have a total of seven rest intervals or a total rest time of seventy seconds. He must therefore start his broken swim on fifty.

Broken 800s.   Broken 800s are usually done as 8 × 100 with a rest interval of ten seconds between 100s. The swimmer should start when the second hand hits fifty.

Broken swims can be of any distance the coach or swimmer wants to select, such as broken 100 (4 × 25), broken 1500 (15 × 100). The rest interval can be five, ten, fifteen, twenty seconds, and so on. If the set of repeats is short, such as 4 × 50 (broken 200), and the rest interval is short, such as ten seconds, the type of training qualifies as a cross between interval (because of the short rest interval) and repetition training (because it will probably be swum at a very fast speed).

TYPICAL SETS OF BROKEN SWIMS

Swim 8 × broken 200s (4 × 50)
Swim 5 × broken 400s (4 × 100)
Swim 3 × broken 800s (8 × 100)
Swim 2 × broken 1500s (15 × 100)

These can be swum with the swimmer trying to keep them at the same time or trying to go each succeeding one faster, as in decreasing time sets.

The swimmer can also do kicking and pulling in the same manner, such as 2 × broken 400 kicks (4 × 100), ten seconds rest interval.

Mixing Broken Swims and Straight Swims

A combination of two methods is the use of alternating broken sets and straight sets, as follows:

Example A.
1. Swim a broken 200 (4 × 50, ten-seconds rest interval).
2. Swim a straight 200.
    Do the above three, four, or five times until a total of 6, 8, or 10 × 200 has been swum, allowing approximately one-minute rest interval between 200s.

Example B.
1. Swim a broken 400 (either 4 × 100 or 8 × 50).
2. Swim a straight 400.
    Do the above two, three, or four times until a total of 4, 6, or 8 × 400 has been swum.

Example C.
1. Swim a broken 400 (4 × 100, ten-seconds rest interval).
2. Swim a straight 400.
3. Swim a broken 300 (3 × 100, ten-seconds rest interval).
4. Swim a straight 300.
5. Swim a broken 200 (4 × 50, ten-seconds rest interval).
6. Swim a straight 200.

Allow one to two minutes rest between swims.

Example D.
1. Swim a broken 1500 (15 × 100, five-seconds rest interval).
2. Swim a straight 1500.
3. Swim a broken 800 (8 × 100, five-seconds rest interval).

4. Swim a straight 800.

5. Swim a broken 400 (4 × 100, five-seconds rest interval).

Allow one to two minutes rest between swims.

Mixing broken swims with straight swims helps relieve the boredom of straight sets. The general pattern is to decrease the time of each effort as the set progresses. In a set of 200s, for example, the third broken 200 might be faster than the second, and the second faster than the first. That is, the times on the broken swims can only be compared to the times on the other broken swims, and the times on the straight swims compared only to those on the other straight swims. The time on the broken swims would, of course, generally be faster than those on the straight swims, thus canceling out the rest intervals.

As can be seen, the swimmer and coach have almost limitless flexibility in the combinations they can devise, using any distance, any rest interval, or any number of repeats. The most common are those mentioned here. They can serve as guidelines until the coach feels comfortable with customizing workouts to suit a particular team situation.

Further examination of the various types of sets listed here demonstrates that, as the swimmer progresses into a set of repeats and becomes more fatigued, he moves from what is still termed the aerobic zone to the anaerobic/non-robic zone. The more intense the effort, the sooner he arrives in the anaerobic zone/non-robic zone. This is the reason the writers dislike assigning the terms *aerobic* and *anaerobic* to particular sets of repeats. Such terminology is misleading because all racing efforts involve both aerobic and anaerobic forms of energy release. That is, while it is true that sprinting is more anaerobic than middle-distance or distance swimming, all three intensities involve all forms of energy release.

MEASURABLE INDICES AS GUIDELINES FOR THE USE OF METHODS

It has become prevalent to use methods and organize sets to conform to mathematical indices related to performance or based on physiological criteria. These parameters allow the coach an objective measure for calculating the response to the training and for comparing with a scientific model that plots the course of change in trainedness.

Some of the more common objective measures include: the estimate of training intensity based on percentage of maximal effort and the estimate of intensity based on heart rate. These indices are used primarily to determine the balance of high intensity and low intensity to ensure the proper *content or mixture of training*.

The Use of Percentages of Maximal Effort as an Estimate of Training Intensity

Swimmers and coaches frequently discuss the effort at which a given swim should be executed in terms of *percentage effort*. This is a subjective, very nebulous term which is relative to so many factors that it has no absolute meaning.

A specific and common understanding might be reached by merely asking each swimmer to think of ten percent slower than the best time of which he is capable for a given distance as being 90 percent, twenty percent slower as being 80 percent effort, and so on.

For example, a swimmer who is capable of swimming 100 yards in fifty seconds would have the following percentage efforts

	_100%_	95%	90%	85%	80%	75%	70%	65%	60%
Seconds	50	52.5	55	57.5	60	62.5	65	67.5	70

There are some considerations that need to be examined when using percentage efforts to determine training intensity. The first involves distinguishing _absolute intensity_ from _relative intensity_. Absolute intensity is derived from maximal swimming velocity, achieved from sprint efforts of extremely short duration. Relative intensity is rated according to the best time for the distance equivalent to the repeat. Percentage efforts can and have been rated on the basis of both absolute and relative intensity, but they are not the same thing. Swimming two hundred yards in one minute and 50 seconds may be 95 percent of relative intensity of the swimmer's best time for the two hundred, but it can be as low as 75 percent of that swimmer's best time for a twenty-five yard allout swim. Thus, in sprint training, times of repeats can be based on absolute intensity; in more prolonged efforts beyond one hundred yards, relative intensity should be used.

When using percentage efforts in training sets, the coach must be aware that changes during the set will take place which disqualify exact percentage efforts as indicators of desired training effects. This is because, as the workload progresses and the swimmer becomes fatigued, the time of execution increases and it can be perceived that intensity decreases. The execution of continued work effort in the presence of fatigue creates a training stimulus that is essential for adaptation. This may not be achieved if the coach decides that the speed is the only factor he needs to consider and he discontinues work when speed drops off. A speed range that accounts for progressive fatigues must be taken into account when using percentage efforts as an indicator of intensity.

The Use of Heart Rate as a Gauge of Effort

The use of heart rate is the preferred method of measuring intensity because it has been shown that heart rate increases linearly with intensity of effort. The most important variables that swimmers should know is their resting heart rate, their maximal heart rate, and target heart rates assigned by the coach to the different methods used in training.

In modern sports training science, ranges of heart rate have been assigned to different work zones of intensity which determine the relative contribution of aerobic and anaerobic/non-robic mechanisms of energy acquisition. In the execution of training loads that are primarily aerobic in nature the heart rate must be kept under 170 to 180 beats per minute. Beyond 180 beats per minute, the work becomes progressively more anaerobic/non-robic in order to sustain performance. In the execution of aerobic loads within the aerobic threshold (lower intensity/subcritical intensity below the anaerobic/lactate threshold), a heart rate of 140 to 170 beats per minute should be maintained. In the performance of anaerobic/lactate threshold work, the heart rate should fall into the range of 170 to 185 beats per minute. Beyond 180 to 185 beats per minute, work will shift to a primarily anaerobic/non-robic emphasis, pushing heart rate to maximal or near-maximal values.

There are a number of precautions to be taken in the use of heart rate. Its use is problematical for swimmers with cardiac anomalies, the most common of which are bradycardia (abnormally slow resting heart rate) and tachycardia (abnormally high resting heart rate). Intensity zones predicated on heart rate are based on a normal resting heart rate of about 70 beats per minute. Swimmers with bradycardia find it difficult to raise their heart rate to the elevations required for intensive work, based on normal heart rate values; swimmers with tachycardia push heart rates to near maximum values even at low intensity work rates.

Another factor to consider is the change in heart rate as the state of trainedness of the swimmer increases. As conditioning improves, it is usually marked by a decrease in resting heart rate. Basal heart rate also changes as a result of the execution of previous work, chronic fatigue, psychological stress, and other factors. The monitoring of resting, morning heart rate is often used to indicate daily basal values. An unusually high, morning resting heart rate in swimmers without tachycardia is often an indicator of over trainedness.

Figure 11-1 is of a swimmer taking his pulse. Average pulse rate and maximal pulse rate are individual, so there are no established norms. Thus, when a swimmer uses pulse rate as a guide to effort, it can only be compared with his own norms.

Determining the Interval of Rest

The use of a measurable index to determine the interval of rest depends on the type of interval. There are several types of intervals: *flat* or *ordinary* intervals, *fixed* or *rigid* intervals, and *work-to-rest ratio intervals*. Flat and work-to-rest ratio intervals designate fixed amounts of rest between repeats, while fixed intervals designate *departure times*. Flat and work-to-rest ratio intervals require no special mathematical formulas to determine their use; they simply follow the rules concerning quantity of rest based on duration and intensity of the repeat.

Mathematical formulas are required for fixed intervals because of the unique conditions that govern their use. Fixed intervals are the preferred form of rest interval because they are considered more challenging than flat or work-to-rest ratio intervals. In many types of work, the interval is decreased when the intensity of training is increased. Determining the fixed interval appropriate for intense, short-rest efforts is one of the most crucial aspects of coaching competitive swimmers, and the use of standard formulas helps to determine the best short-rest interval for individual swimmers.

The coach may rely on three easily obtainable measurements to determine challenging short-rest, fixed intervals: (1) the average time of a set of repeat swims

(a)

(b) **FIGURE 11-1** TAKING PULSE RATES

on a controlled interval, (2) the average number of strokes per length, and (3) the average pulse rate after the repeat swims.

A great deal of variability can be found among individuals on these three measurements. The swimmer and coach must realize that the swimmer is, in essence, comparing his average time for a set of repeats, his stroke number, and his pulse rate with measurements taken from sets of repeats he himself has done previously. Norms taken from a large group of people are not helpful.

These three measurements, especially speed and heart rate, are commonly used in work formulas to designate the level of effort and amount of rest in interval training. Such formulas include the T-8 and the T-20 Test, the PWC-170 Test, and a myriad of others. The T-20 Test, for example, designates departure time based on the average time achieved during a sustained swim (if a swimmer takes twenty-five minutes to swim 2000 yards, his designated interval for a set of one hundreds is 1:20).

Dick Bower* is responsible for devising a method of determining individual departure times, known as *cruise interval* methods. Bower has formalized departure intervals according to the following formula:

> *Cruise Interval = the fastest departure interval at which an individual can swim 5 × 100 repeat swims plus five seconds.*

For example, if the fastest a swimmer can repeat 5 × 100 is on a departure time of 1:05, his cruise interval will be 1:10. When he swims repeats of other distances, the cruise interval can be determined merely by doubling that of the 100 for the 200, tripling it for the 300, and so on. His cruise intervals for the repeat sets of the various distances will be as follows: 50 = 35 seconds, 100 = 1:10, 200 = 2:20, 300 = 3:30, 400 = 4:40, 500 = 5:50, 800 = 9:20, and so on. The departure time of cruise interval sets can be determined by the formula just described, but, for convenience, Table 11–1 provides the approximate interval departure times for freestyle among good swimmers at the various levels, including senior, Masters, and age-group swimmers.

A good time to administer a set of cruise interval repeats is early in the workout, just after the swimmers have warmed up. The cruise interval plus five seconds should be used on the first subset, the cruise interval on the second subset, and the cruise interval minus five seconds on the last subset. One minute

TABLE 11-1 RANGE FOR CRUISE INTERVAL DEPARTURE TIMES (IN YARDS) FOR VARIOUS LEVELS AND VARIOUS DISTANCES

	50s	75s	100s	150s	200s	300s	400s	500s
Senior Men	30.0 to 35.0	45.0 to 52.0	1:00 to 1:10	1:30 to 1:45	2:00 to 2:20	3:00 to 3:30	4:00 to 4:40	5:00 to 5:50
Senior Women	32.5 to 37.5	:46.5 to 55.0	1:05 to 1:15	1:32 to 1:50	2:10 to 2:30	3:15 to 3:45	4:20 to 5:00	5:25 to 6:15
Age Groupers—13&14 Masters—25 to 34	35.0 to 40.0	47.5 to 50.0	1:10 to 1:20	1:45 to 2:00	2:20 to 2:40	3:30 to 4:00	4:40 to 5:20	5:50 to 6:40
Age Groupers—11&12 Masters—35 to 49	37.5 to 42.5	50.0 to 1:05	1:15 to 1:25	1:52 to 2:07	2:30 to 2:50	3:45 to 4:15	5:25 to 5:40	6:15 to 7:05
Age Groupers—9&10 Masters—50 to 59	40.0 to 45.0	52.5 to 1:10	1:20 to 1:30	2:00 to 2:20	2:40 to 3:00	4:00 to 4:30	5:20 to 6:00	6:40 to 7:30
Beginning Swimmers 8 through 12 Masters—60 & over	42.5 to 47.5	55.0 to 1:12	1:25 to 1:35	2:07 to 2:25	2:50 to 3:10	4:15 to 4:45	5:40 to 6:20	7:05 to 7:55

*Dick Bower, Coach of Dick Bower's Swim Club, Metairie, Louisiana. Mr. Bower is a well-known and respected coach of longstanding. His teams have produced many junior and senior national qualifiers. He created the term "cruise interval," a particularly apt phrase in conveying the idea of less than all-out effort.

of rest or more should be allowed between each subset. The swimmers may swim one of the following sets of repeats with the indicated cruise interval:

INDIVIDUALIZED C.I.	SET 1	SET 2	SET 3	SET 4
C.I. plus 5 seconds	8 × 75	6 × 100	4 × 150	3 × 200
Cruise Interval	12 × 75	10 × 100	6 × 150	5 × 200
C.I. minus 5 seconds	6 × 75	4 × 100	3 × 150	2 × 200
(this subset is difficult)				

In repetition training, the use of mathematical formulas to determine rest interval is not a priority. Like flat and work-to-rest ratio intervals, the only major concern is to follow the rules concerning quantity of rest between repeats according to their duration and intensity. The formulation of an individual, challenging short-rest, fixed interval has no place in repetition training.

THE TYPE OF ACTIVITY EXECUTED IN THE USE OF ENDURANCE METHODS

Most swim training is executed under free swimming conditions. That is, under normal conditions in which the technical model remains the same as in competitive conditions with deviations or changes in technical forms, without apparatus that changes technique, isolates certain movements, or changes normal force production, etc. How all four strokes are used within the training plan depends on (1) what events are being prepared for, (2) how the swimmers might use them to achieve comprehensive conditioning (all-sided preparation, which is merely a theoretical dictate), (3) whether or not the athlete can sustain the use of training strokes, and so forth.

Freestyle

Preference is given to freestyle as the main constituent of free swim training. This is because other strokes, such as the breaststroke or butterfly, place greater demands on the swimmer and they cannot always be sustained for long-duration efforts of low to moderate intensity.

Backstroke

Backstroke ranks with freestyle as another stroke that can be used extensively. Among swimmers who specialize in this stroke, backstroke can and is regularly substituted for freestyle to constitute the majority of endurance preparation in free swimming.

Breaststroke and Butterfly

As mentioned earlier, breaststroke and butterfly place very high physical demands on swimmers, thus they are less likely to be used in the development of general endurance. The high demand is not only physiological, it can also be mechanical. There are mechanical problems regularly associated with breaststroke and butterfly that can occur as a result of overuse or poor technique. Shoulder and back problems are common in butterfly and knee problems can develop in breaststroke. The amount of training in the use of these strokes depends on the training capacity and mechanical/structural resiliency of the swimmer.

Medley Swimming

The combined use of all four strokes within single work bouts or throughout sets is viewed not only as a necessity for swimmers who specialize in medley events, but also as a necessary part of increasing the allsided preparedness of the swimmer. It allows the regular but sparing use of butterfly and breaststroke, with the use of all four strokes ensuring the comprehensive technical development, which, on the basis of some sports theory, aids in the more specialized development of chosen competition.

Controlled Breathing

Training with controlled breathing (which is also known as hypoxic training) is a method by which a swimmer induces abnormally high levels of carbon dioxide and low levels of oxygen in the lungs by breathing less often than he would normally, but doing so on a structured basis. If he normally breathes once every arm cycle when swimming a 200-meter repeat swim, he might breathe only half as often, that is, once every second arm cycle, or only one-third as often, once every third arm cycle. Controlled breathing is not so much a training method as it is an adjunct to training that can be used with any of the different training methods. When the swimmer inspires less air, the level of distress increases, becoming an additional stress factor, which may bring about desirable physiological (or perhaps psychological) changes. Several research studies have shown that this additional stress has desirable effects, improving the ability to extract oxygen from inhaled air. The authors used structured breathing patterns for about one third of each total workout and for all the pulling drills, limiting it to not more than one breath every two or three stroke cycles. There are some who believe the improvement is more psychological than physical. They attribute improvement to an enhancement of volitional will, that is, to becoming more accustomed to operating in the presence of discomfort. At the present state of technology, it is not possible to determine the precise mechanisms that may be involved.

The practice of controlling breathing patterns is potentially dangerous, if carried to an extreme, but is not nearly so dangerous as uncontrolled breath holding. This latter technique is not recommended for swimmers. It is an unfortunate fact that any training method which shows promise of improving the margin of success tends to be abused. These writers have heard of coaches who ask young age-groupers to swim 25 yards on one breath. This practice constitutes excessive use and is potentially life-threatening.

Kicking

In kicking drills, the arms are placed in a stationary position with all propulsion being generated by the kicking action of the legs. Keeping the arms stationary is usually accomplished by merely fixing the arms in position, either overhead, at the sides, or through use of such buoyant devices as the kick board. The main emphasis of kicking is to achieve a physiological overload of the leg musculature that cannot normally be accomplished when the kick is combined with the arm pull. It is also used as part of the technical training process to allow the swimmer to concentrate on leg mechanics in order to correct any potential kicking errors and/or to reinforce proper kicking mechanics.

Pulling

In pulling efforts, leg movement is eliminated and propulsion output comes from the arms only. The legs are immobilized through the use of a small inner tube or other elastic material secured to the ankles, or by placing a pull-buoy between the thighs. Pull-buoys are preferred due to the ease of their installation and the buoyancy they provide, which helps maintain streamlined body positioning. Sometimes pull-buoys and ankle straps are used in combination, since it has been found that a minimal kicking action can still be achieved when using pull-buoys, thus thwarting the primary training effect of pulling, which is to create an overload of the arms. This happens most frequently in the breaststroke and butterfly. In freestyle and the backstroke, there are many swimmers who claim that the use of a pull-buoy actually decreases the level of exertion encountered in pulling drills. This is because the legs are kept buoyant without kicking, reducing overall effort. This is especially true with swimmers who possess a kick that increases the total effort required in the armpull. Such a kick can actually reduce forward movement by producing negative force resultants or by simply increasing frontal resistance. In either case, the additional benefit of pulling is to increase availability of oxygen to the arms, through reduction of energy output by the legs, thus allowing greater work output by the arms under conditions which designate this as a desired training effect.

Apparatus Used in Swimming

Besides equipment used in kicking and pulling, other apparatuses are used in swimming in an attempt to create different training effects from those achieved in free swimming. The primary desired training effect is to create conditions of mechanical or physiological overload in order to heighten the effect of adaptation to the training load. The nature of this overload takes on different aspects depending on the apparatus used. They are also used in various combinations with other apparatus and are used in free swimming, kicking, or pulling conditions.

Hand Paddles.   The use of hand paddles is to increase the drag component on the hands by increasing the pressure differential under the hands. In order to maintain stroke cadence and proper mechanics, greater muscular tension must be developed, increasing the display of strength component throughout the entire pull. The amount of drag developed depends on the size and surface characteristics of the hand paddles; that is, larger hand paddles create greater drag and require greater strength efforts. Perforations, rough or smooth surfaces, and protuberances also increase or decrease the drag component. Care must be taken in the use of hand paddles because their excessive or chronic use has been known to aggravate pathomechanical problems of the shoulder.

Swim Fins. Like hand paddles, swim fins also increase the volume of water encountered—in this case, however, by the feet. The purpose of using the fins is also the same: magnification of the drag component in the process of the kicking action. Though greater speeds can be achieved at equivalent physical efforts in free kicking, the main training effect is to use this greater drag component to increase the physical overload of the leg musculature. Comparisons of maximal heart rates between maximal kicking efforts reveal that higher heart rates can be achieved during maximal kicking efforts with swim fins than without. The magnitude of drag achieved depends on the size of the fins. Many swimmers prefer the use of small fins when performing extensive or sustained kicking efforts because, although larger fins produce higher speeds and greater muscular overload, they cause unacceptable levels of discomfort in the feet and ankles.

Swim fins are also said to help improve unaided kicking performance, but this has never been proven definitively. If kicking performance is inhibited by poor mechanics or limited ankle flexibility, and swim fins aid in improving either of these factors, then swim fins may help technical preparation of the kick. Experience has shown this is not highly probable, however.

Tethered Swimming. In tethered swimming, a cord or rope, usually made of some type of elastic material, is secured to a fixed point on the deck or edge of the pool, while the other end is connected to a belt or harness fastened around the swimmer's waist. Tethered swimming is performed with two basic variants: negative and positive tethered conditions. Under negative tethered conditions, the swimmer progresses away from the fixed point and against the resistance or impedance offered by the cord. Depending on the tension developed on the cord, progress is slowed or stopped altogether, with the individual swimming stationary in the water. The training stimulus achieved here is an increase in the level of opposing resistant forces against the swimmer. To remain stationary or not lose ground, the swimmer must increase the level of muscular tension to produce counteractive force. In other words, the nature of the overload is primarily that of developing specific strength abilities for swimming. This increased strength output is only partially possible and worthwhile if the swimmer also attempts to maintain a desired stroke rate and proper stroke mechanics. Tethered swimming creates mechanical conditions in which improper adjustments of stroke mechanics can actually increase or sustain higher force production during tethered swimming. These work conditions, which can be carried over into free swimming, can result in the introduction of undesirable elements into the technical preparation of the swimmer.

In the use of positive tethered conditions, the swimmer progresses towards the fixed point to which the cord is connected. The cord acts as an additional external force in the direction of swimming, contributing acceleration to the mass of the swimmer's body. The result is a condition of speed overload, allowing the swimmer to achieve swimming velocities not available under normal conditions of free swimming. To sustain this effect, the tension on the cord must be maintained by taking up the slack as the swimmer approaches the fixed point. This is accomplished by a number of different mechanical applications.

Weight Belts, Drag Belts, and Drag Suits. The use of weight belts or other such apparatus intended to increase the frictional forces ordinarily encountered in the water are used for various reasons in the development of strength abilities. These have been elaborated upon in Chapter 10, which deals with strength development. The effect of weight belts, whether through the use of lead weights such as are used by scuba divers or specially designed weight belts for competitive swimmers, is to increase the mass of the swimmer in the water, creating conditions for overload. Weight belts are not the preferred choice of swimmers since they reduce buoyancy and, to compensate for this loss, often create improper changes of technique. There are also specially designed weighted cuffs for the wrist and ankles that create different conditions for swimming; but these also may have detrimental effects on technique. Apparatus that increases the frictional forces in the water, such as drag suits or drag belts, are preferred among swimmers because these apparatuses can create hardened conditions without loss of buoyancy.

Kick Boards and Pull-Buoys. Although already mentioned in the section on kicking and pulling, the type of apparatus used in kicking or pulling requires further elaboration. Different types of kick boards and pull-buoys are manufactured or modified "in the field" to produce different mechanical conditions that can change or elicit variations in physical loading during the actual activity. Kick boards and pull-buoys can be made of different materials to produce different conditions of buoyancy. Some of these materials are susceptible to undesirable changes, such as water saturation or normal wear and tear, so care must be exercised when purchasing them. These items may also have different design configurations, which produce variations in mechanical loading. Kick boards are often modified in the field by being cut down to different sizes to produce different conditions of buoyancy. Some programs utilize a variety of different sized kick boards to produce varied loading conditions during kicking. Kick boards are sometimes shaped and modified to be used as pull-buoys, being preferred by some coaches as a way to reduce expense or to eliminate modified kicking action which may occur when pull-buoys are used.

Other Apparatus. Kick sticks consist of resilient plastic rods attached to cuffs which are placed around the thighs and ankles. In addition to creating a mechanical overload, kick sticks also aid in keeping the knees straight on the upbeat of the flutter and dolphin kicks and prevent excessive kneebend on the downbeat of the flutter and dolphin kick that can result in overkicking.

Buoyant gloves/webbed-finger gloves are plastic devices which provide hardened conditions for the armpull. Buoyant gloves are filled with air and make the hands so buoyant that it requires great muscular effort to accomplish an armpull, particularly in the early part of the pull. Webbed-finger gloves achieve an effect similar to that of hand paddles by increasing the volume of water displaced by the hands.

A MIXED PROGRAM OF TRAINING

There appears to be a concensus among leading coaches in the United States that most high-level, competitive swimmers of this country should and do use what is known as a *mixed or integrated* system of training. Also known as complex or heterogeneous training, this system emphasizes the development of several physical abilities in the course of a single training session. This is different from the *multimethod* system of training that makes use of uniform training loads in developing a single physical quality in a training session. The mixed program evolved from pragmatism, the result of trial-and-error, not from a theoretical model. Not much research can be found to either discredit or substantiate its merits. Tables 11–2, 3, and 4 are three workouts which combine the different methods of training in a single workout.

It should be mentioned that the use of a mixed program does not imply that just any arrangements of sets can be put together randomly. In fact, there is evidence to support the idea that, while there may be a high mixture of different methods in each training session, the structure of workout sessions should place emphasis on the development of a single quality (either speed or endurance) every day. The typical ratio emphasizes aerobic work three to four days a week and anaerobic/non-robic work two to three times a week. Aerobic conditioning takes the longest to develop and is the least demanding, therefore it is the quality of emphasis for the majority of workouts throughout the season. This is not only in terms of when aerobic work should be emphasized (early in the season), but also in terms of its secondary role as a means of restoring capacity in that part of the season that emphasizes more anaerobic/non-robic training (end of the season).

TABLE 11-2 EARLY-SEASON MIXED WORKOUT SESSION (USING TWO METHODS)

Procedure	Type of Training	Pulse-rate Range (Low–High)	Quality Developed in Percentage Endurance Speed
1. Warm up 800	Over distance	130	Endurance 90%, speed 10%
2. Swim 16 × 100, 10 sec. rest	Interval training	130–170	Endurance 80%, speed 20%
3. Kick 1000	Over distance	130	Endurance 90%, speed 10%
4. Pull 5 × 200, 15 sec. rest	Interval training (hypoxic breathing)*	130–170	Endurance 80%, speed 20%

Total Distance: 4400 yd. The primary emphasis is on endurance.

*Controlled breathing: every 3, 5, or 7 strokes.

TABLE 11-3   MIDSEASON WORKOUT SESSION
(USING FOUR METHODS)

Procedure	Type of Training	Pulse-rate Range (Low–High)	Quality Developed (Approx. Percentages)
1. Warm up 800	Over distance	120	Endurance 95%, speed 5%
2. Swim 8 × 200 20 sec. rest; 8 × 200 10 sec. rest; 4 × 200 5 sec. rest	Interval training	140–180	Endurance 80%, speed 20%
3. Kick 500	Over distance	140	Endurance 90%, speed 10%
4. Kick 5 × 100, 15 sec. rest	Interval training	135–175	Endurance 80%, speed 20%
5. Pull 500	Over distance	140	Endurance 90%, speed 10%
6. Pull 10 × 50, 10 sec. rest	Interval training (hypoxic breathing)	135–175	Endurance 80%, speed 20%
7. Swim 5 × 150, 3 min. rest	Repetition training	95–180	Endurance 50%, speed 50%
8. Swim 8 × 25, all-out effort, 1 min. rest	Sprint training	85–160	Endurance 10%, speed 90%

Total Distance: 7750 yd. In this workout the main emphasis is on endurance, but a greater percentage of speed is introduced than in the early-season routines.

PLANNING A YEAR'S TRAINING PROGRAM

Effective planning for an annual program consists of establishing a general outline for each of the seasons based on the calendar of major competitions. A preseason session in which the coach outlines the plan to the swimmers may be helpful. It should include a discussion of the training concepts which underlie the coach's training methodology. The coach is not relinquishing leadership by revealing the plan, but rather reassuring the athletes by helping them understand the training process. It lets them know there is a theoretical foundation for the work they will be doing and that the coach is confident enough of the work to subject it to the swimmers' scrutiny. More important, by involving the swimmers, the coach enlists their cooperation via their understanding that sometimes it is necessary to do long, boring sets in order to achieve certain well-defined training goals.

Table 11–5 is an example of an annual training plan. It is quite different from the one carried out by some athletes, particularly those in Eastern European countries where the annual plan is divided into distinct training programs of preparation, competition, and transition. This process is called *periodiza-*

TABLE 11-4   LATE-SEASON WORKOUT SESSION
(RIGHT BEFORE THE TAPER BEGINS, USING FIVE METHODS OF
TRAINING)

Procedure	Type of Training	Pulse-rate Range (Low–High)	Quality Developed (Approx. Percentage)
1. Warm up 800	Over distance	120	Endurance 95%, speed 5%
2. Swim 8 × 200, 15 sec. rest; 8 × 100, 10 sec. rest; 8 × 50, 5 sec. rest	Interval training	130–180	Endurance 80%, speed 20%
3. Swim 20 × 25 variable sprints, 20 sec. rest	Sprint training	95–170	Endurance 20%, speed 80%
4. Kick 10 × 100, 20 sec. rest	Interval training	130–180	Endurance 75%, speed 25%
5. Pull 1000 yards, 2 lengths slow then 1 length fast, etc.	Speed play (hypoxic breathing)	120–170	Endurance 85%, speed 15%
6. Swim at race pace: 200, 150, 100, 75, 50 with one minute rest between each.	Repetition training	95–180	Endurance 50%, speed 50%
7. Loosen down 500	Over distance		

Total Distance: 7175 yd. Here a greater emphasis is placed on speed than in the previous two workouts.

tion. Although there have been efforts to formalize competitive swimming in the same way in the United States, such efforts have not been widely successful. This is because our system is founded on the competitive needs of a school-based system throughout most of the year. This schedule does not lend itself to the periodization of the European model. The need to swim fast several times a season precludes it.

PLANNING EACH WEEK

Table 11–6 is a sample of a weekly plan developed for training collegiate swimmers at the height of hard training for the short-course season. It is not suitable for every age level, but is intended as a guide or starting point.

The coach should try to find time once a week to sit down for an hour to plan the following week's workouts. The plan must contain the training elements appropriate to the particular point in the season, it must balance the week in terms of intensity, volume, and methods, and it must be a suitable component of the training scheme established in the annual plan. As in the case of the annual

TABLE 11-5   AN ANNUAL TRAINING PLAN

	September	October	November	December	January	February
Number of workouts per week	Workouts are optional	5	6	11	11	11
Total time A.M. and distance per week P.M.		1–1½ hr.: 3000–5000 yd.	2 hr.: 6000–7000 yd.	1¼ hr.: 3000–4000 yd. 2¼ hr.: 6000–8000 yd.	1¼ hr.: 3000–4000 yd. 2¼ hr.: 6000–9000 yd.	1¼ hr.: 3000–4500 yd. 2¼ hr.: 6000–9000 yd.
Dry land exercise: How often and how long?	Administer strength, flexibility, and power tests	1 hr.: 4 days/wk. general strength	45 min.: 5 days/wk. general strength	30 min.: 4 days/wk. general strength	30 min.: 4 days/wk. specialized strength	30 min.: 4 days/wk. specialized strength.
Type of training Type of set	Either stay out of the water, play water polo, or swim easy: informal	Over distance and short-rest interval training Sets of 150s, 200s, 300s, 400s, 800s: avoiding short-distance and sprint training	Over distance, short-rest interval training, repetition training and some sprinting. Add 50, 75, 100 repeats plus some 25 sprints	Mixed (integrated) training: combination of all methods. Break team into three groups: sprinters, distance, and others. All types of sets	Mixed (integrated) training, introducing broken swimming. More sprints. Swimmers should begin feeling tired.	Mixed (integrated) training. Swimmers should try to do best repeat times. Watch for good performance in repetition sets.
General plan	This is the best month to take it easy, get away from the pool, try another sport for pleasure and change of pace.	Training begins. Concentrate on building strength and some swimming. This is a good time to work on stroke mechanics, look at stroke films and videos, work on weak strokes.	Tempo of practice picks up; more high-quality work is introduced into training. Strength work continues, but time is reduced by 15 mins. Stroke work and training lectures continue.	For the next 3 months, twice-a-day workouts will prevail. Strength exercise will continue. Improvements in repeat times and reductions in take-off times on short-rest interval training repeats should occur.	Hard work continues, keeping interest high by varying workouts. Don't break training for dual meets. Get a few swimmers ready to make cutoff times in their events. Continue stroke work.	Watch for colds and other upper respiratory illnesses. Tell swimmers to dress warmly, get plenty of rest, and eat properly. Emphasize need for extra calories in the form of carbohydrates.

TABLE 11-5 (*cont'd*)

	March	April	May	June	July	August
Number of workouts per week	8 to 10	6 to 10	5 to 10	12	12	8 to 11
Total time and distance per week — A.M. / P.M.	A.M.: 45 min.–1 hr.: 2000–3500 yd. P.M.: 1–2¼ hr.: 3000–7000 yd.	Short loosen-up workout, 1–1½ hr.: 3000–4000 yd.	1 hr.: 3000–4000 m. 2 hr.: 6000–8000 m.	2½ hr.: 7000–9000 m. 2 hr.: 5000–6000 m.	2½ hr.: 5000–9000 m. 2 hr.: 3000–6000 m.	1–1½ hr.: 3000–5000 m. 1–1½ hr: 2000–3000 m.
Dry land exercise: How often and how long?	20 min.: 3 days/wk.	15 min.: 3 days/wk.	30 min.: 4 days/wk.	30 min.: 4 days/wk.	30 min.: 3 days/wk.	Eliminate all dry land exercise
Type of training / Type of set	Mixed training, avoiding much high-intensity work. Easy swimming, some slow interval training, some sprinting, and pace work.	Mixed training—just enough to stay in shape for U.S. Nationals (if in early- to mid-April).	Mixed training, as in January and February, concentrating on endurance work.	Mixed training, emphasizing improvement in times and decreasing departure times for the various sets of repeats.	Mixed training, spending more time on pace work and sprinting and avoiding too much high-intensity work.	Mixed training, decreasing number of repeat swims, increasing pace work and sprinting.
General plan	Taper-time for all major short-course meets. Gradually reduce yardage until, 3 days before the main event, it is at 2000 to 3000 yds. Prepare mentally for competition.	Resume work, trying to hold taper through Nationals. Two-week break before long-course training begins.	Depending on academic load, swim once or twice daily, primarily over distance and short-rest interval training.	The hardest training of the year takes place in June, due to shortness of season and more time to devote to training. Swimmers must be reminded to observe training hygiene: more sleep, more rest, more calories (carbohydrates especially).	This is the last month of hard training, if Nationals occur in mid-August. Due to short season, taper begins in third week of July.	Swimmers not qualifying for Nationals will adjust their training and taper for National Junior Olympics; zone meets; regional, state, or local competitions.

TABLE 11-6 WEEKLY PLAN FOR MIDSEASON (JANUARY)

	Monday	Tuesday	Wednesday
MORNING	1. W.U. 800 2. S. 16 × 75 Hyp. on :55 (Fly on :60, Back on :60, Br. on 1:10) 3. K. 500 continuously 4. P. 5 × 100 on 1:15 Free to 1:45 Br. Hyp. 5. S. 1000 for time split negative Dis.—W.U. 800, then Swim 4 × 1000 *Total Distance* Others—4000 Dis.—4800	1. W.U. 500 2. S. 10 × 125 Hyp. 3. K. 5 × 100 4. P. 500 continuously Hyp. 5. S. 5 × 300 Dis.—4 × 500 *Total Distance* Others—4250 Dis.—4750	1. W.U. 800 2. S. 3 × 200 3 × 150 3 × 100 3. K. 500 continuously 4. P. 10 × 50 Hyp. 5. S. 12 × 25 Dis.—S. 1650 *Total Distance* Others—3450 Dis.—4700
AFTERNOON	1. W.U. 1200 2. S. Hyp. 10 × 100 on 1:10 Free 1:15 Back Fly 1:25 Br. 5 × 10 on 1:05 Free 1:10 Back Fly 1:20 Br. 5 × 100 on 1:00 Free 1:05 Back Fly 1:15 Br. 3. S. 12 × 25 Every other one fast from a push-off 4. K. 400, then 3 × 200 5. P. 400, then 4 × 150 Hyp. 6. S. 4 × 500 on 7 min. Dis. 2 × 1000 *Total Distance* Others—7500 Dis.—8500 Spr.—6000	1. W.U. 800 2. S. 5 × 200 on 2:20 3 × 200 on 2:15 2 × 200 on 2:10 Dis.—8 × 400 Spr.—Go 100s 3. S. 800—negative split 4. K. 800, then 8 × 25 5. P. 1000 Hyp. 6. a. S. broken 400, 4 × 100—10 sec. R.I. between 100s b. S. straight 400 c. Repeat (a) and (b) for a total of 6 × 400 Spr.—300s *Total Distance* Others—8000 Dis.—8600 Spr.—6400	1. W.U. 1200 2. S. 6 × 150 on 1:45 Free 1:55 Back Fly 2:15 Br. 4 × 150 on 1:40 Free 1:50 Back Fly 2:10 Br. 4 × 150 on 1:35 Free 1:45 Back Fly 2:05 Br. 3. S. 16 × 50 variable sprints 4. K. 600 continuously, then 8 × 50 5. P. 600 continuously, then 2 × 200 6. S. 1000 continuously, concentrating on working turns hard and swimming easy 7. S. 5 × 200 Repetition Training (with long R.I. of 3 min.) Spr.—150s Dis.—4 × 500 *Total Distance* Others—7700 Dis.—8900 Spr.—6450

Note: Most workouts outlined for "Others" are for middle-distance freestylers, breast, back, and butterfly swimmers. In repeat swims the sprinters do either half or three-fourths of the distance assigned the "Others," and unless noted otherwise, the distance swimmers double the distance (i.e., if the "Others" are doing 10 × 100, the sprinters would do either 10 × 50 or 10 × 75, and the distance swimmers 10 × 200).

TABLE 11-6 (*cont.*)

	Thursday	Friday	Saturday	Sunday

MORNING	1. W.U. 500
	2. S. 10 × 100
	3. K. 500 continuously
	4. P. 500 continuously
	5. Complete the workout with anything you want to do to a total of 1500
	
	Total Distance
	Others—4000
	Dis.—5000
	Spr.—3000
		1. W.U. as you would before prelims of NCAAs
		For example:
		a. S., K., or P. a total of 800 yd.
		b. S. 4 to 6 × 50
		c. K. 300
		d. K. 2 × 50
		e. Sprint 2 × 25
		f. Loosen down 200
		2. S. any of the following:
		a. 1 × 400 b. a pace
		  1 × 300 1650
		  1 × 200 c. 20 × 50
		  1 × 100 on :60
		
		Total Distance
		2450 to 3000
			Dual meet at 2:00 P.M.
			All swimmers must work out before the meet.
				Morning off unless you want to be videotaped for underwater stroke analysis, in which case be at the pool between 10:30 A.M. and 1:30 P.M.

AFTERNOON	1. W.U. 1200 :40
	2. S. 20 × 50 on :45
	    :50
	    :35
	  10 × 50 on :40
	    :45
	    :30
	  10 × 50 on :35
	    :40
	  Dis.—30 × 100
	3. S. 1000 split negative
	4. K. 1000 continuously
	5. P. 1000 continuously Hyp.
	6. S. 1 Broken 400—
	  10 sec. R.I.
	  1 Straight 400
	  1 Broken 300—
	  10 sec. R.I.
	  1 Straight 300
	  1 Broken 200—
	  10 sec. R.I.
	  1 Straight 200
	  Dis.—1 Broken 1500
	    1 Straight 1500
	  Spr.—200-20-0-200-150-150-100-100
	
	Total Distance
	Others—7000
	Dis.—9200
	Spr.—6100
		1. W.U. 800
		2. S. 8 × 100
		  8 × 75
		  8 × 50
		  Dis.—Double
		  Spr.—Half
		3. K. 10 × 100
		4. P. 10 × 100 Hyp.
		5. S. Others—3 × 500
		  Dis.—3 × 100
		  Spr.—3 × 300
		6. Work on starts and relay take-offs
		
		Total Distance
		Others—6100
		Dis.—7600
		Spr.—5500
			Dual meet at 2:00 P.M.
			Swimmers come in at 12:30 P.M. and do the following warm-up:
			1. W.U. 800
			2. S. 20 × 50 (Dis.—12 × 100)
			3. K. 400
			4. P. 400 Hyp.
			5. S. Sprints, such as 2 × 25
			After the meet, team members who go 20 × 100 will receive credit for one workout
			
			Total Distance
			Others—4650
			Dis.—4850
			(Not including distance swum in races)
				4:30–6:30 P.M.
				There will be a make-up workout for those who have not done 11 workouts this week.
				1. W.U. 500
				2. S. 8 × 50
				3. K. 400
				4. P. 400 Hyp.
				5. S. 3 × 800
				
				Total Distance
				4100
				All swimmers do same workout.

Code: W.U.—Warm up, S.—Swim, K.—Kick, P.—Pull, Hyp.—Hypoxic, Dis.—Distance Swimmers, Others—Middle-Distance Swimmers, Spr.—Sprinters, Fly—Butterfly, Br.—Breaststrokers, Back—Backstrokers, on 60 sec. refers to departure time, R.I.—Rest Interval. Distance is measured in yards.

plan, the coach should not commit himself to the plan come what may. He will often find by the end of the week that he has changed some items.

The weekly plan assures that the coach will not inadvertently duplicate a set of repeats too close to one another, but will preserve as fully as possible the freshness and variety that is so important to a cyclic sport like swimming. Variety for its own sake is not the goal, but the coach should beware of favoring a specific type of set without realizing he has fallen into a rut. To avoid this trap, he should look at logbooks of the past, check with current publications for new ideas, and trade ideas with other coaches, meanwhile staying within the bounds of his training plan.

Lastly, at some point during the week the coach may find himself rushed for time, in which case a weekly plan set up in advance precludes the need to improvise.

On the other hand, it isn't wise to post the entire week's schedule in advance. Such a practice tends to solidify the plan, leaving no leeway for changing circumstances. Besides, most swimmers don't want to know precisely what they will be doing tomorrow or the day after. They want to know that generally all is on course, but they seem to prefer that the specifics wait their turn.

General Plan—Winter Season. In the following plan, the morning workout is the shortest ($1\frac{1}{4}$ to $1\frac{1}{2}$ hours); the afternoon workout is the longest ($2\frac{1}{4}$ hours). The swimmers are classified in three groups: sprinters, others (all flyers, backstrokers, breaststrokers, and middle-distance crawl swimmers), and distance swimmers.

Morning Session. The total distance is between 3500 and 5000 yards, and the workout time ranges from $1\frac{1}{4}$ to $1\frac{1}{2}$ hours.

1. Warm up 500 to 800 yards, any combination of easy swimming, kicking, and pulling.
2. Swim a set of short rest (five to twenty seconds) interval training repeats that total 1000 to 1500 yards, such as 20 to 30 × 50, 14 to 20 × 75, 10 to 15 × 100, 7 to 10 × 150, 5 to 7 × 200, 4 to 6 × 250. Plan to use a different set each day of the week. Some days mix up the sets—for example, 8 × 100, then 8 × 50.
3. Kick 500 yards—one day kick continuously, the next do the kicking in an interval training method, such as 20 × 25, 10 × 50, or 5 × 100.
4. Pull 500 yards—on the days that kicking is continuous, the pulling should be in an interval-training method, and vice versa.
5. This segment of the workout may be one of the following:
   a. An over distance swim (500, 800, 1000, or 1650 for time—out slow/back hard).
   b. A series of short rest interval training repeats totalling 800 to 1600 yards. The set should be different from the one done in (2) above.
   c. A series of high-intensity repeats (anaerobic/non-robic) with a long rest, such as 3 × 150 with a three-minute rest interval.
   d. Sprints, such as swimming 10 × 50, leaving every $1\frac{1}{2}$ minutes.

The type of repeat swims done in (5) depends largely on what is planned for the second workout. If a high-intensity workout is planned for the afternoon, this section of the morning workout should not be so high, but should be over distance or short rest interval training.

Distance swimmers should do about 5000 yards in the morning. While they may do almost the same workout as the other swimmers, they should double the length of the repeats in (2) and (5) of the workout. Thus, if the "others" are going 10 × 100 in (2), the distance swimmers should go 10 × 200. In (5), if the others are going 800 yards, the distance swimmers should swim 1650 yards.

Stroke swimmers are often called "others" in this chapter. The flyers, back-strokers, and breaststrokers must adjust the total number of repeat swims they do in (2) and (5) by reducing the total number slightly. That is, if the freestylers are going 10 × 100, the flyers and backstrokers will go only 9 × 100, and the breaststrokers only 8 × 100. The sets are organized this way to allow all swimmers to finish that section of the workout at approximately the same time and start the next section together. The distance men have to operate on their own and can do only part of the workout at the same time as the rest of the team.

Sprinters should also change (2) and (5) of the workout by reducing the distance of their repeats. While the "others" are going 10 × 100, the sprinters should go either 10 × 75 or 10 × 50.

Afternoon Session   The total distance is between 7200 and 9000 yards, and the workout time is 2¼ hours.

1. Warm up 800 to 1200 yards (one-quarter swim, one-quarter kick, one-quarter pull, one-quarter swim)
2. Swim a set of short rest interval training repeats with a total yardage of 1800 and 3000 yards using a decreasing rest interval set, such as one of the following:
   a. Crawl—10 × 100 on 1:10 + 5 × 100 on 1:05 + 5 × 100 on 1:00
   b. Breast—8 × 100 on 1:25 + 4 × 100 on 1:20 + 4 × 100 on 1:15
   c. Fly and Back—9 × 100 on 1:15 + 4 × 100 on 1:10 + 4 × 100 on 1:05
   d. Distance—8 × 200 on 2:20 + 4 × 200 on 2:15 + 4 × 200 on 2:05

On other days of the week, other sets of repeats may be done at these distances: 50, 75, 100, 125, 150, 200, 250, 300, 400.

3. On alternate days one of the following types of sets might be chosen:
   a. Swim a set of sprints, such as 12 × 25 with thirty seconds rest.
   b. Swim an over distance effort (400, 500, 800, or 1000), such as out slow/back hard.
4. Kick a total of 800 to 1200 yards, half easy and the rest in repeats (kick 500 easy, then kick 10 × 50 on 50 seconds, or 5 × 100 on 1:40).
5. Pull the same distance as (4) and in a similar manner, except do a different set of repeats. If you kicked 5 × 100, then pull 3 × 200 or 10 × 50.
6. Swim a set of repeats. This is the most important set of the entire day.
   a. Two days a week (Monday and Wednesday) do a high intensity set of repeats (repetition training) with a moderate rest interval and composed of any of the following: 20 × 50 on sixty seconds, 10 × 100 on two minutes, 7 × 150 on three minutes, 5 × 200 on four minutes. Keep a close check on the times and record them in a daily log.
   b. Two days a week (Tuesday and Thursday) do a set of broken swims, such as 4 × broken 200, consisting of 4 × 50 with a ten-second rest interval between 50s.

      c. If the swimmers are tired and appear to have had too much high-intensity work, give them a low-pressure, low-quality workout, such as (1) a continuous 1000 easy swim for no time, (2) a 3 × 400 progressive swim in which each 400 is faster than the previous one, or (3) work on starts and turns.

7. Three days a week finish the workout with some sprinting. These sprints should be done on the days when over distance was done on item 2 of the workout. For example:

      a. Swim 10 × 50 EOOF (every other one fast), moderate to long rest interval, starting a fast 50 every two minutes.

      b. Swim 12 × 25, with thirty-second rest interval.

      c. Time three all-out 50s from a dive.

TRAINING THE DISTANCE SWIMMER

Earlier in this chapter the difference between the type of workouts appropriate for distance swimmers and those for the rest of the team was discussed. This difference is probably obvious to the reader, but more insight into the necessity for different types of workouts may be gained by reading the sections in this chapter devoted to other methods of training, including the one on speed-strength.

For the distance swimmer, the main differences in training are as follows:

1. More aerobic work, including more over distance swimming and short rest interval training.

2. More work, including 20 to 40 percent more total distance in each workout, as time permits.

3. Longer repeat swims than the rest of the team is doing. If the rest of the team is doing a set of repeats such as 8 × 150, the distance swimmer should double the distance, going 6 or even 8 × 300.

Some of the typical sets of repeats for senior-level distance swims, as used in separate workouts, are listed here:

20 to 40 × 100
10 to 20 × 200
8 to 14 × 300
8 to 12 × 400
4 to 8 × 800
1, 2, or 3 × 1500

Chapter 12, "Train with the Experts," gives examples of some distance workouts. These will show that good distance swimmers do not eliminate all speed work (sprinting or high-intensity work—repetition/anaerobic-lactate) from their programs. Although *all swimmers need a mixed program of training*, distance swimmers should emphasize those types of training which develop endurance.

TRAINING THE SPRINTER

As compared with middle-distance and distance swimmers, sprinters need more of the kind of training that develops speed-endurance and speed-strength-endurance (explosive speed-strength or explosive power) and less of the kind that develops aerobic endurance qualities. Although they swim primarily the 50-, 100-, and occasionally the 200-yard/meter events, they will be able to finish those races more strongly if they have acquired some stamina. Second, as mentioned so often before, competitive swimming does not have a purely sprint endurance event. Even the 50-yard/meter race will exhaust the ATP stores in the muscles before the race has ended. This means a sprinter cannot do without endurance work entirely, some over distance and short-rest interval training being needed in order to develop the oxidative system of ATP production, especially in the early stages of training. But, since neither maximal speed-endurance nor maximal aerobic endurance can be packed into a muscle at the same time, one apparently being acquired at the expense of the other, speed-endurance and speed-strength endurance must take priority among sprinters.

The ATP-PCr energy-release system is said to deliver as much as five times more ATP to the muscles of the trained athlete than to those of the nonathlete. This system apparently responds to training via the stress and adaptation mechanism. The elasticity of the sarcolemma (membranous muscle sheath) seems to be improved by sprint training, presumably enabling the muscles to contract more quickly. The sprinter also needs to be able to tolerate the discomfort which occurs when racing and holding one's breath in the short events.

In general, therefore, sprinters need to emphasize the types of training that develop speed. Their training can be adjusted from that of the rest of the team in the following ways:

1. By doing more speed-strength endurance work, composed of all-out sprinting, goal sets, and high-intensity repetition training.

2. By doing less overall distance, as much as 20 to 30 percent less than the middle-distance swimmer, but increasing the intensity of the work.

3. By using shorter repeats and longer rest intervals than the rest of the team. If the team is assigned 8 × 150, the sprinters should do 8 × 100 or even 8 × 75 on the same departure interval as the swimmers who are swimming the 150s.

4. By practicing 25 yard/meter sprints from a dive, flipping the turns and taking one or two strokes after the turns before taking a breath. The coach can time these sprints from take-off to foot-touch.

In order to gain insight into why he should train this way, the sprinter may find it helpful to read the sections in Chapters 7 and 8, which deal with the specific nature of adaptation to stress and the role of speed-strength in sprinting.

TRAINING THE INDIVIDUAL MEDLEYIST

TABLE 11-7   TRAINING FOR THE INDIVIDUAL MEDLEY

Workout Pattern for All Swimmers—Minimum of 11 workouts per week: 6 afternoon practices (2¼ hrs—6000 to 9000 yd.) and 5 morning or evening practices (1 hr. 10 min.—3000 to 5000 yd.)

Monday	Tuesday	Wednesday
Warm up 400	Warm up 400	Warm up 400
Swim 12 × 100 on 1:15	Swim 6 × 150	Swim 6 × 100
Kick 400	Kick 4 × 150	Kick 200, then 3 × 100
Pull 400	Pull 4 × 150	Pull 200, then 3 × 100
Swim 2 × 500	Swim 18 × 50	Swim 400, 300, 200, 100
Entire workout done freestyle	Entire workout swum backstroke	Entire workout swum breaststroke
Warm up 800 (200-s, 200-k, 200-p, 200-s)	Warm up 1200	*Switching workout**
Kick 100, pull 100, swim 100—repeat 10 times alternating strokes	Swim 20 × 50 fly 10 × 50 free	Warm up I.M. Swim 3 broken 400 I.M.s—4 × 100, 10 sec. rest
Swim 800 free	Kick 500, then 5 × 100, free and fly alternating	Sprint 30 × 25—1 kick, 1 pull, 1 swim, alternating
Swim 8 × 200 on 3 min.— 1st 200 fly, 2nd I.M., 3rd back, 4th I.M., 5th breast, 6th I.M., 7th free, 8th I.M.	Swim 30 × 25 sprints, free and fly alternating Swim 16 × 100 on 2 min. in 4 sets of 4 × 100—1st set fly, 2nd free, 3rd fly, 4th free	Kick 600 I.M., then 12 × 50, alternating strokes Pull same as kick Swim 4 × 200 from dive— 1st 2 I.M., 2nd 2 fly
TOTAL: 7000 yd.	TOTAL: 7000 yd.	TOTAL: 6000 yd.

Switching Workout: In this type of workout, emphasis is placed on working on switching from one stroke to another. For example, if the swimmer swims a 400 I.M., he might switch strokes every 25 instead of every 100. Broken swims are also done so that the swimmer will not become accustomed to switching only after a rest interval (i.e., if he swims a broken 400 or 4 × 100 with 10 sec. rest between 100s, he will swim as follows: 1st 100—50 fly/50 back, 2nd 100—50 back/50 breast, 3rd 100—50 breast/50 free, 4th 100—50 free/50 fly.

Individual medley swimmers must decide whether to train all four strokes each day or to train one stroke in one workout, another stroke in the next, and so on. Coaches who have been successful in producing champion individual medleyists vary in their approach, but most agree that there should be a fairly even distribution of time spent on each of the strokes, not necessarily concentrating the same amount of time on each stroke every day. Table 11–7 is a training pattern for individual medleyists coached by these authors. Readers may also want to refer to the workout schedules devised by Richard Shoulberg, renowned coach of many successful individual medleyists. Shoulberg's sample workouts are listed in Chapter 12.

ADJUSTING WORKOUTS TO FIT THE VARIOUS AGE-GROUP LEVELS

When discussing training methods, it is common to use examples from the programs of elite athletes. The authors have used this approach too. While it is true that the training principles which apply to the champion swimmer also apply to age-groupers, high-school swimmers, and even to Masters swimmers, obviously,

TABLE 11-7 (*cont'd*)

Policies for Individual Medley Swimmers

1. Each I.M. swimmer must work on his weakest stroke or strokes at least one whole workout per week.
2. He must *not* practice the I.M. every day.
3. He must do at least two stroke-switching workouts per week. Over half of the Indiana University team swim the I.M. in some meets.

Thursday	Friday	Saturday
Morning off	Swim 3500 any style, concentrating on weakest stroke and breaststroke	Warm up 500 Swim 4 × 400 free progressive Kick 400 fly Pull 400 free Swim 20 × 50 fly
Warm up 800 Swim 6 × 150, concentrating on back and free Kick 400, then 8 × 100, free and back alternating Pull same as kick Swim 6 × 300 on 4½ min. Swim all-out 50	*Switching workout** Warm up 1200 I.M. Swim 10 × 100—1st fly, 2nd I.M., 3rd back, 4th I.M., 5th breast, 6th I.M., 7th free, 8th I.M., 9th fly/back, 10th breast/free Kick 400 I.M. easy kick 10 × 25 all strokes, kick 400 I.M. for time Pull same as kick Swim broken 200, 10 sec. rest 1 straight 200/repeat 6 times	Warm up for meet: 1. Warm up 800 2. Swim 8 × 50—2 of each stroke 3. Swim 200 I.M. in meet 4. After meet swim 20 × 100 freestyle
TOTAL: 6550 yd.	TOTAL: 6400 yd.	

programs have to be adjusted to suit the comparative level of trainedness and the age and maturity level of the swimmers. Having also coached all these levels during the course of our careers, these authors believe they are competent to provide the same workouts they have given their elite swimmers, merely by decreasing both the total time and total distance to fit the needs of younger and less experienced swimmers.

For example, if the team is divided into three levels, the following schedule might be appropriate for age-groupers or high school swimmers:

Beginning Competitive Swimmers—1 hour per day, five workouts per week, consisting of about 2000 yards/meters per workout.

Intermediate Competitive Swimmers—1½ hours per day, six workouts per week, consisting of about 4000 yards/meters per workout.

Advanced Competitive Swimmers—2 hours per day, six workouts per week, consisting of about 6000 yards/meters per workout. During the summer season and part of the indoor season, these swimmers are capable of training twice a day for a total of eleven workouts per week.

By decreasing the number and distance of repeats, the coach can stay within the parameters of the regime described here and yet provide the appropriate kinds and amounts of stress.

For example, if elite swimmers are doing 20 × 150 repeat swims on a departure time of 1:40, this set can be adjusted for the various levels in the following manner:

Beginners—12 × 50 on 2:00
Intermediates—12 × 100 on 2:00
Advanced—20 × 100 on 1:30

An age-group program should make use of the different methods of training described previously for a mixed program, regardless of the level of the swimmer.

It is usually inappropriate for an age-group coach to divide his team into the conventional distance, middle-distance/stroke (others), and sprint categories. Instead the team should be divided according to skill level, and, even then, there will not be very homogeneous groupings. By assigning the best swimmers to a certain lane, the next-best to the next lane, and so forth, the coach will improve the homogeneity of the groupings enough to be able to assign a different number of repeat swims to each lane, using different departure times. For example, Lane 1 (the best swimmers) may swim 10 × 100 with a departure time of 1:30, Lane 2 (next-best) may swim 8 × 100 with a departure time of 1:45, Lane 3 (third best in skill and experience) 7 × 100 with a departure time of 2:00, and so on.

When establishing the groups for an age-group team, it is useful to have an assistant who does nothing but record the statistics the coach will use to make lane assignments for training. Such records provide a basis for the coach's decision as well as evidence of objectivity if there are differences of opinion.

As the swimmers become more skillful and better conditioned, it is inevitable that some assignments will have to be changed. Such changes can be traumatic, but, in the end, if handled sensitively by the coach, are best for all concerned.

Age-group swimmers deserve a well-organized practice that will enhance everyone's feeling of accomplishment and contribute to the positive morale of the team. But, at the same time, there is increasing evidence that young swimmers should not be forced into specialization too soon. Even if the goal of the program were only to select and keep elite athletes in the program, surveys are now beginning to reveal that early specialization does not succeed in that goal. Not many coaches and parents would want to confess to having such a goal, but, even so, it is apparently better for young swimmers to enjoy the experience of age-group swimming without undue pressure either in terms of an overly stressful training load or a winning record.

MASTERS SWIMMING

The Masters program was first organized to accommodate fitness swimmers who hoped to stimulate interest in the program by adding competition to their fitness program. The success of Masters swimming has exceeded all expectations.

At first, Masters swimming operated under the umbrella of the Amateur Athletic Union. It is now an autonomous organization, which holds two championship events annually in this country and cooperates with similar organizations of other nations to hold a world championship event when sponsorship can be found. While the championships are dominated by former competitive swimmers, there are many participants without former competitive experience. The youngest age category is nineteen through twenty-four; the oldest is ninety and older. Most Masters participate for four reasons: fitness, social camaraderie, peer recognition, and desire for competition.

Although some Masters train exceedingly long and hard, most are constrained by job and family responsibilities from making the same commitment as, say, an Olympic contender. It isn't so much a lack of capacity that determines training limitations for Masters swimmers as it is lack of time and energy. Masters swimmers learn to balance their commitments.

In this context, Peder Dahlberg, world-record holder in the forty through forty-four age bracket 200-meter breaststroke *and* commercial building contractor, made the following statement, "If I try to train twice a day, I can't do justice to my job." Mr. Dahlberg trains four to six times a week, averaging 3000 to 4500 yards/meters in a session. He usually trains once a day, though occasionally, on weekends, twice daily. The following samples of Mr. Dahlberg's workouts preceded the world championship event held in July, 1992.

APRIL 13

A. M.	P. M.
400 SKPS (swim, kick, pull, swim)	1200 SKPS
1650 swim	5 × 300 swim
200 kick, 4 × 100 kick	800 kicking drill
200 pull, 8 × 50 pull	500 pulling drill
12 × 100 swim on 1:45, 1:40, 1:35, 1:30	10 × 50 swim
400 swim, negative split	
Total Distance: 4500	4500

APRIL 26 SHORT COURSE	APRIL 27 LONG COURSE
400 Warm-up	400 Warm-up
5 × 150 on 2:30	800 kick
5 × 50 from a dive	800 pull
(29.2, 29.6, 30.1, 29.7, 29.6)	200-150-100-50-50-100-150-200
Total Distance: 1400	3000

MAY 2

400 SKPS	No Swim
4 × 200	
4 × 150	
4 × 100	
4 × 50	
200 kick, 8 × 50	
200 pull, 8 × 50	
200 swim, 8 × 50	
200 swim, 4 × 50	
200 swim, 2 × 100	
200 swim, 8 × 25	
Total Distance: 5400	

MAY 16

400 SKPS
5 × 300 on 5:00
10 × 50 kick, 500
10 × 50 pull, 500
2 × 200
4 × 100
8 × 50
Total Distance: 6200

MAY 27

A. M.	P. M.
400 SKPS	400 SKPS
500 swim progressive	6 × 100 on 1:35,6 × 50 on :45
500 pull progressive	400 kick, 3 × 100 kick
500 kick progressive	400 pull, 16 × 25 pull w/cords
4 × 100 on 1:45	400-200-100-50-50-100-200-100
4 × 100 on 1:40	1 minute rest between efforts
4 × 100 on 1:30	
Total Distance: 3100	4000

JUNE 20 25-METER COURSE	*JUNE 21 25-METER COURSE*
1200 SKPS	A.M.—1800 meters
15 × 100 on 2:00	P.M.—1500 meters
Total Distance: 2700	3300

WARM-UP

Warming up prior to competition or training is so universally accepted a practice that it could be said to have gained the status of an established training principle. It wasn't always so. In the 1940s, two of America's most respected sports theorists stood on opposite sides of the question, "Are there actually benefits to be had from warming up?" While they exchanged pros and cons, most coaches continued to favor warming up, and the practice became entrenched. The theory of the warm-up is that it increases blood flow to the active muscles, raising the temperature by a degree or two. According to van't Hoff's Law, the force a muscle can create is increased, within certain physiological limitations, by raising its temperature. Properly warmed up, the muscles and tendons are less prone to injury. Warming up also stretches out the connective tissue and refines the coordination of the neuromuscular system so the mechanics of the movement are optimized.

Warming up before Practice

Some swimmers warm up entirely on land, using stretching and arm swings for the upper body and stretching for the legs (especially for the breaststroke) in a combined stretching and warming up session. Other swimmers do all their warming up in the water. Still others do a combination of the two, beginning on land with some arm-swinging and stretching-out, then finishing up in the water.

Warming up in the water usually consists of swimming, kicking, and pulling a total of 800 to 1000 yards/meters. A standard set of repeats such as 10 × 200 with a five- to twenty-second rest interval is a good first set of repeats of the day. It is a relatively low-intensity set which loosens up the muscles by stretching the connective tissue at the same time as it prepares the swimmer for more intense efforts to come. Swimmers who warm up sufficiently seldom develop such injuries as bursitis or tendinitis. Since an effective breaststroke kick depends on flexible ankles and feet, breaststrokers should loosen up their legs by kicking easy breaststroke, gradually increasing the pressure on their feet until they feel sufficiently warmed up. They can judge the status of their warm-up by kicking, swimming, or pulling a certain distance and comparing the time with previous times.

The swimmer who has worked out once in the morning and then again in the afternoon need not spend as much time warming up the second time. The warm-up effect carries over for several hours.

Warming up before Competition

Each swimmer should establish the warm-up that suits his needs, allowing the warm-up to evolve until he feels comfortable with it. It is helpful if the coach talks about the purpose of warming up and devotes some time to warm-up practice sessions. The authors often posted a workout in which the first item would read as follows:

WORKOUT—THURSDAY AFTERNOON

1. Warm up as you would before the prelims of the NCAA Championships. For example:
   a. Swim, pull or kick a total of 800 to 1000 yd.
   b. Swim 4 to 8 × 50 on 60 sec. Go each 50 faster than the previous one. Distance men go 4 to 6 × 100 on 1:30.
   c. Kick 200 to 300 yd., then kick 2 × 50 to loosen up legs.
   d. Swim 2 to 4 × 25 yd. from a dive. Distance men swim a couple of 50s hard, but not all-out.
   e. Loosen down 200 yd.

Such a suggested warm-up would then be adjusted to individual needs by the swimmer himself who might do a little more or a little less or make other changes, as he saw fit. It is important that the swimmer have confidence in his warm-up. It should be one he has used with success before practice and minor competitions all season long. Once established, a swimmer may even use the warm-up he believes in throughout his career.

It has become common procedure over the past twenty years for swimmers to do what is called *a wake-up swim* on the mornings of a championship event. They get up early, go directly to the pool for a short loosening-up session, then come back for breakfast and a rest before the preliminaries, which often begin about noon. The idea behind this practice is to make their bodies think it is later in the day than it actually is when they swim the preliminaries. Most swimmers believe they swim better later in the day and the second time they get in the water. There is no good reason not to indulge this conviction.

Warming up before the Finals

Just as not as much warm-up is needed before the second training session of the day, so not as much is needed before the finals of a competition. The wake-up swim, the warm-up just prior to the preliminaries, and the preliminary swim itself all have a carry-over effect. Distance men often want to swim further and work more on pace in their warm-up than sprinters or middle-distance swimmers. Individual medleyists may prefer to warm up by swimming and kicking some of each stroke.

Following is a standard workout for use before any final event. It was used by Mark Spitz before each final in the Olympic Games in which he won seven gold medals:

1. Warm up 400 easy, swimming a little of each stroke
2. Swim 2 × 50 at about 85 percent effort
3. Kick 100 to 200 meters
4. Swim 1 or 2 × 25 meters

THE TAPER

Unquestionably, the aspect of training which causes coaches the most sleepless nights is the taper. Historically, as training for swimming became more rigorous, the need to rest from its rigors just prior to major competition became evident. It was hard to ignore the fact that those who continued to train heavily up to the event often fell short of early season times. At first, this was taken to be evidence of overtraining. Then it began to be understood that the more arduous the program, the longer the rest period had to be. Other factors began to be noticed: Women seemed to need less taper than men; heavily muscled, mature males needed more taper than lightly muscled, immature males; young age-groupers of both sexes needed less taper than mature swimmers. Throughout these observations, distance swimmers were afraid to taper. (Tapering in this group is still more subject to individualization than in the other groups.) Armed with this information, tapering gradually became more effective.

There remains the exception to every generalization, and tapering is still a very individual proposition. Certain ritual behavior as championship events approach appears to be more psychological than physical or physiological, but, until there is more corroborative evidence one way or the other than we have at present, it should be honored in the tradition that athletes usually acquire a lot of emotional baggage as their careers advance.

While the terms *tapering* and *peaking* are used synonymously, tapering seems to be the more common terminology. Peaking has the connotation of arrival at an apex of performance capability; tapering carries the idea of the final phase of rest and diminished workload requisite to optimal performance. When tapering was first introduced, most coaches opted for a period which consisted primarily of speed-strength endurance efforts, that is, time trials and other all-out sprints. That was because they thought of the training season as being devoted mainly to aerobic (endurance) work. It was assumed that when volume was reduced, as in peaking, intensity could be increased. This implemented the idea of getting ready to swim fast by swimming fast. The problem was that this method more often than not failed to produce the desired result. The reason seems to have been that a stress was being imposed on systems which had only been marginally stressed all season. It was in this context that the phrase was frequently heard that "the swimmers had left their races in the practice pool."

The integrated (or mixed) system of training evolved from the failure of a single system to meet all training needs. As training methods were combined at all levels, from age-group through elite teams, the content of the taper period became a process that incorporated the same methods, but in diminishing amounts.

The Four Week Taper

The details of this taper evolved over years of experimentation. Its first version was used with the 1976 Men's U.S. Olympic Team in which the swimmers experienced unprecedented success, winning all the gold medals except two and dominating the silver and bronze medal count. Its statistics show that this taper resulted in 100-percent best times for the first short-course season it was used and 94-percent lifetime bests.

The taper has been used with success on many occasions, by many different teams, ranging from age-group through high school and college. It has been changed in minor ways over the years, but essentially it has remained the same. The success of a taper depends as much on psychological factors as physical ones. As successes have built on one another, this taper has acquired an almost mythical quality.

Each time the taper was requested, a note was sent along, describing the stages the swimmers could expect to undergo. The stages were as follows:

1. The first week, the swimmers will still be training hard. Volume will be reduced slightly, intensity will increase slightly, the number of workouts will remain the same.

2. In the second week, the distance will continue to decrease and the intensity to increase. Having been advised to adjust their schedules as much as possible to match the times of day they will be competing, the swimmers will begin to implement the new schedule.

Swimmers who have been training at peak loads for several months and then begin to taper, commonly experience symptoms of work withdrawal for a week or more before they begin to feel good again. The reason is not known. For lack of a better explanation, the authors believe the swimmers may be feeling a new stress: that of reduced training stimulus. Strange as this notion may seem, it is as reasonable as any that has been advanced. Perhaps the swimmers' bodies have to adapt to a decreased work load. Until they do, they perform poorly or, at least, perceive that they do.

It is helpful to explain to the swimmers in advance that this phenomenon is a precursor to restoration from the fatigue of training. As the symptoms of work withdrawal diminish, they are replaced by emotional and physical exuberance. If the sequence of events has been described in advance, and it happens as predicted, the athletes are reassured and tend to believe that when work withdrawal disappears, they will be ready.

Those who use only a week to a week and a half of taper have been known to state that a short taper is worse than no taper at all. Until the actual reasons—psychological, physical, or physiological—for work withdrawal are understood, coaches must deal with its symptoms. It is an anxious time for the coach and the athlete.

3. The third week brings a change of attitude among most team members. They are full of energy and high spirits. The coach must guard against their desire (and the coach's) to swim them too hard in order to test their speed. The coach should explain that the swimmers' behavior is typical of this stage of the taper and that the coach is pleased to see it happening because it means they are on schedule. If some do not respond as described, the coach should further decrease their work volume. If others appear to be peaking too soon, the coach should add some work, keeping the ratio of distance to intensity the same as in the taper routine.

4. In the fourth week, special emphasis should be placed on swimming the times expected in competition. The team should adhere to the schedule it will

be following throughout competition: sleep, rest, mealtimes, and so on. This is the time to work on starts, turns, and relay take-offs—but not to excess. As mentioned earlier, there should have been drills for these skills all season.

Other Taper Advice

No radical changes in technique should be undertaken at taper time. It is a good time to remind the swimmers of the types of food they should eat and those they should avoid before and during competition. They should already be aware of the foods that disagree with their digestion and of those they can tolerate easily under the psychological and physical stress of competition.

Some swimmers (usually distance swimmers) believe they need a short taper of only a few days. This may be a fact or a matter of subjective mind-set, but it is pointless to argue the merits of such opinions at this crucial stage. Rather than force a reluctant swimmer into a standard taper, it is better to individualize a taper. This taper may include a lot of slow tempo swimming, which, while not demanding, satisfies yet rests the swimmer.

The coach should keep in mind that the taper is the period when the most mistakes are made, and that they are usually errors on the side of too many maximum efforts on the watch. Both the coach and swimmer are intensely interested in how the swimmer is responding, and it is a great temptation to test him.

Several top coaches have admitted to having occasionally fast-timed a swimmer during the taper. They do this to relieve the anxiety that begins to be generated during the taper due to the uncertainty that the taper is working.

Considering all the work that has taken place during the months of training, it is shocking to realize that the season could be for naught if the swimmers' behavior outside the pool during the taper jeopardizes the successful culmination of the season. Reducing a swimmer's workload won't do any good if, when he gets out of practice, he uses his new found energy to play three games of handball and otherwise ignore all the rules of training hygiene. It may be helpful to have a short team meeting to reinforce what every swimmer already knows his behavior should be during the last days before the most important competition of the season.

In Table 11–8 the shortest workouts are in the morning during the short-course season; the reverse happens during the long-course season. Departure times, of course, must be adjusted for long-course training. On the occasion of this taper's first test, the conference championships occurred at the beginning of March, thus the taper began twenty-eight days earlier.

SAMPLE WORKOUTS

Each of the following workouts contains items intended to develop either speed or endurance, but swimmers cannot be stressed maximally for both endurance and speed in every workout. Coaches have discovered that an attempt to do this will result in a negative training effect. That is, endurance work will affect speed negatively and speed work will do the same for endurance. None of this would matter if there were purely speed or endurance events in swimming. If that were the case, a swimmer could concentrate on one or the other. Since there are not, integrated workouts seem to be the best way to go. On the other hand, each

TABLE 11-8   A FOUR-WEEK TAPER

First Day (twenty-eight days prior to meet)

A.M.	P.M.

A.M.

1. WU 200 (S), 200 (K), 200 (P), 200 (S)
2. Swim 200 Neg. Split
3. Swim 20 × 25 EOOF on :25
4. Pull 2 × 400 CB5 or 7 on 5 min.
5. Swim 4 × 100 EOOF on 1:45
6. Swim 4 × 50 on :30 (Cr), :35(Ba/ Fly), :38(Br)
7. Kick 6 × 100 desc each 3 on 1:50
8. Pull 6 × 75 Fly on 1:00
9. Swim 12 × 50 desc each 4 on :40
10. Swim 200 Neg. Split faster than (2) above

P.M.

1. WU 300 (S), 300 (K), 300 (P), 300 (S)
2. Swim:

Sprinters		Distance	
4 × 100 on 1:40		4 × 400 on 4:30	
4 × 75 on 1:05		3 × 300 on 3:10	
4 × 50 on :30		3 × 200 on 2:05	
4 × 25 on :13			
Middle Distance	Ba/Fly	Br	IM
4 × 150 on 1:40	1:50	2:10	1:50
4 × 100 on 1:05	1:10	1:20	1:10
4 × 75 on :50	:55	:60	:55
4 × 50 on :30	:33	:35	:34

3. Kick 400 plus 8 × 50 on :50
4. Swim 16 × 25 on :30, holding times steady
5. Pull 800 Cr plus 4 × 100 own stroke on 1:20; Br on 1:40
6. Swim 20 × 100 desc each 4 on 1:15(Cr), 1:20(Ba/Fly), 1:30(Br) Sprinters go 75 × 100 on 1:15
7. Practice relay take-offs

Second Day (twenty-seven days prior to the meet)

A.M.	P.M.

A.M.

1. WU 300 (S), 300 (P), 300 (K), 300 (S)
2. Swim 8 × 100 IM on 1:30
    8 × 50 on 40/45, two 50s of each stroke
3. Kick 300 plus 8 × 25 on :30
4. Pull 300 plus 8 × 25 on :30
5. Swim 800 ETOF
6. Swim 8 × 25 on :30 EOOF

P.M.

1. WU 400 (S), 400 (K), 400 (P), 400 (S)
2. Swim: 6 × 150 on 1:40(Cr), 2:00(Ba/ Fly), 2:10(Br)
    6 × 100 on 1:05(Cr), 1:15(Ba/ Fly), 1:20(Br)
Dist. go 3000 desc 1000, breaking 31.30 on total dist.
3. Kick 600
4. Pull 600
5. Swim 100 on 1:15, kick 100 on 1:45, pull 100 on 1:15, swim 100, etc., for a total of 1200 y
6. Swim 8 × 25 EOOF on :30 all-out

Third Day (twenty-six days prior to the meet)

A.M.	P.M.

A.M.

1. WU 300 (S), 300 (K), 300 (P), 300 (S)
2. Swim 6 × 100 on 1:50 desc each 3
    6 × 50 on 1:00 desc each 3
3. Kick 200 plus 4 × 25 on :40
4. Swim from dive 4 × 25 all out
Dist. pace 5 × 100 on 1:30

P.M.

             Dual Meet
5. After meet, swim 20 × 100 on 1:15(Cr), 1:25(IM,Ba,Fly), 1:30(Br)

TABLE 11-8 A FOUR-WEEK TAPER *(Continued)*

Fourth Day (twenty-five days prior to the meet)

A.M.	P.M.
1. WU 300 (S), 300 (K), 300 (P), 300 (S)	1. Dist. only—400 (S), 400 (K), 400 (P), 400 (S)
2. Swim: 3 × 300 Cr, CB4 on 3:30 3 × 200 own stroke, desc on 3:00	2. Swim 11 × 150 on 1:40, 1:35 or better
3. Swim 12 × 25 Var. Sprnts on :30	3. Swim 1650 on 17:25 or better
4. Kick 300 plus 4 × 50 on :60	4. Swim 16 × 100 on 1:05, av. :61
5. Pull 300 plus 3 × 100, CB5 on 1:30	
6. Swim 8 × 50 desc each 4 on :50 Dist. only—400, 400, 400, 400 Swim 5 × 300 on 3:15, av. under 3:00 Swim 1650 under 18 mins., av. 1:05/100 Swim 8 × 200 on 2:15, av. 2:08 Swim 1650 under 17:40, av. 1:04	

Fifth Day (twenty-four days prior to the meet)

A.M.	P.M.
1. WU 800	1. WU 400 (S), 400 (K), 400 (P), 400 (S)
2. Swim 300, 1st & 3rd under :57	2. Swim 4 × 125 on 1:30 CB4/5 4 × 100 own stroke on 1:30
3. Swim 10 × 50, odd 50s on :35, even 50s on :30	3. Swim 8 × 25 EOOF on :30
4. Kick 300 plus 4 × 100 on 1:45	*4. Swim 4 × 75 on 3:00 from dive, all-out
5. Pull 8 × 100, CB5 desc each 4 on 1:15 then pull 20 × 25 on :30, each on one breath	5. Kick 600 plus 12 × 25 on :30
6. Swim 2 × 400 on 5:00, build-up each 400	6. Swim 6 × 25 EOOF on :30
7. Swim 2 × 25 plus 1 × 50 from dive	*7. Swim 4 × 75 on 4:00 from dive, all-out
	8. Pull 600
	9. Swim 4 × 25 EOOF on :30
	*10. Swim 4 × 75 on 4:00, from dive, all-out
	*Goal sets of 12 × 75, record average

Sixth Day (twenty-three days prior to the meet)

A.M.	P.M.
1. WU 300, 300, 300, 300	1. WU 400 (S), 400 (K), 400 (P), 400 (S)
2. Swim 8 × 100 broken at 75, wait for clock to hit :50(Cr), :55(Ba/Fly), :60(Br), blast last 25. On 1:30 start next broken 100. Confidence builder in ability to finish hard.	2. Swim 4 × 100 Cr, left arm only on 1:30 4 × 100 Cr, right army only on 1:30 4 × 100 Cr, catch-up stroke on 1:20 4 × 100 Cr, normal stroke on 1:10 Emphasize hand acceleration on this set
3. Swim 4 × 50 Cr on :33, 4 × 50 on :32, 4 × 50 on :31, 4 × 50 on :30	3. Swim 8 × 50 own stroke, desc each 4 on :50
4. Kick 10 × 50 on :50, decreasing departure time 5 secs per 50 until the departure time can't be met. Move departure time back 5 secs. and finish the set.	4. Swim 6 × 25 EOOF on :30
	5. Time 50 Cr, all-out from dive

TABLE 11-8   A FOUR-WEEK TAPER *(Continued)*

Sixth Day (twenty-three days prior to the meet)
A.M.   P.M.

A.M.	P.M.
5. Pull 2 × 200 Cr, Neg. Split on 2:20	6. Kick 300, plus 12 × 25 on :30
6. Practice ten starts, timing at 12½ y.	7. Time 50 Cr, all-out from dive
	8. Pull 300, then 12 × 25 on :30
	9. Swim 6 × 25 Cr, from a dive
	Dist.: after (2) go 5 × 400 on 4:30, 4:20, 4:10, 4:00, then 4 × 300 on 3:30, 3:20, 3:10, 3:00

Seventh Day (twenty-two days before the meet)
A.M.   P.M.

A.M.	P.M.
1. WU 300, 300, 300, 300	1. WU 250 (S), 250 (K), 250 (P), 250 (S)
2. Swim 6 × 150 on 1:50(Cr), 2:00(Ba/Fly), 2:10(Br) desc each 3	2. Swim broken 400 own stroke, 4 × 100 on 10 secs. RI
3. Kick 200 plus 8 × 50 on 45/50	*Swim straight 400 own stroke
4. Swim 12 × 25 Var. Sprnts on :30	3. Kick 300 plus 8 × 75 on 1:15
5. Swim 4 × 75 own stroke, first and last 25 fast on 1:00, Br on 1:10	4. Swim 6 × 75 on 1:00, desc each 3, Br on 1:10
6. Pull 400 Neg. Split	5. Swim broken 200 own stroke, 4 × 50 on 10 secs. RI
7. Swim 4 × 50 own stroke on :45 desc	*Swim straight 200 within 8 secs. of best time
8. Time 2 × 25 from dive and with turn	6. Pull 1000 own stroke
DIST.	7. Swim 16 × 25 Var. Sprnts on :30
1. WU 400, 400, 400, 400	8. Swim broken 100 own stroke, 4 × 25 on 10 secs, RI
2. Swim 15 × 100 on 1:10	*Swim straight 100 within 4 secs of best time
3. Swim 1000 under 10:20	*9. Swim 50 from a dive
4. Swim 5 × 100 on 1:05	10. Practice relay take-offs
5. Swim 500 under 5:00	*RECORD 400, 200, 100, 50 times
6. Swim 6 × 50 on :35	

Eighth Day (twenty-one days before the meet)
A.M.   P.M.

A.M.	P.M.
1. WU 300, 300, 300, 300	1. WU 300 (S), 300 (K), 300 (P), 300 (S)
2. Swim 3 × 200 desc on 3:00	2. Swim 4 × 100 on 1:10(Cr), 1:20(Ba/Fly), 1:30(Br)
3. Kick 200 plus 6 × 25 on :30	4 × 100 on 1:05(Cr), 1:15(Ba/Fly), 1:25(Br)
4. Swim 50 from dive	4 × 100 on 1:00(Cr), 1:07(Ba/Fly), 1:18(Br)
5. Swim 4 × 25 EOOF on :30	
6. Time 50 all-out from a dive	3. Swim 600 desc each 200; Dist. go 800 desc each 200
DIST.:	4. Kick 500 plus 6 × 25 on 20/25
1. WU 300, 300, 300, 300	5. Pull 500 ETOF plus 6 × 25 on 20/25
2. Swim 200 on 2:20	6. Swim 16 × 25
150 on 1:40	7. Twenty turns
100 on 1:05	8. Time 75
100 on 1:00	
50	
3. Pull 600 under 6:30	
4. Repeat (3)	
5. Repeat (4) faster	
6. Repeat as (5) faster	
7. Repeat as (6) faster	

TABLE 11-8 A FOUR-WEEK TAPER *(Continued)*

Ninth Day (twenty days before the meet)

A.M.	P.M.
1. WU 300, 300, 300, 300	1. WU 300, 300, 300, 300
2. Swim 4 × 50 Cr on :40	2. Swim 3 × 125 Cr on 1:30 CB5
4 × 50 Ba on :40	3 × 100 own stroke on
4 × 50 Br on :50	1:05(Cr), 1:10(Ba/Fly), 1:2
4 × 50 Fly on :40	3 × 50 own stroke on :29(Cr),
3. Pull 4 × 100 IM on 1:30	:32(Ba/Fly), :35(Br)
4. Kick 4 × 100 Neg. Split on 2:00	3. Six starts—3 wind-up, 3 grab
5. Swim 8 × 25 EOOF on :30	4. Twelve turns
6. Swim 4 × 100 own stroke desc on	5. Swim 4 × 100 turn relays
2:00	6. Kick 300 plus 12 × 25 on :30
7. 25 from a dive	7. Pull 500 crawl under 5:30
	8. Swim 8 × 50 desc each 4 on :60
	9. Swim 200 turn relay (two swimmers per team). Start in middle of pool. First swimmer swims to the end, flips, and swims back to middle of pool and touches second swimmer. Second swimmer repeats.

Tenth Day (nineteen days before the meet)

A.M.	P.M.
1. WU 300, 300, 300, 300	1. WU 300, 300, 300, 300
2. Swim 8 × 75 Cr on 1:00	2. Swim 9 × 100 Cr on 1:45 desc
8 × 50 own stroke on 40,	3. Six starts—3 wind-up, 3 grab
50(Br)	4. Kick 300 plus 6 × 25 EOOF on :30
3. Swim 400, Neg. Split	5. Swim 6 × 25 EOOF on :30
4. Kick 4 × 75 on 1:15	6. Easy 50
5. Pull 400 Cr	7. 50 from a dive, all-out
6. Swim 4 × 100 own stroke, desc on	8. Pull 500 plus 5 × 50 on :45
1:45	9. Five turns on each wall
DIST.:	DIST.:
1. WU 300, 300, 300, 300	1. Do above workout plus swim 1000
2. Swim 1000, last one under 4:00	under 9:40
3. Swim 800, last 300 under 3:00	
4. Swim 3 × 150 on 1:40	
3 × 150 on 1:35	
5. Swim 5 × 200 desc on 2:30	

Eleventh Day (eighteen days before the meet)
Day off or make-ups

(If swimmer missed a workout during the week, he should do the workout he missed; if he missed due to illness, no make-up is necessary.)

Twelfth Day (seventeen days before the meet)

A.M.	P.M.
1. WU 300, 300, 300, 300	1. WU 300, 300, 300, 300
2. Swim 3 × 200 Neg. Split desc on 4:00	2. Swim 200 Neg. Split
3. Kick 400 plus 4 × 100 on 1:40	3. Swim 4 × 100 desc on 1:40
4. Pull 400 IM plus 100 each stroke on	4. Swim 4 × 75, first and last 25 all-out
1:30, 2:00(Br)	on :60(Cr), 1:10(Ba/Fly), 1:15(Br)
5. Swim 16 × 35 Var. Sprnts on :30	5. Kick 9 × 50 on :60 desc each 3

TABLE 11-8   A FOUR-WEEK TAPER *(Continued)*

Twelfth Day (seventeen days before the meet)

A.M.	P.M.
6. Swim 10 × 50 on 2:00 near maximum effort	6. Pull 2 × 400 crawl on 5:00

Thirteenth Day (sixteen days before the meet)

A.M.	P.M.

1. WU 300, 300, 300, 300
2. Swim 12 × 50 on 1:00 desc each 6
3. Kick 300 plus 6 × 25 on :30
4. Pull 300 plus 4 × 25 on :30
5. Swim 6 × 25 EOOF on :30
 	
DIST.:
1. 400, 400, 400, 400
2. Swim 20 × 100 on 1:05
3. Kick 8 × 100 on 1:30
4. Pull 400 on 4:30
     300 on 3:20
     200 on 2:20
     100 under 1:00
5. Swim 5 × 100 at race pace, each 100 on :55
	1. WU 400, 400, 400, 400
	2. Swim 4 × 100 desc on 1:30
	     4 × 75 desc on 1:20
	     4 × 50 desc on 1:00
	3. Kick 8 × 50 on 1:00
	4. Pull 400
	5. Swim 16 × 25 Var. Sprnts on :30

Fourteenth Day (fifteen days before the meet)

A.M.	P.M.
1. WU 400, 400, 400, 400 2. Swim 6 × 100 on 1:30, 1:45(Br) desc each 3 3. Kick 200 plus 4 × 50 desc on 1:00 4. Pull 200 plus 4 × 50 desc on :50 5. Swim broken 200 plus 4 × 50, 5 secs. RI after first 50, 10 secs. after second 50, 15 secs. after third 6. Swim 200 IM 7. Practice relay exchanges	1. WU as before the meet and follow time schedule for meet 2. Swim 3 × 200 on 3:00 3. Kick 10 × 50 on 50/55 4. Pull 20 × 25 on :30 5. Swim 3 × 100 desc on 2:00

Fifteenth Day (fourteen days before the meet)

A.M.	P.M.
1. WU 500 (S), 400 (P), 300 (K), 200 (IM), then 100 each stroke 2. Swim 20 × 25 on :30 3. Swim 3 × 300 desc on 1:00 RI 4. Swim 3 × 50 at 200 pace 5. Warm down 100	1. WU 400, 400, 400, 400 2. Swim 8 × 50 hard, don't look at clock 3. Six starts and 12½-y sprints for time 4. Kick 300 5. Twelve turns 6. Pull 400 7. Swim 4 × 25 on :40

Sixteenth Day (thirteen days before the meet)

A.M.	P.M.
1. WU 400, 400, 400, 400 2. Swim 8 × 50 no time 3. Swim 800 on the house	1. WU 400, 400, 400, 400 2. Swim 6 × 100 own stroke desc each 3 on 1:45 6 × 100 own stroke desc each 3 on 1:00(Cr), 1:05(Ba/Fly), 1:10(Br)

TABLE 11-8   A FOUR-WEEK TAPER *(Continued)*

Sixteenth Day (thirteen days before the meet)

A.M.	P.M.
	3. Kick 4 × 100, last 25 hard on 2:00
	4. Pull 3 × 100, last 25 hard on 1:30
	5. Swim 8 × 25 Var. Sprnts on :30

Seventeenth and Eighteenth Days (twelve and eleven days before the meet, one workout per day for two days—same workout each day)

1. WU 300, 300, 300, 300
2. Swim 4 × 100 desc on 1:45
3. Swim 4 × 75 on 1:15
4. Swim 4 × 50 desc on 1:00
5. Kick 200 plus 4 × 25 on :30
6. Pull 200 plus 4 × 25 on :30
7. Loosen down 200
8. Swim 4 × 25 EOOF on :30

Nineteenth Day (ten days before the meet)

A.M.	P.M.
1. WU 400, 400, 400, 400	1. WU 300, 300, 300, 300
2. Swim 4 × 100 desc on 1:45	2. Swim 3 × 200 desc on 3:30
3. Swim 20 × 25 on :30	3 × 100 desc on 1:45
4. Kick 200 plus 4 × 50 on 1:00	PR under 160 on set
5. Pull 400	3. Kick 200 plus 4 × 25 on :40
6. Swim 2 × 25 or 50 from dive	4. Pull 12 × 25 Var. Sprnts on :30
	5. Four starts and eight turns, then all-out 25

Twentieth Day (nine days before the meet)

A.M.	P.M.
1. WU 400, 400, 400, 400	1. WU 300, 300, 300, 300
2. Swim 8 × 50 desc each 4 on 1:00	2. Swim 4 × 50 desc on :50
3. Swim 200 Neg. Split, PR 150 or lower	3. Swim 4 × 100 desc on 1:30
4. Kick 4 × 75 on 1:30	4. Swim Cr 500 under 5:00
5. Swim 100 Neg. Split, PR 160 or lower	Ba/Fly 400 under 4:35
6. Pull 200	Br 400 under 5:00
7. Swim 50 Neg. Split from push-off	IM 400 under 4:30
	5. Kick 200 plus 2 × 50
	6. Pull 300
	7. Swim 4 × 50 from dive, last one hard-on, :22(Cr), :24(Fly), :25(Ba), 27.5(Br)

Twenty-first Day (eight days before the meet)

A.M.	P.M.
1. WU 400, 400, 400, 400	1. WU 250, 250, 250, 250
2. Swim 4 × 50 desc on 1:00	2. Swim 4 × 100 on 1:10(Cr), 1:15(Ba/Fly), 1:25(Br)
3. Kick 200 plus 4 × 25 on :40	4 × 100 on 1:05(Cr), 1:10(Ba/Fly), 1:20(Br)
4. Pull 200 plus 4 × 25 on :30	3. Kick 200 plus 3 × 50 on 1:00
5. Pull 12 × 25 with turn	4. Pull 400
	5. Swim 300 Neg. Split

TABLE 11-8   A FOUR-WEEK TAPER *(Continued)*

Twenty-first Day (eight days before the meet)

A.M.	P.M.
	6. Swim 8 × 25 Var. Sprnts on :30
	7. Swim 4 × 50 from dive, last one 95%

Twenty-second Day (seven days before the meet)

A.M.	P.M.
1. WU 300, 300, 300, 300	1. WU 300, 300, 300, 300
2. Swim 16 × 25 Var. Sprnts on :30	2. Swim 6 × 100 desc each 3 on 2:00
3. Swim 150 desc each 50	3. Kick 300 plus 4 × 25 on :30
4. Kick 400	4. Swim 8 × 50 desc each 4 on :50
5. Pull 12 × 25 Var. Sprnts on :30	5. Pull 400 plus 4 × 25 on :30
	6. Swim 4 × 50 build-ups in 3 waves on 2:00
	DIST.:
	1. Do above workout plus
	3 × 150 on 1:35
	3 × 100 on 1:05

Twenty-third Day (six days before the meet)

A.M.	P.M.
1. WU 300, 300, 300, 300	1. WU 300, 300, 300, 300
2. Swim 4 × 75 blast, last 25 on 1:15	2. Swim 8 × 50, hold 1 through 3 steady, 4 moderate on :60
4 × 50 blast, last 25 on :50	3. Kick 300 plus 4 × 25 on :30
3. Kick 300 plus 4 × 25 on :30	4. Pull 300 plus 4 × 25 Var. Sprnts on :30
4. Pull 400	5. Swim 200 Neg. Split, PR 160 or lower
5. Swim 400 no time	6. Swim 4 × 100 desc on 2:00 FLAB-SLAB (Float like a butterfly, sting like a bee) 70% effort, 85% speed concept)
6. Swim 6 × 25 Var. Sprnts on :30	7. Loosen down 200
	8. Practice relay take-offs

Twenty-fourth and Twenty-fifth Days (five and four days before the meet, one workout per day)

A.M. (on the 24th)	P.M. (on the 25th)
1. WU 300, 300, 300, 300	Swim 1000 on the house
2. Swim 4 × 50 hold steady, Cr on :35, Ba/Fly on :40, Br on :45	(This is a good time to use WU of choice)
3. Kick 300 plus 4 × 25 on :30	
4. Swim 4 × 50 desc on :60, last one at 90% effort	
5. Pull 300 plus 4 × 25 on :30	
6. Swim 4 × 25 Var. Sprnts on :30	
7. Swim 200 Neg. Split, Cr under 2:00, Ba/Fly under 2:10, Br under 2:25	
8. Swim broken 100—4 × 25, 10 secs. RI	
Cr :48, Ba/Fly :54, Br 1:02, IM :57 or faster	

TABLE 11-8 A FOUR-WEEK TAPER *(Continued)*

Twenty-sixth Day (three days before the meet)

A.M.	P.M.
Swim 1200 on the house (using WU of choice)	1. WU 300, 300, 300, 300
	2. Swim 8 × 50 on :50, holding first and third steady, fourth at 85% effort, then start over
	3. Kick 200 plus 4 × 25 on :30
	4. Pull 200 plus 4 × 25 on :30
	5. Swim 3 × 100 on 1:05(Cr), on 1:15(Ba/Fly), on 1:30(Br)
	6. Swim 4 × 25 Var. Sprnts on :30
	7. Loosen down 200

Twenty-seventh Day (only two days to go)

A.M.	P.M.
1. Loosen up 1200	1. WU 200, 200, 200, 200
2. Do some 25s from a dive with a turn, but not all-out	2. Swim 8 × 50 on 1:00 desc each 4. Get accustomed to pool. None of this should be hard. (turns, lights, etc.)
	3. Swim 3 × 100 on 2:00. Get used to turning at both ends of pool.
	4. Kick 200 plus 1 × 50 hard, but not all-out
	5. 3 × 25 build-ups from dive
	Dist. swimmers pace 10 × 100 on 1:15, maintaining desired pace for 1650 event

Twenty-eighth Day (meet tomorrow!)

A.M.	P.M.
Follow schedule to be observed throughout meet, getting up at same time, eating at same time; shave down or clip part way. Swim 800 to 1200.	1. WU 300, 300, 300, 300
	2. Swim 4 × 50 desc on 1:00
	3. Kick 200 plus 1 × 50 for time
	4. Pull 200
	5. Swim 1 or 2 easy 50s
	6. Swim 2 or 3 dive 25s
	7. Loosen down

LEGEND OF ABBREVIATIONS

S—Swim	Ba/Fly—back/fly	RI—rest interval
K—Kick	Br—breast	PR—pulse rate
P—Pull	IM—individual medley	WU—warm up
Cr—crawl		

EOOF—every other one fast
ETOF—every third one fast
CB followed by a number—controlled breathing, the number indicating a single arm stroke
Desc—each one faster than the previous
Neg.Split—negative split (swimmer goes out slower than he comes back)
Var.Sprnts—variable sprints
Dist.—distance
min.—minutes
secs.—seconds
y—yards
av.—average

workout should have an emphasis. About twice a week, early in the season, the major emphasis should be speed; the other four to six workouts should stress endurance. As the season progresses, the emphasis should shift to more speed work, especially for sprinters.

Each of these workouts may be adjusted to suit the different age levels and the various levels of skill or sports mastery.

Early Season Workouts

During the first two weeks of this short-course season very little speed work was done. The following one-a-day workout (September 15) fell within the first two weeks. A record was kept of the times for Item 4, the 800-yard pulling effort. The times ranged from 9:24 to 12:41, the slowest being for a swimmer who had not trained during the summer.

SEPTEMBER 15

1. Warm up 300 swim, 300 kick, 300 pull.
2. Swim 10 × 50 Fly, Hyp.* 2 on :45.
10 × 50 Back on :45.
3. Kick 6 × 100 on 1:50 or better.
4. Pull 800 Free for time, Hyp. 4.

5. Swim 14 × 100 own stroke,	Free	Back/Fly	Breast
	1:20/1:25	1:25/1:30	1:35/1:40

6. Dive 50
Total Distance: 4750 yards
*Hypoxic or controlled breathing

September 29 was the final one-a-day workout. Beginning September 30, doubles began three days a week, making a total of nine workouts per week.

SEPTEMBER 29

1. Warm up 500.
2. Swim 4 × 200 own stroke on C.I.* + 10.
4 × 150 Crawl on 2:00 Hyp. 4.
4 × 100 own stroke on C.I. + 5.
3. Kick 500 straight
4. Swim 12 × 50 Fly, Hyp. 2 on :60.
5. 1000 crawl, Hyp. 5.
6. Swim 800 negative split
7. Swim 20 × 20 in dive well on :45.
Total Distance: 5600 yards
*C.I. = Cruise Interval

October 14 was a double workout day. Note that more speed work has been added and that the workouts have begun to be differentiated among the sprinters, middle-distance, and distance swimmers.

OCTOBER 14   A.M.

1. Warm up 500
2. Swim 12 × 100, descending each 4 on C.I. + 10.
3. Swim 2 × 400, neg. split on 3:45.
4. Kick 200, then as 12 × 25 on :25.
5. Pull 200, then 12 × 25 no breathers on :20.
6. Swim 4 × 200 on 2:30.
Total Distance: 4300 yards

P.M.

1. Warm up 400-swim, 400-kick, 400-pull, 400-swim.
2. 32 × 25 no breathers on :30.
3. Swim

Distance	Middle-Distance	Sprinters
15 × 200 descending each 3 on 2:30	15 × 100 on 1:30, descending 3	15 × 75 first 5 on :60, last 25 hard; second 5 on 1:15, last 50 hard; third 5 on 1:30, all hard

4. Pull 3 × 500 Crawl, descending on 6:00; Dist.: Hyp. 4/5.
5. Swim 16 × 25 EOOF*, no breathers on :60; Dist.: 22 × 50 on :35.
Total Distance: Distance swimmers—8000
  Middle-Distance swimmers—5800
  Sprinters—5425
*Every Other One Fast

Midseason Workouts

Doubles are being done five days a week and a single workout is done on Saturday for a total of eleven practices each week. Make-ups are held on Sunday morning for those who may have had to miss a workout for academic or other reasons.

DECEMBER 3   A.M.   P.M.

A.M.

1. Warm-up 8 × 100 I.M.* (swim straight through as an 800).
2. Swim 10 × 50 Free on :35,
   Breast on :50,
   Back on :45,
   Fly on :45,
3. Swim 400 neg. split.
4. Kick 4 × 200 I.M. on 3:30.
5. Pull 6 × 100 I.M. pm 1:20.

Total Distance: 3100 yards

*Individual Medley

P.M.

1. Warm up 300-swim, 200-kick, 200-pull, 300-swim.
2. Swim 40 × 100 (first 10 × 100 on 1:15; second 10 × 100 on 1:10; third 15 × 100 on 1:05/1:10; 5 × 100 on :60/1:05; no break before last 5 × 100).
3. Pull 300, then 8 × 25 (first 25 easy, second one hard).
4. Swim 5 broken 150s (break at 100, leave on C.I. + 5, blast last 50—total interval 2:00).

Total Distance: 6250 yards

The following workouts occurred during the end-of-semester exam period. Swimmers were given the option of doing only half of each workout. In the morning, five of total roster of twenty-five did the whole workout, the rest missed the workout entirely; in the afternoon sixteen exercised the option, six did the whole workout.

DECEMBER 14   A.M.   P.M.

A.M.

1. Warm up 500.
2. Swim 6 × 200 on C.I. + 10 own stroke; Breast 5 × 200.
3. Swim 18 × 50 on :35/:40.
4. Kick 200, then 12 × 25 on :25.
5. Pull 200, then 12 × 25 on :25 one breathers.
6. Swim 4 × 100, descending on 1:20/1:30.
7. Swim easy 800 I.M., changing strokes every length.

Total Distance: 4800 yards

P.M.

1 Warm up 200-swim, 200-kick, 200-pull, 200-swim (same for half workout option).
2. Swim 6 × 200 own stroke, descending each 3 on 3 minutes, last one hard (half option did 3 × 200).
3. Kick 6 × 100 on 1:45, neg. split (half option did 4 × 100).
4. Swim 10 × 100 on C.I. + 5 (half option did 6 × 100). Swim 6 × 100 on C.I. (half option did 4 × 100).
5. Pull 3 × 200 I.M. (half option swam one easy 50, then one hard 50 from a dive, repeating four times).

6. Swim 400, look at time at 300
   300, look at time at 200
   200, look at time at 100
   100, descending all efforts
   in (6)
7. Swim 8 × 25 EOOF.

Total Distance: 6000 yards for total
workout
3200 half option

This workout took place in the Canary Islands. Following Christmas with their families, the team went to the island of Tenerife for holiday training. Training was long-course meters.

DECEMBER 29   A.M.

Distance
1. Warm up 800.
2. Swim 2 × 400 neg. split on 5:00.
3. Swim 6 × 200 on 2:45, working second and fourth 50.
4. Pull 1000 Hyp. 6, 500 Hyp. 4/5, 200 Hyp. 3/4.
5. Kick 300, then 6 × 100 on 1:50/2:00.
6. Swim 14 × 50 on 1:45 EOOF.

Total Distance: 6100 meters

Middle Distance
1. Warm up 800.
2. Swim 3 × 200 on 2:45, working second and fourth 50.
3. Swim 8 × 100 on 1:15.
4. Kick 300, then 5 × 100 on 2:00.
5. Pull 300, then 8 × 100 on Hyp. on first 50, working second 50.
6. Swim 4 × 100 Fly on 2:00.
7. Loosen down 200.
8. Swim 20 × 50 EOOF on 1:45.

Total Distance: 5700 meters

Sprinters
1. Warm up 800.
2. Swim 20 × 50 on 1:45 EOOF.
3. Kick 300, then 4 × 100 on 2:15, working first 25 of each 50.
4. Pull 300, then 8 × 50 breath control (first 25 no breath, second 25 easy).
5. Swim 8 × 100 on 1:30, first 50 constant moderate, second 50 crescendo.
6. Swim 5 × 50, from a dive, 80 percent effort.
7. Swim 8 × 50 on 1:45 EOOF.

Total Distance: 4650 meters

P.M.

Distance
1. Warm up 800.
2. Swim 1000.
3. Swim 4 × 200, descending on 2:30.
4. Pull 2 × 400.
5. Swim 1000, (Broken 5 × 200).
6. Kick 300, then 6 × 100 on 1:50/2:00.
7. Swim 1000, (Broken at 400, rest 10 secs.
   Broken at 700, rest 10 secs.
   Broken at 900, rest 10 secs.)
8. Swim down 200.

Total Distance: 6500 meters

Middle Distance
1. Warm up 800.
2. Swim 12 × 100 on 1:25, descending each 4.
3. Kick 200, then 6 × 100 on 2:00.
4. Swim 400, using catch-up.
5. Pull 6 × 200, first 100 Hyp. 6, second 100 faster (not Hyp.).
6. Swim 4 × 50 on :60, one of each stroke in "I.M." order, repeat 6 times for a total of 24 × 50, first one straight, second one broken at 50, third one broken at 100.
7. Swim 3 × 200.

Total Distance: 6200 meters

Sprinters
1. Warm up 800.
2. Swim 8 × 100 on 1:30, first and last 25 hard.
3. Kick 200, then 4 × 100 on 2:15, first and last 25 hard.
4. Pull 400 catch-up.
5. Pull 3 × 200 on 3:00, first and third Hyp. 6, second faster, no hypox
6. Swim 8 × 100, first 25 all-out sprint.
7. Swim 6 × 100 on 1:30, first and last 25 hard.
8. Swim 3 × 50 from a dive, build-ups.

Total Distance: 4750 meters

Peak of Training Density

The team has returned from holiday training to the beginning of the second semester. Upon their return, some swimmers participated in an international competition, resting for only a few days prior to the meet. The team is now back into the hardest phase of training. In two weeks, those who make the Conference Championship Team will begin the four-week taper. The only exceptions will be the elite swimmers who will use a modified taper and will swim tired through the Conference meet, beginning their full taper about a week after the meet.

JANUARY 21   A.M.   P.M.

1. Warm up 1000.
2. Swim 8 × 100 on C.I. + 5, hold steady.
3. Kick 100 on 1:45/1:50; Pull 200 on 2:30, repeating four times for a total of 400 kicking and 800 pulling.
4. Swim 16 × 50, odd 50s on :40, even 50s on :35.
5. Loosen down 200.
Total Distance: 4000 yards

1. Warm up 250-swim, 250-kick, 250-pull, 250-swim.
2. Swim 9 × 100 on C.I. + 10, descending each 3.
3. Swim 400 own stroke, neg. split.
4. Kick 12 × 50 on :60, neg. split.
5. Pull 1 × 200 I.M. on 3:00.
      1 × 200 Free on 2:30.
      1 × 200 I.M.
6. Swim 16 × 50 on 1:30, EOOF; distance: 5 × 200 on 2:15.
7. Swim 2 50s from a dive.
8. Loosen down 300.
Total Distance: Sprinters and middle-distance swimmers—4700 yards
                          Distance swimmers—4900 yards

Hard training will continue for those who are not tapering for the Conference Championship. Note the appearance of goal sets at this stage of training. They have been used sparingly up to this point. Goal sets are highly challenging, but also very demanding.

FEBRUARY 1   A.M.

1. Warm up 250-swim, 250-kick, 250-pull, 250-swim.
2. Swim 4 × 50 Fly on :40,
        4 × 50 Back on :40,
        4 × 50 Breast on :50,
   Swim 4 × 50 Free on :35.
3. Swim 3 × 200 own stroke, neg. split on third effort.
4. Kick 5 × 100 on 2:00, neg. split.
5. Swim 4 × 100 own stroke, C.I. + 5,
        4 × 100 own stroke, C.I.
6. Swim 16 × 25 variable sprints on :30.
7. Swim 50 from a dive.
Total Distance: 4150 yards

P.M.

1. Warm up 200-swim, 200-kick, 200-pull, 200-swim.

2. Swim   Distance   Middle-Distance   Sprinters
            5 × 300 on 3:30.   6 × 150, C.I. + 5.   6 × 100 on 1:30,
                                  4 × 150 on C.I.   descending
            3 × 300 on 3:20.   4 × 100 on C.I.   each 3.
            3 × 300 on 3:10.   4 × 100 on C.I.
                                                       4 × 50 on :30.

3. Kick 24 × 25 on 25 (for all three groups).

4. Pull 4 × 100 Fly/Back on 1:30.
        4 × 100 Breast/Free on 1:30.
        4 × 100 Free on 1:05/1:10.

5. Goal set:
        8 × 100 on 4/5 minutes—Middle Distance.
        12 × 50 on 3:00/3:30—Sprinters.
        3 × 400 on 10 minutes.

Total Distance: Distance Swimmers—8500 yards

Middle-distance Swimmers—7100 yards

Sprinters—6400 yards

SUGGESTED READING

1. Tudor Bompa, *Theory and Methodology of Training* (Dubuque, IA: Kendall/Hunt Publishing Co., 1983), 132 pages.

Train with the Experts

Throughout the history of the sport of competitive swimming in the United States, the leading coaches have been a highly individualistic group: not unlike pioneers in other fields of endeavor in this relatively young country. When they spoke at clinics, they were willing to share ideas, but only to a point. It often happened that the conceptual foundation of their training methods eluded their listeners. Was that because they didn't want to reveal professional secrets? In some cases, perhaps. Or was it that they couldn't be more specific because they didn't *have* a scientific basis for the way they trained their swimmers? Anyone who has persevered to this point in the book has probably already guessed that these authors believe the latter was the case. The overwhelming majority of swimming coaches in the United States were themselves once swimmers. Their methods evolved from what could be described as *informed trial and error*. Their ideas originated from the way they had been trained, what they gained along the way from other coaches, and what their own creativity dictated. Successful coaches developed their own style. Much that same situation continues today, although it is changing.

One of the coaches who was interviewed for this chapter speaks of coaches as being *either intuitive or pattern coaches*. He thinks of himself as being an intuitive coach: one who knows intuitively what each swimmer needs on a given day. It is clear that he feels a mild contempt for a coach who allows himself to be the prisoner of a rigid plan or pattern, from which he refuses to deviate no matter how disastrous may be the training response of his swimmers. Yet, operating within at least a general plan is very reassuring to both a coach and his athletes, providing the plan is not too radical and the coach has a history of success with his methods. The point here is that many different coaching styles have worked in this country, and there is no single type of successful coach. In fact, there are almost as many personality types in our profession as there are coaches of our sport. It just isn't possible to generalize about whose personality and whose methods are the best. It can be said that our leading coaches enjoy a prominence in the swimming community that is unique in the sports world.

This is substantially different from the circumstances which have prevailed in the Eastern European countries and which have been widely imitated throughout the rest of the world. Their books and periodicals suggest that a whole new profession grew up around the need to provide sports methodology to athletic coaches, or trainers, as they were called. (The term *trainer*, by the way, exemplifies the difference in status between the charismatic coaches of the United States and the anonymous trainers of the Communist system. In the latter case, the coach was merely one member of a team of professionals dedicated to the total sports preparation of the athlete.)

In keeping with the prevailing political philosophy in Eastern Europe following World War II, highly centralized sports bureaus were organized for the express purpose of developing sports theory. Technical research in all the disciplines proliferated, and training schemes were developed on the basis of the results of that research. These schemes were promulgated to local sports centers throughout the various countries. This tremendous effort was made in the belief that healthful, wholesome, and successful athletics were the best public relations stratagem to promote the political system. It is a testimony to the effectiveness of the effort that, even after the political system itself had collapsed, the sports system continued to produce athletes who won most of the medals in the 1992 Olympic Games. Chapter 8 presents an overview of the sports theory that was created in the USSR.

This chapter will try to show how trial-and-error methods have guided American thinking about training. The material is based primarily on interviews with and replies to a questionnaire sent to some of the current coaching leaders of this country. As stated before, the opinions expressed have been based on the pragmatism of performance results rather than on scientific theoretical approaches. The stopwatch being the usual deciding criterion, what informs this process and prevents it from being too haphazard to be effective is that the people in the top rank of a small group of its best practitioners are insightful, astute coaches, whose programs have served widely as models for the competitive swimming community, usually to the improvement of results.

In the authors' opinion both the centralized method of the Eastern Europeans and the pragmatic one of the Americans have obvious strengths and weaknesses. In the centralized plan, swimming is only one of a full range of activities in a total training design created for all so-called cyclic sports, of which swimming is one. As such, the plan does not allow for individualization. Either the individual athlete was expected to adjust his training needs to the dictates of the plan, or it was assumed that local trainers would quietly adjust the plan.

On the other hand, European sports scientists are incredulous when they are told that, until recently, the United States did not even have a certification program for its coaches. Anyone who wanted to become a coach was free to do so. We now have an education and certification program, operated by the American Swimming Coaches Association. It ensures that a novice coach can acquire a basic knowledge in all the disciplines which relate to the coaching of swimming: physiology, biomechanics, psychology, administrative skills, strength-building, and so forth. There have been efforts by the leadership of U. S. Swimming to assume this responsibility, but, so far, to no avail.

We are trying to improve the basis of our sports theory and the expertise of our coaches, but we don't want to gain these assets at the cost of losing intuitive perception. That is the reason the authors have decided to present the predominating ideas of some of our most successful coaches and even those of the coach of another country.

Most coaches who have achieved national prominence train their swimmers four hours or more per day, six or seven days a week, at the height of the training season. This includes time spent on dry-land or in-water strength-building programs. There may be exceptions in which swimmers have succeeded on as little as two hours per day of training. They are usually sprinters. The current buzzwords are *cross-training*, which implies the use of nonspecific activities to achieve a desired training effect, and *stroke drills*, which employ technique drills in repeat sets rather than whole strokes. Time will prove or disprove the efficacy of these techniques, as performance results will again decide whether they become permanent parts of the training effort.

Several interviews and sample workouts follow.

EDDIE REESE
MEN'S SWIMMING COACH, UNIVERSITY OF TEXAS

Eddie Reese, Men's Swimming Coach of the University of Texas, was the 1992 U.S. Men's Olympic Coach. Mr. Reese is an acknowledged expert at bringing his teams to the peak of performance at championship time.

Question: When do you begin training for the indoor season?

Answer: We have a team meeting on the first day of classes. That's when we do all the paper work the NCAA likes to have you do, which is at least an hour's worth nowadays. Then the first allowable day we start in the water. Usually the day after that, we'll go in the weight room. We have a videotape that the team watches for orientation. The film is designed with safety considerations in mind and to familiarize the kids with the kinds of equipment we use. There may be some who have never lifted at all or are unfamiliar with certain kinds of equipment. The tape shows them the proper techniques; so, basically, we're interested in safety and technique.

Question: Do you make the tapes yourself?

Answer: No, the strength people in the weight room have the film and it's specifically for our weight room.

Question: How do you start them off?

Answer: I'm one of those guys who believe in starting off easy. We begin the first week with maybe 2000 to 2500 [yards]. I'll appoint a different person each day to stop me, when we get to that point. And it's all technique: It's all turns, push-offs, starts, the stroke drills we use in practice—especially early in the year.

Question: Do you show any films?

Answer: We show films of *them* at that time. Maybe not of the past, but of what they're doing now, and then there's bound to be somebody in practice who's been there and does it right, and then we'll show 'em that. We'll run a comparison, but it'll be films we take that week.

Then, the next couple of weeks, we work up to about a thousand a week. I feel that, if you work into your practices, you can work harder longer because the swimmers [will] have adjusted better. Instead of jumping out and starting with 4000, and soon you're at 6000, and in three weeks you're starting doubles, I think that's too hard on 'em and they get too tired quicker. It seems like you can't push 'em as long as I want to push 'em, unless you start out gradually. We go hard till basically the middle of January with no break. We don't shave or taper in December; in fact, not shaving, tapering, and emphasizing meets goes back a long way. You [James E. Counsilman] wrote an article early in the fifties that had to do with depletion of the adrenal system, remember that? Well, I went back when I was in graduate school—that was in '64—and got hold of every study I could locate. The one you did concerning swimming used two or three groups: one group that was swimming only, one group that was swimming and exercising, and so forth. So I remember all that stuff. You talked about the de-adrenalization: about trying to get 'em up too much in every practice or get 'em up every weekend for a meet, and how they'd get to the end of the year and have nothing left. . . . I remember you saying that it might be next year before they had recovered enough to go good. And I've seen that [happen].

All right, so I'll give you some workouts from the various times of the year or an idea of how my schedule goes (see pp 364–370).

Question: What do you emphasize at the beginning of the season?

Answer: In the weight room and in the water, we emphasize technique. And in the weight room: safety. But in the water, we work on streamlining, teaching them to do all the simple things they may not have been taught in high school.

Question: You said you use movies and videos. Specifically how do you use them?

Answer: Oh, yes. We've got films that we've taken the last few years to show what we want out of the starts, the turns, and so forth. . . .

Question: Do you do any running, and, if so, at what times of the season?

Answer: We've done running at different times in our program. This year, I tried to help my flutter kickers by warming them up and then having them run some quarters.

Question: Quarter miles? Did you time 'em?

Answer: Yeah, timed 'em. I gave them their times to go in different groups and we ran four or five quarters.

Question: What would their times be like? A minute or under?

Answer: No. I never had them going under a minute. I didn't want 'em running that hard. I would worry about their legs. But they were in the sixty-five range and another group that was in the seventy range. Generally, there were two groups, and sixty-five was at eighty-five or ninety percent [effort] for one group, and seventy was [at about the same percentage of effort] the second group. At the same time, we were doing hops, like the Russians did that time they came to Santa Clara. Or jumps, whatever you want to call them. We had a sequence of things we did down on the football field. We'd do five lunges—that's what we'd call 'em—where they'd just step forward, touch their back knee, then stride forward. Those five lunges mean five on each side. They'd alternate and then they'd do ten lunges and ten hops, then maybe fifteen lunges and fifteen hops and they'd be at the end of the football field. I'd give 'em a minute to rest and then we'd do like twenty hops as high as they could hop. And that's one of the hardest things you can do. And then *that's* when we'd do our quarter-mile runs, after we'd done the lunges and the hops. We'd keep up the quarter miles well into the first semester, maybe till mid-November.

Question: Is there anything else special?

Answer: Yes, we started running up the stadium steps this year.

Question: One at a time?

Answer: Oh, yeah.

Question: Did you take any measurements to see if they improved their vertical jump or their times for any given distance?

Answer: Not for a given distance, but we did [measure] their vertical jumps this year. When we first started exercising, the vertical jump went down, and as we hopped and everything else. But, pretty soon, it went back up higher than the starting level. It was about five weeks before it did that. Then there were exceptions: like Shawn Jordan [the top sprinter on the Texas Men's Team in the early 1990s]. Shawn's a 35-inch vertical jumper, and he didn't get back to that height until the end of the year. I mean he started at 35 and he went down to 30, 29, and then he came back up, but he never got back to 35.

[Authors' Note: In studies at Indiana we found that athletes with a high vertical jump improved very little in a regime of exercise with the Biokinetic

Leaper, an accommodating resistance device designed to improve leaping ability, while those with an initially low vertical jump improved significantly.]

Question: Did you find that your distance swimmers had a lower vertical jump?

Answer: Distance swimmers' vertical jumps are not very good. But the strange thing is that I also had a sprinter who went :43.8, 1:35.8 on the hundred and two hundred free and was right at :20 flat for the fifty and he had only a 23-inch vertical jump, yet he's got a start like a guy with a 30-inch vertical jump. But I think that's because he streamlines so well and he weighs about 180, so he's got the body weight for momentum and does a real impressive job. His start was second on the team to Shawn Jordan.

Question: So is it your opinion that the vertical jump is not always a reliable predicter of potential in particular events? That there may be other factors which can override it?

Answer: Yes, I would say that sums up my feelings. I remember Kent Benson improving it from 22 to 27 inches a long time ago, when you used the Leaper. I remember that. I don't know. Maybe the jury's still out on that. Because, here's Shawn with a 35 vertical jump and Josh Davis with a 23 . . . and Josh is, you know :43.8 in the hundred and that's the first year in our program. I mean he's 1.2 seconds faster than Shawn was in his first year.

Question: What kind of dry land exercises do you do?

Answer: We climb ropes, we do wheels up the ramp—you remember those—the 6-inch lawn mower wheels with a 16-inch two-by-four, and you bolt 'em into the two-by-four, put a little foam rubber on the top of the two-by-four and wrap it with tape. You put that below your knees and you walk up ramps with your finger tips turned in. And, surprisingly, it is better for your postural muscles than it is for your arms. The way you bring your arms in is when you hop . . . do it two arms at a time. All right—other dry lands? We do lunges, hops, we do some walking up stadium steps, we hop up stadium steps, but, as I said before, this can get you hurt.

Question: Do you take any special kinds of measurements?

Answer: Yes. We do strength tests every three or four weeks in the weight room, depending on how long [the swimmers have] been in the program. If they're freshmen, we do it every three weeks because the strength test we do is just a variation of a workout. Our normal workout for, let's say, our 200 and under people, is a set of eight and three sets of six in the weight room [Authors' Note: barbells of different weights]. It's oriented towards strength, so, on the third week for freshmen, two weeks of this will really hurt 'em. On the third week we do a set of eight, six, four, and two and we test 'em on the two is all. I never test 'em on a single repetition in the weight room, because that's when they're likely to get hurt.

Comment: Yeah, there are calibration tables that can help predict max from a given number of repetitions of a lesser weight.

Answer: Right. Basically that's it. . . . We also do a standing long jump that will do coordination and explosive power.

Question: Do you measure how far they can jump?

Answer: Yes.

Question: And does that correlate highly with their explosive power and with vertical jump?

Answer: I haven't done that, and I'd like to try it. Talking with you now makes me think that might be fun to do.

Question: Do you use any other special devices that you feel have been particularly effective and also are unique to your program?

Answer: I also like swimming with surgical tubing. [Authors' Note: In this type of drill, one end of the surgical tubing is attached to a belt around the swimmer's waist and the other end to one end of the pool.]

Question: Do you swim down, flip the turn, and come back, or what?

Answer: If they're real strong, they can flip, but we have different sizes of surgical tubing and, as they progress and increase the speed on how soon they can get down to the other end, then we go up a gauge on the surgical tubing, or we just cut two feet off of it. But, it's done on an individual basis and we haven't really recorded anything on that. We *do* know that that is one of the hardest things we can do in the water. I used to think that, when they'd swim against it to the other end, the overload was the hardest part . . . but they tell me that what I call the overspeed part of it, when they come back with it pulling them, is very, very hard.

Question: They have to keep their hands moving fast, right?

Answer: Yes. And maybe it's hard because, usually, it's after the overload part. And I control their breathing, too; that is, when they come back fast, if it's fly or free, I ask 'em not to breathe. If it's backstroke, it's usually dolphin kick underwater. That's hard. It's only for eight or ten seconds, but it's all-out. I'm also experimenting with something this year, and you might be able to help me with that. I've had a couple of kids in my program for a long time—this is their sixth year. So I want to come up with something a little bit different. [Authors' Note: It's a good policy to devote 10 percent of the total training distance to experimental techniques. This relieves boredom for both the coach and swimmer, each of whom may learn something of value.] Like the kick drill I'm having the breast-stroker do now. You remember when butterfly was with the breaststroke kick? Well, now, on the kick drill, I have him kick three breaststroke kicks with his head down and without breathing. Then he gets to breathe by taking a butterfly stroke. And when he does a butterfly stroke, he finishes it with one of his kicks.

It's basically the same thing: teaches him to get his head down fast, and . . . it's different.

Question: Do you do it every day? It's different, right?

Answer: Oh, yeah. It kills 'em too. They don't like it, so I know it's good for 'em.

Question: Do you continue with your strength program once you're into hard training in the water?

Answer: Yes, we do. . . . As we start training harder and harder, the first six or seven weeks everybody's strength keeps going up and up. Then, as time goes on, what they can do in the weight room starts dropping off. They don't like that, because they don't like to start going backwards in the amount of weight they can lift. But we lift—if the first week of March is our goal—we lift pretty strong with most everybody till early January, middle January, then we taper. We start cutting back on our repetitions and, if we're at six repetitions, the first week of taper, we'll cut to four; and the next week, we'll cut to two and we'll do two for two or three weeks in a row.

Question: The same amount of weight?

Answer: No, the weight'll go up. It's just the same way as when you taper for swimming. [Authors' Note: The analogy is that tapering with weights allows the swimmer to manage heavier weights; tapering for swimming allows the swimmer to go faster.]

Question: Do you use any special exercises for your breaststrokers?

Answer: No, I just kind of put 'em on a bicycle, since [Mike] Barrowman came out with that. And we do squats for a while and then we go [back] to the bicycle for the last half of the season, because squats really take it out of their legs and I think [squats are] really a hard thing to do.

Question: Do you do any hypoxic work, that is, breathing every two or three strokes on the breaststroke?

Answer: The hypoxic we do on breaststroke is a curve at two times. When we do a kick drill, one of them is without a board. We kick four kicks with the head down, then two full strokes, and that's when they breathe. And that's hypoxic—either they learn to hold their breath or to kick faster, one of the two. 'Cause if they kick faster, they get to the air quicker.

Question: One of the keys to your success, in my opinion, has been your ability to see talent in a swimmer and predict that he will improve. What do you look for in a swimmer when you go out to recruit him as a future [University of Texas] athlete?

Answer: Well, when I shake their hand—I've got an average-sized hand—and, if their hands are bigger than mine, that's a start. When I'm shaking their hand, I look down at their feet. There's another start. [But] what I really look for, very simply, is distance per stroke. I miss a lot of people who have long arms, but not the strength to use them, so they're at a mechanical disadvantage. There are so many people that, in order to get better, just need to swim. Just give 'em time. There are hundreds out there. Like there are some college programs that will say, "Well, you can't get a scholarship unless you make an NCAA standard." . . . In fact, this past season, we would have had no one that had an NCAA standard out of high school.

Question: Well, I think there's something else there. It's not intuition, but don't you recognize something there?

Answer: You could be right about that.

Question: And, I don't mean to brag, but I always thought I had a similar ability. I'd often contact a kid and you would already have contacted him. And I thought, well, we're seeing something and we can't put a finger on it. Right?

Answer: Right. Okay, I like that, that's right. Sometimes I'll watch how well they push off the walls, how well they start. I remember my first year at Auburn, I went to the Florida high school meet. I was late recruiting, and they had their state meet the second weekend in May at that time. I watched a butterflyer go :55.6, but he almost had to duck to go under the flags. By his senior year, he was :48.4 on the medley relay for me. There aren't many :55 flyers that ever go that fast, but he had it, you know, and he was willing to try. I think there are a lot of people that have got the talent, and, whether you see it or not, getting it out of them is maybe a bigger step than finding it. And that's because it's all in how you treat people. That may be the most important ingredient.

Question: All right, back to your dry land program. Do you think your exercise program has helped your sprinters more than your distance swimmers?

Answer: This is a great question, and, without a doubt, yes. I have fished around for a program for distance swimmers, and I've found that, if you put them on a heavy weight program, they get a little bit faster, but you kill their mile. You know, their 500 and 200 may get better, but I've had guys at the mile actually dip. I don't care how fast you get 'em, they're not gonna swim a great 200. So now anybody I get for the mile, I'm real careful with 'em. They do mostly body-weight exercises and only if they can do numbers, like fifteen to fifty repetitions. I don't mess with the shorter repetitions. I definitely feel that my sprinters are helped more than my distance swimmers by my dry land program. But I am proud of the fact that my distance swimmers graduate as milers and keep going faster, and that's because, each year, I increase a little bit what they do in the water.

Question: In the past you've been known for success as a sprint and middle-distance coach, and now your distance swimmers are showing. Have you made changes in your distance regimen? If so, what are they?

Answer: I've always felt I had the best distance program in the country, but I never recruited [distance swimmers], because I thought—sure it would be great to get a good distance man like Brian Goodell, for example, because he could do it all—but that your 200 man is the basis of your team. And you know, now, it's more that way than ever. I mean, even your 50 free, 100 free, and 100 flyers are the backbone of your team.

But, no, I've always swum my distance swimmers a lot; whatever "a lot" means. And now I've made an attempt to recruit distance swimmers. That's because right now, the distance events are a joke. The 500 free, the mile, and even the 200 free and 200 fly this year were terrible events. You know, we used to have the 500 man, the Craig Beardsleys, who could also swim a great fly. [Even now, we have a few.] Melvin Stewart is a 4:16 500 man and he swims a great butterfly. So they've gotta have a great background to do that. In other words, in the training events, except for the 400 I.M., which I don't really understand, we're dropping out of sight.

Anyway, you know what I think might have helped my distance swimmers? It's that I'm slowly realizing how important it is, if you've got a half hour left in your distance program and you've gotta decide whether you do 100s, 200s, 400s, or swim it straight—I've about decided that you're better off swimming it straight. I also believe that we shouldn't do a whole lot of 100s in practice, we should do 200s instead. I think 100s are something to do in taper, because they're easy to do and they're easy to do with no rest, and they're easy to do fast. With 200s, you get [them] to do ten . . . on two minutes, and you're asking for under 1:55, then you are really getting some elevated physiological values. But you give 'em twenty 100s on a minute, and high school kids can do that. It's nothing. It's the same length of time, same yardage, maybe even a second faster per hundred, but it's not the same. A 200 seems to me a better distance. If you normally do 50 percent of your program in 100s, you need to change . . . all but ten percent of [the program] to 200s instead of 100s. That's just a guess, but my distance swimmers get better every year. That's all I can go by, but I think those are some of the reasons for the improvements.

Question: One last question. You're aware of the controversy about all the supposedly different styles of breaststroke. Do you think there is such a thing as separate styles? That is, do you think there's a big difference between the wave-action breaststroke, the traditional breaststroke, and the pop-action breaststroke?

Answer: No, not a whole lot. I think the key to Mike Barrowman's success [a wave-action practitioner] is that he trains hard and that he's very, very tough mentally and physically. But he's eliminated resistance throughout his stroke, as much as you can do for breaststroke. I think there are certain mechanical principles in all the strokes that we need to stick to, and then there are individual differences.

SAMPLE WORKOUTS FROM EDDIE REESE

Included are an early-season, short-course workout; a midseason, long-course morning session; a midseason, short-course afternoon session; and a short-course, taper workout.

EARLY SEASON/SHORT COURSE (ONE WORKOUT DAILY)

Warm-up Distance Swimmers

200 free on 2:45
100 left-arm fly 1:30 } All four
100 right-arm fly 1:30 } sets × 3
4 × 50 kick on :50

Warm-up All Others

200 free on 2:50
100 left-arm fly 1:35 } All four
100 right-arm fly 1:35 } sets × 3
4 × 50 kick on :50

All Swimmers

16 × 25 (odd numbered—breast pull; even numbered—kick on back) on :30

Distance Swimmers

3 × 200 free 2:20
2 × 200 IM 2:30 } × 4
4 × 50 fly :50

Middle-Distance Swimmers

3 × 200 free 2:25
3 × 200 IM 2:30 } × 4
4 × 50 fly :50

Others

4 × 150 free 2:00
1 × 200 IM 2:40 } × 4
6 × 25 choice :30

MIDSEASON/LONG COURSE (MORNING)

Distance Swimmers

Warm-up

2 × { 400 free on 5:20
      fly/free on 5:30

3 × { 800 free pull on 10:30
      pull on 10:00
      swim on 10:00

100 fly—25 left arm,
25 right arm, 25 swim, 25 stroke drill

4 × { 200 back on 3:00
      200 breast pull on 4:00

All Other Swimmers

Warm-up

4 × { 200 free on 3:00, 2:50, 2:40, 2:30
      100 IM or SD on 1:50, 1:45, 1:40, 1:35
      100 kick on 2:10, 2:05, 2:00, 1:55

5 × { 400: odd free, breast #3 on 5:00–5:15
      even fly, back by 100s
        or
      breast pull on 6:30–7:00
      back pull on 6:30–7:00

Surgical Tubing: 8 × 50 on 1:15 (odd: go down fast; come back fast; even: go down fast free/others easy)

MIDSEASON SHORT COURSE (AFTERNOON)

Distance Swimmers
Warm-up
200 free on 2:30
100 kick on 1:45, 100 IM on 1:30 (fly/stroke drill)
200 free on 2:30
100 kick on 1:45, 100 IM on 1:30 (fly/stroke drill)
220 free on 2:30
100 kick on 1:45, 100 IM on 1:30 (fly/stroke drill)
230 free on 2:30
100 kick on 1:45, 100 IM on 1:30 (fly/stroke drill)
250 free on 2:30
100 kick on 1:45, 100 IM on 1:30 (fly/stroke drill)

Breaststrokers
Warm-up
100 IM on 1:30 (fly/stroke drill), 100 kick on 1:45
150 breast on 2:30
100 IM on 1:30 (fly/stroke drill), 100 kick on 1:45
160 breast on 2:30
100 IM on 1:30 (fly/stroke drill), 100 kick on 1:45
170 breast on 2:30
100 IM on 1:30 (fly/stroke drill), 100 kick on 1:45
180 breast on 2:30
100 IM on 1:30 (fly/stroke drill), 100 kick on 1:45
190 breast on 2:30
100 IM on 1:30 (fly/stroke drill), 100 kick on 1:45
200 breast on 2:30

Backstrokers, Butterflyers, and Individual Medleyists
Warm-up
100 IM on 1:30 (fly/stroke drill), 100 back on 1:45
150 free on 2:10
100 IM on 1:30 (fly/stroke drill), 100 back on 1:45
160 free on 2:10
100 IM on 1:30 (fly/stroke drill), 100 back on 1:45
170 free on 2:10
100 IM on 1:30 (fly/stroke drill), 100 back on 1:45
180 free on 2:10

100 IM on 1:30 (fly/stroke drill), 100 back on 1:45

190 free on 2:10

100 IM on 1:30 (fly/stroke drill), 100 back on 1:45

200 free on 2:10

Sprinters and Middle Distance Swimmers

Warm-up

150 free on 2:15

100 back on 1:30, 100 kick on 1:45

160 free on 2:15

100 back on 1:30, 100 kick on 1:45

170 free on 2:15

100 back on 1:30, 100 kick on 1:45

180 free on 2:15

100 back on 1:30, 100 kick on 1:45

190 free on 2:15

100 back on 1:30, 100 kick on 1:45

200 free on 2:15

100 back on 1:30, 100 kick on 1:45

Distance Swimmers

Main Set

3 × 200 free on 2:15, 150 fly on 2:15, 50 back, breast, free on 2:15, rest 1 minute

3 × 200 free on 2:10, 150 back on 2:10, 50 back, breast, free on 2:10, rest 1 minute

2 × 200 free on 2:05, 150 fly on 2:05, 50 back, breast, free on 2:05, rest 1 minute

2 × 200 free on 2:00, 150 back on 2:00, 50 back, breast, free on 2:00

Backstrokers and Individual Medleyists

Main Set

3 × 50 free, back, free on 2:20, 150 fly on 2:15, rest 1 minute

8 × 50 fly on :50 (look good)

2 × 50 stroke drill on 1:15

3 × 50 free, back, breast, free on 2:20, 150 back on 2:15, rest 1 minute

8 × 50 fly on 1:50 (look good)

2 × 50 stroke drill on 1:15

10 × 50 breast pull on 1:10 (fast 2 or 3 or S)

Breaststrokers

Main Set

8 × 100 IM on 1:00

100 breast on 1:20

75 breast kick on 1:20

3 × 400 free on 5:00, each one between 4:10 and 4:30

10 × 50 breast on 1:30, fast—between :32 and :34

Break—Break—Break

400 IM stroke drill

5 × *fast* turns

Middle Distance and Sprinters

Main Set

6 × 400 freestyle

    1st on 4:20,

    2nd and 3rd on 4:10

    4th, 5th and 6th on 4:00

        Two minute break

6 × 200 freestyle

    1st on 2:20,

    2nd and 3rd on 2:10

        Two minute break

9 × 100 freestyle

    1st on 1:20,

    2nd, 3rd and 4th on 1:10

    5th, 6th, 7th, 8th and 9th on 1:00

Swim down

SHORT COURSE—TAPER

Warm-up Distance	*Warm-up All Others*
800 free	500 free
400 IM/stroke drill	400 IM/stroke drill
300 kick	300 kick
4 × 50 IM	4 × 50 IM
100 free	100 free

Distance and Middle-Distance (Together)

4 × 200 free pull on 2:15

4 × 50 (25 fly and 25 free) on :45

4 × 100 free pull on 1:10

4 × 50 (25 fly and 25 free) on :45

Distance	*Middle-Distance*
2 × { 175 free on 2:15 / 200 free on 2:15	2 × { 100 free on 1:30 / 125 free on 1:30
2 × { 175 free on 2:10 / 200 free on 2:10	2 × { 100 free on 1:25 / 125 free on 1:25

$$2 \times \begin{cases} 175 \text{ free on } 2:05 \\ 200 \text{ free on } 2:05 \end{cases} \qquad 2 \times \begin{cases} 100 \text{ free on } 1:20 \\ 125 \text{ free on } 1:20 \end{cases}$$

$$2 \times \begin{cases} 175 \text{ free on } 2:00 \\ 200 \text{ free on } 2:00 \end{cases} \qquad 2 \times \begin{cases} 100 \text{ free on } 1:15 \\ 125 \text{ free on } 1:15 \end{cases}$$

Breaststrokers

$$4 \times \begin{cases} 200 \text{ (25 breast, 25 free) on } 2:30 \\ 4 \times 25 \text{ breast kick drill (3 kicks, 2 full strokes) on } :30 \\ 2 \times 50 \text{ breast, fast on } :45 \end{cases}$$

Easy 50 on 1:00

Break—Break—Break

400 IM stroke drill

5 × *fast* turns

Sprinters

3 × (75 free at :45 on :55

(25 fast on :25

(Easy 50 on 1:00

(50 free at :30 on :35

(25 fast on :25

(Easy 50 on 1:00

(25 free at :15 on :20

(25 fast on :25

(Easy 50 on 1:00

Break—Break—Break

5 × *fast* turns

Relay exchange work

Individual Medleyists and Flyers

200 IM (4 × 50 IMs) on 2:30

4 × 25 breast pull on :30

100 dolphin kick on 1:45

2 × 50 fly, fast on :45

Easy 50 on 1:00

200 IM (2 × 100 IMs) on 2:30

4 × 50 breast pull on :30

100 back kick on 1:45 (flyers go dolphin kick here)

2 × 50 back, fast on :45 (flyers go fly)

Break—Break—Break

Easy 50 on 1:00
200 IM on 2:30
4 × 50 breast pull on :30
100 breast kick on 1:45
2 × 50 breast, fast on :45
Easy 50 on 1:00

Break—Break—Break

Easy 800 IM stroke drill
5 × *fast* turns

Backstrokers

4 × (200 (25 back, 25 free) on 2:30
(4 × 25 reverse dolphin kick on :30
(2 × 50 back, fast on :45
(Easy 50 on 1:00

Break—Break—Break

Easy 400 IM stroke drill
5 × *fast* turns

RICHARD SHOULBERG
SWIMMING COACH, GERMANTOWN ACADEMY
AND FOXCATCHERS FARM

Richard Shoulberg has the reputation for training swimmers harder than any other successful coach in the United States. We were interested in hearing about his program and identifying the factors that make it unique.

Question: Can you give us a brief outline of your schedule from the beginning of the training season onward; how your program is designed on a yearly basis; the amount of break your swimmers take between the indoor and outdoor seasons—that sort of general information?

Answer: We put the boys in polo at the end of August, and they play polo twice a day up to about the third week of September. Then they start to do normal stroke drills. Our girls get in the water once a day in early September, up to the third week of September, and then we go two sessions of fitness every day in September. One of these is strictly land work—where we do "dollies," run, jump rope, use medicine balls, things of that nature—and the other being water work. [Authors' Note: Dollies are roll-arounds fitted with castors, similar to those used by automobile mechanics. The swimmers use them to pull themselves up an incline or even on a level surface. The idea is to improve strength in the pulling muscles.]

Each week we increase our workload in the water. At the heaviest time of year, in seventy minutes our distance and top I.M.ers go about fifty-two to fifty-three hundred yards before school, plus twenty minutes of medicine balls and twenty minutes of free choice, which means they may do any type of dry land work they like for that period of time. They do a lot of Bio-Bench, do a lot of Vasa-trainer, and a lot of individual things on stationary bikes; but I would say that, primarily, the Vasa-trainer [Vasa Swim Trainer] and the Bio-bench [Bio-Kinetic Swim Bench] for approximately sixteen to twenty minutes every day, doing different speeds and movements. [Authors' note: The Bio-Kinetic Swim Bench is an inclined bench fitted with a set of pulleys attached to a shunted generator which exploits the swimmer's own muscular effort to power the electronic resistance as well as the electronic readout. The resistance accommodates to the degree of effort throughout the range of motion. The Vasa Swim Trainer is a commercial device which stands about 4 feet high at its highest point and about 2 feet high at its lowest. It is equipped with a slanted benchlike arrangement on rollers which allows the swimmer to use his own body weight as resistance as he pulls himself up the incline and lowers himself.] We also do a lot of stroke recovery muscle group work.

In the afternoon, in the heavy season, we go 130 minutes during which we go about 10,200 yards. And so, on a normal day, five days a week, we're going about 16,400 [yards] Monday through Friday, allowing the athletes to go to a slower time standard if they're off pace in order to work on technique.

Saturday is our big day. We go long course, when we do what we call a four-forty. It's four hours and forty minutes of interval training, not at a high intensity, as during a normal weekly practice, but, because of the number of minutes, it's very, very difficult. Sunday is a recovery day and I allow some of the athletes to take one academic day off a week from dry land and a sixty-minute swim, and then make Sunday an intense day for that athlete to use as a make-up.

Question: Please mention any other forms of dry land exercises you have used, and do you incorporate stretching exercises in your dry land program?

Answer: As for stretching, I don't think—I know I don't do enough stretching with my athletes, I guess that's one of the weakest parts of our program. But we do a lot of drill work in the water, and I think that improves flexibility. We do some running, particularly with those who have a weight problem, or we do a lot of stationary bikes. All our dry land equipment is installed around the perimeter of the pool. This enables me to oversee both dry land work and swimming conveniently. We do some Nautilus work in the spring, maybe for about six weeks, three days a week ... not extremely heavy, and we do some Nautilus work and some heavier free weights for about eight weeks in the fall. I'd rather do endurance-type of weight work or Bio-bench or Vasa-trainer because I'm dealing primarily with the high school athlete. When my college athletes come back in the summertime, I notice a lot of them like to do heavy lifting with few repeats, and I sometimes wonder if it really makes them swim any faster, although it may make their bodies look stronger. I think they give up some important cardiovascular work going into the pool—so there are trade-offs. We've done some testing with the Vasa-trainer, using the heart monitor, and I'm amazed at the pulse rates we're getting out of the athlete going up the incline very fast and down extremely slow. The ratio is about one to eight or one to ten, and they go down really, really slow and their heart rates are monitoring about 184 to 190, which I think is pretty amazing for something that is only a few sets of muscle movements or muscle patterns. We do a lot of strength work, going forearms, wrist, and hands—probably more than most programs. We have jungle gyms that I made, which do a lot of strength-building of the wrists and forearms and hands. I think it's an area that is overlooked; I think it affects sculling, and if you can't scull, you're not going to swim very fast. We do a lot of the basic things too, but the other thing we do that I think is different is what we call "recovery muscle" work. We do it with surgical tubing, the Vasa-trainer incline—either on the Vasa-trainer boards or the Bio-bench. We do that every day—some form of recovery muscle work.

Question: The United States has declined in swimming in terms of international standings. In 1976 we won three-fourths of all the medals in the men's events and all but one gold medal at the Olympic Games. Now we're at a point here we're lucky to grab a fourth of the medals. Do you have any idea why this has happened?

Answer: Yes, I have a lot of ideas. First of all, I question the double or triple shave in the short-course season and I also question the level of training—maybe I should say lack of training—taking place in the United States in April and May, because I believe it has a definite effect on the results in August. I question the addition of the short events, the short relays, but, more than anything, I question the yardage per minute that we're doing now, compared to what we were doing in 1976. I've got the feeling that we're doing less yardage per minute and we're doing more quality, quality, quality or racing type of work. I think swimming at slower speeds had some real benefits in learning muscle movements or muscle patterns—as I explain it to my athletes, "hooking the toes or fingers to the brain"—and we don't do enough of that, in my view. We must do more swimming and spend less time in the weight room. It's not as glamorous, but I think we can design our training to make it more acceptable to the athlete.

I also really wonder if we're serving our elite athletes as we should, when we make them shave so many times during the short-course season. In my opinion we need to rethink our system for meeting time standards. In talking with some of the great European athletes, I've found out they don't have to focus on a lot of dual-meet swimming; they only have to focus on international swimming. Their federations have a protection system that allows their athletes to train and not have to worry about competing locally. We worry about competing locally and we fail to put enough emphasis on international competition.

There's too much emphasis on fast swimming every day. We don't emphasize building a base and we don't take the time to develop stroke technique. We're more interested in winning local meets; our goals are too shortsighted. I definitely feel that it takes many, many years of preparation to develop a great athlete.

The other thing that affects performance is shaving more than once or twice a year. Some of my college athletes come back after three or four shaves in the wintertime, and then have to reshave to make their standards in the summer. I wish we could carry our standards longer, reward excellence at our Nationals or NCAAs by allowing the top nine or twelve or sixteen athletes to carry their standards for eighteen months. That would then allow them to train for a whole year's cycle without having to worry about resting and tapering just to get into the big meets. Instead, we worry about a four-year cycle.

Question: Can you tell us a little about your program at Germantown Academy and about Team Foxcatcher? At what age do your swimmers begin? Do most of them attend the Academy or do you have some swimmers, especially during long-course season, who come in from other areas?

Answer: When we went to the Olympic Trials in 1988, eighteen athletes represented our school/club program. The majority of them had about six years service in our program on an average. I think that number is one of the highest in the country from a grass-roots program that allows athletes to strive towards the Olympic Trials. It is also a program which allows both athletes with minimal talent to enjoy swimming and to pursue other activities and those with great talent to attain great levels of success.

First of all, our age-groupers do minimal competition. We do not have any competitive outlet for them, other than the local ones they might choose to represent on their own, such as US[Swimming] Teams. They come to us two or three days a week, strictly for technique. We work on the development of technique every day with all our athletes, even up to the world-class level. I think it's the key to our program, plus we work on all four strokes every day. We're not a boarding school, but the headmaster allows me to find housing for four or five athletes every year, and I tell the parents that the kids' responsibility is their academics, the second responsibility is swimming, or the second can be social—whichever you want to decide. We do a lot of training every day, but school is first.

Question: Are you coaching both men and women? Both sprinters and distance swimmers? If you are coaching all of these, how do you break up your workouts? Can you classify the different groups?

Answer: First of all, I coach both men and women. I coach sprinters, distance, and middle-distance. I design four levels of practice every day, and it's highly organized. We work to yards per minute and I keep a record—in fact, I've kept a record ever since 1971. I have four groups, and I swing around the pool every day and watch all the groups. I certainly have some favorite athletes that I gravitate to more than others, but I get to know the pace of the individual swimmers as well as their training cycles, and I rotate them in and out of lanes. Our high school boys team, two years ago, went 3:01, which is still the national age-group record for seventeen-, eighteen-year-olds in the 400-yard freestyle relay. Three of those boys qualified for senior Nationals in the I.M. In the girls events, our 1987 team broke the national record in the 400 freestyle relay, with each girl averaging :51.1. All four of those girls qualified for the I.M. at Nationals. So, I don't think I.M. training is detrimental to sprinting. I don't try to develop sprinters in high school. I try to develop a well-rounded athlete and then allow the next level of coach, that is, the NCAA coach, to decide on a specialty. And again, I think that rotating athletes in and out of different groups gives the distance swimmers more respect for the sprinter. When they work a lot of high quality, they see how tough it is. We do minimal high quality work in our practices. We do a lot of descending work and a lot of controlled swimming. I like controlled swimming which I monitor by heart rate. I don't have a lactate machine, but I do have heart monitors that the swimmers wear. We fluctuate our speeds on a regular basis, holding different paces and using different drills. It's amazing that a swimmer will do a 5000 straight—either meters or yards, we'll take yard times—do 100 on a 1:10 [departure time] drill, that is, do 100 and go 1:04, do 100 in 1:08 technique, and then race 100. We'll do four or five thousand this way and the heart monitor really doesn't know what hundred we're on, but the heart rate stays up quite high during the whole five thousand swim even though we're doing drill-controlled work. So we try to outsmart the heart and save the limbs a little bit.

Question: We were looking at some of the material you sent. On a particular day you have the swimmers in the pool for twenty-four hours. They swim for three hours and then rest for three. Can you tell us a little about this special workout: how far the kids go, what the purpose or strategy of this activity is?

Answer: Well, I try to do it twice in a 365-day cycle. We call it "mountain climbing," where we'll swim approximately thirteen hours out of the twenty-four-hour cycle, starting with three to four hours in the water, interval training—intense interval training—with approximately an hour and a half rest and then two-and-a-half hours with the rest factor increasing. We'll start at seven in the morning, we'll go until eleven in the evening, and then we'll sleep on the deck. Mr. DuPont makes us sleep in the wrestling room now because he has more compassion than I do and doesn't let the kids sleep on the deck anymore. Then we get up at 3:20 A.M. and we stretch, we eat, and then we race from four o'clock until seven. During that last three hours is the highest yardage or meters per minute of the entire session. When it's over, we've gone 64,500 short-course yards, we've gone 52,000 long-course meters, plus using all four strokes and basic interval training. I think it makes the athlete tougher mentally. . . . I don't know if it does anything other than that, but I do think mental toughness plays an important role in our sport. When we do the twenty-four practices, no assistant coaches are present, only I am in the pool. We tell the athletes that any time they can't maintain the intensity, to increase rest, increase intake of calories, and try to get back on the next cycle. And, when we leave there, we know we've accomplished a lot. I wouldn't advocate doing this more than once or twice a year because it makes me too darned tired.

Question: We're always looking for new approaches in coaching. Do you have anything new in mind for this current season?

Answer: Each year, I try to focus on some new aspect of training. Two years ago we did a lot of fin work. We're not doing that again, but I'm not afraid of trying things like that. I think the single most important thing we do in the water is "bucket" swimming, where we have a chlorine bucket tethered to the athlete's waist on a five-foot rope, and we swim three days a week, pulling the bucket at high rest or straight swimming, depending on what I want. I think it works on stroke technique, gives stroke awareness: When the bucket is in the water and the swimmers have a dead spot in their stroke, they know it. I have videotapes of one of my elite swimmers. I took the video because some of the Olympic coaches told me I was wrong for allowing him to pull the bucket. They were sure it would hurt his technique. So, we videotaped him underwater, and he had perfect fly technique with the bucket. It gives the athlete instant feedback on feel for his stroke. So we've done a lot of bucket swimming: It decreases yardage per minute, but it increases strength and awareness in the water, and that is more important than yardage.

Question: You've had a lot of success with your swimmers in the individual medley, and it seems logical that you are doing a lot of your work using all four strokes. Is that the case, and do you plan to continue with this practice?

Answer: First of all, I have plotted it out, and in my most successful seasons my athletes, we never went more than 52 percent of our total training in freestyle. The least successful season was when we went a high percentage in freestyle and just touched the other strokes. So we try to design our training to have 50- to 52-percent freestyle.

Question: Do you see anything new on the horizon, that is, possible innovations that may be helpful to the progress of swimming in this country?

Answer: The thing that worries me about the horizon is too many coaches in the United States don't want to work. And I hate seeing my athletes leave a highly intensive, well-structured program and go on to new programs, and not have a real structured environment to train under. They come home very bored with their training or they come home with the new-found knowledge that hard work is not necessary to swim fast. I think there has to be a steady progression of intensity and change, which is manipulated by the coach to help the athlete. I'm not in favor of pound, pound, pound all the time; but you have to learn that you can challenge your athletes to become better.

Question: There are a lot of ambitious young coaches out there, all looking for the secret of success. Can you offer any advice to these people as to how to acquire more knowledge about training, mechanics, the psychology of handling athletes, and so on?

Answer: First of all, they need to go to as many clinics as possible—the ones where they can meet and talk to the masters of their sport. I think U.S. Swimming has a responsibility to use the great coaches of today. . . . U.S. Swimming should seek out a way—or maybe it should be the [American Swimming Coaches Association]—of inviting aspiring young people to clinics where the great masters of our sport can . . . explain their sports secrets. Of course, I'm not sure there are any real secrets, other than hard work and organizing priorities. . . .

I'm very, very structured in organizing my practices. I love watching my athletes try to improve on my challenges. I don't go on the deck unprepared. I ask my athletes to be prepared academically, so I have to be a role model. And I use my athletes in my program every day to help each other. I think the best coaches in our sport are the present athletes, who have success and then go on to help the younger athletes.

But I don't know. Be organized, be willing to try new things, and don't train the fifteen-year-old athlete like a twenty-two-year-old. Realize that there are changes taking place in your athletes' bodies, and that, therefore, you must train them in accordance with those changes. You can't look at one great coach's success and copy his or her log. It probably won't apply to your program. I think you must control the environment where the kids train. We do ten practices a week during the winter in a 25-yard, six-lane pool. In the morning we go seventy minutes with twenty minutes of free-choice dry land and twenty minutes of structured dry land. In the afternoon, we go 130 minutes in the water for our more aggressive athletes and fifty minutes of structured dry land. Maybe you can't apply that in your program. What you can apply is the control of the environment in your particular program and with your particular circumstances to the best advantage of your swimmers.

SAMPLE WORKOUTS FROM RICHARD SHOULBERG

The following workout is taken from the Twenty-four-Hour Camp which Mr. Shoulberg described in his interview. The workout took place on November 30, when the team had been training nearly two months. This version was planned for the middle-distance swimmers on the Germantown Academy/Foxcatcher Team. This phase of the Twenty-four-Hour Camp lasted from 7:00 A.M. to 12:01 P.M.; the next phase would begin at 1:45 P.M.

One minute rest is allotted between sets.

1. 16 × 100 on 1:30 (free 50 drill, built = odd-numbered 100s consist of technique 50s, coming back with build-up 50s; even-numbered 100s consist of stroke-of-choice 50s, coming back stroke-of-choice 50s which are faster than going out, that is negative split).
2. 3 × 700 on 9:55 (free pace 85, n/s, 5/1 = if freestyle pace is 1:25/100, that equals no rest; negative split the 700, controlled breathing of 5 double arm cycles to 1 breath).
3. 1 × 400 on 5:30 (back).
4. 8 × 100 on 1:25 (free des 1 to 4 = freestyle, descending times—i.e., #1–4, #5–8, #5 being faster than #1, slower than #4, #3 faster than #4—concentrating on technique).
5. 3 × 800 on 10:35 (free pace = 79.3 secs/100; most go faster than this for rest, faster effort than Item 2 above).
6. 18 × 100 on 1:35 (odd r.IM, even 50 br/fr = on odd-numbered 100s, swimmer reverses the normal order of the strokes in the IM; on even-numbered, swimmer swims 50 each of breast and free).
7. 3 × 900 on 13:10 (free fins = using fins, pace each 100 at 1:27, technique being more important than time; will be slower than Item 5 above).
8. 8 × 300 on 4:58 (odd 150 IM/fr, ev free 88 = odd-numbered 300s are to be swum half I.M., half freestyle; even-numbered 300s are to be swum freestyle, each 100 to be under 1:28).

9. 18 × 50 on :45 (free des 1 to 3 = freestyle, descending times, first effort through third 50s, repeating six times—#4 faster than #1, slower than #3; #7 slower than #6, faster than #4, etc.).

10. 1 × 800 on 11:25 (total race back = all-out effort backstroke).

11. 12 × 250 on 3:55 (free pace 94, padd, 7/1 = freestyle pace is 1:34 or under, swum with paddles, controlled breathing at a rate of 7 single arm pulls to 1 breath).

12. 1 × 500 on 6:55 (free race pace 83 = freestyle pace is 1:23 per 100).

Total distance: 19,400

The following samples are middle-distance, morning and afternoon workouts taken from an early-season log, when the team had been training about a month and a half for the short-course season. Mr. Shoulberg wishes to emphasize two points: (1) In all their training they work both ends of the pool—every set; every session. (See Item 2 in A.M. workout.) This doubles their number of leaders. Swimmers get in at both ends of the pool. By having an odd number of repeats in a set of 75s, athletes change ends of the pool for the next set. (2) They use only the Counsilman Pace Clock (analog dial as opposed to digital) for all training. With odd-numbered send-offs, the athlete must think more and must use the pace clock. This ensures they will learn pace. (See Item 3 in A.M. workout.)

A.M.

1. 45 minutes dry land exercise.

2. 11 × 75 on :55 (4/53, 4/51, 3/49 free = first four 75s should be under :53, next four under :51, next three under :49).

3. 4 × 175 on 2:40 (back, 100 drill; 75 bu sp = 100 drill means any backstroke drill the swimmers like; 75 build-up to top speed).

4. 10 × 100 on 1:36 (kicking fins).

5. 1 × 1000 on 12:00 (free swim with fins).

Total distance: 3525

P.M.

1. 48 minutes dry land exercises, consisting of 30 to 33 different exercises—11 could be Nautilus—rotating on regular basis.

2. Team Warm-Up: Success Drill—announce all three sets at same time. Repeat sets four times with no rest between sets.
   a. 6 × 25 on :22 free
   b. 4 × 25 on :20 free
   c. 2 × 50 on :45 bk/br

3. 11 × 250 on 1:54 (free des 1/3, pace is :35—for coach's reference only).

4. 4 × 375 on 4:50 (free paddles & bands, 5/1 = freestyle, using paddles and bands; controlled breathing at a rate of 5 double arm strokes to 1 breath).

5. 11 × 100 on 1:18 (free with fins un 62 = swim freestyle with fins, each 100 under 1:02)

6. 4 × 600 on 8:45 (300 bk/br p 87.5 = 300 each of back and breast in each repeat, pace is 1:27.5 per 100)

7. 8 × 100 on 1:35 (odd I.M., even back)

Total distance: 9850

The final sample workouts from Mr. Shoulberg are taken from the late-season log. They are a morning and an afternoon session done on February 18, about a month before a championship event.

A. M.

1. 8 × 75 on :57 (free 25 surf; 25—5 R, 5 L; 25 bu = 25 kick only with hands streamlined out in front, 25 consisting of 5 strokes right arm and 5 strokes left arm, and 25 build-up for speed).

2. 2 × 400 on 5:45 (200 bk/fr, padd = 200 each of backstroke and freestyle, swum with paddles).

3. 8 × 75 on 1:12 (25 fly 8/1, 25 fkyb, 25 race = 25 fly, swum with 8 kicks and 1 stroke; 25 fly, kick on your back; 25 fly, all-out).

4. 1 × 600 on 9:00 (2 lanes swim down).

Total distance: 2600

P. M.

1. 12 minutes of dry land exercise

2. 12 × 50 on :38 (25 hh, 25 bu = 25 swim with head high, chin on surface of water, head set; 25 build-up for speed).

3. 1 × 550 at 8:05 (25 surf 75 built = 25 kick only with hands streamlined out in front, 75 building speed within each 75, plus 50 swim).

4. 4 × 100 on 3:00 (race from a dive = all-out, choice of stroke).

5. 5 × 300 on 4:15 (free pull/buoy, 9/1 = freestyle pulling only, using pull buoy; controlled breathing at a rate of 9 double arm strokes to 1 breath).

6. 6 × 100 on 1:40 (back 50 drill, 50 build = backstroke, each one faster than the last)

7. 8 × 50 on 1:25 (kick board race)

8. 8 × 100 on 1:40 (75 fl/25 bk, rotate = swim 75 fly, then 25 back, 25 fly, then 75 back).

9. 1 × 300 on 4:10 (100, −3, −2, −1 race swim = all-out 100s, swum with three fewer strokes than normal, then two fewer, then 1 fewer).

10. 1 × 300 on 5:00 (swim down 2 lanes = all athletes in two lanes, simulating conditions at championships—extremely crowded warm-up and warm-down—*get used to it, so you can go fast at meet*).

Total distance: 5450

CHEN YEUNG CHI
NATIONAL HEAD COACH,
PEOPLES REPUBLIC OF CHINA

The following conversation took place in Bloomington, Indiana, during Mr. Chen's visit to the United States in March and April, 1991. Because Mr. Chen had difficulty with English and the authors do not speak Chinese, we have been forced to paraphrase some portions of the interview conducted by the senior author.

Question: We are talking about macrocycles, and I have asked Mr. Chen about Chinese training: the number and types of cycles they use in the periodization of their quadrennial plan, and to explain whether or not this system is similar to the East German model, in which four major cycles per year are undertaken. I have told him that we use two macrocycles in this country, primarily because they fit into our competitive seasonal plan.

Answer: Yes. I think [our system of three to four macrocycles per year is similar to the East German plan].

Question: How many weeks in each macrocycle?

Answer: For example, East Germany, they use four cycles per year. First one, maybe up to Europe Cup, usually in middle of December. The first cycle maybe thirteen to fifteen weeks' duration. Then, second cycle, maybe they use ten to thirteen weeks. After they finish the cycle, they usually have a dual meet with the Soviet Union. And third cycle is usually thirteen to seventeen weeks, then Nationals or [some international competition]. Then, last cycle is of eight weeks, usually East Germany cycle separate. For example, in 1988 they were preparing for the Olympic Games. End of first cycle they joined the Europe Cup on the 12th and 13th of December. Then Soviet Union with East Germany, they meet together on March 14th and 16th. The end of third cycle, Nationals in July, 20th to the 25th. Then, last cycle, Olympic Games in September, 18th to 23rd. So, in China, we use the East German four-cycle plan up until July, but the last one, [in which] East Germany used eight weeks to the Olympic Games, China used twelve. So the third cycle, East Germany used thirteen to seventeen weeks, but China's third cycle was ten weeks. Not very hard in third cycle, just preparing. The last cycle we did very, very hard training—twelve weeks.

Question: And you had very good results?

Answer: Yes, yes.

Question: So, will you continue this four-cycle plan, do you think?

Answer: Yes.

Question: It's similar, in that you will be leading up to a championship event?

Answer: When Rudolf Klaus [East German national coach] trained in China, for example, in the third cycle of thirteen weeks, Klaus did two weeks general physical conditioning, one week transition to specific strength, two weeks specific strength training, and this is dryland exercise. While in water, Klaus emphasized kicking, pulling and speed works. After that, two weeks aerobic training, three weeks high attitude, one week adaptation on sea level, two weeks taper for the competition. That was thirteen weeks in third cycle training when Rudolf Klaus taught us in China. When arranging cycle, we must go to the altitude training. So second, third, fourth cycle we have to go to altitude training for three weeks—so very helpful. [Authors' Note: This was interpreted as following the universally accepted principles of the periodization of training—that is, resolving training to suit the need of peaking for major competition by organizing the training period into major cycles, the nature of which is determined by the length of time between major competitions.]

The following is an outline of Mr. Chen's thirteen-week (third cycle) program:

A. Two weeks general physical preparation—introductory cycle.
B. One week integral general physical preparation and special physical preparation—three week involving.
C. Two weeks specific strength training.

In the previous five weeks in pool, Klaus emphasizes kick pull and speed work.

D. Two weeks aerobic training.
E. Three weeks high altitude training.
F. One week adaptation to sea level.
G. Two weeks taper.

Question: How high do you go train—7000 feet?

Answer: I'm not sure in feet, but in meters it is 1893.

Question: That would be . . .

Answer: In Mexico City, that is 2300 meters, I think.

Question: Yes, Mexico City is 7000 feet so you are training at a little under that altitude.

Answer: Rudolf Klaus is the East German who went to China. When he was there in 1986, he told us, "I had nineteen times altitude training experience." So from 1986 up to now we have fifteen times altitude training experience with the Chinese team. I think this is one of the leaders [in this sort of training, in the world] and we have progressed rapidly, I think.

Question: But not so much in the distance, huh?

Answer: [Chuckling] No—but sprints.

Author: Because in distance, anything over 150 to 200 meters at altitude is slower. One-hundred meters time similar at sea level and at altitude. But 200 meters, you start getting slower, and 1500 meters—much slower at altitude; so you are swimming at a slower pace, and I think this is a disadvantage for distance events. In 1968, when competition was at Mexico City, I had Don MacKenzie, who won the breaststroke, and Charlie Hickcox, individual medley winner, second in the backstroke, and won three gold medals. . . . And, I didn't train them at altitude that year and they won, swam very well at high altitude in Mexico City. Many of the swimmers that train at altitude had bad results [in the past]. So I decided not to take my swimmers—Hickcox, and so on, all of my swimmers—to altitude. But we did a lot of controlled breathing—did a lot of it. We had fantastic results. [Authors' Note: Altitude training is controversial because results have not been uniform. Further study is needed.]

Question: Did the Chinese like the altitude training?

Answer: Yes. They like altitude training very much. And Soviet Union, East Germany, Bulgaria and China do a lot but Hungary not too much.

Author: I think if you stay too long, it can be bad.

Mr. Chen: Our experience, maybe the longest—four weeks. Maybe three to four weeks would be better.

The following workout was provided by Mr. Chen as typical for members of the East German team. The swimmer was Barbara Meineke of then East Germany. Her times were :55.18 for 100 meters free (1983), 1:58.75 for 200 meters free (1984), and :26.08 for 50 meters free (1984).

A.M.

1. 1000 Warm-up.
2. 5 × 100 freestyle pulling with paddle and buoy on 1:30, averaging 1:07.8.
3. 400 easy.
4. 1500 freestyle pulling with paddle and buoy—17:17.0.
5. 600 freestyle with fins.
6. 10 × 100 kick on 2:15, averaging 1:33.
7. 600 fly free with fins.
8. 8 × 50 free on 1:15, averaging :29.5 (90% effort).
9. 1500 easy.
   Total distance: 7500

P.M.

1. Swim Bench.
2. 1500 Warm-up.
3. 6 × 200 freestyle rest 1′, averaging 2:12.4 (89% effort).
4. 1500 pull, swim, kick, swim.
5. 6 × 200 freestyle rest 1′, averaging 2:07.3 (93% effort) × lactic acid—7.7 mM.

6. 1500 (4 × 25 speed).

Total distance: 6900.

EVENING

1. 800 Warm-up.

2. 10 × (100 fast 100 easy) first through fourth 100—freestyle swim with paddle, averaging :58.5

(Fifth 100—75 fast/25 slow, :48.2)

(Sixth thru ninth 100—freestyle swim with paddle, averaging :59)

(Tenth 100—Max. :59)

3. 700 easy.

Total distance: 3500

Total for the day: 17,900 (6 hours)

SKIP KENNEY
MEN'S SWIMMING COACH, STANFORD UNIVERSITY

Skip Kenney was the successful coach of a prominent age-group program before he moved to Stanford. He has served as an Olympic coach and has trained many NCAA titlists. Mr. Kenney responded to a written questionnaire submitted to him by the authors, providing a set of sample workouts in the context of the questionnaire.

Question: Do you divide your team into various groupings? If so, what are the categories?

Answer: Yes, I do. We have a separate lane for butterfly, for back, for breast, for sprint freestylers, and for distance freestylers.

Question: Do you break your season into different phases of training, such as definite macroperiods, which are then further differentiated into microperiods, or do you gradually shift the emphasis from less to more speed work as the season progresses? Would you give us the range of volume throughout the season (that is, early season yardage through the point of highest yardage and down to taper yardage)?

Answer: We gradually shift from zero to greater quality and distance

Early season—6000 per workout

Highest—8000 per workout

Taper phase—2500 to 4000 per workout

Question: Please provide some early-season, mid- to late-season, and taper workouts for each category of swimmer.

MIDDLE-DISTANCE SWIMMERS

1. Swim 800.
2. Swim 20 × 100 on 1:10, odd numbered easy, even numbered fast.
3. Swim 16 × 25 on :30, 25 easy, 25 fast.
4. Pull 2000, each 500 faster.
5. Kick 6 × 200 on 3:00 (descend 1–3).
6. Kick 10 × 25 fast.
7. Swim 400 easy (for form).
8. Swim with zoomers 30 × 50 on :60 (50 easy, 50 fast), from a dive on the last six.

   Total distance: 8550

DISTANCE SWIMMERS

1. Swim 20 × 50 (10 on :45, 5 on :40, 5 on :35).
2. Swim 4-4–1-1 × 2 (4 easy, 4 fast)
   (3 easy, 3 fast)
   (2 easy, 2 fast)
   (1 easy, 1 fast).

   Hypoxic 5 or 6 entire set.
3. Pull 3 × 1000 on 12:00 (descend 1–3).
4. Kick 2 × 300 on 4:15.
5. Swim 4 × 800 on 9:00 (descend 1–4).
6. Swim 20 × 50 on :45, (50 easy, 50 fast).

   Total distance: 9800

BREASTSTROKERS

1. Swim 1200, last 300 stroke drills.
2. Swim 16 × 50 on :50 (breast arm pull with flutter kick).
3. Pull 2 × 400, 20 seconds rest—all breast.
4. Swim 6 × 200 on 3:15 (descend 1–3).
5. Kick 400.
6. Kick 16 × 25, 10 seconds rest—all fast.
7. Swim 10 × 150 on 2:15 (25 fly, 100 breast, 25 free).
8. Swim 12 × 25 I.M. order.

   Total distance: 6600

Question: Do you have an organized strength program? If so, what types of exercise do you include, how much time do you devote to the program each day, and do you change its content during the course of the season (in type of exercise—lighter to heavier weights, for example—or use of different equipment, and so on)?

Answer: Yes. Most exercises are general body-strength oriented: traditional lifts such as bench press, lat pulls, leg extension and curls, and so on. Specificity and endurance are achieved at the pool through water work. We train at this type of work three days a week, usually Monday-Wednesday-Friday, for about one hour. Some of the keys to our program include: 1) lifting before workout, 2) being consistent with three days a week, 3) doing cycle strength cycle (i.e., four weeks on, one week off), 4) having variety, and 5) changing cycle intensity. In other words, we don't do the same exercise the same way all year!

Question: What types of strength-building equipment do you use?

Answer: Almost all of it is free weights, with a few Nautilus.

Question: Do you terminate strength-building exercises before the most important competition of the season? If so, explain when and how.

Answer: We usually terminate our weight program six to eight weeks from our goal meet. At that point we focus on transferring general body strength into specific swimming power.

JACK SIMON
COACH, U.S. SWIMMING CLUB

Jack Simon has been highly successful with both men and women swimmers, having placed many swimmers on national teams, including U.S. Olympic Teams. Jack is particularly recognized as a developer of distance swimmers. He answered our questionnaire and provided some sample workouts.

Question: Do you divide your team into various groupings? If so, what are the categories?

Answer: Yes, but later in the season. At the beginning I do general work with all, mostly over distance and I.M. training along with lots of technique work. When we do break, we go with the following groups: distance, middle-distance, I.M., back, breast, fly, and sometimes (rarely) a sprint free group.

Question: Do you break your season into different phases of training, such as definite macroperiods which are then further differentiated into microperiods, or do you gradually shift the emphasis from less to more speed work as the season progresses? Would you give us the range of volume throughout the season (that is, early season yardage through the point of highest yardage and down to taper yardage)?

Answer: Yes, using a period of time twenty weeks prior to a National Championship. The first eight weeks are used as a time for working on mechanics, developing the aerobic system, and team-building. We also start building on small amounts of speed work.

The next six weeks we change the emphasis of training to encompass training at more intense levels. While a large portion of this period is still at submaximal levels, sessions of anaerobic threshold, Max VO(2), and anaerobic work are cycled in several times a week. Short speed work (13 meters and 25s) continues to build in this period. [Author's note: These terms designate how methods of training are organized to achieve certain physiological effects. Such factors as distance of repeat, optimal number of repeats, rest interval between repeats and between sets, and training speed represented as percentages of race speed are manipulated to achieve these goals.]

I believe it's important to reiterate that we start with small amounts of speed work early in the season and build throughout the season.

Question: Please provide some early-season, mid- to late-season, and taper workouts for each category of swimmer.

Answer: Sample workouts will appear at the end of the interview.

Question: Do you have an organized strength program? If so, what types of exercise do you include, how much time do you devote to the program each day, and do you change its content during the course of the season (in type of exercise—lighter to heavier weights, for example—or use of different equipment, and so on)?

Answer: Yes. Approximately thirty to forty-five minutes six days per week.

Since I work with athletes who are mostly eighteen and under, we do no free or machine weights. I believe strongly in body-weight exercises, complemented with lots of medicine ball work and a sensible amount of work with cords.

Our program during the aerobic phase of the season is building repetitions and decreasing rest. Later in the season we will build extreme speed into the exercise (that is, three to five sets of as many reps as possible in twenty seconds with one to one-and-one-half minutes of rest.

This past year I have had six athletes, the oldest being eighteen and the youngest a fourteen-year-old girl, who were power tested [at the U.S. Olympic Center] in Colorado Springs. All six tested well above the National Team average. We also do a large percentage of our work in the core (torso) area. Front and back.

Question: What types of strength-building equipment do you use?

Answer: Medicine balls that range from 1 kilo to 4 kilos, cords, box approximately 5 inches high (for pliometric push-ups), climbing rope, pull-up and dip bars, resistive jumping board, bleacher.

Question: Do you terminate strength-building exercises before the most important competition of the season? If so, explain when and how.

Answer: We taper those down near championship season. Approximately seven to ten days out, we eliminate power-type exercises [from] the program, but we retain . . . core exercise at a reduced level.

Question: Please provide any information about your strength or stretching program that you think is unique.

Answer: I feel sure that stretching is important, but I don't have the time to make it an integral part of our program. We teach many different stretching exercises as well as shoulder- and knee-strengthening exercises at the beginning of the season. I have to rely on the athletes to do them at home. Good luck!

General stretching covers the shoulders, torso, and legs; stroke-specific stretching is implemented for those who need it.

SAMPLE WORKOUTS FROM JACK SIMON

NOVEMBER 22—LONG COURSE

1. 3 × 100 IM, 100 stroke, 100 free finger tip, 100 back wrist flick drill, 100 kick no board, 30 seconds between rounds.
2. *Main Set*

    (Instructions are to keep the heart rate at 160. We use the scoreboard pace clock for this set.)

    8 × 100 on 1:15.

    4 × 200 on 2:28.

    2 × 400 on 4:52.

    1 × 800 on 9:38.

    2 × 400 on 4:48.

    4 × 200 on 2:22.

    8 × 100 on 1:11.

    200 easy.

    4 × 25 power kicks underwater.

    300 easy.

    Total distance: 6200 meters

NOVEMBER 24—LONG COURSE

1. 3 × 200 free.

    200 IM.

    100 stroke.

    800, 700, 600, 500, 400, 300, 200 with 15 seconds rest.
2. *Main Set*

    3 × (2 × 200 IM straight with 10 seconds rest.

    (1 × 400 IM straight with 30 seconds rest.

    2 minutes rest between rounds.

    1 × 1200 IM (3 × 400 IM swum straight).

    All three 400 IMs were recorded, the object being to go faster on the straight 1200 IM.

    Total distance: 8600 meters

DECEMBER 28—LONG COURSE

1. 2 × 400 free, 300 back, 200 breast, kick 100 (choice of style).

    300 free, 200 back, 100 breast, kick 2 × 50 choice.
2. 2 × 400 IM, 100 fly, 400 IM, 100 back.

    400 IM, 100 breast, 400 IM, 100 free.

20 seconds rest after stroke swim, second time through, go 200 IMs and 50s of stroke.

3. 20 × 50 fly on 1:00.
4. 100 easy.
5. 10 × 50 fly on 1:00.
6. 100 easy.
7. 15 × 100 pull on 1:30, controlled breathing 1/5.

Total distance: 9800 meters

JANUARY 28—LONG COURSE

1. 12 × 200 (3 free on 3:00, 3 IM on 3:30, 3 back on 3:20, 3 free on 2:45).
2. 24 × 50 on 1:30 from a dive—record.
3. 400 swim on 6:00.
4. 2 × 200 pull on 2:50.
5. 4 × 100 swim on 1:15.
6. 400 free.
7. 12 × 25 from a dive, walk back, choice of stroke.
8. 600 swim (heart rate—150).

Total distance: 6100 meters

FEBRUARY 17—LONG COURSE

1. 400 swim, kick, pull.
2. 300, 2 × 150, 3 × 100, 6 × 50—all on a base of 1:30.
3. 300 easy.
4. 3 × (2 × 100 on 1:30
   (1 × 200 on 3:30 (heart rate-150).
   Three minutes rest.
5. 6 × 25 on 1:30 from a dive.
6. 20 × 50 on :40, holding :32s.

Total distance: 4250

RICHARD QUICK
WOMEN'S SWIMMING COACH,
STANFORD UNIVERSITY

Mr. Quick consented to let us publish his dry land exercise program for the short-course season of a pre-Olympic year. The program began with three weeks of training at the U.S. Olympic Center in Colorado Springs. This was followed by approximately six weeks of early-season work, beginning in mid-September and lasting through October. The fall and winter program phase began at the end of October and ended in mid-December. Next came the pretaper phase, starting six weeks before the taper began, followed by the taper weight program.

FALL QUARTER DRY LAND TRAINING:
(weeks 1–3 at Colorado Springs)

Basic Strength	Circuit Training
Leg Press	Lunges with Dumbbells
Lat Pulls	Bench with Dumbbells
Leg Extensors	Medicine Ball with Partner
Bench Press	Leg Press
Lateral Raises	Seated Rows
Biceps Curls	Lateral Raises
Triceps Press	Tubing Pulls
Wrist Curls	Triceps Press
Back Extensors	Squat Thrusts
Abdominals and Stretch	Abdominals and Stretch

Week 1: 1 × 12 @ 70% of Max.—30 sec. on, 30 sec. switch—1 round
Week 2: 2 × 12 @ 70% of Max.—40 sec. on, 20 sec. switch—2 rounds
Week 3: 3 × 10 @ 70% of Max.—40 sec. on, 20 sec. switch—3 rounds

FALL QUARTER:
(weeks 1–4 on campus, on their own)

Hip Sled	3 × 10–12 @ 70%	Triceps Push-down	3 × 10–12
Bench Press	3 × 10–12	Arm Curl	3 × 10–12
Lat Pull-down	3 × 10–12	Arm Rotators	1 × 30
Lateral Raises	3 × 10–12	at 40%–50%	
Leg Extensors	3 × 10–12	Wrist Curls	2 × 15
Leg Curls	3 × 10–12	Abdominal Work and Back	
(minimum of 60% leg extension)		Extension	

FALL/WINTER QUARTER:
(weeks 1–6 on campus, strength phase, using hip sled, bench press, & lat pull-down in Cycle Program)

	Freestylers and Backstrokers		
	Warm-up	Workout	Additional Routine*
Week 1: Monday	2 @ 70%, 2 @ 75%	6 × 2 @ 80%	A
Wednesday	2 @ 70%, 2 @ 75%	6 × 3 @ 80%	B
Friday	2 @ 70%, 2 @ 75%	6 × 2 @ 80%	A

Week 2:	Monday	2 @ 70%, 2 @ 75%	6 × 4 @ 80%	B
	Wednesday	2 @ 70%, 2 @ 75%	6 × 2 @ 80%	A
	Friday	2 @ 70%, 2 @ 75%	6 × 5 @ 80%	B
Week 3:	Monday	2 @ 70%, 2 @ 75%	6 × 2 @ 80%	A
	Wednesday and Friday—Holiday Break			
Week 4:	Monday	2 @ 70%, 2 @ 75%	6 × 6 @ 80%	B
	Wednesday	2 @ 70%, 2 @ 75%	6 × 2 @ 80%	A
	Friday	2 @ 70%, 2 @ 75%	5 × 5 @ 80%	B
Week 5:	Monday	2 @ 70%, 2 @ 75%	6 × 2 @ 80%	A
	Wednesday	2 @ 70%, 2 @ 75%, 2 @ 85%	3 × 3 @ 95%	B
	Friday	2 @ 70%, 2 @ 75%	6 × 2 @ 80%	A
Week 6:	Monday	2 @ 70%, 2 @ 80%, 2 @ 90%	2 × 2 @ 100%	B
	Wednesday	2 @ 70%, 2 @ 75%,	6 × 2 @ 80%	A
	Friday	2 @ 70%, 2 @ 80%, 2 @ 90%	1 × 2 @ 105%	B

*Additional Routine	A		B
Leg Extension	2 sets of 8	Leg Extension	2 sets of 6
Seated Rows	2 sets of 8	Pullovers	2 sets of 6
Leg Curls	2 sets of 8	Arm Curls	2 sets of 6
Upright Row	2 sets of 20	Shoulder Rotators	2 sets of 20
Wrist Curls	2 sets of 20	Wrist Curls	2 sets of 20
Back Extensors	2 sets of 10	Back Extension	2 sets of 10
Leg Raises	2 sets of 20	Leg Raises	2 sets of 20
Kickbacks	2 sets of 8	Kickbacks	2 sets of 6
		Dumbbell: Supinator/Pronator	2 sets of 20

FALL/WINTER: DRY LAND CIRCUIT TRAINING

Stations:

1. Pull-ups (partner-assisted)
2. Jump Rope
3. Surgical Tubing Pulls
4. Stair Climbing
5. Vasa-trainer
6. Step-ups
7. Medicine Balls
8. Abdominals and Stretching (as a group)

Initially, rotation occurred after each exercise. As the season progressed, the set system was built up to six sets before rotating.

Early in the fall thirty seconds work with thirty seconds rest was done, then forty/twenty, then sixty/fifteen.

In the winter quarter, an hour of step aerobics was added; two times per week at first, then three times per week.

POWER AND MUSCLE ENDURANCE (SIX WEEKS BEFORE TAPER):

Monday and Saturday	*Wednesday*
1. Swim Bench—10 × 30 @ 1 min. @ 55 cycles/min.	1. Swim Bench—8 × 15 @ 1 min. @ 60 cycles/min.
2. Dumbbell Bench—1 × 50 @ 40%–50% in 1 min.	2. Hip Sled—2 × 6 @ 80%, 1 × 12 @ 40%–50% *fast.*
3. Nautilus Pullovers–1 × 50 as above.	3. Bench Press—2 × 6, 1 × 12 as above.
4. 30 sec. Jump Rope or Bike *fast.*	4. Lat Pulls as above.
5. Upright Rows—1 × 50 as above.	5. Upright Rows.
6. Lat Pulls—1 × 50 as above.	6. Triceps Press.
7. 30 sec. Jump Rope or Bike *fast.*	7. Arm Curls.
8. Straight Leg Kicks 1 × 100 in 1 min.	8. Abdominals and Stretching.
9. Jump Machine—1 × 30 in 30 sec.	
10. 30 sec. Jump Rope or Bike *fast.*	
11. Triceps Press—1 × 50 as above.	
12. Leg Extensors—1 × 30 in 30 sec.	
13. 30 sec. Jump Rope or Bike *fast.*	
14. Abdominals and Stretching	

Supplementary Exercises for Both Sessions

Arm Rotators—1 × 20

Back Extensors—1 × 20

Wrist Curls—1 × 20

TAPER WEIGHT PROGRAM

1. Swim Bench—5 × 30 @ 1 min. @ Race Rate or 5 × 15 @ 1 min. @ Race Rate plus 5%.
2. Jump Machine—1 × 30 in 30 sec.
3. Lat Pulls—1 × 25 in 30 sec.
4. Dumbbell Bench Press—1 × 25 in 30 sec.
5. Lateral Raises—1 × 25 in 30 sec.
6. Abdominals and Stretching (maintenance only).

Roster of Elite Swimmers Pictured in Text

CHAPTER 1

Figure 1–10	Rick Thomas	NCAA qualifier; member of NCAA 1st-Place Free Relay
Figure 1–11	Charlie Hickcox	U.S. Olympian, 1968, 3 Gold and 1 Silver; 8 NCAA titles
Figure 1–12	James Sweeney	Big Ten Champion; NCAA Finalist, 1650 Yards
Figure 1–13	Mark Spitz (A)	U.S. Olympian, 1968 and 1972, 9 Gold, 1 Silver and 1 Bronze
	James Montgomery (B)	U.S. Olympian, 1976, 3 Gold Medals; 8 NCAA TITLES
	Nobutaka Taguchi (C)	Japanese Olympian, 1972, 1 Gold Medal
	Charlie Hickcox (D)	See above
Figure 1–16, 17, 18	Mark Spitz	See above
Figure 1–19	Rowdy Gaines	U.S. Olympian, 1984, 3 Gold Medals
Figure 1–20	Alex Baumann	Canadian Olympian, 1984, 2 Gold Medals

| Figure 1–21 | Nobutaka Taguchi | See above |
| Figure 1–22 | Jim Halliburton | NCAA qualifier & finalist |

CHAPTER 2

Figure 2–2	Mike Burton	U.S. Olympian, 1968 and 1972, 1 Gold Medal in each
	Don Schollander	U.S. Olympian, 1964
Figure 2–5	James Montgomery	See above
Figure 2–6	Jennifer Hooker	U.S. Olympian, 1976; NCAA & Nat'l. AAU Champion
Figure 2–7	Chuck Sharpe	Big Ten Champion; NCAA qualifier
Figure 2–10	Roy Saari	U.S. Olympian, 1964 NCAA Champion
	Ulrike Richter	GDR Olympian, 1976, 1 Gold Medal
	Cornelia Ender	GDR Olympian, 1976, 4 Gold Medals
Figure 2–12	Mark Spitz	See above
Figure 2–13	Jenny Turrall	Australian Olympian & World-Record Holder
	Joe Hudepohl	U.S. Olympian, 1992
	Rowdy Gaines	See above
	Gustavo Borges	Brazilian Olympian, 1992, 1 Silver Medal
Figure 2–14	Artur Wojdat	See above
Figure 2–16	Rick Thomas	See above

CHAPTER 3

Figure 3–2	Romulo Arantes	Brazilian Olympian, 1976; NCAA qualifier
Figure 3–3	David Berkoff	U.S. Olympian, 1988 and 1992; 1 Bronze Medal; NCAA titlist; World-Record Holder
Figure 3–4	Lea Loveless	U.S. Olympian, Silver Medal
Figure 3–5	Tracy Caulkins	U.S. Olympian, 1976; National Champion, 47 titles
Figure 3–6	Rick Thomas	See above
Figure 3–7	Jeff Rouse	U.S. Olympian, 1992; 1 Silver Medal

CHAPTER 4

Figure 4–1	Mel Nash	Pan-Am Champion, 1974
Figure 4–2	Rick Thomas	See above
Figure 4–4	Mary T. Meagher	U.S. Olympian, 1984 and 1988; World-Record Holder
	Gary Hall	U.S. Olympian, 1972 and 1976; 2 Silver & 1 Bronze

	Rafal Szukala	Polish Olympian, 1992; 1 Silver Medal
	Anthony Nesty	Surinam Olympian, 1988 and 1992, 1 Gold, 1 Bronze
Figure 4–5	Mary T. Meagher	See above
Figure 4–6	Carl Robie	Silver Medal, 1964, Gold Medal, 1968; 200 Fly
	Rafal Szukala	See above
	Mary T. Meagher	See above
Figure 4–7	Pablo Morales	U.S. Olympian, 1992, Gold Medal
Figure 4–8	Kevin Berry	Australian Olympian, 1964, Gold Medal

CHAPTER 5

Figure 5–1	Megan Kleine	U.S. Olympian, 1992
	Nobutaka Taguchi	See above
Figure 5–2	Unidentified National qualifier	
	John Hencken	U.S. Olympian, 1972 and 1976, 1 Silver and 1 Gold
Figure 5–3	Mike Barrowman	U.S. Olympian, 1992; Gold Medal; World-Record Holder
Figure 5–4	Mike Barrowman	See above
Figure 5–5	Marc Schlatter	NCAA runner-up
Figure 5–6	Mike Barrowman	See above
Figure 5–7	Megan Kleine	See above
Figure 5–8	Nobutaka Taguchi	See above
Figure 5–9	Chet Jastremski	U.S. Olympian, 1964 and 1968, 1 Bronze Medal

CHAPTER 6

Figure 6–1	James Montgomery	See above
	Steve Clark	U.S. Olympian, 1964, Gold Medal
Figure 6–2	James Montgomery	See above
Figure 6–3	James Montgomery	See above
Figure 6–4	Rick Carey	U.S. Olympian, 1984, Gold Medal
Figure 6–6	Gary Hall	See above

APPENDIX 2

Theoretical Considerations in Special Strength Training

Enhancing both the intramuscular and intermuscular coordination of muscular activity will hopefully achieve the main purpose of strength training for sport, which is defined as "increasing the working effect of movement." Increasing the working effect of movement depends on the particular nature of the sport; in this case, placing specific demands on the qualitative character of strength for swimming.

The working effect of movement is analyzed by examining the *resultant force production* of the sports movement. The science used here is called *tensio-dynamography*. It involves the measurement of force production in movement on special apparatus, recording it on what are known as tensiograms or dynamograms. It can involve measuring the force production of a single movement within the entire sequence or pattern of movement within the sport or that of the entire movement. In competitive swimming, this is accomplished by measuring the force production during the propulsive phase of the individual stroke cycle. The force production is plotted on a graph which typically shows variations in force production over time (that is, from the beginning of the movement until the end of the movement). In all cases of movement, the variation in force production normally describes a hyperbola or curve on the graph, and this curve is often referred to as a strength impulse or force curve. This force curve defines the force/time pattern of movement.

Each sport displays its own unique force curve, and individual athletes display minor variations in their curves which demonstrate differences in both force capacity and force application in strength displays. Changes in the force curve during training indicate changes in the strength preparation of the athlete.

The force curves measured in swimming are uniquely different when compared to those of other sports. While most sports display a *one peak* force curve, competitive swimming typically displays a *two peak* curve. The two peaks are separated by a *notch*. The first peak represents the initial part of the pull and is referred to as the *pull phase* of the stroke. The notch, which is located in mid-stroke, is followed by the second peak, which is designated the *push phase* (see Figure Appendix 2-1). The notch indicates the weakest point of the pulling action; the sticking point at which force application diminishes. The notch occurs as a result both of loss of leverage and of the fact that the different muscle groups are switching from the pulling musculature to the pushing musculature. In the science of tensiodynamography, it is at the middle part of the pull where pulling strength is tested in the isometric regime and used as an indicator of absolute pulling strength.

Force curves are used to determine the *speed-strength characteristics* of movement. These characteristics are determined by measuring the force curve and breaking down these measurements into speed-strength indices, which are based on force or time parameters or a combination of both. For example, the

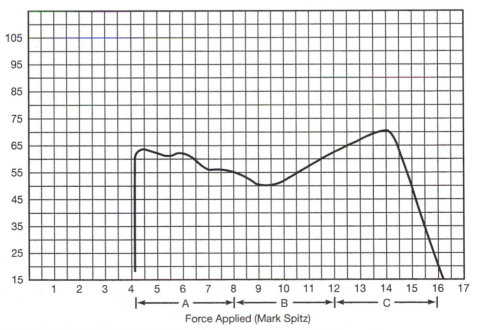

FIGURE APPENDIX 2-1   TYPICAL TWO-PEAK FORCE CURVE IN THE PROPULSIVE PHASE OF THE SWIMMING MOVEMENT

length of the curve determines the time taken to execute the movement and is quantified as the speed of movement. The height of the curve indicates magnitude of force production, with the highest point of the curve indicating maximal force production. The steepness or gradient of the curve indicates the rate or speed of force production. The following section outlines the methods of assessing speed-strength indices and how they are plotted on the force curve.

Figure Appendix 2-2 indicates the fundamental aspects of the force curve. The area under the curve is impulse force (I). The highest point is referred to as maximal force production (F max). Also plotted on the graph is the resistance (P) to be overcome.

Figure Appendix 2-3 illustrates the method of assessing the speed-strength indices which define the strength ability of explosive strength. Explosive strength is defined as the time it takes to reach maximal force production: the less time it takes to reach F-max, the more explosive the movement.

Because of the unique character of the force curve in competitive swimming, there are different speed-strength indices that are illustrated in the following graph (Figure Appendix 2-4).

Under the influence of strength training, there are definite changes in the force curve, which reveal differences in how the impulse force is expressed. In such cases, the magnitude of maximal force production has increased, and the time it takes to achieve maximal effort has decreased (see Figure Appendix 2-5). This indicates that the perfecting of the working effect is dependent upon the display of a larger maximum force in a shorter period of time. While this may be the case with most sports movements, it is not necessarily the desired effect in competitive swimming. An increase in the efficiency of swimming movement is usually associated with increasing force production over a longer period of time, which is marked by a reduction in stroke rate. Bulgakova[1] compared changes in

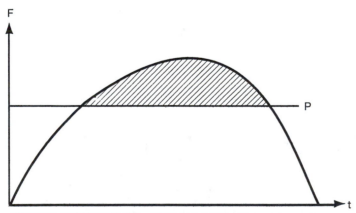

FIGURE APPENDIX 2-2   TYPICAL DISPLAY OF FORCE PRODUCTION PLOTTED ON A FORCE/TIME GRAPH

This force curve (or strength impulse) illustrates the development of working force (F), over time (T). P = the weight or resistance to be overcome. F-Max = the highest level of working force developed during the movement. I = the impulse force which is the shaded area under the curve.

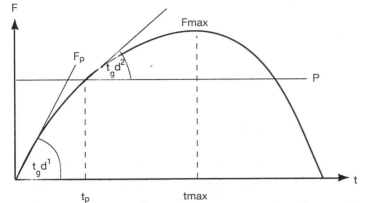

$$I = \frac{F_{max}}{t_{max}} \quad I = \text{explosive strength}$$

$$Q = \frac{F_p}{t_p} \quad Q = \text{starting strength}$$

$$G = \frac{F_{max} - P}{t_{max} - t_p} \quad G = \text{acceleration strength}$$

FIGURE APPENDIX 2-3 FORCE/TIME GRAPH ILLUSTRATING THE METHODS OF ASSESSING EXPLOSIVE, STARTING, AND ACCELERATION STRENGTH (VERKOSHANSKY, 1986).

the force curve between swimmers conducting dry-land strength training and swimmers utilizing in-water strength training. They determined that, while both forms of strength work boosted strength capabilities, dry land strength training had a negative impact on swimming technique through decreasing the magnitude of the pull gradient and that of arm stroke time (see Figure Appendix 2-6).

On the basis of these findings, it would appear that the essential strength ability required in swimming movements is explosive strength. Although explosive strength is not associated with the stroking movement, Rasulbekov[2] demon-

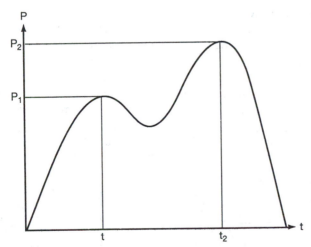

FIGURE APPENDIX 2-4 SPEED-STRENGTH INDICES OF A TWO-PEAK FORCE CURVE IN SWIMMING

P = the amount of hydrodynamic pressure on the hand
T = the time in seconds
The force gradient in the pulling phase (Gradient 1) = P (1):T(1) and the force gradient in the pushing phase (Gradient 2) = P(2):T(2).

FIGURE APPENDIX 2-5   CHANGES IN THE FORCE
CURVE OF A SPORTS MOVEMENT:
1. Before training,
2. After training

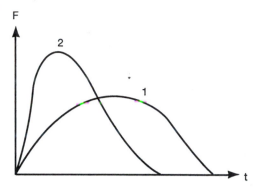

strated that the improvement of swimming strength in pulling is not only
associated with an increase in the magnitude of power output, but also with a
decrease in the time of achieving maximal effort. This is indicative of an increase
in explosive strength in the pull (see Figure Appendix 2-7).

Thus the nature of competitive swimming is expressed in the cyclic repetition of *explosive* efforts which maintain an optimal power output for a relatively
long period of time. The character of the display of explosive strength depends
upon the condition of resistance, which determines the presence of speed-
strength characteristics. In explosive acyclic-type movements, such as the start
or push-off, Verkoshansky[3] has broken down the force curve into special strength
abilities, which fall along a continuum, based on the load-velocity relationship.
These serve as parts of units of the total muscle tension regime, being referred
to by Verkoshansky as *componential* strength abilities, and their display or realization in the muscle activity always follows a sequential pattern. The four special
strength abilities include absolute strength, acceleration strength, starting
strength, and absolute speed of muscle contraction.

Absolute speed of muscular contraction is defined as the highest velocity of
an unloaded movement. Starting strength is defined as the ability to display force
production rapidly at the beginning or onset of the development of muscle
tension. Starting strength is displayed in the isometric regime until force production reaches a level that approximates or exceeds the external force (resistance)
at which joint muscle contraction actually begins and movement takes place.

FIGURE APPENDIX 2-6   COMPARISON OF
CHANGES IN SWIMMING STRENGTH BETWEEN
SWIMMERS CONDUCTING IN-WATER AND DRY-
LAND STRENGTH TRAINING

Force curves of crawl swimmers (A, in-water group
and B, dry-land group). Dotted line indicates before
training; solid line indicates after training.

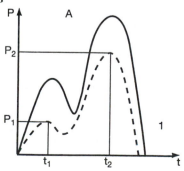
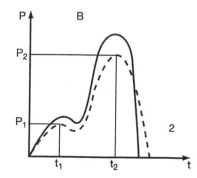

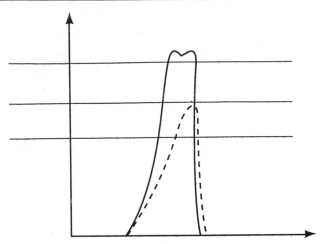

FIGURE APPENDIX 2-7 CHANGES IN THE EXPLOSIVE POWER OF A RUSSIAN BUT-
TERFLIER

Comparison of Explosive Power of V. Belov.
(1980—dashed line, 1981—solid line)

Acceleration strength is defined as the ability to develop maximal force production rapidly for a given load, once the onset of actual muscle contraction takes
place. Absolute strength is defined as the highest possible level of force production
in the isometric regime without time limit.

It is believed that the essential strength ability required for swimming is
speed of muscular contraction. This ability assumes great significance due to the
unique aspect of force production in swimming, when compared to those of other
athletic movements. It can be seen in the force curves of other sports movements
that force production diminishes rapidly in an inverse proportional manner when
the speed of movement increases (see Figure Appendix 2-5). According to Plyashko[4] the reverse pattern occurs in a water environment. In the water the
amount of applied force is directly proportional to the quadrant of the speed. This
phenomenon emphasizes the importance of strength training for swimming by
placing priority on speed-strength preparation of swimmers for the achievement
of superior movement speed. More precisely, this involves the achievement of an
appropriate pattern of hand acceleration, while attempting to increase peak hand
acceleration at critical phases of the arm pull.

In addition to indicating strength abilities, force curves are also used to
assess technical attributes of the swimming movements. Thornton and Flavell[5]
developed techniques of stroke analysis based on the force curves generated
by swimmers using the Biokinetic Swim Bench. Semiaccommodating resistance,
which is a feature of the Biokinetic Swim Bench, has become a tool in tensiodynamography which allows more precise analysis of stroke deficiencies by comparing
individual force curves with those of ideal curves. A weakness of so-called "ideal
force curves" is that they assume a constant application of force. Although such
an assumption is not physically possible, the comparison between "individual"
and "ideal" force curves allows a comparative modeling which indicates strengths

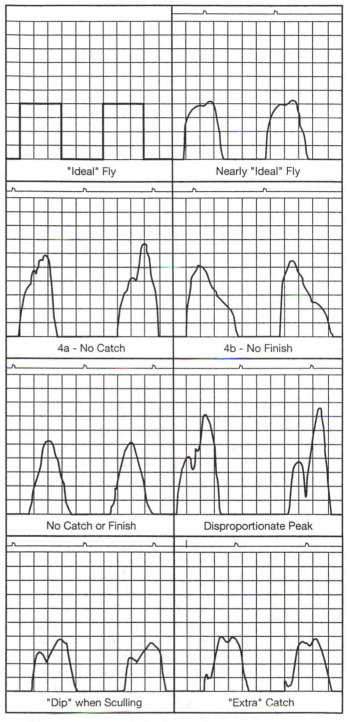

FIGURE APPENDIX 2-8 TYPICAL DEVIATIONS FROM CONCEPTUAL "IDEAL" FORCE CURVE IN THE BUTTERFLY STROKE

and weaknesses of segments of the strokes as they are realized over time. Figure Appendix 2-8 shows typical deviations from a conceptual, ideal force curve in the butterfly stroke.

In summary of our position on the various means of strength training:

1. The use of dry land strength preparation and traditional strength-training modes is essential in the initial stages of the swimmers' careers as part of their general physical preparation, as well as part of an integral approach to correct strength deficiencies or imbalances that cannot be corrected by more specialized means of strength training.

2. As the swimmers progress further into their careers they should discard the means of strength training that have not only lost their ability to produce beneficial strength-training effects, but also may result in adaptive restructuring that can be detrimental to swimming performance. Kiselev[6] compared the use of both traditional and more specialized strength training means in the strength preparation of swimmers. It was determined that while traditional strength training led to greater gains in absolute strength, it did not increase swimming strength as significantly as the more specialized means, but resulted in greater gains in muscle hypertrophy, considered an undesirable effect in competitive swimming. This is done only when it has been determined that the swimmers' strength preparation has reached a level that warrants such a progressive shift to more specialized means.

3. While speed of muscular contraction is the essential special strength ability required in competitive swimming, this does not mean that the other strength abilities should be neglected. To achieve balanced strength, a sufficiently high level of absolute or maximal strength is needed in *all* muscles. This is especially true of the shorter, broader muscles, more proximal to the chest and lower trunk, serving not only as prime movers, but as stabilizers of important joint movement. Once the proximal and more distal muscles have achieved a sufficient level of strength proper, then attention can be turned to the enhancement of speed-strength of the distal muscles.

FOOTNOTES

1. N.Z. Bulgakova, et al., "Improving the Technical Preparedness by Using Strength Training," *Teoriya i Praktika Fizicheskoi Kultury*, 7, 1987, 31–33.

2. R.A. Rasulbekov, et al., "Explosive Strength in Pulling," *National Strength and Conditioning Association Journal, vol. 8, no. 2* (1986), secondary reference.

3. Y.A. Verkoshansky, *Fundamentals of Special Strength Training in Sport* (Moscow: Fizikultury I Spovt, publishers, 1986). Translated and reprinted by Sportivny Press, Livonia, MI., pp. 61–67.

4. G.I. Plyashko and G.A. Gilev, "Concerning the Speed-Strength Preparation of Swimmers," *Teoriya i Praktica Fizicheskoi Kultury,* 6, 1988, 28–30.

5. N. Thornton and E.R. Flavell, "Electronic Assisted Dry Land Stroke Analysis," (Albany, CA: ISOKINETICS, INC., Publisher, 1980–81), pp. 60–63.

6. A.P. Kiselev, "The Use of Specific Resistance in Highly Qualified Swimmers' Strength Training," *Teoriya i Praktika Fizicheskoi Kultury*, 5, 1990, 46–47.

Glossary

Absolute intensity   This level is derived from maximal swimming velocity, achieved from sprint efforts of extremely short duration.

Addisonoid state   State of training apathy.

Adenosine diphosphate (ADP)   An ester composed of adenosine and diphosphoric acid which is created by the breakdown of ATP to liberate energy for physiological reactions.

Adenosine triphosphate (ATP)   An ester composed of adenosine and triphospheric acid which serves as a source of energy for physiological reactions, especially muscle contractions.

Aerobic energy system   ATP is resynthesized by a complex biochemical process known as oxidative phosphorylization, which involves the Kreb's citric acid cycle and electron transport chain.

Anaerobic/non-robic energy system   The term *anaerobic* literally refers to the creation of energy in the absence of oxygen. In human physiology this involves the phosphocreatine and glycolytic pathways in the resynthesis of ATP. According to some researchers the term anaerobic is inappropriate in defining human ergogenesis for work. They prefer the term *non-robic*. This term has no literal justification.

Arm recovery   The non-propulsive phase of the stroke.

Athletic character   This includes the establishment of proper long-term motivation, appropriate sports-ethics behavior, and comprehensive educational and intellectual development for sport.

Autogenic training   The training used to achieve what is considered an optimal emotional state using methods of self-regulation.

Back crawl stroke   A stroke executed in the supine position resembling an inverted crawl stroke; making use of a flutter kick and an alternating armpull.

Backstroke, elementary   Double overarm backstroke with either the frog or scissor kick.

Basedowoid state   State of training agitation.

Breaststroke   A stroke executed in the prone position, which combines the whip kick, a glide or thrust with the arms overhead, and a double arm pull downward and to the side. In modern parlance, three styles have been identified; the flat or traditional breaststroke, the pop-up or vertical breaststroke, and the wave, wave-action, or undulating breaststroke.

Buoyancy   The ability to float or rise in water, affected by the swimmer's body type, bone size, muscular development, weight distribution, relative amounts of fat tissue, and lung capacity.

Butterfly stroke   A stroke executed in a prone position that combines a dolphin (fishtail) kick and a double arm pull with an over-the-water recovery.

Calisthenics   These exercises allow the full brunt of the athlete's body weight to bear on the movements. Resistance is often further enhanced by combining the exercise with certain objects (e.g., dumbbells, medicine balls, weighted balls).

Central fatigue   Failure of neural drive, resulting in reduction in the number of functioning motor units and reduction in motor unit firing frequency.

Central nervous system (CNS)   The part of the nervous system involved in voluntary control of movement.

Chronobiology   The science or the study of changes in biological systems over time.

Controlled breathing (hypoxic training)   This method induces abnormally high levels of carbon dioxide and low levels of oxygen in the lungs by breathing less often than the swimmer normally would, but doing so on a structured basis.

Crawl stroke   A stroke executed in the prone position that combines a flutter kick with an alternating, overarm action.

Cross-training   The use of nonspecific activities to achieve a desired training effect. Also known as general physiological preparation.

Cruise interval methods   Methods devised by Dick Bower to determine individual departure times.

Curling   This refers to the formation of vortices in back of the moving body. These vortices may interfere with the creation of optimal lift.

DIRT   A cue word that represents the four factors influencing the use of interval training methods: D—Distance to be swum; I—Interval of rest between each repeat swim; R—Repetitions (number of bouts of exercise or repeat swims); T—Time (average time assigned to each repeat swim).

Dolphin (fishtail) kick   This kick is made by keeping the legs together and kicking them up and down in the vertical plane.

Dorsiflexion   Ankle flexion in which the top of the feet are brought up toward the shins. It aids in the sculling action of the kick.

Dynamic correspondence   This principle states that the dynamic characteristics of the strength training exercise must conform to the competitive exercise as closely as possible.

Eddy resistance   Water resistance caused by the water that is not able to fill in instantaneously behind poorly streamlined parts of the body. The result is that the body is forced to pull along large numbers of water and air molecules.

Electrostimulation   Direct electrical stimulation at the point of the muscle innervation.

Emotional tone   This psychoemotional index refers to the intensity of the athlete's positive or negative experiences.

Endurance   The ability to resist physical stress over a given time period, the ability to resist fatigue, and the onset of fatigue or time to fatigue.

Endurance reserves   A theoretical psychophysiological state that allows the individual to maintain or increase work capacity in the presence of an advanced state of exercise-induced fatigue.

Extensive interval training   Efforts at low to moderate intensity with short rest intervals.

External resistance   The main means of stimulating the display of greater muscle tension. These main means take the form of external objects, apparatus, or other media which the athlete is required to overcome through the production of higher levels of muscle tension.

Failing adaptation   Inability of the organism to adapt to the training load. This includes training staleness and overloading, both of which designate the failure to adapt and improve as a result of the training load. It involves the cumulative effect of both physical and mental stress factors, which interfere with the training process of the athlete.

Flexibility   This is the degree of range of movement of a joint. Bone structure and the degree to which muscles around the joint will permit it to move (its elasticity) are two limiting factors.

Force application   The ability to convert the force capacity of a muscle into joint movement.

Force capacity   The ability of the individual muscle to produce tension.

Frontal resistance   The resistance to forward progress that is created by the water immediately in front of the swimmer or any part of his body.

Full circumduction   The biomechanical term to describe the full, overhead elevation of the arms.

General adaptation syndrome (GAS)   The reaction to stress which occurs as a predictable syndrome. There are three steps that typify GAS (see Figure 7-1).

General strength training   This training is concerned with the development of balanced, comprehensive, whole body strength.

Hand pitch   The angle of attack of the hand relative to the pull pattern.

Helix models of periodization   A principal training model in which the volume/intensity ratio oscillates in such an antiphasic manner as to produce a spiral configuration.

Heterochronicity of adaptation   The variability in the rate of improvement of specific physical abilities within the biological systems.

Ideomotor training   Special psychological training often required to enhance psychic faculties and referred to as mental imagery or mental rehearsal.

Inertia   The tendency of a body to remain in one state, either in motion or at rest.

Integrated (mixed) training   This system suggests that several physical abilities can be stressed in a single training session.

Intensive interval (repetition training)   Efforts of submaximal to maximal intensity with long rest intervals.

Interval training   This type of training is characterized by intermittent physical activity. Different forms include extensive interval, intensive interval, and repetition training.

Kick   Stabilizes and keeps the feet from dropping, preserving streamlining.

Kinematic chain   The entire body which is composed of kinematic links, or body segments. There are two types of kinematic chains: the *closed kinematic chain,* in which the body is in contact with a solid surface, and the *open kinematic chain,* in which the body is not in contact with a solid surface against which it can act. A swimming body is considered to be an open kinematic chain.

Kinetic energy   Energy that is created through preliminary movement and is stored in the elastic component of the muscle.

Lift (Bernoulli effect)   The pressure differential created by the movement of water over a foil (i.e., the hands and feet), resulting in the generation of lift forces. These lift forces depend on the *aspect ratio* or shape of the foil and the *angle of attack* or pitch of the foil relative to the path of motion.

Load distribution schemes   These schemes break down training organization into simple numerical tables.

Loads, extensive   These training loads are executed at the lower ranges in intensity, guided by constant load and the interval principle.

Loads, intensive   These loads are executed at higher ranges of intensity and in relatively low volumes. They are guided by the interval principle and use intensive interval and repetition methods.

Local adaptation   The specific training effect of exercise.

Over distance training   Continuous swimming of long distances (e.g., 400 meters, 1650 yards).

Macrocycle   The largest type of training cycle, it includes semiannual, annual, and multiyear (usually quadrennial) cycles.

Macrotapering   This theory establishes a succession of training years in which each year places primary emphasis on the development of one principle physical ability, ending with the successive unification of the holistic performance state in the last year ending with major competition.

Medial rotation   The inward rotation of the upper arm and forearm so the palm faces diagonally outward.

Mesocycle   This training cycle is an average of intermediate cycle, anywhere from two weeks to a month in duration, and usually containing a finalized number of microcycles.

Methodology of training   The specific approaches with the means of training to achieve certain training effects. The means of training are physical exercises, which are specially selected, organized, and formed movements; methods refer to the manner of repetition of the means of training.

Microcycle   The most fundamental cycle of training, usually several days to a week in duration.

Mixed (or integrated) training system   Also known as complex or heterogeneous training, this system emphasizes the development of several physical abilities in the course of a single training session.

Model training methods   A variant of specialized endurance preparation which uses training loads that simulate the conditions of competition as closely as possible.

Motor image   The sum of notions in the athlete's mind about the structure of the sports activity: the technique of the sport's movement, the competitive event, and the environment in which it takes place.

Motor orientation   The inner readiness to carry out a trained skill in a strictly defined way.

Motor unit   The combination of a single alpha fiber and the number of muscle fibers it innervates.

Multimethod training system   This method makes use of uniform training loads in developing a single physical quality in a training session.

Peaking   Peaking refers to the arrival at an apex of performance capability.

Perceived exertion   This is the swimmer's identification of sensations that result from the application of a given amount of effort. These sensations arise from the accumulation of fatigue products in the muscles and the strain upon the metabolic system.

Periodization   An annual training plan that divides training programs according to preparation, competition, and transition.

Periodization of training   First advanced by Metveyev in 1965, the approach divides the training plan into major stages and periods to give an organization structure of the time-course of the training plan.

Peripheral fatigue   Failure of force generation of the whole muscle, resulting in impaired neuromuscular transmission and impaired excitation contraction coupling.

Physical loads   The expression of stress through increased physical activity which results in increases in the level of physiological work.

Physical preparation   Its purpose is to develop the abilities of endurance, strength, speed, and mobility. These abilities are interrelated in total performance and have been resolved into complex abilities.

Plan periods   Periodization breaks training years or seasons into major periods, which include the preparatory period, the competitive period, and the transitional period.

Pliometrics   Also known as shock exercises, these exercises are used to achieve a forced extension (stretch) of the muscle prior to the actual active work of the muscle or movement involved.

Principle of dominance   This stipulates that concentration is enhanced when certain cortical nerve centers are able to increase their levels of stimulation and dominate other centers in order to filter out minor random external stimuli and create a focal point of excitement or stimulation in the cerebral cortex.

Pronation   The forearm turns the palm downward; the reverse is called *supination.*

Propulsion   The resultant action which drives the swimmer and is created by the muscular contractions of the arms and legs as they exert pressure against the resistance of the water.

Psychological tension   A psychoemotional index that refers to the athlete's emotional excitement level.

Psychological tonus   This psychoemotional index refers to the activeness or passiveness of the athlete's attitude toward his performed activities.

Psychophysiological phenomenon   A combination of central nervous system resistance to fatigue and athletic will power.

Relative intensity   This level is rated according to the best time for the distance equivalent to the repeat.

Residual effect of training   Changes due to adaptation to physical loads that can be maintained for long periods of time or can be recalled quickly after the potential for long lasting training effects has elapsed.

Resistance (Drag)   In swimming, the hydrodynamic forces, which act upon the swimmer's body and tend to reduce forward motion. In swimming research the terms *active* and *passive* drag are used to describe relative amount of drag at different phases of the stroke.

Sets   These are the most rudimentary forms of implementing and realizing training methods as actual work loads.

Simulators   This method of training executes a training load equivalent to the competitive distance, which is broken up into smaller work bouts.

Specificity of training   The concept states that a specific stress brings about a specific physiological change or adaptation.

Specific resistance modes   These refer to strength exercises and apparatus which are developed to meet the requirements of special strength training based on the principle of dynamic correspondence. There are two basic types: dry land specific resistance and in-water strength training.

Speed   In sports training theory, speed is subdivided into different speed abilities. They include the speed of motor reaction time, the speed of single acyclic movements, and the speed or frequency of repeated cyclic-type movements.

Sports training physiology   The study of changes in the organic capacity of the athlete as a result of the stress of training and the adaptations to that stress.

Sprint training   All-out sprinting of extremely short distances.

Start fever, start apathy   Negative psychoemotional states at the moment of competition.

Streamlining   Positioning the body to offer the least possible resistance.

Strength   The ability of a muscle or group of muscles to create high levels of tension or to overcome external resistance through muscle contraction.

Strength abilities   There are three types of strength abilities: maximal or absolute strength; speed-strength or explosive strength; and strength endurance. Maximal (absolute) strength deals primarily with the magnitude of muscle tension development; speed-strength (explosive) is concerned primarily with the speed of muscle tension development and muscle contraction; and strength endurance is concerned primarily with strength work under conditions of fatigue.

Stroke drills   A training method that employs technique drills in repeat sets rather than whole strokes.

Surface drag   The resistance caused by the water immediately next to the body.

Systemic adaptation   The non-specific, whole body training effect of exercise.

Tapering   The final phase of rest and diminished workload requisite to optimal performance.

Tensiodynamography   This scientific method involves the measurement of force production in movement on special apparatus, recording it on tensiograms or dynamograms.

Tethered swimming   A cord or rope is secured to a fixed point on the deck or edge of a pool, while the other end is connected to a belt or harness fastened around the swimmer's waist.

Theoretical square law   The resistance a body creates in water (or any other fluid or gas) varies approximately with the square of its velocity.

Training complex   This is a training unit that pursues the development of one physical ability, but uses different methods and exercises to fulfill the training task.

Training load distribution   The distribution of different types of training loads throughout the different stages and cycles of the plan periods.

Training models   This type of modeling allows for the clarification of the structure of training and is usually expressed in graphic diagrams such as flow charts or bar graphs.

Training plan   Logically conceived strategy that controls the process of training to allow the swimmer to achieve short-term and long-term competitive performance goals.

Training units   A practice session in pursuit of a single training objective. A workout may be composed on one or several training units.

Uniform workloads   Training sessions of units (workouts) devoted to the development of a single physical ability.

Visualization   The unification of ideomotor and autogenic preparation to achieve an optimal state of technical, tactical, and emotional readiness for competition.

Whip Kick   A kick used in the breaststroke, characterized by a preparatory phase in which the hips and knees are flexed and the thighs are rotated medially, and a thrust phase in which the hips and knees are extended and the thighs are rotated laterally.

Index

Abduction (joint action), 257
Abilities, 195
    complex, 195, 196
    componental strength, 400
    reactive, 263–64
    speed, 215–20
Absolute intensity, 309
Absolute speed of muscular
    contraction, defined, 400
Absolute strength, 257
    defined, 401
    methods of developing, 262–63
Acceleration in butterfly stroke, 103
    hand, in crawl, 58–59
    hand speed and, 22–29
Acceleration strength, defined, 401
Accommodating (isokinetic)
    resistance, 266
Achilles tendon stretcher exercises,
    300, 301
Acidosis, 161
Action-reaction, 8–10, 16
    in crawl stroke, 37–38
    in whip kick, 111–12
Active drag, 3
Adaptation(s)
    categories of, 165
    chronobiology of, 169–82
    compensatory, 173, 174
    cyclic nature of, 169–73
    defined, 158
    to endurance training, 165–67
    failing, 172, 181–82, 222
    heterochronicity of, 173
    intracellular, 180
    models of, 168–73
    neurophysiological, 164
    short-term, 158–59
    to specific means and methods of
        training, 165–68
    to strength training, 167–68
    training effects and, 174–81
Addisonoid state (state of training
    apathy), 227
Additional acceleration training,
    218–19
Adduction (joint action), 257
Adenosine triphosphate (ATP), 159,
    160
ADP, 159
Aerobic conditioning in mixed
    program of training, 319
Aerobic endurance, 177–78, 198, 248,
    249

Aerobic endurance loads, 246
Aerobic zone, 309
Afternoon training session in weekly
    training plan, 327–28
Age-groupers, 373
Age-group levels, adjustment of
    training program for, 330–31
"Age of highest achievement," notion
    of, 231
Agitation, state of, 227
Agonistic muscle, 257
Agonistic swimmers, 152
Alactate endurance, 177–78
Alarm reaction, 169
Alekseev, A., 226
Alligator shoes (exercise), 300
All-sided preparation, principle of,
    191–95
Alternating sprints, 216–17
Altitude training, 175–76, 380–81
Amateur Athletic Union (AAU), 333
American Swimming Coaches
    Association, 357, 375
Anaerobic-aerobic/aerobic-anaerobic
    regime, interval training in,
    204–5
Anaerobic-alactate/alactate endurance
    regime, interval training in,
    207
Anaerobic-alactate endurance loads,
    246
Anaerobic alactate training, 216
Anaerobic (lactate) endurance,
    177–78, 198, 248
Anaerobic lactate/glycolytic regime,
    interval training in, 205–7
Anaerobic-lactate loads, 246
Anaerobic/lactate threshold regime,
    interval training in, 204
Anaerobic/non-robic training in mixed
    program of training, 319
Anaerobic/non-robic zone, 309
Anaerobic threshold, 160–61, 166
Anaerobic threshold endurance, 248
Ankle extensors and flexors, 278
Ankle flexibility, 88
    breaststroke kick and, 117
    in flutter kick, 46
    tests of, 298–99
Ankles, plantar-flexion of, 278, 296,
    298, 299
Ankle stretcher exercise, 299
Annual training models, 243–54
    principal training models, 244–49

quantitative training models,
    249–50
Annual training plan, 320–23
Annual (yearly) periodization, 230–31,
    233–36
Antagonistic muscle, 257
Apathy
    start, 222
    training, 227
Arantes, Romulo. 394
Arc start, 142
Arm depressor muscles, 275
Arm pull
    for back crawl stroke, 70–79, 80–81
    for backstroke, 11–15
    bent-arm, 72–74
    in breaststroke, 11–15, 121–30, 133
        coordination with kick, 123–26
        long, after dive and turn, 126–30
    "Buggy whip," 73–74
    in butterfly stroke, 11–15, 91–95
    in crawl stroke, 11–15, 48–60
        application of propulsive force,
            49–50
        elbow bend, 51–53
        high elbow in, 53–55
        medial rotation of upper arm,
            55–57
        shoulder and body roll, 58
        wrist flexion and, 50–51, 52
    elliptical pattern of, 50, 53, 59
    hand position in, 19–22
Arm recovery
    in back crawl stroke, 74–75, 79–85
    in backstroke, 9
    in butterfly stroke, 10, 95–98
    in crawl stroke, 9–10, 47–48, 49
    rushed, 31
    transfer of momentum during, 30
Arm rotator drills, 55, 282
Arm stroke
    in breaststroke, 118–22
        arm-pull pattern, 11–15, 121–30,
            133
        elbow bend, 118–21
        high-elbow position, 121
    in crawl stroke, 47–60
        pull, 11–15, 48–60
        recovery, 47–48, 49
        relationship of kick to, 41, 42, 43
Arm-swing (wind-up) start, 30, 133,
    134, 135, 138–39
Arousal, 221
Assistant mover muscle, 257

Asthenic emotions, 220
Athletic character, 223
Athletic hygiene, 182
ATP, 159
ATP-PCr (phosphocreatine) system of
    energy, 159, 160, 329
ATP resynthesis, 159, 160
ATP turnover, 159
Attack mesocycle, 239
Autogenic training, 221, 226–27
Auxiliary gymnastic exercise, 270, 272

Back crawl stroke, 65–85
    arm pull for, 70–79, 80–81
    arm recovery for, 74–75, 79–85
    body position for, 66
    breathing in, 85
    kick for, 66–70, 71
    rules governing, 66
Back hyperextensors, 274
Backstroke
    arm pull patterns of, 11–15
    elbow position in, 19, 21
    elementary, 66
    for endurance preparation, 314
    evenness of application of force in,
        29
    past and present form of, 4
    path of middle finger in, 15
    recovery in, 9
    sample workouts for, 366–67, 370
    turn, 146, 147–49
Backstroke start, 135–41
Ballistic exercises, 263
Barbell, exercises using, 271, 272,
    278–89
Barrowman, Mike, 362, 364, 395
Basedowoid state (state of agitation),
    227
Baumann, Alex, 25, 26, 393
Beardsley, Craig, 364
Bench press, 272, 281
Benson, Kent, 360
Bent-arm pull, 72–74
Bergen, P., 234
Berkoff, David, 70, 394
Bernardi, Oronzio de, 65
Bernoulli effect. See Lift (Bernoulli
    principle)
Berry, Kevin, 99, 395
Bibbero, Marquis, 65
Bicarbonate loading, 161–62
Bicep curls (exercise), 272, 279
Biokinetic Leaper, 359–60
Biokinetic resistance, 266, 268, 269,
    401
Bio-Kinetic Swim Bench, 371, 372,
    401
"Biomechanical Analysis of Freestyle
    Aquatic Skill, A" (Schleihauf),
    22
Biomechanics. See Mechanical
    principles
Biondi, Matt, 25
Biopsy needle, muscle, 183
Body position
    for back crawl stroke, 66
    for breaststroke, 110
    in butterfly, 87–88
    for crawl stroke, 34–38

Body roll
    in backstroke, 74
    crawl arm stroke and, 58
Bondarchuk, A., 235, 238
Bone structure, flexibility and, 295
Borges, Gustavo, 394
Bower, Dick, 313
Bradycardia, 311
Breaststroke, 104–31
    arm stroke in, 118–22
        arm-pull pattern, 11–15, 121–30,
            133
        elbow bend, 118–21
        high-elbow position, 121
    body position, 110
    breathing and head action, 122–23
    common mistakes in, 130
    different styles of, 364
    elbow position in, 19, 20
    for endurance preparation, 314–15
    evenness of application of force in,
        29–30
    evolution of, 105–7
    exercises for, 362
    kick in, 111–18
        ankle flexibility and, 117
        coordination with pull, 123–26
        dorsiflexion in, 278
        knee injuries and, 117–18
        warming up for, 335
    mechanical problems associated
        with, 315
    path of middle finger in, 15
    rules governing, 109–10
    sample workouts for, 366, 367, 369,
        383
    styles of
        "pop-up"/"high rise"/undulating,
            107–9, 112–15, 122–23,
            124–26
        traditional (flat), 107–9, 116, 122,
            127–29
        "wave-action," 107–9, 122–23
    turns, 143–45
Breaststroker's sit-down test, 299
Breathing
    in back crawl stroke, 85
    in breaststroke, 122–23
    in butterfly stroke, 99–103
    controlled, 315, 362
    in crawl stroke, 36–37, 60–64
    explosive, 61
    late, 60
Broken swims, 156, 307–9
    mixing straight swims and, 308–9
"Bucket" swimming, 374–75
"Buggy whip" pull, 73–74
Bulgakova, N.Z., 398–99
Buoyancy, 31
Buoyant gloves, 318–19
Burton, Mike, 394
Butterfly stroke, 86–103
    acceleration in, 103
    arm pull in, 11–15, 91–95
    arm recovery in, 10, 95–98
    body position, 87–88
    breathing action and timing in,
        99–103
    dolphin kick in, 88–91
    elbow position in, 19, 20

for endurance preparation, 314–15
hand pitch in, 18–19, 98
lift in, 17
mechanical problems associated
    with, 315
path of middle finger in, 15
rules governing, 87
sample workouts for, 366–67, 369
turns, 143–45
typical deviations from conceptual,
    ideal force curve in, 402, 403

Calisthenics, 270, 271
    hopping and jumping, 290
Cardiac anomalies, 311
Carey, Rick, 395
"Catch-up" style of crawl stroke, 29
Caulkins, Tracy, 394
Central fatigue, 164
Central nervous system (CNS), 168
Character, athletic, 223
Chen Yeung Chi, 379–82
Chinning exercises, 275
Chronobiology of stress and
    adaptation, 169–82
Clark, Steve, 395
Clinics, 375
Closed kinematic chain, 58
Coaches
    interviews with leading, 355–91
        Chen Yeung Chi, 379–82
        Kenney, Skip, 382–84
        Quick, Richard, 387–91
        Reese, Eddie, 357–70
        Shoulberg, Richard, 370–78
        Simon, Jack, 384–87
    intuitive vs. pattern, 355–56
Coaching, 3–4
Combative exercise, 270, 273
Combined exercise, 270, 273
Combined/partner exercises, 270
Compensatory adaptation, 173, 174
Competition(s)
    amount of time between, 212–13
    conditions of, 213–15
    local vs. international, 372
    mobilizational readiness for, 227
    model. See Model training
    number within training plan, 212
    successive days of, 214
    warming up before, 335–36
Competitive exercises, 196, 199
Competitive loads, 195, 211–14
Competitive microcycles, 239–41
Competitive period, 234, 235
    percentages of load distribution in,
        252–53
Competitive-specific training, 195,
    200, 211–15
Complex abilities, 195, 196
Complex training. See Mixed program
Componential strength abilities, 400
Comprehensiveness, principle of, 190
Concentrated variant of training load
    organization, 245
Concepts, 188
Conditioning, 5, 311
Conjugate-successive system of loading
    organization, 245, 246
Consciousness, principle of, 188

Constant load principle, 200
Constant methods. *See* Overdistance training
Continuous loads, 200–201, 203
Controlled breathing, 315, 362
Controlled swimming, 374
Cook, James, 2
Counsilman, James E., 358
Counsilman model of stress and adaptation to physical loads, 170, 172
Counteractive exercise, 270, 273
Crawl stroke, 33–64
    action-reaction in, 37–38
    arm opposition in, 84
    arm stroke, 47–60
        pull, 11–15, 48–60
        recovery, 9–10, 47–48, 49
        relationship of kick to, 41, 42, 43
    Bernoulli principle applied to, 59–60
    body and head position for, 34–38
    breathing, 36–37, 60–64
    "catch-up" style of, 29
    drag in, 60
    elbow position in, 19, 20
    for endurance preparation, 314
    evenness of application of force in, 29
    flutter kick, 38–46
        mechanics of, 44–46
        patterns of, 41–44
        role of, 38–41
        timing of, 41
    hand acceleration in, 58–59
    hand position at recovery, 36
    lateral reaction in, 9–10
    origins of, 33
    path of middle finger in, 15
    riding too low in water during, 9
    rules for competition, 33–34
    turn in, 146, 150–51
Crossover kick, 38, 42, 44, 45
Cruise interval, 253, 313, 314
Curling, 60
Cyclic activities, 29
Cyclical-endurance sports, training models for, 249
Cyclic nature of training, 197, 236–41
    macrocycles, 236
    mesocycles, 236–39
    microcycles, 239–41, 242, 253

Dahlberg, Peder, 333
Daland, Peter, 253
Dalton, Davis, 111
Dead lift (exercise), 274, 284
De-adrenalization, 358
Decreasing rest interval sets, 305–6
DeLorme Method, 262
DeLorme Principles of progressive resistance, 261–62
Density (external load factor), 261
    load dynamic of, 191
Departure times, determining individual, 313, 314
Descending-time sets, 305
Distance events, kick rate in, 39–40

Distance swimmer(s)
    sample workouts for, 365, 366, 367, 368–69, 383
    training program for, 328, 363–64
        morning sessions, 327
    vertical jumps of, 360
Distributed variant of training load organization, 245
Dive, sailor, 142
Dollies, use of, 370
Dolphin kick, 68, 70, 71–72
    in butterfly stroke, 88–91
Dominance, principle of, 221
Dorsiflexion, 296
    Achilles tendon stretcher exercise to increase, 300
    in breaststroke kick, 278
    test of, 299
Double wrist curl, 283
Drag. *See also* Resistance
    active, 3
    in backstroke, 72, 78
    in boats vs. swimmers, 12
    in crawl stroke, 60
    hand paddles to increase, 316–17
    head position and, 34–35
    passive, 3
    swim fins to increase, 317
Drag belts and drag suits, 318
Drag kick, 41
Dry land apparatus
    speed-strength endurance work using, 268, 269
    strength-endurance work using, 269
Dry land exercises, 360, 363, 371–72
    from Richard Quick, 388–91
Dry land specific resistance, 266
Dry land strength training, 399, 403
Duration loads, 201, 203–4
Duration methods. *See* Overdistance training
Dynamic correspondence, principle of, 259, 266

Early season program, samples of, 348–49, 365, 377–78
Eastern Europe
    centralized training methods in, 356–57
    periodization in, 320–21
East German four-cycle plan, 379–82
Eddy resistance, 7, 9
Edwards, R.H.T., 164
Efficiency, 16
Elasticity of muscle, flexibility and, 295–96
Elbow bend
    in breaststroke arm stroke, 118–21
    in pull of crawl arm stroke, 51–53
Elbow extensor (exercise), 274, 278, 281, 282
Elbow position, 19–21
    high
        in breaststroke arm stroke, 121
        in pull of crawl arm stroke, 53–55
Electrostimulation, 260
Elementary backstroke, 66
Elite swimmers, roster of, 393–95
Elliptical pull pattern, 50, 53, 59
Emotional tone, 221

Ender, Cornelia, 394
Endurance
    aerobic, 198
    anaerobic (lactate endurance), 177–78, 198, 248
    effects of strength training on, 179
    special-strength training for, 178–79
    speed-strength, 199, 207, 267–69, 329
    strength-endurance work, 198, 207, 258, 264–66, 269
    workouts stressing, 348
Endurance abilities, 197–99
    classification of, 198–99
    development of, 197
Endurance methods, activities
        executed in use of, 313–19
    apparatus used, 316–19
    controlled breathing, 315
    kicking drills, 316
    pulling drills, 316
    strokes, 314–15
Endurance preparation, 165, 199–215
    different levels of, 199–200
    means and methods of, 200–202
    special endurance methods, 203–15
Endurance reserves, 164, 221
Endurance sports, training models for, 245–49
Endurance training, 198
    adaptations to, 165–67
    maximal loads in, 241
    specialized, 199, 204–15
Energy systems, 158–64, 329
Entry, normal reach, 48
Entry mesocycle, 239
Environment, 222
    control of training, 376
Enzymes, 159
Ermolaeva, M., 220
Evans, Janet, 40
Exchanges, relay, 146
Excitation, 221
Exercise(s)
    Achilles tendon stretcher, 300, 301
    alligator shoes, 300
    arm rotator, 55, 282
    ballistic, 263
    for breaststroke, 362
    competitive, 196, 199
    for development of strength, 259–60, 269–90
        with barbell, 271, 272, 278–89
        for flexibility, 299–301
        general-preparatory, 265, 270–74
        shock exercises/pliometrics, 260, 263–64, 290, 291–92
        special-preparatory, 265, 270–78
    dry land, 360, 363, 371–72
        from Richard Quick, 388–91
    stretching, 298–301, 385–86
    training, 195
Exertion, perceived, 153, 156, 157
Exhaustion, 169
    organic, 164
Exogenous stress factors, 181–82
Experimental techniques, using, 361
Experts, training with. *See* Coaches
Explosive breathing, 61
Explosive isometric efforts, 264

Explosive strength/power, 135, 247, 258, 399–400
  defined, 398
  methods of developing, 263–64
  training for, 168, 329
  vertical jump as measure of, 290–94
Extension (joint action), 257
Extensive interval training, 164, 166, 303
Extensive loads, 200
Extensive training, 164
External load factor, 261. *See also* Intensity
External resistance, increased, 259

Failing adaptation, 172, 181–82, 222
Fast twitch glycolytic (FG) fibers, 182–83, 185
Fast-twitch oxidative/glycolytic (FOG) fibers, 182–83
Fatigue
  defined, 197
  nervous system, 164
Fats, 162
Feathering, 55
Fever, start, 222
Filin, V.P., 244
FINA (Fédération International de Natation Amateur), 86
Finals, warming up before, 336
Finger flexors, 275–78
Fishtail kick. *See* Dolphin kick
Fitness and Sports Review, 187
Fixed (rigid) intervals, 303, 311
Flat (ordinary) intervals, 303, 311
Flat (traditional) style breaststroke, 107–9, 116, 122, 127–29
Flavell, E.R., 401
Flexibility
  ankle, 88
    breaststroke kick and, 117
    in flutter kick, 46
  bone structure and, 295
  defined, 295
  exercises for, 299–301
  muscle elasticity and, 295–96
  strength abilities and, 295–301
  strength and, 5, 6
  stretching exercises to improve, 298–301
  tests of, 296, 297–98
Flexibility training, 227
Flexion (joint action), 257
Flexor muscles, 275–78
Flip turn, 146, 150–51
Fluid mechanics, 2–3
Fluid pressure, lift and, 16
Flutter kick
  ankle flexibility in, 46
  in backstroke, 68–70
  in crawl stroke, 38–46
    mechanics of, 44–46
    patterns of, 41–44
    role of, 38–41
    timing of, 41
  six-beat, 67
F max (maximal force production), 398
Force capacity of muscle, 256
Force curves, 397–403

fundamental aspects of, 398
"individual" and "ideal," 401–3
Forearm
  inward rotators of, 275
  supination of, 55
Forward bend (exercise), 287
Forward raise (exercise), 284
Forward trunk flexion test, 298
Four-week taper, 337–39, 340–47
Free-fall properties of resistance apparatus, 264
Freestyle. *See* Crawl stroke
Free swimming conditions, 207
  strength training using, 267, 269
Free swim training for endurance, 313–15
Frog stroke, 105
Frontal resistance, 6, 7, 9
Full circumduction position, 264
Full squat (exercise), 285
Furukawa, Masura, 106

Gaines, Rowdy, 25, 393
Gathercole, Terry, 106
General adaptation syndrome (GAS), 168
General endurance preparation, 199
General-preparatory stage, 234, 235
General-preparatory strength exercises, 265, 270–74
General strength training, 258–59
Gloves, buoyant, 318–19
Glucose, 162
Glycolysis, 160, 161
Glycolytic system, 160
Goal set, 253
Goersling, A., 105
Goodell, Brian, 363
Good Mornings (back hyperextensors), 274
Grab start, 133, 134, 135, 136–37
Gradualness, principle of, 191
Guzhalovsky, A.A., 241, 243
Gymnastic exercise, auxiliary, 270, 272

Half squat (exercise), 284
Hall, Gary, 394
Halliburton, Jim, 27–28, 394
Hamuro, Detsuo, 106
Hand acceleration in crawl, 58–59
Hand paddles, 316–17
Hand pitch, 21–22
  in butterfly stroke, 18–19, 98
Hand position in crawl stroke, 36
Hand speed
  acceleration and, 22–29
  in backstroke, 76
  in good swimmers, 25–28
  in poor swimmers, 28–29
Harre, Dietrich, 188, 222, 236, 237
Hay, James, 5
Head action and breathing in breaststroke, 122–23
Head position
  for crawl, 34–38
  drag and, 34–35
Health promotion, principle of, 190

Heart rate
  controlled swimming monitored by, 374
  as gauge of effort, 310–11, 312
  use of swim fins and, 317
Heel raises, 274
Helix models, periodization based on, 253
Hencken, John, 395
Heterochronicity of adaptation, 173
Heterogeneous training. *See* Mixed program
Hickcox, Charlie, 381, 393
Hierarchy of Needs, 222
Higgins, John, 106
"High rise" (undulating) breaststroke, 107–9, 112–15, 122–23, 124–26
Hip extensors and flexors, 278
Hip flexion, 112–15
Hip rotation, 58
Hi-walking, stationary, 288, 289
Hole-in-the-water start, 142
Homeostasis, 158
Hooker, Jennifer, 394
Hopping and jumping calisthenics, 290
Horizontal rowing, 280
Horne, R.H., 105
Hourglass pattern, 95
Hudepohl, Joe, 394
Hydrolysis, 159
Hygiene
  athletic, 182
  nutritional, 227
  psychological, 222
Hypnoideomotor training, 220, 226
Hypoxic (controlled breathing) training, 315, 362

Ideomotor training, 220–21, 225–26
Imagery, mental, 220
Impulse force, 398
Impulse unit resistance apparatus, 264
Impulse units, 290
Increasing rest interval sets, 306
Individualization, principle of, 191
Individual medley
  pace of, 156–57
  sample workout for, 366–67, 369
  training program for, 330–31
Inertia, 3
Informed trial and error, 355. *See also* Coaches: interviews with leading
Integral-approximated modeling, 208–11
Integrated system of training. *See* Mixed program
Intensification of training, principle, 191
Intensity, 261
  absolute vs. relative, 309
  in competitive period, 234
  heart rate as gauge of, 310–11, 312
  percentage efforts as indicator of, 309–10
  zones of, 203
Intensive loads, 200
Intensive training, 161
  interval, 161, 166–67, 303

Intermittent work, 303–4
International competitions, 372
International sports training theory, 185–227
  endurance abilities, 197–99
    classification of, 198–99
    development of, 197
  endurance preparation, 165, 199–215
    different levels of, 199–200
    means and methods of, 200–202
    special endurance methods, 203–15
  fundamentals of, 188–97
    methodology of training, 195–97
    physical abilities of athletic performance, 195
    sports training principles, 188–95
  psychological preparation, 220–27
    assessment of psychic qualities, 221–22
    general and special, 223–27
    hierarchy of psychological preparation, 222
    psychological hygiene, 222
  speed abilities, 215–20
    defining, 215
    nontraditional methods for enhancing, 217–20
    specialized speed preparation, 215–16
    traditional vs. conventional methods, 216–17
Interval of rest, determining, 311–13, 314
Interval principle, 191
Intervals, types of, 311
Interval training, 201–2, 303–4
  in anaerobic-aerobic/aerobic-anaerobic regime, 204–5
  in anaerobic-alactate/alactate endurance regime, 207
  in anaerobic lactate/glycolytic regime, 205–7
  in anaerobic/lactate threshold regime, 204
  extensive, 164, 166
  to improve strength component of special endurance, 207
  intensive, 161, 166–67
  for twenty-four hour period, 374, 376–77
  types of sets for, 304–9
Intuitive coach, 355–56
Inward rotators of upper arm and forearm, 275
In-water strength training, 266–67
  for speed-strength endurance, 269
Isokinetic resistance, 266
Isometric efforts
  explosive, 264
Isometrics, 260
  for maximal-strength development, 262–63

Jastremski, Chet, 30, 107, 395
Joint actions, 257
Joints, flexibility and movement of, 295–301
Joint strength exercises, partial/single, 272
Jordan, Shawn, 359, 360
Jump, vertical, 290–94, 359–60
Jumping quarter squat (exercise), 288

Kenney, Skip, 382–84
Keyhole pattern, 95
Kick(s)
  in back crawl stroke, 66–70, 71
  in breaststroke, 111–18
    ankle flexibility and, 117
    coordination with pull, 123–26
    dorsiflexion in, 278
    knee injuries and, 117–18
    warming up for, 335
  in crawl stroke, 38–46
    crossover, 38, 42, 44, 45
  dolphin, 68, 70, 71–72
    in butterfly stroke, 88–91
  drag, 41
  flutter
    ankle flexibility in, 46
    backstroke, 68–70
    in crawl stroke, 38–46
    six-beat, 67
  two-beat
    crossover, 38, 42, 44, 45
    straight, 41–43
  wedge, 111, 118
  whip, 111–17, 118
Kick boards, 44, 318
Kicking drills, 44, 68–69, 316
Kicking performance, swim fins and, 317
Kick sticks, 318
Kindermann, W., 253, 254
Kinematic chain, closed and open, 58
Kinetic energy, 259–60, 264
Kiseley, A.P., 403
Klaus, Rudolf, 379–80
Kleine, Megan, 395
Knee extensors and flexors, 274, 278
Knee injuries in breaststroke, 117–18
Koshkin, Igor, 239
Kubelin, A.B., 253, 254

Lactate endurance, 177–78, 198, 248
Lactate threshold (OBLA--Onset of Blood Lactic Acid threshold), 166
Lactate tolerance work, 205
Lactic acid, 160–61, 166
Lactic-acid-ATP, glycolytic system, 160
Late-season workout, sample from Richard Shoulberg, 378
Latissimus device, 289
Lat pulls, 274, 275
Leading method of training, 217–18
Leg curls, 274
Leg extensors and flexors, 278
Lift (Bernoulli principle)
  applied to crawl stroke, 59–60
  in backstroke, 72, 78
  in butterfly stroke, 17
  effect of, 10–22
    pull and hand position, 19–22
  fluid pressure and, 16
Load(s)
  competitive, 195, 211–14
  continuous, 200–201, 203

  duration, 201, 203–4
  extensive, 200
  intensive, 200
  maximal, 241, 243
  physical, 159, 190
  physiological, 190
  principles of, 190–91
  training, 190, 213
  zones of intensity, 203
Load degree, 191
Load demand, 191
Load distribution. *See* Training load(s)
Loading microcycles, 239, 241, 242
Loading rhythm, 191
Load procedure, 261
  for general strength-endurance training, 265
Load process, 191
Load/recovery ratio, 240, 241, 252
Load structure, 191
  weekly, 253, 254
Local adaptation, 165
London Medical Dictionary (Parr), 2
Long-distance events
  pace of, 152
  training model for, 247–49
Loveless, Lea, 394
Lower extremities, streamlining of, 8

McCloy Method, 262
MacKenzie, Don, 381
Macrocycles of training, 236, 379
Maglischo, Ernie, 253
Mantevich, D.E., 241, 243
Maslow, A., 222
Masters program, 332–35
Maturation, individual
  performance detriments and process of, 232
  specialized strength training and, 243
Matveyev, L.P., 188, 230, 232, 244, 245
Matveyev model of stress and adaptation to physical loads, 172–73
Maximal force production (F max), 398
Maximal loads, 241, 243
Maximal speed (speed-strength) endurance, 199, 207, 267–69
  training sprinter for, 329
Maximal strength, 257
  general versus specialized, 263
  methods of developing, 262–63
Meagher, Mary T., 394
Mechanical principles, 1–32
  action-reaction, 8–10, 16
  buoyancy, 31
  effect of lift, 10–22
    pull and hand position, 19–22
  hand speed and acceleration, 22–29
  propulsion, 3, 5, 7
    evenness of application of, 29–30
  resistance, 3, 5–7, 9
  theoretical square law and, 30–31
  transfer of momentum, 30
Mechanics of breathing in crawl, 60–64
Medicine ball throws, 290, 291

Medley swimming for endurance
  preparation, 315
Meineke, Barbara, 381
Mental imagery (mental rehearsal),
  220
Mental toughness, 374
Mertens-Huttel exerciser, 268
Mesocycles of training, 236–41
  defined, 236
  load/recovery ratios in, 240, 241
  periodization and, 236–39
Methodological approach, 261
  in strength-endurance training, 265
Microcycles of training, 197
  correct and incorrect variants of
    structuring, 254
  defined, 236
  periodization and, 239–41, 242, 253
  of primary training emphasis, 254
  two-peak, 253
Middle distance events, pace of, 152
Middle-distance swimmers
  sample workouts for, 365, 368, 383
  training-load distribution for,
    245–47
Middle finger, path of, 15
Midseason program, long and short
  courses, 365–68
Midseason workout, sample, 349–52
Mitochondria, 160
Mixed program, 319–20, 321
Mobilizational readiness for
  competition, 227
Model competition. *See* Model training
Modeling and systemization of
  training, 241–54
  annual training models, 243–54
    principal training models, 244–49
    quantitative training models,
      249–50
  multiyear training models, 241–43
  of weekly cycles, 250–54
Model training, 196, 208–11
Molonosov, A.S., 226
Momentum, transfer of, 30
Monogarov, V.D., 221
Montgomery, James, 25, 393
Morales, Pablo, 90, 395
Morning training session in weekly
  training plan, 326–27
Motion, Newton's Third Law of
  (action-reaction), 8, 9, 72
Motor abilities, interconnections
  between, 179
Motor actions, speed of, 215
Motor image, 220
Motor orientation, 220
Motor reaction, speed of, 215
Motor unit, 168
Movement stereotypes, 219
Movies for training, 357, 358
Multimethod system of training, 172,
  319
Multi-year load distribution scheme,
  249–50, 251
Multiyear training models, 241–43
  periodization of, 230, 231–33
Muscle(s), 6
  contraction of, 256
    speed of, 258, 400, 401, 403

elasticity of, 295–96
  force capacity of, 256
  prime mover, 257, 275–78
  recovery, 47
  speed and energy expenditure of, 31
  synergistic, 257, 279
Muscle biopsy needle, 183
Muscle charts, 276–77
Muscle fiber typing, 182–85
Muscular activity, various roles of,
  256–57
Muscular tension development, speed
  of, 258, 267–69
Musculoskeletal adaptations, 167–68
Muth, Guts, 105
Myers, Henry, 86, 106
Myoglobin, 183

NAD, 161
Nash, Mel, 394
Neck, hyperextension of, 99
Needs, Hierarchy of, 222
Negative split, 305
Negative tethered conditions, 317
Nervous system fatigue, 164
Nesty, Anthony, 395
Neural adaptations, 168
Neuro-motor system, 164–65
Neurophysiological adaptation, 164
Neutralizer muscle, 257
Newton, Isaac, 8
Newton's Third Law of Motion, 8, 9,
  72. *See also* Action-reaction
Normal reach entry, 48
Notch in two-peak force curve, 397
Nutritional hygiene, 227

OBLA (Onset of Blood Lactic Acid)
  threshold, 166
Olympic cycle, 233
Omelyanenko, 226
100–yard/meter distance, pace of, 146
Open kinematic chain, 58
Operative plans. *See* Cyclic nature of
  training
Ordinary (flat) intervals, 303, 311
Ordinary microcycles, 239
Organic exhaustion, 164
Organization of training, logical
  process involved in, 230, 232
Out-slow/back-hard sets (negative
  split), 305
Overcompensation, 169–72, 173, 175
Overdistance training, 164, 166,
  200–201
Overloading, 181, 191
  apparatus used to create, 316–19
  signs of, 225
Overreaching, 48
Oxford Method, 262
Oxidative phosphorylization, 160
Oxidative (steady-state) system, 160
Ozolin, N.P., 188, 191, 192, 225–26

Pace, 146–57
  factors affecting, 152–53
  of individual medley, 156–57
  learning, 153–56
  middle and longer distances, 152
  of 100–yard/meter distance, 146

simulators to teach, 211
  steady pace chart, 153, 154–55
Pace clock, 377
Paddles, hand, 316–17
Panting, 85
Parr, Bartholomew, 2
Partial/single joint strength exercises,
  272
Partner exercise, 270, 273
Passive drag, 3
Pattern coach, 355, 356
Peaking, 337. *See also* Taper, the
Peak of training density, sample
  workout for, 352–54
Pendulum effect, 253
Perceived exertion, 153, 156, 157
Percentage efforts as indicator of
  intensity, 309–10
Performance objectives of training
  plan, 229–30
Periodization of training, 173, 206,
  230–36
  based on helix models, 253
  in China, 379–81
  in Eastern European countries,
    320–21
  macrocycles and, 236
  Matveyev's principal model of
    traditional, 244, 245
  mesocycles and, 236–39
  microcycles and, 239–41, 242, 253
  multiyear training plans, 230,
    231–33
  variants of, 235–36
  yearly training plan, 230–31,
    233–36
Peripheral fatigue, 164
Perkins, Kieren, 49–50
Personality tests, 221
Petrovich, G.I., 243
Phosphocreatine (ATP-PCr) system of
  energy, 159, 160, 329
Phosphorylization, oxidative, 160
Physical loads, 159, 190
Physical preparation, 195
Physiological basis for training
  swimmers, 158–85
  adaptations to training methods and
    means, 165–68
  chronobiology of stress and
    adaptation, 169–82
  energy systems, 158–64
  muscle fiber typing, 182–85
  neuro-motor system, 164–65
Physiological loads, 190
Pike start, 142–43
Plan, training, 229–30. *See also*
  Training theories involved in
  planning process
Plan periods of training, 229, 233–34
Plantar-flexion of ankles, 278, 296,
  298, 299
Platonov, V.N., 253
Pliometrics, 260, 263–64, 290,
  291–92
Plyashko, G.I., 401
"Pop-up" (undulating) breaststroke,
  107–9, 112–15, 122–23,
  124–26
Positive tethered conditions, 317–18

Power (speed-strength), 135
Practice, warming up before, 335
Precompetition mesocycle, 239
Preliminary-specialized preparation, 195, 199, 203–4
Preparation. *See also* Training
  all-sided, 191–95
  endurance, 165, 199–215
    different levels of, 199–200
    means and methods of, 200–202
    special endurance methods, 203–15
  levels of, 165, 188
  preliminary-specialized, 195, 199, 203–4
  psychological, 220–27
    assessment of psychic qualities, 221–22
    general and special, 223–27
    hierarchy of psychological preparation, 222
    psychological hygiene, 222
  types of, 192–94
  unity of general and specialized, 190
Preparatory period, 233–35, 236
Prime mover muscles, 257, 275–78
Principal training models, 244–49
Principles, 188
Prins, Jan, 184
Profile of training, 230
Progressive resistance method, 262
Propulsion, 3, 5, 7
  in the crawl, 38–40, 49–50
  evenness of application of, 29–30
  lift, 10–11
Psychoemotional preparedness, 220–22
Psychological preparation, 220–27
  assessment of psychic qualities, 221–22
  general and special, 223–27
  hierarchy of psychological preparation, 222
  psychological hygiene, 222
Psychological tension, 221
Psychological tonus, 221
Psychophysiological phenomena, 164
Pull. *See* Arm pull
Pull-buoys, 316, 318
Pulling drills, 316
Pullovers exercise, 275
Push phase of stroke, 397
Pyruvate, 160
Pyruvic acid, 161

Quadrennial plan, 233, 234
  load distribution in, 250, 251
Quantitative training models, 249–50
Quick, Richard, 387–91

Rasulbekov, R.A., 399–400
Reactive ability, methods of developing, 263–64
Reactive properties of nervous system, 168
Recovery
  in back crawl stroke, 74–75, 79–85
  in backstroke, 9
  in butterfly stroke, 10, 95–98
  crawl stroke, 9–10, 47–48, 49

  mechanics of, 9–10
  rushed, 31
  transfer of momentum during, 30
Recovery microcycles, 239, 241, 242
Recovery muscle, 47
"Recovery muscle" work, 372
Recruiting athletes, 362–63
Reese, Eddie, 357–70
  sample workouts from, 364–70
Rehearsal, mental, 220
Relative fiber-type distribution, 183
Relative intensity, 309
Relay exchanges, 146
Repetition(s)
  ballistic exercises in, 263
  defined, 261
  principle of, 190
  for strength-endurance training, 265
Repetition maximum method, 261
Repetition training, 161, 166–67, 202, 303–4
  determining rest intervals in, 313
  types of sets for, 304–9
Repetitive display of explosive effort, 267
Repetitive effort method, 262
Reserves, endurance, 164, 221
Residual effect of training, 180–81
Resistance, 3, 5–7, 9, 169
  DeLorme Principles of progressive, 261–62
  on force/time graph, 398
  forms of, in strength exercises, 259
  increased external, 259
  semiaccommodating, 266, 268, 269, 401
  specific modes of, 259, 266–67
    speed-strength endurance work, 267–69
    strength-endurance work, 269
  traditional, 259, 262–66
  types of, 6–7
  velocity and, 30–31
Rest
  intervals of, 311–13, 314
  nature of, 174
Rest cycle, 239
Reverse double wrist curl, 283
Reversibility, 191
Richter, Ulrike, 394
Rigid (fixed) intervals, 303, 311
Rise on toes exercises, 286
Robie, Carl, 395
Roll, body
  in backstroke, 74
  crawl arm stroke and, 58
Rope jumping, 281, 290
Rotation (joint action), 257
Rouse, Jeff, 394
Rowing exercises, 275, 280–81
Rubin, V.S., 244
Running, 359
  stationary, 288, 289
Rushed recovery, 31
Russians, variation in arrangement of mesocycles proposed by, 239

Saari, Roy, 394
Sailor dive, 142
Salnikov, Vladimir, 40, 153

Sarcolemma, elasticity of, 329
Sargent Standing Vertical Jump Test, 183
Scapula, rotation of, 49, 275
Schlatter, Marc, 395
Schleihauf, Robert, 22, 25
Schollander, Don, 394
Scoop start, 142
Sculling, 15–16, 59
Self-regulation, 221
Self-suggestion methods, 227
Selye, Hans, 169
Semiaccommodating (biokinetic) resistance, 266, 268, 269, 401
Sets
  defined, 261
  for distance swims, 328
  types of, 304–9
    broken swims, 307–9
    decreasing rest interval sets, 305–6
    descending-time sets, 305
    increasing rest interval sets, 306
    out-slow/back-hard sets (negative split), 305
    straight sets, 304, 308–9
    varying-distance sets, 306–7
Sharpe, Chuck, 394
Shaving, 6–7, 372
Shock exercises (pliometrics), 260, 263–64, 290, 291–92
Shock microcycles, 239
Short-term adaptations, 158–59
Shoulberg, Richard, 330, 370–78
  sample workouts from, 376–78
Shoulder flexibility, 295–96
  tests of, 297
Shoulder press, 274
Shoulder roll, crawl arm stroke and, 58
Shoulders, elevation of, 49
Shoulder shrug (exercise), 281
Side bend exercises, 286, 287
Simon, Jack, 384–87
Simulators, 156, 208–11
Simulatory electrostimulation, 260
Simulatory stage of training, percentages of load distribution in, 252
Sit-down test, breaststroker's, 299
Sit-up with knees bent, 288
Six-beat kick, 41, 67
Skill level, age-group swimmers divided by, 332
Sliding filament theory, 256
Slow-twitch oxidative (SO) fibers, 182–83, 185
Soviet Sports Review, The (now *Fitness and Sports Review*), 187
Special endurance, interval training to improve strength component of, 207
Specialization
  age-group swimming and, 332
  age of, 231, 232, 233
  maximal loads based on event, 241–43
  principle of, 190

Specialized endurance training, 199, 204–15
Specialized-foundation (preliminary-specialized) preparation, 195, 199, 203–4
Specialized speed preparation, 215–16
Specialized strength training, 259
    individual maturation and, 243
    theoretical considerations in, 396–403
Special-preparatory stage, 234, 235
Special-preparatory strength exercises, 265, 270–78
Special-strength training, 258–67
    for endurance, 178–79
    general, 258–59
    means of, 259–60
    methods of, 260–67
    specialized, 259
Specificity of training, 165, 172, 191
Speed
    vertical jump as measure of, 290–94
    workouts stressing, 348
Speed abilities, 215–20
    defining, 215
    nontraditional methods for enhancing, 217–20
    specialized speed preparation, 215–16
    traditional vs. conventional methods, 216–17
Speed-assisted training, 219–20
Speed barrier, 219–20
Speed-endurance, 198, 329
Speed of muscle contraction, 258, 401, 403
    absolute, 400
Speed of muscular tension development, 258, 267–69
Speed range, 219
Speed-strength, 258
    methods of developing, 263
    training models for, 249, 250
Speed-strength characteristics of movement, force curves to determine, 397–403
Speed-strength (maximal speed) endurance, 199, 207, 267–69
    training sprinter for, 329
Speed-strength (power), 135
Speed-strength training. See Explosive strength/power
Spitz, Mark, 22, 23, 24–25, 336, 393
Split times, 152–53
Sport Verlag, 187
Sprint-endurance, 199
Sprinter(s)
    sample workouts for, 367, 369
    training program for, 329, 363
        morning sessions, 327
Sprints, breathing in, 64
Sprint training, 160, 167, 216–17, 303
Squats, 272
Squatting exercises, 284–85
Stabilization from kick, 38–40
Stabilizer muscle, 257
Stabilizing cycles, 238
Stabilizing stage, percentages of load distribution in, 252
Staleness, training, 181

Start(s), 133–43
    arm-swing (wind-up), 30, 133, 134, 135, 138–39
    backstroke, 135–41
    common mistakes in, 142–43
    grab, 133, 134, 135, 136–37
    "step-up," 135
    track, 133, 134
Start fever or apathy, 222
Starting-in mesocycle, 239
Starting strength, defined, 400
Stationary hi-walking and running, 288, 289
Steady pace chart, 153, 154–55
Steady state, 162
Steady-state (oxidative) system, 160
"Step-up" start, 135
Stereotypes, movement, 219
Sthenic emotions, 220
Stimulating cycles, 238
Stimuli. *See* Stress(es)
Straddle lift with squat, 285
Straight goal sprints, 216
Straight sets, 304, 308–9
Straight swims, mixing broken swims and, 308–9
Straight two-beat kick in crawl stroke, 41–43
Streamlining, 7, 8
Strength, 135
    absolute, 257
    componential, 400
    defined, 256
    flexibility and, 5, 6
    maximal, 257
    nature of, 256–57
    speed-strength/explosive. *See* Explosive strength/power
Strength abilities, development of, 257–301
    exercises for, 259–60, 269–90
        with barbell, 271, 272, 278–89
        for flexibility, 299–301
        general-preparatory, 265, 270–74
        shock exercises/pliometrics, 260, 263–64, 290, 291–92
        special-preparatory, 265, 270–78
    flexibility and, 295–301
    identifying different abilities, 257–58
    special-strength training, 258–67
        general, 258–59
        means of, 259–60
        methods of, 260–67
        specialized, 259
    specific resistance modes for, 259, 266–67
    speed-strength endurance work, 267–69
    strength-endurance work, 269
    traditional resistance methods for, 259, 262–66
    vertical jump as measure of, 290–94
Strength-building equipment, 385
Strength-endurance, 198, 207, 258, 269
    methods of developing, 264–66
Strength imbalances, 270
Strength impulse (force curve), 397–403

Strength tests, 360
Strength training, 29, 165, 198, 372, 383–84, 385
    adaptations to, 167–68
    dry land, 399, 403
    effects on endurance, 179
    in-water, 266–67
        for speed-strength endurance, 269
    main purpose of, 396
    maximal loads in, 241, 243
    positive effects of, 178
    specialized, 259
        individual maturation and, 243
        theoretical considerations in, 396–403
Stress(es)
    chronobiology of, 169–82
    defined, 158
    exogenous factors in, 181–82
    prolonged or repeated exposure to, 159
Stretching exercises, 298–301, 371, 385–86
Stroke(s). *See also specific names of strokes*
    endurance training using, 314–15
    push phase of, 397
    training for, 372, 374–75
Stroke swimmers, morning training session for, 327
Summation, 168
Superadaptation, 175
    cycle of, 170, 172
Surface drag, 6–7
Surgical tubing, swimming with, 361
Sustained speed endurance, 198
Sweeney, James, 393
Swim fins, 317
Synergistic muscles, 257, 279
Systematic adaptation, 165
Systemization of training, 241–54
    annual training models, 243–54
    multiyear training models, 241–43
    principal training models, 244–49
    principle of, 190
    quantitative training models, 249–50
    of weekly cycles, 250–54
Systems of training, 196
Szukala, Rafal, 395

Tachycardia, 311
Taguchi, Nobutaka, 25–27, 30, 393
Taper, the, 234, 337–39, 362, 385
    four-week, 337–39, 340–47
    sample workout for, 368–70
Tapering, 6
Tempo of work, 266. *See also* Pace
Tensiodynamography, 396, 401
Tension, psychological, 221
Tension development, 256
Tethered swimming, 267, 269
    endurance preparation with, 317–18
    negative tethered conditions, 317
    positive tethered conditions, 317–18
Theoretical preparation, 188
Theoretical square law, 30–31, 152
Theories, 188. *See also* International

sports training theory; Training theories involved in planning process
Thevenot, Melchisedech, 104
Third Law of Motion, Newton's, 8, 9
Thomas, Rick, 393
Thornton, N., 401
Time course of training plan, 229
Times, split, 152–53
Time standards, system for meeting, 372
Toeing in, 46
Tone, emotional, 221
Tonus, psychological, 221
Topchiyan, Y.S., 249
Toughness, mental, 374
Track start, 133, 134
Training. *See also* International sports training theory; Interval training; Periodization of training; Physiological basis for training swimmers; Preparation; Strength abilities, development of; Strength training
  adaptation to specific means and methods of, 165–68
  additional acceleration, 218–19
  at altitude, 175–76, 380–81
  anaerobic alactate, 216
  autogenic, 221, 226–27
  competitive-specific, 195, 200, 211–15
  effects of, 163, 173–81
    adaptation and, 174–81
    categories of, 173–74
    positive and negative, 176–80
    residual, 180–81
    short- and long-term delayed, 174–76
  endurance, 198
    adaptations to, 165–67
    maximal loads in, 241
    preliminary-specialized, 203–4
    specialized, 199, 204–15
  for explosive-strength (speed-strength), 168, 329
  extensive, 164
  flexibility, 227
  hypnoideomotor, 226
  ideomotor, 220–21, 225–26
  integrated, 172
  intensive, 161
  leading method of, 217–18
  logic of controlling, 230, 231
  methodology of, 195–97
  models of, 196, 208–11. *See also* Modeling and systemization of training
  movies and videos for, 357, 358
  multimethod system of, 172, 319
  number of competitions in plan, 212
  organization of, 230, 232
  overdistance, 164, 166, 200–201
  plan for, 229–30
  plan periods of, 229, 233–34
  repetition, 161, 166–67, 202, 303–4
    determining rest intervals in, 313
    types of sets for, 304–9
  special-strength, 258–67

general, 258–59
  means of, 259–60
  methods of, 260–67
  specialized, 259
  specificity of, 165, 172, 191
  speed-assisted, 219–20
  sprint, 160, 167, 216–17, 303
  systems of, 196
  transfers of, 179–80
  transitive, 207–8, 209
  types of, 163
  unidirectional, 253
  variable resistance, 218
  volitional, 223–26
Training complex, 196
Training exercises, 195
Training load(s), 190, 244
  principal models of, 244–49
  quantitative models of, 249–50
  ratio of competitive loads to, 213
  schemes, 249–50, 251
  over weekly cycles, 250–54
Training microcycles, 239–41
Training program, organizing, 302–54
  adjustments for age-group levels, 330–31
  annual training plan, 320–21, 322–23
  for distance swimmer, 327, 328, 360, 363–64
  endurance methods, activities executed in use of, 313–19
    apparatus used, 316–19
    controlled breathing, 315
    kicking drills, 316
    pulling drills, 316
    strokes, 314–15
  for individual medleyist, 330–31
  intermittent work, 303–4
  Masters program, 332–35
  measurable indices as guidelines in, 309–13
    heart rate as gauge of effort, 310–11, 312
    interval of rest, determining, 311–13, 314
    percentage efforts as indicator of intensity, 309–10
  mixed program, 319–20, 321
  sample workouts, 339–54
    early season, 348–49
    midseason, 349–52
    peak of training density, 352–54
  sets, types of, 304–9
    broken swims, 307–9
    decreasing rest interval sets, 305–6
    descending-time sets, 305
    increasing rest interval sets, 306
    out-slow/back-hard sets (negative split), 305
    straight sets, 304, 308–9
  varying-distance sets, 306–7
  for sprinter, 329, 363
  the taper, 234, 337–39, 362, 385
    four-week taper, 337–39, 340–47
    sample workout for, 368–70
  warm-up, 335–36
  weekly training plan, 321–28
Training staleness, 181

Training theories involved in planning process, 230–55
  cyclic nature of training, 197, 236–41
    macrocycles, 236, 379
    mesocycles, 236–39
    microcycles, 239–41, 242, 253
  modeling and systemization of training, 241–54
    annual training models, 243–54
    multiyear training models, 241–43
    principal training models, 244–49
    quantitative training models, 249–50
    of weekly cycles, 250–54
  periodization of training, 230–36
    multiyear training plans, 230, 231–33
    yearly training plan, 230–31, 233–36
Training units, 196
Transitional period, 234
Transitive training, 207–8, 209
Trial and error, informed, 355
Trunk muscles, 279
T-20 Test, 312
Turns, 143–46
  backstroke, 146, 147–49
  butterfly and breaststroke, 143–45
  freestyle, 146, 150–51
Turrall, Jenny, 394
Twenty-four-Hour Camp, 374, 376–77
Two-arm press exercises, 279, 280
Two-beat kick
  crossover, 38, 42, 44, 45
  straight, 41–43
Two-peak microcycle, 253

Undulating style of breaststroke, 107–9, 112–15, 122–23, 124–26
Unidirectional training, 253
Unidirectional variant of training load organization, 244, 246
Uniform workloads, 171–72
U.S. Swimming, 375
Unity of general and specialized preparation, principle of, 190
Universalism, principle of, 191–95
Upper arm
  inward rotators of, 275
  medial rotation of, in crawl stroke, 55–57
Upright rowing, 280–81
Utility principle, 190

Van't Hoff's Law, 335
Variable resistance efforts, 263
Variable resistance training, 218
Varying-distance sets, 306–7
Vasa Swim Trainer, 371, 372
Velocity, resistance and, 30–31
Verbal formula, 226
Verkoshansky, Yuri, 230, 244–48, 400
Versatility, principle of, 190
Vertical jump, 290–94, 359–60
Videos for training, 357, 358
Visualization, 227
Volitional capabilities, 164

Volitional effort (isometric), 260
Volitional preparedness, 221
Volitional training, 223–26
Volkov, N., 173
Volume (external load factor), 261
Volume/intensity ratio in principal
    training models, 244

Wake-up swim, 336
Warm-up, 335–36
Wave-action style of breaststroke,
    107–9, 122–23
Way of life, 222
Webb, Matthew, 105
Webbed-finger gloves, 319
Wedge kick, 111, 118
Weekly cycles, 236, 250–54
Weekly training plan, 321–28
Weight belts, 318
Weightlifting, 271, 278–89
    fundamental exercises, 272–74
Whip kick, 111–17, 118

Whole body strength exercise, 272,
    274
Wiggling, 74
Wind-up (arm-swing) start, 30, 133,
    134, 135, 138–39
Wojdat, Artur, 50, 153
Work
    intermittent, 303–4
    lactate tolerance, 205
    nature of, 174
Working effect of movement, 396
Workloads, uniform, 171–72
Workouts
    distance, 328
    of East German team, 381–82
    for individual medley, 330–31
    for mixed program of training, 319,
        320, 321
    sample, 339–54
        early season, 348–49
        from Jack Simon, 386–87
        midseason, 349–52

peak of training density, 352–54
    stressing endurance, 348
    for weekly training plan, 326–28
Work regimes in utilization of specific
    resistance, 259, 266–67
    speed-strength endurance, 267–69
    strength-endurance, 269
Work-to-rest ratio intervals, 311
Work withdrawal, tapering and
    symptoms of, 338
Wrist curls, 283
Wrist flexion, 50–51, 52, 275–78

Yakovlev model of stress and
    adaptation to physical loads,
    169–72
Yearly training plan, periodization of,
    230–31, 233–36
Yessis, Michael, 187

Zones of intensity, 203